TEACHER SUPPLY, DEMAND, AND QUALITY

Policy Issues, Models, and Data Bases

Proceedings of a Conference

Erling E. Boe and Dorothy M. Gilford, Editors

Committee on National Statistics
and
Division of Education, Training, and Employment

Commission on Behavioral and Social Sciences and Education

National Research Council

NATIONAL ACADEMY PRESS
Washington, D.C. 1992

NOTICE: The project that is the subject of this report was approved by the Governing Board of the National Research Council, whose members are drawn from the councils of the National Academy of Sciences, the National Academy of Engineering, and the Institute of Medicine. The members of the committee responsible for the report were chosen for their special competences and with regard for appropriate balance.

This report has been reviewed by a group other than the authors according to procedures approved by a Report Review Committee consisting of members of the National Academy of Sciences, the National Academy of Engineering, and the Institute of Medicine.

The National Academy of Sciences is a private, nonprofit, self-perpetuating society of distinguished scholars engaged in scientific and engineering research, dedicated to the furtherance of science and technology and to their use for the general welfare. Upon the authority of the charter granted to it by the Congress in 1863, the Academy has a mandate that requires it to advise the federal government on scientific and technical matters. Dr. Frank Press is president of the National Academy of Sciences.

The National Academy of Engineering was established in 1964, under the charter of the National Academy of Sciences, as a parallel organization of outstanding engineers. It is autonomous in its administration and in the selection of its members, sharing with the National Academy of Sciences the responsibility for advising the federal government. The National Academy of Engineering also sponsors engineering programs aimed at meeting national needs, encourages education and research, and recognizes the superior achievements of engineers. Dr. Robert M. White is president of the National Academy of Engineering.

The Institute of Medicine was established in 1970 by the National Academy of Sciences to secure the services of eminent members of appropriate professions in the examination of policy matters pertaining to the health of the public. The Institute acts under the responsibility given to the National Academy of Sciences by its congressional charter to be an adviser to the federal government and, upon its own initiative, to identify issues of medical care, research, and education. Dr. Kenneth I. Shine is president of the Institute of Medicine.

The National Research Council was organized by the National Academy of Sciences in 1916 to associate the broad community of science and technology with the Academy's purposes of furthering knowledge and advising the federal government. Functioning in accordance with general policies determined by the Academy, the Council has become the principal operating agency of both the National Academy of Sciences and the National Academy of Engineering in providing services to the government, the public, and the scientific and engineering communities. The Council is administered jointly by both Academies and the Institute of Medicine. Dr. Frank Press and Dr. Robert M. White are chairman and vice chairman, respectively, of the National Research Council.

This project was supported with funds from the the National Center for Education Statistics, U.S. Department of Education.

Library of Congress Catalog Card No. 92-50735
International Standard Book Number 0-309-04792-7

Additional copies of this report are available from:

National Academy Press
2101 Constitution Avenue, NW
Washington, D.C. 20418

B033

Printed in the United States of America

COMMITTEE ON NATIONAL STATISTICS

Contents

PART V DATA BASES **225**

PART VI CONCLUSION **285**

Contributing Authors

STEPHEN M. BARRO is president of SMB Economic Research, Inc., Washington, D.C. Since earning a Ph.D. in economics from Stanford University in 1974, he has conducted research in education finance, teacher supply and demand, and comparative education, as well as in other topics. His monograph entitled *Cost-of-Education Differentials Across States* was published in 1991.

ROLF BLANK is project director, State Education Assessment Center, Council of Chief State School Officers. He has conducted research in education and program evaluation on such topics as magnet schools and high school organization and management. He is currently directing research on systems of indicators of science and mathematics education in the fifty states. He earned a Ph.D. in sociology from Florida State University in 1976.

ERLING E. BOE served as codirector of the conference. A professor of education at the University of Pennsylvania, he has conducted research on the role of incentives in behavior and in psychometrics, as well as on other topics. He is currently investigating teacher supply, retention, transfer, and attrition topics with national data bases and state policies designed to restructure public education. He received a Ph.D. degree in experimental psychology from Washington State University in 1962.

CHRISTOPHER T. CROSS is executive director-education initiative, The Business Roundtable, Washington, D.C. Previously he was assistant secretary for educational research and improvement in the U.S. Department of

Education. As such, he was responsible for the department's efforts in statistics gathering, assessment, research and development, and information dissemination. Cross's other prior experiences include serving as vice chairman of Macro Systems, Inc., a Maryland-based professional services company; president of University Research Corporation, a Maryland-based professional services research and information services company; Republican staff director and senior education consultant for the U.S. House of Representatives' Committee on Education and Labor; and deputy assistant secretary for legislation (education) in the U.S. Department of Health, Education and Welfare (1970-1973). His publications and presentations include an elementary/secondary education data redesign project for the National Center for Education Statistics in 1985.

EMERSON J. ELLIOTT is acting commissioner of education statistics, U.S. Department of Education, and director of the National Center for Education Statistics. A federal agency administrator and policy analyst, he headed the Department of Education planning and evaluation office and issues analysis staff and directed a Congressionally mandated school finance study. He was the first deputy director of the National Institute of Education and has headed the Institute for Educational Leadership educational staff seminar. Prior experience with the U.S. Office of Management and Budget included serving as chief of the Education Branch and a deputy chief of the Human Resources Programs Division. He received an M.P.A. from the University of Michigan.

DOROTHY M. GILFORD served as codirector of the conference. Formerly, she served as director of the National Center for Education Statistics and as director of the mathematical sciences division of the Office of Naval Research; currently she is director of the National Research Council's Board on International Comparative Studies in Education. Her interests are in research program administration, the organization of statistical systems, education administration, education statistics, and human resource statistics. A fellow of the American Statistical Association, she has served as vice president of the association and chairman of its committee on fellows. She is a member of the International Statistics Institute. She received B.S. and M.S. degrees in mathematics from the University of Washington.

GUS W. HAGGSTROM is a statistical consultant at RAND. Since earning a Ph.D. in mathematics from the University of Illinois in 1964, he has conducted research in education and human resources, statistical methods and research design, marriage and the family, as well as in other topics. His recent work has included studies of high school graduates, scientists and engineers, and assessing teacher supply and demand.

THOMAS L. HILTON is senior research scientist, Division of Cognitive Assessment Research, Educational Testing Service. Since earning a Ph.D. in educational psychology from Harvard University in 1956, he has conducted research on student achievement in high school and college and on the origins and supply of scientists and engineers, as well as on other topics. He is currently pursuing studies in talent flow in higher education and persistence in science of high-ability minority students.

MARY M. KENNEDY is professor of education and director of the National Center for Research on Teacher Education at Michigan State University. She has conducted evaluative research of the Chapter 1 Compensatory Education Program and the Education for All Handicapped Children Act of 1975, as well as research in other topics. Her recent work includes publications on teacher education. She received a Ph.D. in educational psychology from Michigan State University,

RONALD E. KUTSCHER is associate commissioner, Office of Employment Projections, U.S. Bureau of Labor Statistics. Since completing graduate study in economics at the University of Illinois in 1956, he has conducted research on economic and technological development, including implications for employment patterns and skill and education requirements of the work force, as well as in other topics. He is currently directing development of medium-term economic projections of the U.S. economy and the preparation of the *Occupational Outlook Handbook.*

RICHARD J. MURNANE is professor of education at the Graduate School of Education, Harvard University. Since earning a Ph.D. in economics from Yale University in 1974, he has conducted research in labor markets in education, school effectiveness and quality, as well as in other topics. He recently chaired the National Research Council's Committee on Indicators of Precollege Science and Mathematics Education. His recent research has concerned the operation of teacher labor markets and the connections between education and the productivity of the work force.

PAUL PLANCHON is associate commissioner for elementary/secondary education statistics of the National Center for Education Statistics. Since earning a M.A. in sociology and anthropology from Kent State University in 1966, he has served in several federal government positions conducting survey research on physicians and civil litigation and on educational, welfare, and income statistics, as well as on other topics. He is currently directing a number of projects on large-scale national survey research and data base development in elementary and secondary education.

ALBERT SHANKER has served as president of the American Federation of Teachers, AFL-CIO, since 1974. Among a large number of appointments, he has been a public school teacher, president of the International Federation of Free Teachers' Unions, and a member of the National Academy of Education and the President's Education Policy Advisory Committee. Since December 1970, he has written a weekly column, "Where We Stand," on education, labor, economic, and human rights issues, for the Sunday *New York Times*.

LEE S. SHULMAN chaired the Conference on Teacher Supply, Demand, and Quality. He is the Charles E. Ducommun professor of education at Stanford University. He served on the Faculty of Education at the Michigan State University before moving to Stanford University in 1982. He has conducted research on teaching and teacher education, as well as on other topics. He is currently investigating new strategies for the assessment of teaching at the elementary and secondary education levels. He is past president of the American Education Research Association and the current president of the National Academy of Education. He received a Ph.D. in educational psychology from the University of Chicago in 1963.

JAMES B. STEDMAN is a specialist in social legislation for the Congressional Research Service of the Library of Congress. Since earning an M.A. in history from Harvard University, he has performed nonpartisan research for members and committees of Congress in teacher reform, school reform, school desegregation, as well as in other topics. He has recently authored a report entitled *Teachers: Issues for the 102d Congress*.

JAMES M. WILSON, III, is senior project analyst and principal investigator for the Northeast Teacher Supply and Demand Study of the Institute for Social and Economic Research of the University of Massachusetts. He has conducted research on various aspects of teacher supply and demand, population forecasting, and minority access to and retention in postsecondary education. He is currently pursuing various studies of teacher supply and demand in the Northeastern region and the Virgin Islands. He earned an M.S. in resource economics from the University of Massachusetts in 1984.

ARTHUR WISE is president of the National Council for the Accreditation of Teacher Education. Since earning a Ph.D. in educational administration from the University of Chicago, he has conducted research on legislated learning, school finance, and teacher supply and demand, as well as in other topics. He also currently serves as chair of the board of directors of the National Foundation for the Improvement of Education and as chair of the Government Liaison Committee of the American Educational Research Association.

Acknowledgments

The Committee on National Statistics and the Division of Education, Training, and Employment gratefully acknowledge the contributions of the many individuals who participated in the Conference on Teacher Supply, Demand, and Quality and gave generously of their time and knowledge.

The conference was convened in March 1991 at the request of the National Center for Education Statistics (NCES), the Office of Educational Research and Improvement of the U.S. Department of Education. The center's generous support of the conference and the participation of NCES staff members in the conference were essential to its success and are gratefully acknowledged. In particular, thanks are due to Emerson Elliott, acting commissioner of NCES, for his introductory remarks on the background to and purposes of the conference; to Paul Planchon, associate commissioner of NCES, for framing the relationship of the conference to NCES programs and plans; and to a number of other NCES staff members who contributed to planning the conference and these proceedings.

The contributions of several individuals to the identification and analysis of national data bases leading to the preparation of the tables of Appendix C are also recognized with appreciation. Alan Fechter of the National Research Council presented a helpful discussion of this topic at the conference and provided consultation leading to the development of this appendix. In addition, the initial review and organization of national data bases presented by W. Ross Brewer, of the Vermont Department of Education, and Stephen P. Coelen and James M. Wilson III, of the University of Massachusetts, served as the basis for developing the framework and content of Appendix C.

On behalf of all the conference participants, I want to acknowledge with gratitude the contributions of the staff. Jane Phillips and Laura Lathrop managed the logistical arrangements for the conference. Jane cheerfully and efficiently handled the numerous rounds of revisions in preparing the conference proceedings. Laura drafted many of the data base descriptions and identified the data elements relevant to teacher supply, demand, and quality in these data bases. Dorothy Gilford and Erling Boe served as codirectors of the conference. They shared responsibility for the conference, with Dorothy assuming primary responsibility for organizing the conference and administrative matters and Erling for preparing the draft proceedings. The conference report also benefited from the thoughtful comments of reviewers and the editorial assistance of Christine McShane and Eugenia Grohman of the Commission on Behavioral and Social Sciences and Education.

Lee S. Shulman, *Chair*
Conference on Teacher Supply, Demand, and Quality

I

INTRODUCTION

Introductory Remarks

CHRISTOPHER T. CROSS

This conference brings together statisticians, researchers and policy makers, three groups that must talk together, but—as we know—sometimes have difficulty finding the time.

But this type of communication is vital. Surveys and other data collection systems must provide the information policy makers need at the time they need it and in a form they can use. For their part, policy makers need to be more clear about what their needs are and about what information is most useful. This conference provides an opportunity to engage in this sort of give and take.

The subject of this conference—teacher supply, demand, and quality—is clearly of central importance to education. The implications of the relevant statistics and research affect the most important determinant of learning—classroom teachers.

Yet this is a field still very much in its infancy. As seen in the papers presented at this conference, debate continues over such basic issues as what to measure, how to measure it, and even when to measure it. Even more work remains to be done in designing models that predict shortages ahead of time, so that policy makers can respond in time.

Nonetheless, progress is being made on a number of important issues. We have learned, for example, that yearly attrition rates can be deceptive for predicting future needs since many departing teachers eventually return to teaching after a few years. Nearly 40 percent of current teachers have taken just such a break and returned to the classroom (Feistritzer, 1990).

We have also learned that, while aggregate data is important, more attention must be focused on key subject fields that may face particular difficulties. We know, for instance, that two-thirds of secondary school principals are having a difficult time hiring chemistry and physics teachers. Other studies have shown that many teachers in these subjects lack a degree in the field.

One policy tool several states are experimenting with for dealing with such shortages is alternative certification for teachers and principals. Such alternative routes can bring to education talented individuals who, while they may lack formal certification, may nevertheless be well qualified. This is especially important in critical shortage areas such as science, mathematics, and foreign languages.

But better, more systematic data on alternative certification (and its potential as a tool for bringing needed teachers into the classroom) are needed. Policy makers look to educational statisticians and researchers to provide the information needed to weigh such matters.

Action to ensure an adequate supply of qualified teachers is also under way at the federal level. One example is the Federal Coordinating Council for Science, Engineering, and Technology (FCCSET). Through its Committee on Education and Human Resources, FCCSET seeks to coordinate the myriad science and education programs of several federal agencies and departments into a coherent national strategy. FCCSET has made teacher education and training its number one priority.

This leads to a subject that is critical—*teacher quality.* Teacher supply and demand are only part of the picture. Even if we have enough teachers in critical subjects, even if teachers know the subjects well that they are teaching (which we know is not always the case), subject knowledge does not necessarily translate into teaching quality. We need indicators that give us a true picture of teacher quality, which includes teaching practices.

Studies tell us that today's teachers still tend to rely on many of the same methods teachers used at the start of this century. They "deliver" education through lectures, and they ask students to repeat lessons back on tests, often simple multiple-choice tests.

This common practice reflects an inadequate understanding of the nature of knowledge and results in a flawed approach to learning. We now know that to attain true understanding, students must be able to use facts to think and analyze for themselves, not just to recall isolated bits of data. Such new, and more demanding, expectations require approaches to teaching that are more interactive—approaches that engage students in thinking *as a matter of course.* But educators are expected to lead a charge into territory many of them have never experienced.

As we move toward what Lauren Resnick calls "the thinking curriculum," we face a dilemma. Teachers were taught according to the old ways we are trying to leave behind. And they have internalized the premises underlying these practices into deeply held attitudes and beliefs. Teaching practices are drawing lots of attention lately. They should. Changing them is vital to our objectives for improving education.

During the 1980s, we decided, as a nation, that all children can learn. And that all children can learn to think. That was a main point of the national education goals. As President Bush and the governors agreed, "All our people, not just a few, must learn to think for a living." Never before has a nation set its sights so high for all its people—and all its children.

States are struggling to implement these very basic changes. California has found that one of the greatest obstacles to implementing the impressive curriculum embodied in its Frameworks and other reform efforts has been the difficulty teachers experience in revising their assumptions about how children learn. As they begin to make this shift—through training, professionalization, etc.—statistics derived from surveys can help in the following ways:

- They can help us see how teachers adapt to, implement, and enact changes;
- They can allow us to gauge teacher attitudes and practices;
- They can establish a baseline;
- They can help us monitor changes in those attitudes and practices over time; and
- They can help us examine these changes in relation to shifts in policy.

As our changing understanding of learning demonstrates, teachers and other educators need to become consumers of education research. They must stay in touch with the research community so that they can implement, or at least experiment with, new findings such as "wait times" and new approaches to student assessment.

Much remains to be done to bring this about, both on the part of teachers and on the part of those producing the research. It might be helpful to consider research consumption as a component of teacher quality. How aware are teachers of relevant research and how much are they experimenting with new approaches in their classrooms?

One final note. In her paper, Mary Kennedy makes a recommendation that is particularly worth considering. She recommends that National Assessment of Educational Progress (NAEP) surveys include context-specific questions that tap teachers' basic educational beliefs and values. Such questions, she points out, "could improve our understanding of teachers' fundamental orientations toward teaching and the kinds of outcomes they promote in their students." If tied to NAEP, responses to such questions will provide a means for examining the link between teacher attitudes and student performance. Student learning, after all, is the critical feature of education—the one we all care about most.

It is the potential for providing policy makers with useful, actionable data that we, in the Department of Education, see statistics and research on teacher supply, demand, and quality—and the proceedings of this conference—as so important.

REFERENCE

Feistritzer, C. Emily
1990 *Profile of Teachers in the United States, 1990.* A National Center for Education Information survey. Washington, D.C.: Feistritzer Publications.

Conference Background

EMERSON J. ELLIOTT

The National Center for Education Statistics (NCES) was pleased to sponsor the Conference on Teacher Supply, Demand, and Quality (TSDQ) and this collection of papers based on the proceedings. This publication represents a continuation of work undertaken by the National Research Council that focused on the supply, demand, and quality of precollege science and mathematics teachers. The purposes of the conference were to reassess the status of TSDQ a year after the 1990 report *Precollege Science and Mathematics Teachers: Monitoring Supply, Demand, and Quality* to update our understanding, and to help establish an agenda for future work in this important facet of public education.

Several important recommendations for NCES were forthcoming during the course of the Research Council's earlier work that we have accepted and implemented. For example, it was recommended that NCES should suspend projections of teacher supply until better data were available and better models were built. Accordingly, we did suspend such projections. Other recommendations we acted on pertained to collection of data on recent college graduates, schools, and the staffing of schools. We look forward to receiving further useful and compelling recommendations as an outgrowth of the conference.

Teacher supply, demand, and quality are of particular importance to the mission of NCES because they are built into our authorizing legislation. Back in 1974, NCES was charged with conducting surveys to determine the demand for and the availability of qualified teachers and administrative personnel, especially in critical areas. This charge was enacted about the time Washington concluded that there was a teacher glut, and that the Education Professions Development Act should be abolished because it was no longer needed.

In 1986, the interest in teacher supply, demand, and quality—especially for mathematics and science teachers—was renewed. Congress gave NCES the additional assignment to address needs for teachers in various subject areas; to examine possible teacher shortages; to identify the sources of teacher supply; to monitor the teaching force in terms of its demographic characteristics, academic qualifications, job preparation, experience, and skills; and to determine the rate at which teachers leave the profession along with their reasons for leaving.

At the present time, much attention and energy are being devoted to the development and measurement of progress toward national education goals. The performance of U.S. students in science and mathematics is one topic of great concern, and this relates to the supply and quality of science and mathematics teachers. How to measure progress toward achieving national goals and the quality of teachers are still unresolved issues.

The NCES Perspective

PAUL PLANCHON

NCES hopes this conference will produce three benefits for its work. First, we expect it will provide us with an opportunity to keep abreast of public policy and methodological issues in TSDQ. Second, it should provide us with an opportunity to continue dialogue about TSDQ among policy researchers, educators, and those in federal and state statistical agencies. Finally, it will provide an opportunity to take stock of innovations recently introduced into NCES programs. We are interested in your assessment of them in terms of strengths and limitations, and whether they measure up to your expectations. Perhaps more important, we hope to receive your advice about how our existing programs and surveys should evolve in the future, about new components or surveys that we should consider adding, and about how value might be added to our data bases by integrating or linking them.

The scope of our interest is typified by the structure of the conference. It is organized into discussions first on TSDQ policy issues, then on modeling teacher supply and demand behavior, next on the utility of national data bases for supplying the data needed by the models, and last, on state teacher data bases.

In terms of policy issues, it is interesting to note that, in the last few years, there has been less concern about teacher shortages; rather, the major policy issue is now becoming teacher quality. The Kennedy paper does a very good job of elucidating the quality issue. While we recognize the importance of teacher quality, we also recognize that our metrics for measuring teacher quality are woefully inadequate at this time. Your guidance on how we might proceed in this area is sought.

With respect to modeling teacher supply and demand, the Barro paper was quite useful in summarizing the progress that has been made since he wrote a similar paper several years ago for the first National Research Council report on teacher supply and demand. NCES would value your advice on what our role, along with that of the Office of Research in the Office of Educational Research and Improvement and the National Science Foundation, ought to be in stimulating (and perhaps even funding) research into developing better TSDQ models. We at NCES clearly have a stake in the further development of models relevant to our teacher supply and demand projection methodology. In addition, we might stimulate TSDQ research with state data bases. This would be within the scope of our mandate in the National Cooperative Education Statistics System, wherein we have authority to undertake research and demonstration projects.

Although NCES has a number of data bases relevant to TSDQ, they are managed in different parts of the organization. It is therefore very useful to have someone scan across and analyze these data bases, including other existing national data sets, to give us a better perspective of how they all contribute to TSDQ research.

With respect to state data bases, it is encouraging to know that their use in studying TSDQ issues continues to be valued. The work of individual states summarized in the Barro paper is indicative of such interest. The teacher common market project in the New England states and New York indicates interest in these issues not only at the state level, but also at the regional level. There is growing interest as well in the Southern and North Central states for regional data bases on teachers. In addition, the National Science Foundation clearly has an interest in issues of teacher supply and demand at the state level as evidenced by the State Science/Mathematics Indicators Project, which it sponsors at the Council of Chief State School Officers.

It is clear that a national analysis of teacher supply and demand without further disaggregation is inadequate. Our interest at NCES needs to go beyond this. Obviously there are subnational variations in this phenomenon, which we need to study. Even though our newest survey, the Schools and Staffing Survey (SASS), was explicitly designed to obtain state-level data, SASS is limited in fully exploring TSDQ issues at the state level because sample sizes will simply not support many of the needed analyses. Another advantage of state data bases is that many of them have a longitudinal component because states have been collecting teacher data for many years.

In conclusion, I will mention a few new NCES initiatives. Feedback from you on some of the actions we are currently planning to undertake and others that we are contemplating will be very useful.

With respect to SASS, we are now budgeted to readminister the Teacher Followup Survey (TFS) several times. Currently, SASS is designed as a cross-sectional survey, complemented with the TFS, which after one year follows samples of teachers who (a) have left the profession, (b) transferred between schools, and (c) remained in the same school. Beginning with the 1992-93 SASS, we plan to follow these samples of teachers longitudinally as long as it proves fruitful to do so.

Another SASS innovation that we are pilot testing this year is the addition of a student component, the concept being to draw samples of students instructed by the individuals in the teacher sample. The feasibility and utility of this approach is now being explored. One of the advantages for including students in SASS is to understand better student course-taking patterns, one factor related to teacher demand.

NCES has also introduced (for fiscal 1989) collection of fiscal data in our state aggregate collection. This provides a much more powerful fiscal data base at the state level than we have had for at least 10 years. These new data should be useful for analyzing selected fiscal aspects of TSDQ.

We have also been working closely with the U.S. Bureau of the Census in collecting fiscal data at the school district level. Every five years, the Bureau's F-33 data collection entails a census of school districts, while in the off years these data are only state representative. In 1991, NCES provided additional funding to the Census Bureau so that the 1990 F-33 collection could be expanded to include all school districts. We will be able to link financial data from the district level with the many population characteristics generated by the census mapping project when information from the mapping project becomes available in late 1992 or early 1993, thereby enhancing the analytic utility of that data base. In the coming years, NCES will work closely with the Census Bureau in a number of ways to enhance the school district finance data.

NCES also has a new survey, the National Household Education Survey (NHES). The first administration of this survey was conducted in early 1992. Using a random digit dialing telephone survey method, we plan to survey a sample of 60,000 households. It is possible that the NHES will provide opportunities to explore some of the difficult issues in measuring the teacher reserve pool.

Choosing Teachers and Choosing to Teach

ALBERT SHANKER

In February 1991, I was invited to address the opening session for the first presentation of a group of papers on the issue of teacher supply and demand. I was unable to attend that evening, but I have had a chance to review the work and to think about ways to consider the process of estimating the need for teachers and the supply of those willing to teach. I am grateful to Dorothy Gilford, who has continued to encourage me in this endeavor, as well as to Stephen Barro, Mary Kennedy, Richard Murnane, and others who have contributed to my thinking about this issue. I certainly share their concerns about the lack of adequate models to predict the elements of supply and demand.

I will leave to these expert authors the technical discussion of model development and of teacher quality and practice issues. Their papers are important and useful and will reward all who read them. I will concentrate on the issue of teacher quality and how it affects supply and demand.

Let me begin with an example of how standards of quality are thrown out the window when the demand exceeds the supply of quality recruits. In Baltimore a few years back, the district set out to identify top candidates for its teacher vacancies. It tested applicants, had them provide samples of letters they would write to parents, and asked them to respond to questions that teachers would ordinarily encounter in their work. A number of candidates were identified as unacceptable for hiring and received letters from the district to that effect. Then in September, the city hired the same candidates it had earlier identified as unacceptable. Why? Because after the supply of successful candidates had been hired, vacancies still remained. The district placed conditions on these "Labor Day Specials," such as a requirement that they go to school at night to improve their literacy and math skills. The point, however, is that in the face of an inadequate supply of teachers, the district immediately abandoned its interest in quality.

The Baltimore example is troubling because most of the rest of our nation's school systems would do, and have done, the same thing. We hear a lot about high standards for entering teaching, but even the modest standards our states now set are routinely set aside when supply lags. We hear a lot about teachers' knowing their subjects, but misassignment and out-of-license teaching are commonplace. In some countries, if there is an insufficient number of qualified teachers, students are sent home until a qualified teacher can be found. The custodial function of schools is compromised, not standards of teaching quality. Here it's just the opposite.

The future supply of teachers in our nation will come from the high school classrooms of America, where from 4 to 7 percent of students are achieving at the highest levels, as measured by various tests administered by the National Assessment of Educational Progress. Whether it is reading, mathematics, science, or other subjects just a scant few of our twelfth graders are demonstrating a level of knowledge and skills that is reasonable to expect of the majority of our prospective high school graduates—certainly the ones that go on to college, and that's half of them. That half is the source of our future supply of teachers. The highest achieving of these high school graduates are snapped up by our elite postsecondary institutions; few of them become teachers. Judging from the NAEP scores, the overwhelming majority of the students who go on to college are getting their high school education there. That's our future labor source, and that's the pool from which we'll be drawing our future teachers.

Contrast our situation with that of our competitors. In France, Germany, and other nations, the students who enter postsecondary education have passed very rigorous exams, far more demanding than anything you'll see on the NAEP tests. They send 20-35 percent of their high school students on to college, while we send 50 percent, but 100 percent of their college entrants have met standards that are at least as high as those attained by only 4-7 percent of our twelfth graders. You can safely say, then, that 100 percent of our competitors' future teachers come from the equivalent of our top group of students. Even if all our best students chose careers as teachers, the United States would still have a substantial quality gap to close.

Teaching in a nation as large as the United States is a mass profession, and it is hard to get uniformly high quality in a mass profession. And yet we continue to organize our schools on the basis of self-contained classrooms, which require large numbers of teachers and which mitigate against our avowed desire to have a qualified teacher in every one of them. Perhaps instead of consistently compromising on quality, we could experiment with organizing work differently. Instead of one teacher per classroom—a teacher who may or may not be qualified—we could try differentiated teams of educators. The head of the team would be a fully qualified teacher who planned and taught the main lessons and who organized the work of other adults—interns paraprofessionals, etc.—who assisted groups of children in discussing and working through the lessons. The point of this illustration is not to endorse a model but to suggest that the demand question may have an organizational or structural solution that allows quality to be retained in the face of inadequate supply.

Another approach to the teacher quality issue might be pay for knowledge systems, similar to those found in industry. Currently, teachers advance on the salary schedule in part based on advanced degrees and credits. By and large, any postgraduate courses or programs are accepted. It's also the case that many teachers take courses to qualify themselves as school administrators, who get paid much more than teachers. There is no reason why employers and unions can't use the existing system to line up incentives in the right direction: Instead of rewarding any course taking, why not reward taking courses and completing programs that boost teacher quality? For example, most states do not require elementary school teachers to know much math and science, and, as far as I can tell, these teachers do not go on to take courses in these subjects (and how to teach them). Might this change if financial incentives were offered for them to do so?

As you can see, I view the issue of quality as both competency in subject matter and in how to teach subjects to youngsters. In this country, we've put methods over content and are generally satisfied if prospective teachers know content at about the level they will teach. But one characteristic of teachers in countries that are doing a better job of educating youngsters than we are is their high level of subject matter competency compared with that of U.S. teachers. Here, we value the sensitivity of the elementary school teacher above his or her knowledge and teaching skills in math. I fail to see how we can expect to have our students perform at world-class standards in math when we don't care whether or not our elementary school teachers know math. When we address the question of supply and demand, we must do so in the context of supplying those who clearly know the subjects we wish our youngsters to master and who can demonstrate that they know how to reach youngsters.

Now, on the brink of real shortages of teachers, is the best time for us to insist on a change in how we organize schools and in the requirements for subject mastery for prospective teachers. We are in difficult financial constraints. But rather than insist on business as usual, we should take our difficulties as an opportunity to move ahead with the development of new organizations for the schools of the next century.

You will see in the chapters of this book models for forecasting both supply and demand for teachers. These models traditionally rely on fixed pupil/teacher ratios to determine demand. Supply estimates are quite often a function of counting those certified, and they ignore the questions of who remains in teaching, or ever teaches, and for how long. Supply and demand models also tend to ignore public policy issues.

Let me give you two examples of the kind of public policy issues that can wreak havoc with even the most sophisticated estimates of how many teachers we will need and of who and how many will be available to fill vacant positions. Take an issue like private school choice. Right now, most Americans are opposed to allowing public dollars to follow kids to private and parochial schools. But if public schools don't improve, pressure for privatization will probably increase and gain more converts. Consider the effect on teacher demand if large numbers of private schools grew up. Consider the effect on quality if their standards for teachers were even lower than those of the public schools, which they probably would be absent regulation.

Another issue that must be considered is the increasing cost of a college education and the decisions that are affected by those changes. Students who pay $40,000 and up to get an education must ask about the long-term consequences of borrowing money to get a teaching degree that allows them to go to work for low wages in a situation in which they have little autonomy and lousy working conditions. If we contrast that with other options available, we may find that, given the financial consequences alone, teaching will be a viable choice for fewer and fewer, regardless of the demand.

So interest in teaching is an economic issue, but it is also a social issue. We have seen evidence of this in the behavior of those who chose teaching as a career in the past. For example, social factors made teaching the occupation of choice for educated women and minorities who were barred from other professions. People chose teaching and did not choose the alternatives because of the conditions of their time, as well as their personal interests.

Political considerations can lead to changes in vocational interests and choices. During the Vietnam War, record numbers of people entered teacher education programs in order to get a draft deferment, and many have stayed to teach our children. Right now, we have an opportunity to take advantage of another political development to help schools get more teachers. Some look at the reduction in world hostilities and see a peace dividend in the form of retiring military personnel who may be interested in teaching. Tens of thousands of career military personnel may become available through programs jointly supported by the Department of Defense and the Department of Education. Similarly, many of the technical and professional staff likely to be laid off in defense-related industries are promising sources of math and science teachers.

The point is that supply and demand estimates need to include or be analyzed in conjunction with the political, social environmental, and labor conditions that exist in the target and alternative occupations. Before college students invest in education as a career, they ask, "Will there be work for me when I graduate? Will that work be satisfying and earn me respect?" What kind of message are we sending to prospective teachers when pay is poor, prospects for advancement are lousy, and when the ratio of teachers to students is 1:18 in primary schools while the ratio of supervisors to teachers is 1:11?

Demand for services is one part of the equation; how many teachers we have to provide service is the other. This number will depend on such things as attrition, retirement, and the new people we attract to the profession. Attrition means, literally, the wearing down by friction, and I am certain that many teachers who have left the profession in recent years would find this definition apposite. Teachers have been worn down by increasing violence in schools, larger classes, overzealous supervision, and poor and dangerous school facilities. All these things take their toll and often lead some of our best teachers to cut short their teaching careers by a number of years. It would be difficult, if not impossible, to include these intangibles in equations of supply. However, we need to evaluate data in light of conditions teachers face and keep in mind the importance of fixing some of the conditions that drive teachers away.

We also need to pay attention to the new teachers who will need support systems if they are to survive. Studies tell us a number of troubling things about new teachers: that those with the highest credentials are the first to leave, that half leave within a short period of time, and that our present system of teacher induction fails 50 percent of those who use it. A 1990 report from the Department of Labor tracked education graduates from 1985-86. It reported that, in 1987, 7 percent of the graduates who had prepared to teach were out of the labor force, 2 percent were unemployed, 16 percent were working part time, and just 75 percent were working as elementary or secondary teachers. Imagine, though, if we were to create a support system for new teachers that allowed them to begin their professional lives the way young professionals do in other fields. They might have mentors, limited work assignments—rather than a full class load on the first day—and internships with a variety of school personnel. Under this system, we could save potentially excellent teachers who are now lost to the profession at the same time as we eliminated those who could not make the grade. Based on current projections of attrition at 5.6 percent of the teaching force, and our experience of hiring about half new teachers and half experienced teachers for vacancies, we could retain 22,000 more teachers each year, increasing the supply and actually doing something about the quality issue as well.

Retirement is another important factor in teacher supply, and it will rise in importance as the teaching force ages. According to the Department of Labor, in 1988, 48 percent of teachers were over 40, and 18.5 percent over 50. By 1990, the number had grown by 83,000 to 19.9 percent over 50, with 1 in 10 being 55 or older. We will see an increase in the retirement rates as we near the end of the century, and we need to look on this as an opportunity to accelerate restructuring. We need to use the changeover to introduce new patterns of instruction and supervision and to focus resources where they can be of most use to children instead of simply allowing for incremental increases and decreases in our budgets.

Moreover, we must begin recruiting while young people are still trying to decide what career they will follow. Each increase of 1 percent in the retirement rate means we will need 30,000 more teachers. It means our current share of graduates who can qualify to teach, which may be 10 or 11 percent of all college graduates, must increase by 25 to 30 percent to accommodate the retirement increase. If an increase of that magnitude seems impossible under the present education system, then our consideration of supply models must include a discussion of the consequences of not changing.

I am pleased to have had an opportunity to offer my thoughts on these matters and especially honored to appear with people for whose work I have the greatest respect. Read on, and there will be a quiz at the end.

II

SUMMARY

Summary of Conference Proceedings

ERLING E. BOE AND DOROTHY M. GILFORD

INTRODUCTION

Since instruction is delivered primarily by teachers, the size, composition, and distribution of the teaching force are vital to the effectiveness of U.S. public education.[1] In turn, public education is widely regarded as central to the nation's social and economic well-being and to its international competitiveness. Consequently, the adequacy of the supply of teachers (in terms of numbers, composition, and distribution) in relation to the demand for them has been a matter of continuing concern among educators and policy makers responsible for ensuring the effectiveness of public schools.

During the current phase of educational reform commencing in the early 1980s, the teaching force has been widely characterized, on the whole, as inadequate to meet current national requirements. In contrast with earlier decades, we no longer define the inadequacy of the teaching force in terms of either its size or the general level of its members' formal credentials. Instead, we are concerned with the ability of the teaching force to deliver high-quality classroom instruction as ultimately measured by student learning outcomes. Numerous recent reports by blue ribbon commissions have concluded that education as a whole, and teachers in particular, are not producing public school students with the level of knowledge, skill, and discipline required in today's complex and competitive economic climate.

Note: Since this chapter summarizes the entire proceedings, some of the summary text is excerpted from material contained in subsequent chapters without specific citation. These contributions of conference participants to the summary are acknowledged collectively.

As a result of this broad and critical conclusion about the condition of U.S. public education, numerous policy responses have been, and continue to be, made. Among the policy responses is the recent specification of national education goals by President Bush and state governors, coupled with procedures to monitor progress toward these performance targets. As a major initiative for achieving these goals, the federal administration launched its America 2000 program, a massive effort to develop and test new and better ways to organize and operate schools and to measure student outcomes. Similarly, a number of policy initiatives are under way to upgrade the quality of the nation's teaching force. Among many that could be cited are policies that create alternative entry routes for new teachers, provide federal support for teacher preparation in several fields, and establish a national system for certifying teachers at a high level of teaching competence.

Given the current size (about 2.5 million) and complexity of the nation's teaching force in public education, the development of effective, manageable, and affordable policies to improve the overall quality and distribution of this work force is a formidable task. This task surely would benefit from reliable, detailed information about teacher supply, demand, and quality (TSDQ).

In response to the need for such information, the National Center for Education Statistics (NCES) asked the National Research Council (NRC) to convene a Conference on Teacher Supply, Demand, and Quality: Policy Issues, Models, and Data Bases. The proceedings published here are based on this conference, which was convened by the NRC's Committee on National Statistics (CNSTAT) and Division of Education, Training, and Employment (DETE) in 1991. The overarching purpose of the conference was to contribute to the development and retention of a teaching force of the highest possible quality for U.S. elementary and secondary schools through three activities:

- Identification of the major issues that policy makers can expect to face in the decade to come in developing and retaining a teaching force of the highest possible quality, and of their information needs in doing so;
- Review of the adequacy of leading TSDQ projection models in relation to these information needs and delineation of specific directions in which such models should be developed further to meet these needs more completely; and
- Review of the adequacy of state, regional, and national data bases relevant to TSDQ with respect to the basic data required to generate the information needed by policy makers and delineation of specific directions in which data bases should be developed further to meet these data requirements more completely.

Given this focus on policy issues, projection models, and data bases, conference presentations naturally do not provide a comprehensive review of current knowledge about teacher supply, demand, quality, and shortage. Such reviews are available in the literature. The conference was designed to generate a variety of ideas about the topics addressed rather than to reach a consensus expressed as formal recommendations. These proceedings contain background papers prepared for the conference, invited discussions of these papers, and summaries of open discussion of the ideas presented. Accordingly, the proceedings represent the individual views of conference participants and do not necessarily reflect the views or policies of CNSTAT, DETE, or NCES.

The conference was designed to stimulate discussions and suggestions (a) concerning information needed by policy makers and others in addressing current and emerging TSDQ issues, and (b) for further development of models and data bases needed to generate this information. From the perspective of NCES, the conference was also intended to provide information about the utility and role of its existing data bases and programs in analyzing TSDQ issues and to provide suggestions for enhancing its contributions to this topic.

The conference brought together a broad spectrum of individuals with interests in TSDQ from the perspectives of policy making, modeling, data base development, practice, and research. Sessions were organized around the papers prepared on teacher quality issues, projection models, and data bases, along with prepared discussions of these papers followed by open discussion among conference participants. The conference agenda and the list of conference participants appear in Appendix A.

This volume is organized for the most part in accordance with the agenda: each of the three main topics is followed by a summary of the open discussion among participants, entitled "general discussion." Finally, summary descriptions of national data bases containing information relevant to TSDQ are presented in Appendix B, and the specific TSDQ data elements (i.e., variables) recorded in these data bases are organized and presented in tabular form in Appendix C.

This summary chapter provides a synopsis of the entire conference including TSDQ information needs and suggestions for action made by participants during open discussions of each major topic. Following an overview of teacher supply, demand, and shortage, the remainder of this chapter provides sections on (a) a major policy issue: teacher quality; (b) TSDQ projection models; and (c) teacher data bases at the state, regional, and national levels. Particular information needs and suggestions for action associated with each of these topics are included in these sections. The summary concludes with several general suggestions for action.

The information needs and suggestions for action reported here are not formal recommendations adopted by vote of conference participants and therefore are not referred to as recommendations. Instead, such needs and suggestions emerged during the course of numerous open discussions by participants occurring during the course of the conference. The editors of this volume organized them in the form reported in this summary.

OVERVIEW OF TEACHER SUPPLY, DEMAND, AND SHORTAGE

Teacher Demand

The national demand for public school teachers is defined operationally, and in the aggregate, as the total number of teaching positions funded by local education agencies (LEAs), i.e., the number that LEAs are able and willing to employ at a given time. Total demand thus defined is the end result of a number of considerations leading to the establishment of teaching positions. The main factors determining teacher demand in any particular year are the number of students enrolled in public schools, policies pertaining to curriculum and teacher-pupil ratios, prior commitments to employed teachers, LEA funding capacity, and the prices that must be paid for various types and qualities of teachers.

Aggregate demand, however, is of little use in understanding the dynamics of demand for the teaching force or in designing policies to ensure an adequate supply of teachers. For these purposes, total demand must be specified in greater detail, i.e., disaggregated by teaching assignment and geographic distribution of the teaching positions.

More specifically, computations of disaggregated teacher demand should be stratified by subject matter, grade level, preparation for serving the special needs of students (especially handicapped students and those with limited English proficiency, region of the country, and urbanicity of schools within which teaching positions have been established. In addition, demand should be specified by the attributes of teachers desired, especially teacher qualifications (their training, degree level, licensure, and experience) and race/ethnicity. When specified at this level of detail, teacher demand can be compared with information about teacher supply to examine supply-demand relationships.

Teacher Supply

The national supply of public school teachers in any year is defined, in the aggregate, as the number of eligible individuals available from all sources who are willing to supply their services under prevailing conditions. The supply includes qualified individuals who (a) currently hold teaching positions, (b) seek to enter the profession by applying for open positions, and

(c) would apply for positions if suitable openings existed. The main factors determining who is available to teach are considered to be the availability of teaching positions relative to the availability of positions in other occupations, teacher wages relative to wages in competing occupations, and working conditions in teaching relative to conditions in other occupations. Unfortunately, no sources of data are capable of providing adequate information about the total supply of teachers thus defined (Gilford and Tenenbaum, 1990).

What is known with reasonable precision is the annual number of teachers hired from among those available through several sources of supply. That is, the number of individuals continuing in public school teaching from one year to the next is known, as is the number of individuals entering public school teaching annually. The former group is often called continuing teachers, and the latter group is often called entering teachers or new hires. Collectively, continuing and entering teachers constitute the cohort of individuals employed as teachers (in short, the teaching force[2]), a group representing an unknown proportion of the potential total supply of teachers.

Aggregate information about the size of the teaching force is of only modest value for understanding teacher supply. In practice, it is virtually the same as aggregate demand. To be useful in understanding the teaching force, information is needed about various sources of supply of individuals hired as teachers, as well as about the composition and distribution of the teaching force. Information at this level of detail could then be related to comparable information about teacher demand in efforts to understand the degree to which teacher demand is being met by qualified individuals, as well as the sources of teachers that might be manipulated by policy in order to provide a more adequate supply.

In practice, the term *supply* (as in teacher supply and demand) is typically used imprecisely. Instead of referring to total potential supply, the expression *teacher supply* is used loosely to refer to the composition of the actual teaching force, to potential sources of entering teachers such as recent graduates of teacher preparation programs, and to teacher supply shortages that occasionally occur in some subject matter fields at various geographic locations. The total potential supply of hireable individuals almost always equals or exceeds the number of available teaching positions. Therefore, in the aggregate, the size of the teaching force is usually determined by the demand for teachers as defined by the number of funded teaching positions, not by supply constraints.

Sources of Supply

As previously mentioned, the teaching force is composed of two large groups—employed teachers continuing from year to year and entering teachers in any year. Both are broad categories drawn from more specific sources. Continuing teachers typically have the option of remaining in the same position from one year to the next. Nonetheless, many practicing teachers choose to apply for teaching positions in other schools, in other subject matter fields, or both. Furthermore, some employed teachers may be reassigned to different teaching assignments within a school or reassigned to a different school within the same LEA. Thus, the flows of practicing teachers within the public education system constitute a major source of teachers hired into, or reassigned to, open teaching positions. Their transfer within the system creates openings in positions they vacate, assuming such positions continue to be funded by the LEA. Due to attrition of teachers from the profession and gradual expansion of the total number of teaching positions, a large number of additional individuals are also hired by the public education system each year (Rollefson, 1992). Such entering teachers are drawn from four sources:

- A reserve pool of qualified teachers composed of:
  (a) experienced former teachers and
  (b) graduates of teacher preparation programs from prior years (sometimes called delayed entrants);
- Recent graduates of teacher preparation programs (some of whom are also experienced teachers);
- College graduates who have not completed a teacher preparation program and who have not previously taught (sometimes referred to as entrants via alternate routes); and
- Teachers employed in private schools who migrate to teaching positions in public schools.

In view of this complexity in the sources of employed teachers, detailed information about flows of teachers into and within the profession is vital to understanding the relative importance of these sources of teacher supply.

Teaching Force Composition

The composition of the teaching force is a multifaceted concept that includes teacher qualifications (especially in relation to specific teaching assignments); subject matter specialty; grade level; preparation for serving special needs of students (especially handicapped students and those with limited English proficiency); and teacher characteristics such a race/ethnicity, gender, and age. Existing teacher data bases can provide good information about these and other attributes of the teaching force. This information makes it possible to determine how well the supply of teachers yields a teaching force that corresponds to the demand for teachers with desired characteristics, for various subject matters, grade levels, etc. It would also be very desirable to have similar information about the composition of applicant pools for open teaching positions and, in fact, about the total potential supply of teachers.

Teaching Force Distribution

The teaching force is distributed among public schools that vary by type, grade level, and location. A major concern is that teachers are maldistributed among schools in terms of qualifications, experience, race/ethnicity, and other dimensions of the teaching force. For example, high schools in large urban areas usually attract a teaching force that is less experienced, younger, and less well prepared to teach high school subjects than teachers hired at nearby suburban schools. Therefore, information about the distribution of the teaching force needs to be presented in terms of teacher variables (such as qualifications) to understand fully how well the supply of teachers meets the demand for teachers at schools of various types, levels, and locations. Such analyses of the teaching force are possible with existing teacher data bases. Little is known, however, about the characteristics of applicants (from which entering teachers are selected) as a function of school location. Unless information about applicants is known, it is not possible to determine whether the supply of teachers available to various schools is adequate, or whether difficulty in hiring qualified teachers is due to hiring practices or other factors. This distribution problem stems from teachers' behavioral response to school location, one of the many variables affecting the supply of teachers available to a school. Supply obviously can vary from school to school since supply is a relationship between the number of qualified individuals who would be willing to teach and such incentives as the salary, working conditions offered, the location of the school, and other alternative career opportunities.

Teacher Shortage Issues

Policy makers responsible for ensuring the effectiveness of public education are necessarily concerned that the supply of qualified teachers is sufficient for all schools. Consequently, the topic of actual and potential teacher shortages is being addressed continually. Only occasionally is there concern about teacher surpluses, although that, too, can be a significant policy issue (especially for state governments) if the capacity for preparing teachers in certain fields is well in excess of demand.

Quantity: A Nonproblem

In recent decades, there has been little or no shortage of individuals available to fill open teaching positions; in 1987-88, only one percent of U.S. teaching positions in the public sector were unfilled (NCES, 1991a). The supply of teachers—in gross numbers—has generally been well in excess of demand. During the early 1980s, however, it appeared that general teacher shortages could develop in the late 1980s and 1990s.[3] The following trends seemed to appear in several variables that affect teacher supply and demand in a direction that would increase demand and reduce supply:

- High teacher attrition from the profession partly due to low salaries and poor working conditions,
- Increasing teacher retirement rates due to an aging teacher force,
- Rising public school enrollments due to the echo of the baby boom,
- Continuing decline in teacher-pupil ratios,
- Falling enrollments in teacher preparation programs,
- Decreasing interest among women in teaching due to more lucrative opportunities in other professions, and
- Constriction in the numbers of entering teachers because of more stringent entry standards including entry-level teacher tests and early performance assessments.

Most of these trends did not develop, nor did teacher shortages materialize. Both attrition and retirement rates were lower than expected, a behavioral response on the part of teachers, which for some teachers was probably due to the desire for a high quality of life combined with financial conditions that required a family to have two incomes. Consider the actual trend for each of the projected trends.

High Teacher Attrition. In the early 1980s, attrition rates for public school teachers were estimated to be 8 percent based on an old study (Metz and Fleischman, 1974). More recent data show that the annual teacher attrition from 1987-88 to 1988-89 was 5.6 percent in the nation as a whole (Bobbitt et al., 1991). This lower attrition rate is one of the main reasons why the projected teacher shortages have not materialized. There are several reasons for the lower attrition rate. First, the proportion of young teachers was considerably smaller in the late 1980s than in the early 1970s, and middle-aged teachers have a lower attrition rate than young teachers. Second, women are leaving teaching at all-time low rates, and when they do leave they more often return and take shorter breaks from teaching (Grissmer and Kirby, 1991). This shift has little to do with salary or working conditions, but rather is due to the increasing importance of women's salaries as part of family income over the last 20 years. Third, new teachers are more often drawn from the 30-45 age group (Murnane and Olsen, 1989; Kirby et al., 1991; Murnane and Schwinden, 1989), and individuals who enter at a later age have lower attrition than those entering at younger ages. Fourth, teacher salary levels began to rise in the early 1980s, and much recent work has shown that attrition rates decline as salary increases (Murnane and Olsen, 1989, 1990; Murnane et al., 1989; Grissmer and Kirby, 1991).

Increasing Teacher Retirement Rates. Because the average age of the teaching force has been gradually increasing for a number of years, teacher retirement rates have been increasing and are expected to continue to increase during the next 15 years. Since the average age of teachers is approximately 42, half of all teachers are within 13 years of retirement eligibility. However, most teachers do not retire at age 55; instead, retirement in the 62-65 age range is becoming more common. This slower rate of retirement means that new teacher demand is increasing more slowly than previously thought, and it is more likely that large numbers of teachers will retire during the 2000-2010 period than during the 1990s.

Rising Enrollments and Falling Teacher-Pupil Ratios. Expected higher public school student enrollments nationally have materialized and probably have been higher than originally predicted due to immigration. Teacher-pupil ratios have continued to decline, especially for earlier grades and for mathematics and English courses in high schools. However, further declines in teacher-pupil ratios appear unlikely, at least in the near future, since many states have severe budget problems. In some cases, increases in teacher-pupil ratios may occur.

Falling Enrollments in Teacher Preparation Programs. Although falling enrollments in teacher preparation programs were projected, actual enrollments have been increasing fairly strongly in recent years. Assumptions made in the early 1980s did not take into account student reaction to the perceived increased job opportunities in teaching. Perhaps even more important is recent research showing that new graduates from teacher preparation programs usually fill one-half or less of teacher vacancies each year (Murnane et al., 1989; Kirby et al., 1991). Other sources (former experienced teachers, previously trained but inexperienced teachers, and migrating teachers from private schools) meet a large share of the annual demand for entering teachers. Therefore, new teacher education graduates, instead of being needed to fill most of the demand for entering teachers, are needed to fill only part of this demand.

Decreasing Interest Among Women in Teaching. With increasing opportunities for women to enter medicine, law, business, and other professions during recent decades, forecasters anticipated a decline in the proportion of women in the teaching profession. Instead, the increasing proportion of women in the overall labor force and the increasing role they play in providing family income seems to have resulted in stronger interest by women in teaching, at least as measured by increases in the proportion of women in this profession. In Indiana, for example, women have become a larger percentage of the teaching force during the past 20 years (Kirby et al., 1991; Grissmer and Kirby, 1991). A similar trend occurs in national statistics. In 1966, 69.0 percent of public school teachers were women. This percentage dipped to a low of 65.7 in 1971, but then gradually rose to a new high of 70.2 percent in 1988 (NCES, 1991a). Although it is true that more women are entering other professions, it is also true that more women are entering teaching. The large increase in the population of women ages 20-25 and their greater labor force participation has resulted in more women in almost all professions.

More Stringent Entry Standards. Little evidence exists to support the hypothesis that fewer teachers enter and continue in the profession due to either fear or failure of entry tests or of performance assessments. The evidence from Indiana is that attrition rates of young teachers have declined—not increased—over the last five years, roughly the period when testing was introduced. Most teacher testing may simply delay entry into teaching. While individuals may fail a teacher qualifying test the first time, the failure rates after multiple chances at passing are generally very low. Furthermore, few states or LEAs have adopted testing programs that could serve as barriers to aspiring teachers.

The Problem of Composition

Although most people now recognize that the supply of teachers is generally adequate to fill the ranks of the nation's teaching force, a major concern remains about a shortage of teachers who are able to deliver high-quality instruction in the classroom. In other words, the match between the composition of the teaching force (in terms of subject matter knowledge, instructional skills, fluency in multiple languages, and demographic characteristics) and the demand for teachers with such abilities and characteristics is far from optimal.

In short, there are too few teachers who are able to perform at a high level in their particular teaching assignments. For example, there are shortages of highly qualified teachers in certain subject matters such as science and mathematics (Gilford and Tenenbaum, 1990) and in teaching fields such as bilingual education (Schmidt, 1992). Likewise, there is a shortage of minority teachers (American Association of Colleges for Teacher Education, 1987). Thus, the problem of teacher shortages is now construed in terms of certain inadequacies in the qualifications and characteristics of the teaching force, but not in its size in relation to gross demand.

The Problem of Distribution

Just as the problem of teacher shortage is now construed in terms of inadequacies in the composition of the teaching force, it is similarly construed in terms of inadequacies in the distribution of the teaching force. Teachers are needed, of course, in schools that vary by grade level and by location in urban, suburban, and rural areas. While almost all teaching positions are filled in all these schools, the qualifications of teachers are unequally distributed among them (Oakes, 1990). For example, the shortage of highly qualified teachers in many urban schools is considered to be greater than the overall shortage of such teachers. In this instance, the concern about teacher shortages is defined in terms of the distribution of qualified teachers among schools of different characteristics, not about a general shortage of teachers.

Equilibrating Supply and Demand

Since there is a shortage of highly qualified teachers in some teaching assignments at some locations, it might be expected that a significant proportion of teaching positions would remain unfilled. Yet that is not the case. Hiring practices in the field of education ensure that "teachers" are present to staff almost all classrooms. Only one percent of teaching positions nationally were unfilled in 1987-88 (Hammer and Gerald, 1991).

In particular, three strategies are used to equilibrate supply and demand, two of which work on the supply side and one on the demand side. The main mechanism used is to relax qualification requirements during hiring. If a highly qualified applicant is not available to fill an open teaching position, a less qualified applicant typically will be hired. In fact, many teachers are hired on emergency certificates shortly before a school year begins, a strong indication that a fully qualified candidate was not available. Other ways to compromise on applicant qualifications include hiring experienced teachers with poor performance records or hiring otherwise qualified teachers out of their fields of competence. These compromises with qualifications, which are made to equilibrate teacher supply and demand, are counterproductive to efforts by policy makers and administrators to improve the quality of teaching practice.

Another supply side mechanism used to equilibrate teacher supply and demand is to offer financial incentives for teachers to enter and continue in the profession, i.e., to enhance teacher supply. Some of these incentives entail bonuses offered to teachers in shortage teaching fields, such as bilingual education, and at shortage locations, such as schools in large urban centers. Other financial strategies for enhancing teacher supply are to raise overall teacher salaries so as to make the profession more competitive with other occupations and to raise entry-level teacher salaries substantially so as to attract more novice teachers to the profession.

If the supply of hireable teachers is still not sufficient to fill open teaching positions, then the demand for teachers can be reduced and brought into line with available supply by increasing the workloads of employed teachers. This can be done by increasing class sizes and by increasing the average number of classes assigned to teachers. Both approaches increase the teacher-pupil ratio. While these strategies can be effective in equilibrating teacher supply and demand and thereby ensuring that all classrooms are staffed with a teacher, they do little to enhance the quality of teaching practice. On the contrary, increasing workloads can have an adverse effect on the quality of teaching and the morale of teachers.

TEACHER QUALITY: A MAJOR POLICY ISSUE

Currently the principal policy issue relevant to teacher supply and demand is how to improve teacher quality while simultaneously maintaining a sufficient supply of teachers to meet demand. This issue is particularly important because it is widely presumed that higher-quality teachers will engage in higher-quality teaching practices in their classrooms, which will lead directly to improved student learning outcomes—the prime objectives of all stakeholders in public education. While this presumption may be intuitively obvious, education researchers have found it difficult to demonstrate robust relationships between potential indices of teacher quality, on one hand, and student learning outcomes, on the other (Hanushek, 1986).

The design of effective policies to improve teacher quality has been impeded by three problems. First, there is little general agreement about what specific characteristic of teachers indicates quality. Second, existing models of teacher supply and demand do not address the subject of teacher quality and therefore offer no guidance. Third, data on variables that might indicate teacher quality are very limited, a circumstance that restricts research that might lead to practical measures of quality.

In spite of these problems in defining teacher quality, education policy makers, administrators, and researchers have given considerable attention to five dimensions presumed to indicate quality in education. Two of these dimensions, teacher qualifications and tested ability, are characteristics of individual teachers; they pertain specifically to "teacher quality." The third dimension, the demographic matching of teachers and students, pertains to the quality of a teaching force such as the faculty of a particular school. The fourth dimension, teacher professionalism, involves the degree to which teachers are given responsibility for and authority over their work; it represents a quality dimension of LEA policy. Finally, the fifth dimension, classroom teaching practice, refers specifically to teaching quality, as distinguished from teacher quality. Each of these dimensions is considered in turn in the following sections.

Dimensions of Quality

Teacher Qualifications

Traditionally, teacher quality has been defined by a teacher's formal qualifications, which include completion of a teacher preparation program, accreditation status of the program completed, course work or earned degree(s) beyond the baccalaureate, subject matter majors and minors, credentials by subject matter (state certification/licensure status), and prior teaching experience. A standard or full credential (as contrasted with probationary, temporary, emergency, etc.) in some particular subject matter is intended to serve as a summary indicator of at least minimally adequate training and experience as defined by the particular state issuing the certificate. Thus, an individual holding, or eligible for, a standard certificate is presumed to be of higher quality for teaching in the subject matter of certification than an individual without a certificate.

There are at least three problems with using teacher certification as an indicator of teacher quality. First, standards and procedures for teacher certification vary widely by state. To qualify for standard certification, some states require a master's degree, a qualifying examination, participation in a teacher induction program, and/or a major in the subject matter of certification; others do not. These variations cause problems in equating credentials in conducting cross-state analyses and research on teacher quality. Second, a teacher who holds a standard certificate in two subject matters (e.g., biology and chemistry) but not a third (e.g., mathematics) may be assigned to teach classes in all three—a not uncommon event in a small high school. In this circumstance, it is not clear whether the teacher should be considered to be qualified. Third, past research has not demonstrated reliable or substantial associations between any of the dimensions of teacher qualifications and student learning outcomes (Gilford and Tenenbaum, 1990; Hanushek, 1986).

Nonetheless, teacher certification serves the symbolic function of defining professional qualifications for the teaching profession, a necessary condition for defining any recognized profession. Furthermore, it is argued by some that defining *teacher* quality in terms of credentials is all that can be done reasonably, and that this is precisely the practice used in other professions. A license to practice medicine, for example, is defined by completing an accredited program of medical education and the passing of a qualifying test. This defines, at the very least, a minimum level of quality of a person meeting these standards. Just as physician quality is not defined formally by the morbidity or mortality statistics of patients treated, so the argument goes, teacher quality should not be defined by associating teacher credentials with student learning outcomes.

In recent years, education policy makers have attempted to strengthen teacher credentials in several ways. Several states have moved to regulate teacher education curricula by increasing course requirements in subject matter fields, while decreasing or limiting courses in professional education. However, these policies, even if effective, will affect only newly prepared teachers, not practicing teachers or individuals in the reserve pool of potential entering teachers. A related, but partially contrary, development comes from The Holmes Group, a consortium of education deans of research universities, which strongly advocates a more demanding credential for teachers. This group maintains that a four-year teacher preparation program at the baccalaureate level is insufficient, that instead the education of prospective teachers should be concentrated in subject matter disciplines at this level. They further propose that the professional preparation of all beginning teachers should be provided by some means, e.g., a five-year baccalaureate or a master's degree.

Another policy initiative to strengthen teacher credentials has been the formation of the National Board of Professional Teaching Standards (NBPTS). The board plans to conduct examinations that highly capable teachers can take to qualify for board certification as master teachers. This plan, still in the development phase, uses the board certification system in the medical profession as a model.

Finally, another initiative, the use of alternative routes to certification, has gained momentum in recent years. A total of 33 states now have provisions for some form of alternative route to certification (Feistritzer, 1990). Through alternative routes, individuals who have earned baccalaureate (or higher) degrees but who have not completed a traditional teacher preparation program are allowed to short-circuit normal requirements for obtaining a teaching credential. Instead, some teacher training is typically provided by a variety of means, such as intensive summer programs before teaching commences, inservice training after teaching commences, and/or close supervision by experienced teachers once teaching begins. The use of alternative routes into the teaching profession was first proposed as a means of increasing the supply of math and science teachers, but proponents of this approach argue that it will also enhance teacher quality by attracting new teachers who are brighter, better educated in subject matter fields, and more experienced than the typical teacher education graduate. The general effectiveness of alternative route programs in achieving these objectives remains to be demonstrated.

Tested Ability

There is evidence that college students who enter teacher preparation programs tend to score lower on tests of academic aptitude than students entering other career tracks; that, among teacher education graduates, lower-scoring students are more likely to enter the teaching profession; and that, among employed teachers, those who score higher on the National Teacher Examination (NTE) tend to leave the profession sooner (Murnane et al., 1989; Murnane and Olsen, 1990). Thus, throughout the supply pipeline, lower-scoring individuals tend to be selected for and retained in the teaching profession.

While these trends appear to be contrary to the objective of securing a teaching force of high quality, the general relevance of tested ability of teachers to the task of teaching and to the quality of student learning outcomes has not been demonstrated.[4] One reason for this may be that tests used to measure teacher abilities are much too narrow and have been limited to the multiple-choice format. The ability to select the correct answer on an aptitude or achievement test may not indicate anything about a teacher's ability to solve open-ended problems, to explain solutions to students, or to create problems for teaching students. While intellectual ability is obviously relevant to teaching, it is not known how low ability test scores must be before teaching performance is adversely affected.

Nonetheless, a substantial majority of states include some form of teacher assessment in the certification process for new teachers. Yet no state has been able to demonstrate the job relevance of these test scores. To avoid lawsuits, cutoff scores are set very low and ample opportunities are provided for those who fail to be retested. Even if test performance were demonstrated to be relevant to teaching performance, the use of tested ability in initial teacher certification would affect only new teachers, not teachers certified before the tests were introduced.

Two national initiatives are currently under way to develop better teacher ability tests. The process being developed by NBPTS for certifying master teachers involves a test, and the Educational Testing Service is developing a new version of the NTE. In addition to measuring subject matter knowledge, the tests being developed by both sources will include major performance components that will require teachers to demonstrate teaching practice skills.

Demographic Matching of Teachers and Students

Demographic matching refers to the similarity between the distribution of demographic characteristics (such as race/ethnicity, gender, and age) of the teachers in a school and those of the students. It has been argued that the distribution of the teaching force by race/ethnicity constitutes a significant dimension of quality relevant to the outcomes of schooling for minority students who need role models. There is concern about the teaching force in this respect because it is largely white, suburban, middle class, and female. By contrast, demographic trends in the nation as a whole (and especially in the population of public school students) are clearly moving dramatically in the direction of a larger proportion of minority populations (especially of Hispanic background) and of an increasing proportion of students from young families with substandard incomes.

Even if the demographics of the teaching force matched the demographics of public school students on a school-by-school basis, it would not be possible to match teachers and students on a class-by-class basis, since classes of students are usually heterogeneous. Given this difficulty, perhaps the main concern should be with improving the quality of classroom teaching practice because of its centrality to academic outcomes, rather than teacher-pupil demographic matching.

Nonetheless, students are generally aware of the demographic characteristics of teachers in their schools, not just their own classroom teachers. Representative diversity of the teaching force is considered to be important because minority students will be exposed to role models of like characteristics who are achieving in the teaching profession. Moreover, diversity within a school's teaching force may increase knowledge and understanding of different cultural groups in both students and teachers and improve students' chances of interacting successfully with different cultural groups that they are likely to encounter later in the workplace. For these reasons, demographic matching of teachers and students is considered to be a quality dimension of education.

Policy initiatives to increase demographic matching have concentrated on the supply of new teachers by attempting to increase the numbers of minority students entering college, with the hope that these increased numbers will yield more minority students who elect teaching as a career. The main inducement used for increasing minority enrollment in college has been the provision of financial assistance. To be effective, this strategy must be sustained over many years because it addresses only the production of new teachers, not the demographic mix of the active teaching force and the reserve pool of potential teachers.

Teacher Professionalism

The fourth dimension of quality of interest to policy makers is the professional lives of teachers. In view of the complexity and context-specificity of teaching, it is widely advocated that teachers should have professional autonomy and responsibility similar to that typically accorded members of other professions. Advocates of conferring professional autonomy on teachers argue that it will enhance the attractiveness of the profession as a career choice and will improve the quality of classroom teaching practice. Though these arguments are often made and are cogent, there is little research evidence to support them, and so there is ample room for skepticism.

Several major trends in education policy promote teacher professionalization. The rapidly proliferating practice of decentralizing authority over major aspects of school operations from district offices to school councils (under the rubric of school-based management) usually places teachers in key decision making roles as council members. Likewise, programs involving merit pay, career ladders, and/or peer evaluation typically entail enhanced professional responsibility for teachers. These programs are often resisted by teachers because they are difficult and time-consuming. They require special training for decision making and management and, in addition, require released time from instruction—resources that all too often are not made available. In addition, policies that require teachers to collaborate with each other and to observe and evaluate peers are counter to the traditional culture of teaching. Not surprisingly therefore, policies promoting the professionalization of teaching often do not originate with teachers, but instead with educational administrators and policy makers.

Classroom Teaching Practice

The quality of classroom teaching practice has been widely criticized in recent years because of its emphases on basic skills instead of higher-order thinking, on discrete facts instead of problem solving, on teaching for exposure instead of for understanding, and on competition among students instead of cooperation. In general, teaching has been watered down and too little has been expected of students.

Several recent reports on U.S. education argue that schooling must better prepare students for the world of work they will be entering, which will require problem-solving skills, adaptability, and the ability to work in teams. Not only must the content and strategy of teaching change, but teachers must also become increasingly prepared to teach a different kind of student, one that has been alienated traditionally from schools and that is unlikely to be similar to the teacher demographically.

Of the five quality dimensions reviewed here, the quality of teaching practice is most directly connected logically to the objective of increasing the quality of student learning. This is what students experience every hour of the school day. However, there are no clear indicators of the quality dimension of classroom teaching that correlate with student learning outcomes (Hanushek, 1986), and therefore it is difficult to assess strategies intended to change practice.

Improvements in teaching practices are also very difficult to implement, particularly since research indicates that there is a strong tendency for teachers to emulate the teachers they observed as students. We are caught in a vicious cycle of mediocre practice modeled after mediocre practice, of trivialized knowledge begetting more trivialized knowledge. But traditional teaching is no longer good enough.

Improved teacher training is a critical component of improving teaching practice. Because the teaching force is so large and the vast majority of teachers continue from year to year, inservice training for practicing teachers is needed if rapid change is to occur. Yet there is no broad-based policy initiative (such as school-based management, for example) specifically addressed to upgrading the quality of classroom practice by active teachers. To be sure, there is some inservice training for active teachers, but most state and locally sponsored programs do not incorporate the strategies for influencing teaching practices that have been demonstrated to be effective during two decades of research.

Some policy actions have been initiated to improve the quality of teaching practice of new teachers. For example, several states prescribe a probationary period of a year or two for new teachers during which their teaching practice is assessed. The research on which these assessments are based was conducted at the elementary level, where the content is weighted toward basic skills and therefore has not much relevance to the teaching of higher-order thinking. Another strategy for improving the practice of new teachers is an induction program now required by 13 states. Under these programs, LEAs must provide first-year teachers with some sort of guidance, usually by experienced teachers. However, to the extent that experienced teachers themselves do not engage in the kind of quality classroom practice that is needed today, new teachers are socialized into traditional, but increasingly inadequate, teaching practices through such induction programs.

An alternative model for improving teaching practice currently under development is the professional development school (PDS), in which student teachers receive their practical experience and active teachers have opportunities to learn more about teaching. In contrast to traditional lab schools operated for decades by many colleges of education, PDSs are genuine collaborations between university-based teacher education programs and public schools. So far, although PDSs are intended to improve both the preparation of new teachers and the practice of the existing teaching force, they have emphasized the preparation of new teachers and have not developed means by which benefits will ripple to other schools within a LEA. Consequently, the potential of this model to upgrade teaching practice on a substantial scale remains to be demonstrated.

Finally, major policy efforts are being made in many states and by the federal government to restructure schools, the basic intent of which is to improve the quality of educational outcomes. Although these efforts may lead to significant improvements in teaching practice, as well as other aspects of school organization and operation, they are not targeted specifically at improving the quality of classroom practice. Hard data are not yet available about the educational benefits of restructured schools, including improvement in teaching practice.

Limits of Teacher Quality

As stated earlier, it is widely presumed that higher-quality teachers will engage in higher-quality teaching practice in their classrooms, which will lead directly to improved student learning outcomes. The general validity of this presumption is examined critically here in light of available knowledge and in terms of prospects for attaining further improvements in teacher quality.

If we recognize improved student learning outcomes as the prime objective of public education yet to be attained, then it is certainly important to identify factors that can be manipulated by educational policy that will yield progress toward achieving this objective. Improving teacher quality further is one major possibility—one that has been manipulated by policy for more than a century.

However, it should not be assumed that improvement in teacher quality (i.e., credentials or tested ability) will lead automatically to improvement in the quality of teaching practice or in other aspects of educational quality (i.e., demographic matching of teachers and students and teacher professionalism). For example, the selection of teachers who have earned master's degrees or who have scored high on ability tests will not result automatically in better teaching, unless they are taught how to teach more effectively. Likewise, improving the match between teachers' credentials and their teaching assignments will not necessarily improve practice, nor will reducing demographic disparity between the teaching force and the student population or adding programs to professionalize teaching. Conversely, improving classroom practice will not necessarily improve teacher credentials or reduce demographic diversity. Improvement in any one of the five dimensions of educational quality reviewed here will not necessarily improve any of the other dimensions. To the extent that these dimensions of quality are considered to be important, then improvement of each should be addressed directly, and any intended impact on teaching practice should be assessed instead of assumed.

An important question is whether the potential for further improvement in teacher quality is sufficient to affect student outcomes favorably. There are practical limits on gains that might be possible in indices of teacher quality. Given the sheer size of the teaching force in public education—approximately 2.5 million individuals employed as teachers (NCES, 1991a), the task of raising overall teacher quality is indeed formidable. About 10 percent of college-educated women and 4 percent of college-educated men are employed as teachers in the United States; no other profession draws such a large proportion of college-educated adults (Lanier, 1986). If entering the teaching profession were made so attractive in terms of compensation and working conditions that many more of the best and brightest went into teaching, then we would soon be worrying about a tested-ability problem in other professions in the private sector such as medicine, law, and engineering. Salaries in these professions would no doubt escalate to compete with the higher salaries for teachers. Under any likely scenario, the size of the teaching force would simply be too large to be filled by individuals from the upper levels of tested ability.

As previously stated, research on measures of teacher credentials and tested ability has demonstrated only very limited associations with student learning outcomes. There are several plausible reasons for this lack of association. First, available measures of teacher quality may have little relevance to the quality of teaching practice, though this cannot be determined with certainty because independent measures of the quality of teaching practice do not exist. Second, policy efforts over many decades to improve teacher credentials may have so restricted the range of differences among teachers that the remaining variability is irrelevant to the student learning outcomes. For example, a minuscule 0.6 percent of public school teachers have not earned a baccalaureate degree (NCES, 1991a). Thus, for all practical purposes, the range of variability on the degree credential is restricted to the difference between baccalaureate and master's degrees. Third, variables other than teacher quality, such as school policies, student readiness, and parents' expectations, may be so strongly associated with student learning that the contribution of the remaining variability in teacher quality is obscured. Finally, current measures of student learning outcomes may not capture critical aspects of student learning and therefore may not reflect adequately the contribution of classroom practices. These measures have been predominantly paper-and-pencil tests of the multiple-choice type, which primarily measure basic skills. Dissatisfaction with such measures of student learning is leading to the development of alternative performance-based measures.

The several limitations reviewed here in understanding and improving teacher quality as currently measured do not suggest that teacher quality is irrelevant. Basic command of subject matter knowledge is obviously vital in order to teach mathematics or Russian, for example. What is not clear is the relative importance of variations in teachers' subject matter knowledge and teaching skill above some threshold level when compared with the importance of other variables related to student learning.

Teacher Quality: Information Needs and Suggestions for Action

During the course of conference presentations and discussions, participants identified additional information needed to address teacher quality issues. Much of this information is relevant to planning improvements in TSDQ data bases, and some can be useful in designing future research with existing data bases. Conferees also made a number of suggestions for actions to enhance knowledge about teacher quality. These information needs and suggestions are reported as such below. However, they are not formal recommendations adopted by vote of conferees, and should not be interpreted as such.

Information Need 1: Teacher Quality Indicators. Since understanding the importance of teacher quality is severely limited by the lack of accepted measures of this attribute, measures are needed that give a truer and more useful indication of teacher quality. Information is also needed about what such indicators reveal with respect to teacher quality-quantity tradeoffs, quality-price relationships, and projections of quality and quantity of teacher supply.

Information Need 2: Teacher Credentials. Since states license teachers under widely differing systems, better information is needed for individual states about approved and rejected applications for teaching credentials by type (i.e., permanent, emergency, etc.) and source (e.g., out-of-state teachers, range of college curricula leading to initial entry to teaching, including alternative routes) and about the match between teaching credentials and assignments and about the importance of teaching credentials to teaching practice. Information is also needed about the qualifications of teachers who fill new vacancies. More information is needed about whether and how teachers' credentials influence school district hiring, salary, and promotion practices. Finally, information is needed about whether and how credentialing policies influence the attractiveness of teaching. Do course requirements influence a student's decision to enter teaching?

Information Need 3: Demographic Matching. Given the widespread interest in promoting minority representation in the teaching force and the presumed relevance of demographic diversity of this force to desirable educational outcomes, information is needed at the school level about demographic mix of the teaching force and about how well this mix matches the demographic mix of enrolled students. In addition, more information is needed about the race/ethnicity of members of the teacher supply.

Information Need 4: Teacher Professionalism. The large number of broad policies intended to promote teacher professionalism (some of which are opposed generally by teachers) make research into their effectiveness difficult. As an interim step, it would be useful to document teachers' attitudes about taking more professional responsibility. Data are needed about teacher perceptions of their control over various aspects of their work and about the relationship of variations in such perceptions to teacher retention, transfer, and attrition.

Information Need 5: Programs to Improve Practice. Data should also be gathered about some of the actual programs designed to improve practice. More specific data are needed about selection of and characteristics of participants in induction programs, assessment programs, and professional development schools. Detailed data are also needed on the total volume of inservice activities provided and the character and duration of these activities.

Information Need 6: Assessment of Quality of Teaching Practice. It is difficult to develop and expensive to apply direct measures of the quality of teaching practice. One feasible approach to tapping an important aspect of teaching practice would be to document teachers' beliefs about what should be taught and about their role in facilitating learning. Information about teacher beliefs and their relation to student learning could be helpful in assessing the quality of teaching practice.

Suggestions for action on the topic of teacher quality centered around its definition and measurement. Without consensus on appropriate and useful measures of teacher quality, relevant components of data bases cannot be developed, and analyses of the quality dimension within teacher supply and demand are not possible. Specific suggestions made are presented in the following paragraphs.

Suggestion 1: Teacher Quality Indicators. Sustained research should be undertaken on various indicators of teacher quality with the intent of developing consensus about valid indicators of teacher quality that can be measured and included in teacher data bases. The new indicators of teacher quality that will be generated by NBPTS and the revised NTE, as well as by efforts of states (such as Vermont) to develop new performance measures of teacher effectiveness, should be included in the NCES data systems. More generally, it was also suggested that for teachers, as for physicians and lawyers, credentials become the prime indicator of quality.

Suggestion 2: Tested Ability of Teachers. Emphasis should be placed on research on test development. Tests of pedagogical subject matter knowledge that are directly relevant to effective teaching need to be developed and used in place of present tests, which emphasize general ability and general subject matter knowledge and have little demonstrable relevance to teaching practice. Such test development should be undertaken under the auspices of specialized test development organizations rather than by NCES. However, NCES should play a role in the validation of these new assessments by adding some items from such tests to the Teacher Questionnaire for the National Assessment of Educational Progress (NAEP) so the teachers' responses could be correlated with student achievement scores.

Suggestion 3: Teaching Practice. NCES should develop items about teaching practice for inclusion in its Teacher Questionnaire for NAEP. Items might include teachers' beliefs about subject matter content that should be taught and about the role of teachers in facilitating student learning. Teacher responses to such items could be correlated with student learning outcomes.

Suggestion 4: Demographic Matching. Efforts to improve minority representation in the teaching force so as to better match the proportion of minority pupils could be enhanced by better tracking and projections of the race/ethnicity attribute of the teachers. Specifically, a race/ethnicity item should be incorporated routinely in all national surveys of teachers. As indications of potential new minority teachers in the pipeline, NCES should consider making routine projections of (a) the total pool of minority high school pupils who are eligible for college and (b) the total pool of minority college graduates.

Suggestion 5: Successful Schools of Education. Schools of education vary in the degree to which they are successful in producing teacher graduates that are actively recruited by LEAs. As an approach to understanding the nature of teacher training leading to LEA satisfaction with teaching practices, it was suggested that characteristics of successful schools of education be compared with those of schools considered to be poor in this respect.

TSDQ PROJECTION MODELS

The continuing concern of educational policy makers over the adequacy of the prospective supply of teachers in relation to demand has stimulated efforts over the years to produce data that could be used in projections of future supply-demand balance. Many of these efforts have focused on producing data bases fundamental to teacher supply and demand analyses (the topic of the following major section). Simultaneously, other efforts have focused on developing the analytic tools required to use these data to provide information needed by policy makers and others.

Prominent among these tools are teacher supply-demand projection models that have been developed to predict trends in the teacher labor market, especially to estimate imbalances or deficiencies in time for policy makers to take corrective action. An assessment of the adequacy of TSDQ projection models with respect to predicting trends in the teacher labor market is presented in the following sections. In short, useful teacher demand models—which depend on student enrollment and pupil-teacher ratio—have been developed. Little has been done, however, to create behavioral demand models that will show how the pupil-teacher ratios will change with future changes in causal factors such as economic, demographic, or fiscal conditions. At the national level, NCES has moved to develop such a model.

By contrast, teacher retention/attrition models are more advanced, and recent research findings and improved data bases can be expected to lead to further progress in the development of such models. Finally, models for projecting the supply of entering teachers from multiple sources have not been developed because of lack of data about the number of eligible individuals willing to enter the teaching profession at any given time. People enter teaching for a variety of reasons: for economic reasons, to have a schedule similar to that of their own children, to work with children, because of an outstanding teacher who served as a role model, or because of the satisfaction of helping others. Teachers also leave teaching for a variety of reasons—to engage in fulltime child rearing or to follow a spouse whose job has been relocated. Although it is known that teacher supply, like the supply of skilled labor for other occupations, is sensitive to financial incentives (Freeman,1971), data are not available to model the effect of other determinants of teacher supply.

Almost all of the existing models deal only with numbers of teachers and not with teacher quality. One exception is a model (Manski, 1987) consisting of two parts: one which explains occupation choice (between teaching and nonteaching) as a function of the earnings and nonmonetary characteristics associated with alternative occupations. The second explains occupation-specific earnings as a function of academic ability and other factors. This behavioral model is of interest because, in principle, it could be used to answer policy questions about improving the average ability of the teaching force by maintaining minimum ability standards in combination with sufficient salary increases. As Manski notes, the model is dependent on the intuitive assumption that SAT score is a measure of teacher quality, although there is no research that supports this assumption.

Types of TSDQ Models

A teacher supply-demand projection model consists of a set of mathematical relationships that can be used to estimate future levels of teacher supply and demand. Ideally, these projections are linked to future economic and educational conditions and policies. A complete model consists of three main components, or submodels, for projecting: (a) the demand for teachers, (b) the supply of teachers retained from year to year (or, equivalently, a model of teacher attrition), and (c) the supply of potential entrants into the active teaching force. The latter two components, taken together, constitute projections of total teacher supply, which (ideally) can be compared with projections of total demand. In contrast with projection models, system models provide only a cross-sectional identification and organization of major variables involved in understanding teacher supply-demand:

they do not involve other variables and equations needed to estimate future trends in supply and demand.

The types of information that can be generated with a supply-demand projection model depends on several model characteristics. One such characteristic is the extent of *disaggregation* of teachers by subject matter specialty and other variables. Some models deal only with teachers in the aggregate; others disaggregate in ways that make it possible to respond to detailed policy questions.

Another key characteristic is whether a teacher supply-demand projection model is *mechanical* or *behavioral*. Mechanical models estimate only what will happen in the future if established trends continue. Behavioral models, in contrast, link demand and supply estimates to changes in pertinent conditions and policies. Only behavioral models can be used to address "what if" questions about the effects of hypothetical changes in circumstances on teacher supply and demand.

A third critical attribute of teacher supply-demand projection models is whether and how they deal with teacher *quality*. Unfortunately, nearly all projection models avoid the quality dimension and focus only on numbers of teachers. Nonetheless, teacher quality is considered here because of the growing urgency of this topic.

Teacher Demand

The total national demand for public school teachers is defined by the sum of the number of teaching positions funded by all LEAs, i.e., the number of teachers that LEAs are able and willing to employ at a given time. The size of the employed teaching force is virtually the same (99 percent) as total demand (NCES, 1991b). Projections of demand less projections of the supply of retained teachers estimate the number of individuals that will have to be hired into the teaching force to replace those who leave, to adjust for changes in student enrollment and to respond to changes in educational policy such as in teacher-pupil ratio.

The concept of teacher demand as the number of funded teaching positions is an economic definition that treats teacher demand as contingent on how much teachers cost and how much money LEAs are able and willing to spend on teachers. An alternative concept of teacher demand is framed in terms of fixed requirements for teachers, such as set by predetermined teacher-pupil ratios. The significance of this difference for modeling is that the requirements notion is expressed in mechanical projection models based on teacher-pupil ratios (or trends therein); whereas the economic definition points toward behavioral models in which estimates are derived from multivariate equations linking demand to various economic and demographic variables. Thus far, mechanical models dominate the field of teacher demand projections.

The prevailing method for projecting demand is the mechanical method of multiplying projected student enrollments by current or extrapolated teacher-pupil ratios. The simple, standard demand model of this type can be expressed as follows: (Projected number of teachers demanded in year t) = (Projected student enrollment in year t) x (Projected teacher-pupil ratio in year t). This method yields no information on how the teacher-pupil ratios themselves, and hence the numbers of teachers demanded, can be expected to change in the future in response to changes in school policy, course enrollment patterns, and economic and demographic conditions. This does not mean that such projections are necessarily inaccurate, but it minimizes their utility in policy analysis. Although there do not appear to have been any state-level efforts to create behavioral demand models, NCES has moved in the direction of such a model at the national level by shifting from a mechanical to a regression-based projection method. Although the present NCES model needs to be developed further, it represents an important step in the right direction and a point of departure for further national and state-level modeling efforts.

Models incorporating disaggregated projections of teacher demand by level of education and subject specialty have become relatively common, but the methods used to disaggregate by subject are crude. The standard approach is simply to assume that the distribution of enrollment among subjects at each level of education will remain constant.

An important implicit assumption underlying all the current demand projection models is that the teacher market has been and is in a condition of excess supply. This assumption is reasonable in the aggregate and for most subject areas, but currently it may be wrong for certain fields, such as science, mathematics, and special education. Wherever the excess-supply assumption is violated (i.e., where unmet demand exists), projections based on actual numbers of teachers employed in the past will understate the numbers of teachers likely to be wanted in the future.

Ideally, behavioral demand models should be developed in which projections are based on multivariate econometric models relating numbers of teachers demanded to economic and demographic factors such as per student expenditure, per capita fiscal capacity, student/population ratio, the makeup of the student population, and salary levels both inside and outside teaching. Such models will probably have to be constructed at a level of aggregation one rung below the level at which they are to be used; that is, state-level demand models will have to be constructed with district-level data, and a national model with state-level data. Since necessary data appear to be available nationally and for at least some states, such modeling seems eminently feasible and could proceed if necessary resources were available.

Apparently no existing teacher demand projection model incorporates teacher quality variables. The fact that teacher salary schedules typically are scaled by experience and training indicates that qualifications matter to LEAs. These variables define dimensions of teacher quality, just as number of funded positions define demand for teacher quantity, so it is meaningful to speak of a demand for quality. Other aspects of teacher quality that warrant investigation are quality-price relationships (how much extra LEAs are willing to pay for valued attributes of teachers) and quality-quantity (the extent to which LEAs would be willing to accept lower teacher-pupil ratios to gain higher quality but more expensive teachers) tradeoffs. Conceivably these relationships might be included in future projection models, but there are formidable obstacles to designing models incorporating both teacher quantity and quality, and it is unlikely that this will be accomplished soon.

Teacher Retention and Attrition

The primary source of supply of total teachers in any year is the active teaching force during the prior year. Typically, 92 to 96 percent of a state's teaching force continues from one year to the next. The remainder constitute annual attrition from the active teaching force. The simple, standard retention model can be expressed as follows: (Projected number of teachers retained from year t to year $t + 1$ = (Number of teachers employed in year t) x (Projected teacher retention percentage for year t). The difference between total teacher demand and retained teachers represents the number of entering teachers that need to be hired to satisfy demand fully. Hence, it is very important to be able to estimate teacher retention (or attrition) accurately because even a small percentage error in estimating teacher retention translates into a large percentage error in estimating the number of entering teachers to be hired.

At their best, state projection models for teacher retention differentiate extensively among various categories of teachers. The more sophisticated state retention models now project numbers of continuing teachers by applying age-specific attrition rates to age distributions of teachers, differentiating also by level of education and subject specialty. Nonetheless, many states still project the supply of retained teachers simply by applying statewide average attrition rates to all categories of teachers. However, recent research on teacher attrition has yielded findings that could translate into further improvements in models for projecting numbers of retainees. Among these are findings about male-female differences in attrition patterns, changes in attrition rates over time, and, perhaps most important, effects of salary levels, working conditions, and other economic factors on exit rates from teaching. If the estimates of effects of salaries, working conditions, etc., can be refined, the present mechanical (albeit sophisticated) models could be transformed into behavioral models of teacher attrition.

Until recently, data limitations at the national level have constrained the number of separate average attrition rates used by NCES to two: rates for elementary teachers and rates for secondary teachers. National projections can be expected to improve, however, because of the availability of more accurate and detailed data from SASS and TFS questionnaires. It will soon be possible to project national as well as state teacher retention on the basis of disaggregated age-specific and subject-specific attrition rates. Research now under way may also lead to the incorporation of certain behavioral elements (e.g., responses to salary changes) into the national models.

Though it would be desirable to be able to estimate the quality of retained teachers, apparently no retention/attrition model has included teacher quality variables. However, a major concern that higher-quality teachers (to the extent that the NTE score signifies quality) are more likely to leave the profession has been borne out by some research (Murnane, Singer, and Willet, 1989; Murnane and Olsen, 1990). Although the problem of measuring teacher quality remains, it would be relatively easy to include a quality variable in retention/attrition models because there would be no need to estimate what quality would have been under hypothetical conditions.

In sum, retention/attrition projection models are the most advanced elements of teacher supply-demand models, and further progress using recent research findings can be expected, widening the sophistication gap between attrition models and those for other components.

Entering Teachers

To satisfy teacher demand fully, entering teachers usually must be hired to augment the number of teachers retained from the prior year. The four sources of supply of potential entering teachers—the reserve pool, recent graduates of teacher preparation programs, entrants via alternate routes, and private school teachers—yield the number of entering teachers that are hired annually into public education to augment the number of retained teachers. Estimates of future demand for entering teachers can be obtained by subtracting the projected number of retained teachers from the projected demand for teachers. Then comparisons between the projected numbers of entrants needed and the projected supply of entrants should lead to conclusions about the adequacy of supply and therefore the likelihood of future teacher shortages or surpluses. Although the number of teachers entering the profession annually can be measured and projected, the supply of potential entrants cannot be measured or projected, at the present time, for any of the sources of supply. Little credence should be given, therefore, to any projections of teacher shortage or surplus based on comparisons between projections of demand and purported projections of supply.

The main problem in modeling entering teacher supply is that the number of eligible individuals willing to supply their services as teachers at a given point in time under the conditions prevailing at that time is not known with respect to any of the sources of supply. While estimates can be made, for example, of the number of experienced (but inactive) teachers and the number of recently trained teachers, no data are available about the proportion of these groups that are available to enter the teaching profession.

The lack of adequate methods, or even a sound conceptual framework, for projecting the supply of potential entrants into teaching continues to prevent the development of complete supply-demand models that can be used to assess the supply-demand balance. Many current models offer no projections at all of the supply of potential entrants into teaching. Those that do rely on one or the other of two unsatisfactory approaches. The first approach, equating the projected supply to the projected stock of persons certified to teach in a state, is clearly inadequate. Many certified persons are not in the supply (i.e., willing to teach under current conditions), and many persons in the supply may not (yet) be certified. The second approach, projecting supply by applying past entry rates to numbers of persons presumed to be in various supply pools, is invalid because past entry rates are more likely to have been determined by numbers of open teaching positions (demand) than by numbers available (supply). Most model developers have not yet come to grips with the fundamental problem that, if past hiring mainly reflects demand, then supply cannot be inferred from it. Consequently, data on employment and hiring cannot be used to measure current teacher supply nor to project future supply. Additional information is needed to estimate how many teachers would be available to take teaching jobs if hiring were not limited by demand.

Fortunately, some progress may be possible in modeling the reentry behavior of inactive experienced teachers by using essentially the same methods as have been used to model teacher attrition. These methods do not apply, however, to the other major sources of potential entrants. Although satisfactory methods of projecting the supplies of these other sources of entrants are unlikely to be developed soon, several strategies do seem worth pursuing. One is to estimate supply from information on numbers of applicants for teaching positions. Such information is collectable either from individuals or school districts. Serious problems would arise in interpreting it because a teacher may submit applications to multiple districts, but the resulting estimates, even if flawed, might be substantially better than what is now available. A related approach is to derive supply estimates from survey data on the job-seeking behavior and intentions of persons in selected groups. Although this method would be subject to all the usual problems of using responses to hypothetical questions to infer labor market behavior, the issue is whether substantial gains could be made, compared with the present unsatisfactory situation.

We consider briefly the feasibility of introducing a quality variable into the supply model. The principal available strategy for improving teacher quality is to use a higher quality standard in hiring entering teachers, thereby gradually altering the quality of the teaching force. However, both the feasibility of improving teacher quality and the rate at which quality can be improved depend on the distribution of quality in the supply of prospective new hires. In principle, prospective entrants could be classified by quality, and separate entry rates or propensities to apply for positions could be determined for persons in the different quality strata. At present, the unsolved basic conceptual problems of supply modeling are so severe that taking the quality dimension into account is a remote prospect.

Projection Models: Information Needs and Suggestions for Action

In addition to quality related topics, participants identified a number of information needs pertaining to various aspects of teacher demand, supply, and their equilibration. Conferees also suggested a number of actions that could be undertaken to improve projection models. These information needs and suggestions are reported as such below. However, they are not formal recommendations adopted by vote of conferees, and should not be interpreted as such.

Information Need 7: Subject-Specific Course Enrollment. With respect to projecting teacher demand by subject matter field, more refined information is needed about trends over time in subject-specific course enrollment rates. Methods will also have to be developed for projecting such rates.

Information Need 8: Reserve Pool. Although the reserve pool of certified teachers is the major source of entering teachers hired into public education and is probably in decline, very little is known about its size and composition. Information is needed about the current and projected size of this pool as a function of teacher quality and other characteristics. Adding a brief survey of applicants for teaching positions in the Demand and Shortage Questionnaire of the Schools and Staffing Survey would increase knowledge about characteristics of the active portion of the reserve pool and changes in this group over time.

Information Need 9: Teacher-Pupil Ratios. Information is needed about conditions under which teacher-pupil ratios change, because this ratio can serve as an equilibrating factor in supply-demand models and as an indicator of teacher workloads. More needs to be known about the impact of economic factors, changes in student demographics, and the introduction of instructional technology on teacher-pupil ratios, as well as teacher receptivity to tradeoffs between teacher-pupil ratios and teacher salaries.

Information Need 10: Teacher Migration. Although teacher migration from one school to another is one of the major sources of supply to, and attrition from, schools, LEAs, and states, little is known about this phenomenon. Therefore, information is needed about patterns of migration as a function of teacher characteristics and attributes of schools and LEAs from which and to which teachers migrate.

Information Need 11: Teacher Support. Since support provided to teachers—especially novice teachers—is presumed to be related to the quality of teaching practice and to teacher retention, better information is needed about the usefulness of various kinds of support provided to teachers.

Information Need 12: Supply-Demand Analysis of Science and Math Teachers. In view of the importance of science and mathematics teachers to national education goals and the discrepant findings about their retention in the teaching profession, much better information is needed to assess the potential for shortages in these subject matter fields. More specifically, information is needed about sources of entering supply, migration and reassignment, attrition and reentry, and retirement for teachers in the various science disciplines and mathematics.

Information Need 13: Teacher Mobility. Since teachers have opportunities for employment in the general labor market as well as in the teaching profession, more extensive comparative data related to occupational choice are needed for teaching and other occupations. Information is also needed about factors related to occupational choices made by individuals who hold teaching credentials, whether or not currently employed as teachers.

Information Need 14: Teacher Retirement. Since the average age of teachers has gradually increased during recent decades, there is the clear prospect of accelerated attrition due to retirement. To project the magnitude of this attrition and to develop retirement policies, information is needed to project retirement rates as a function of teacher characteristics and tradeoffs between salary levels and various retirement options and benefits.

The present inadequate state of development of TSDQ projection models generated a number of suggestions about actions that could be taken to develop models more fully and about variables that need to be taken into account during the course of such development. These are identified in the paragraphs below.

Suggestion 6: Comprehensive TSDQ Model Development. A comprehensive model (or models) of teacher supply and demand needs to be developed to improve the accuracy and utility of estimates of supply-demand balances and imbalances, and to serve as a framework for determining the relevance of data to analyses of teacher supply-demand issues. In this regard, it was also suggested that NCES work toward integrating their supply-demand model into a larger model that encompasses the entire economy, and that NCES explore the use of both cross-sectional and time-series approaches in their modeling.

Suggestion 7: Guidebook for TSDQ Model Development. Given the fairly rudimentary state of TSDQ models in most states and the many technical issues involved in model development, it was suggested that NCES or some other organization prepare a guidebook for states. The guidebook should incorporate basic TSDQ modeling concepts, practical step-by-step guidance on how to develop a functional TSDQ projection model, and guidelines for assembling data from state records in a form suitable for making supply-demand projections.

Suggestion 8: Theoretical Basis of TSDQ Modeling. Though discussion revealed that a considerable theoretical base (drawing on theories of human capital, career progression, and imperfect information in the labor market) exists for TSDQ modeling, it has not been systematically explicated. It was suggested that a statement of the theoretical underpinnings of TSDQ projection models would be useful for policy makers and others who are concerned about teacher supply-demand issues.

Suggestion 9: Teacher Demand Projections. It was suggested that certain changes in NCES teacher demand projection modeling can yield more useful estimates. As a major example, the use of pooled time-series, cross-sectional data from states for the past 10 years would permit development of a more detailed model than the current use of 30-year national-aggregate time-series data and avoid the assumption of a stable relationship between educational and fiscal variables over a 30-year period. It was also suggested that a few states might experiment with the development of econometric projection modeling similar to that used in the 1988 and 1990 NCES projections.

Suggestion 10: Teacher Retention/Attrition Projections. A number of suggestions were offered about improving projections of teacher retention/attrition. First, methods must be developed to project changes or trends in attrition rates, and then these projected rates should be used in computing projections of the size of the retained teaching force, instead of the present practice of assuming fixed attrition rates based on the rate observed in a prior year. Second, a teacher quality variable, e.g., teacher test scores, should be incorporated into teacher retention/attrition projections when feasible. Third, as more than one or two teacher characteristic variables are built into retention/attrition projection models the use of multivariate methods will be required to sort out the relationships of teacher variables with attrition rates and to estimate the effects on attrition of hypothetical or projected changes in particular teacher characteristics. Fourth, in modeling the supply of retained teachers, a clear distinction should be made between voluntary attrition (a supply-side phenomenon that reflects the decisions of individual teachers) and involuntary attrition (a demand-side phenomenon that reflects decisions of employers). Fifth, it was suggested that modeling teacher flows at the school level should be attempted because of the many changes in assignment of retained teachers within schools and between schools. Finally, recent research on teacher retention/attrition has yielded a number of findings pertaining to attrition and reentry, such as attrition rate differences and differences in attrition patterns among categories of teachers, that have direct implications for the improvement of retention/attrition projection models and should be used to this end.

Suggestion 11: Entering-Teacher Projections. Since data are not available on the quantity and quality of individuals in supply pools of potential entering teachers, methods for modeling projections of teacher supply and entry are underdeveloped. Both relevant data bases and methods to model teacher supply and entry are needed to achieve a complete TSDQ model and to make meaningful projections of imbalances of teacher demand and supply. To this end, some useful data could be collected from applicants for teaching positions. Data could also be collected about the job-seeking behavior and intentions of persons in selected groups of the population—an approach subject to the problems inherent in inferring labor market behavior from responses to hypothetical questions.

Suggestion 12: Teacher Compensation and Working Conditions. Because variables pertaining to teacher compensation and working conditions are of particular relevance to teacher entry, retention, and attrition, it was suggested that such factors be incorporated in teacher supply-demand projection models. Suggested variables include teacher salary levels, teacher salaries relative to salaries in other occupations, and relative unemployment by occupation. In addition, various school and student variables can be used as indices of working conditions.

Suggestion 13: Differentiated Staffing. In addition to teachers, teacher aides and specialists in instructional technology are involved in providing instruction to students. It was suggested that the effect of prospective or hypothetical changes in the numbers and instructional roles of these auxiliary personnel on teacher demand and supply be examined.

TEACHER DATA BASES

The need by education policy makers and others for factual and reliable information about the teaching force, including future estimates of supply-demand relationships generated by projection models, has led to the development of teacher data bases at the state, regional, and national levels. The data must be of reasonable quality, timeliness, and accessibility, however, to be useful for projection models and decision making.

Fortunately, there are now several data bases that will support rather sophisticated analyses of a number of important aspects of teacher supply and demand. At the national level, teacher surveys are particularly rich sources of data about many supply-demand variables. A brief description and assessment of teacher data bases is presented here.

State Data Bases

Much information about teachers practicing in a state is contained in state administrative records. Typically, relevant information is contained in different sets of records such as those pertaining to teacher certification (or licensure) and to retirement, each of which can be used separately for study of some aspect of teacher supply and demand.

The use of state data for investigating teacher supply and demand is especially promising because of the wealth of detailed, longitudinal information typically residing in state records. In practice, however, these records vary considerably in the breadth of teacher supply-demand data maintained and in the degree to which teacher supply-demand variables are linked to individual teachers. Though various state records often can be linked to create integrated or comprehensive teacher data bases, states do not ordinarily maintain such integrated data bases incorporating longitudinal information by teacher. Instead, the data must be assembled at considerable effort and cost by researchers interested in studying teacher supply-demand phenomena at the state level. In fact, it is common for researchers to spend several years creating usable data bases from state administrative records before beginning to conduct analyses of teacher supply-demand issues.

A number of variables relevant to teacher quality are contained in state records. For the most part, these are variables pertaining to teacher qualifications. Commonly (though not uniformly) found in state records is information about teachers' educational attainment, academic major, field of certification, type of certification, and years of teaching experience. A few states also record teachers' tested ability scores.

The quality of state records raises several major concerns about the use of data from these sources for studying teacher supply-demand issues. One concern is about incomplete data. Problems include incomplete reporting of data by teachers and LEAs and periodic purging of state records. Another concern is the inaccuracy of recorded data. Inputs from teachers and LEAs may contain errors, and state data management procedures can be inadequate. A third concern is inadequate documentation of the recorded state data, an important consideration for researchers attempting data analyses. The comparability of data among states is a serious issue in making cross-state comparisons. For example, a major incompatibility of data among states arises from their different categories and requirements for teacher certification. Finally, the timeliness of data is of concern. All data files used should be reasonably current if analyses based on them are to be of maximum value to policy makers and others.

Nonetheless, the difficulties inherent in using state data for teacher supply-demand analyses can be managed, and experience has demonstrated that there are substantial benefits to be derived from research with teacher data bases. These sources of data, at their best, contain a remarkable degree of detailed, longitudinal information about teachers, students, and schools. In recent years, several research programs (e.g., Richard Murnane and associates from the Harvard Graduate School of Education; David Grissmer and associates from RAND; James Wilson and associates from the Massachusetts Institute for Social and Economic Research) have used state data successfully to investigate major supply-demand issues such as trends in teacher licensure, entering teachers, attrition, reentry, and retirement as a function of teacher characteristics such as age, gender, race/ethnicity, subject matter specialty, and tested ability. The long time-series on individual teachers available from state records is particularly valuable in studying the course of teacher career development over time and the changing trends in how such careers develop.

Regional Data Base

The only regional teacher supply-demand data base (the Northeast Regional Data Base) currently operational has been developed for New York and the New England states by the Massachusetts Institute for Social and Economic Research (MISER).[5] In cooperation with these states, MISER has taken the lead in assembling useful data bases for seven states by extracting information available from multiple sources within each of the seven states in the Northeast region. However, MISER has not generated original teacher data through sample surveys or other means.

With funding from federal, state, and private sources, MISER worked closely with the seven states of the Northeastern region to improve and to expand the collection and management of teacher data within each state and has begun to create linkages among the emerging state data bases for analytic purposes. The development of these data bases goes beyond what the cooperating states would have implemented on their own initiatives.

Since the Northeast Regional Data Base is comprised of seven state data bases constituted from administrative records within each state, the virtues and limitations of state data bases described in the prior section likewise apply to this regional data base. Being a collection of data bases from all states of a region, however, it has the special advantage of permitting study of reciprocal cross-state migration of teachers within the region. In addition, cross-state comparisons of teacher data has gained the attention of chief state school officers and has led to the emergence of policy changes such as regionalizing teacher credentialing.

This regionalized teacher supply-demand data base is a new phenomenon, which has generated a great deal of favorable attention. In fact, the Southern Regional Education Board is developing a comparable data base using the MISER model. Although the development of the MISER data base has been limited by the availability and quality of information in state records and by the availability of funding to develop and sustain the MISER data set, it has already produced some useful findings and benefits for the region. MISER plans to continue testing the feasibility and utility of a regional data base for the Northeast.

National Data Bases

Several data bases useful for analyses of TSDQ issues now exist at the national level. With one or two exceptions, none of these are derived from data collected and reported by state or local education agencies. Instead, most national data relevant to TSDQ have been generated by sample surveys with questionnaires—the prime example being the Schools and Staffing Survey (SASS) and its longitudinal component the Teacher Followup Survey (TFS), conducted by NCES. SASS was administered during the 1987-88 and 1990-91 school years and is scheduled to be conducted every three years thereafter.

SASS was designed to collect extensive information especially relevant to teacher supply, demand, and quality, as well as the status of schooling generally. For schools in the public sector, SASS includes separate questionnaires designed to obtain information from teachers, from principals of schools to which the teachers are assigned, from schools to which the teachers are assigned, and from LEAs sponsoring these schools. With this design, teacher, principal, school, and LEA data are linked. TFS is administered in years following each SASS to three groups of teachers included in the prior SASS sample: (a) teachers who continued teaching in the same school; (b) teachers who continued in the profession but transferred to a different school; and (c) teachers who left the teaching profession, thereby permitting detailed study of teacher mobility and attrition.

More specifically, data generated by SASS and TFS serve the following five purposes: (a) to profile the nation's teaching force; (b) to improve estimates and projections of teacher supply and demand by teaching field, sector, level, and geographic location; (c) to allow analyses of teacher mobility and turnover; (d) to enhance assessment of teacher quality and qualifications; and (e) to provide more complete information on school policies and programs, administrator characteristics, and working conditions. Accordingly, SASS includes a great deal of information about representative samples of teachers from each state and from the nation as a whole.

NCES has established several other national data bases that provide data relevant to teacher supply and demand topics. Among them are the Common Core of Data, High School and Beyond, the National Longitudinal Study, the National Education Longitudinal Study (NELS:88), Surveys of Recent College Graduates, and the National Assessment of Education Progress (NAEP). Survey data from these sources and SASS typically include information about teacher qualifications. The Longitudinal Study of American Youth sponsored by the National Science Foundation (NSF) provides an opportunity to study the relationship between teacher qualification variables and student academic achievement. This is also possible with NELS:88 and NAEP. A complementary component of NELS:88 was the NSF sponsored Teacher Transcript Study (Chaney, 1991), which obtained transcripts of the academic records of science and mathematics teachers within the NELS:88 study. The analysis for this study focused on teachers' backgrounds in terms of their own college-level preparation in science and mathematics as a prediction of their students' achievement.

Several national data bases relevant to teacher supply and demand have been sponsored by organizations other than NCES. Two examples are the National Surveys of Science and Mathematics Education, sponsored by NSF, and the Status of the American Public School Teacher, sponsored by the National Education Association, both of which include extensive information about national samples of teachers. In addition, tested ability measures of prospective teachers and practicing teachers can be found in data bases of the Graduate Record Examination and the Scholastic Aptitude Test.

Data Base Comparisons

There are major differences between state and national data bases, as well as complementary strengths. In contrast with data from national sample surveys, state records contain a wealth of detailed data about populations of teachers, students, and schools. These records are maintained year by year, thereby permitting examination of trends over time and permitting cohort studies of teachers as their careers develop. In contrast, national surveys are usually based on samples of these populations, and limited sample sizes often do not permit detailed analyses of many variables and their cross-tabulations.

Unfortunately, state data bases are beset by a number of limitations. One is that teachers from any particular state, or from a combination of a few states, do not constitute a representative sample of the national teaching force. Furthermore, variations among states in definitions of variables and in policies pertaining to teachers limit the generalizability of state-level findings. Another limitation of state data bases is their inability to distinguish between teachers that leave the teaching profession or simply migrate to out-of-state schools. Without this information, attrition studies lack precision and may yield misleading interpretations.

For the most part, the strengths of national data bases relevant to TSDQ are the limitations of state data bases, while the limitations of national data bases are the strengths of those at the state level. At their best, national data bases, such as SASS, include a great deal of information about probability samples of teachers for each state and for the nation as a whole, thereby providing (a) a national perspective of the teaching force, (b) opportunity for state-by-state comparisons, and (c) a basis for analysis of teacher migration among all states. In addition, the surveys on which they are based define variables uniformly across all units sampled and use a standardized procedure, thereby permitting interpretations of data that are generalizable nationally.

National data bases, however, are as yet very limited in the extent to which they can support time-series analyses for nationally representative samples of teachers. In addition, practical limitations on the length of survey questionnaires do not permit the level of detailed information gathering that is often possible with administrative records from which state data bases are derived. Finally, resources available for national surveys limit sample sizes, thereby restricting many important analyses.

Since the best currently available state and national data bases are complementary in their respective patterns of strengths and limitations, there is great advantage not only in having both types available, but also in being able to link data bases at these two levels. From the perspective of NCES, there is considerable potential for linking SASS with state data bases, and it is important to work toward achieving this dual strategy.

Data Bases: Suggestions for Action

Major advances in the development of data bases relevant to TSDQ projections and research have been made in recent years at the national, regional, and state levels. Nonetheless during the course of open discussions occurring throughout the conference, participants suggested many further steps that could be taken to strengthen and expand such data bases. These suggestions are reported as such below.

Suggestion 14: State Record Management. Since state administrative records are the information source for state data bases relevant to TSDQ, it is important that these records be maintained so as to be suitable for TSDQ projections and research. Three related suggestions were made about management of these records: (a) that states design and maintain pertinent state records in ways that support TSDQ research as well as administrative functions; (b) that the experience of recent researchers with state data bases be used to improve state record management; and (c) that guidelines for state data management be developed to assist states in responding to this need.

Suggestion 15: Funding State Data Base Development. Since most states do not have sufficient resources to produce high-quality data bases of the type described in Suggestion 11, it was suggested that NCES, or some other federal agency, provide states with capacity-building grants for this purpose.

Suggestion 16: Teacher Demand Data. NCES should develop a more elaborate behavioral model for teacher demand projections that includes economic and fiscal variables, especially at the state and local levels.

Suggestion 17: Longitudinal Supplements to SASS. Although SASS has a longitudinal supplement for teachers in the TFS, it was suggested that NCES give high priority to sustaining this component over time, that TFS content on teacher attitudes toward teaching and teaching styles be increased, and that ideally observations of direct classroom teaching be made in addition to using survey questionnaires.

Suggestion 18: Unused National Data Bases. There are a number of national data bases (e.g., the Longitudinal Study of American Youth, the Scholastic Aptitude Test, and the Graduate Record Examination) relevant to analyses of teacher quality that have not been used for this purpose. A suggestion was made that these data be used to study the quality of teacher supply starting in high school at the beginning of the pipeline.

Suggestion 19: Linking SASS and State Data Bases. Inasmuch as data bases derived from state administrative records and from national sample surveys with questionnaires are both extremely valuable for teacher supply-demand analyses but in distinctive and complementary ways, it was suggested that steps be taken to link SASS data with state data to enhance the range and depth of possible analyses.

Suggestion 20: Linking SASS with Work Force Data Bases. The teaching force is a component of the larger national labor force in which eligible teachers compete for jobs in a wide variety of occupations. Similarly, a very large, but unknown, number of educated adults can compete for jobs in the teaching profession and enter through widely available alternative routes, even though they have not undertaken teacher training. Consequently, it was suggested SASS be linked to larger work force data bases so that the transfer of workers among occupations (including teaching) can be analyzed, thereby providing a broader understanding of factors involved in teacher supply and shortage.

Suggestion 21: International Education Data. It was suggested that data from the United States included in international assessments of education should be used more extensively, especially data relating teacher characteristics to student outcomes.

GENERAL SUGGESTIONS FOR ACTION

In addition to the suggestions for action related to teacher quality, projection models, and data bases as described above, conference participants made the following suggestions pertaining to broader aspects of teacher supply-demand projections and research:

Suggestion 22: On-Line Classroom Computers. It is now technically possible to connect NCES with a national sample of teachers electronically through on-line classroom microcomputers. It was suggested that NCES explore the possibility and utility of having a standing national sample of teachers who routinely transmit data on classroom events to a central repository so that teacher behavior and student learning can be observed as it happens.

Suggestion 23: TSDQ Research Consortium. The value of SASS and other national data bases for analyzing teacher supply and demand issues is much greater than can be exploited by NCES and contract analysts. Accordingly, it was suggested that NCES create and fund a consortium of independent TSDQ researchers in order to capitalize more fully on the potential of these data bases.

Suggestion 24: Annual TSDQ Conference. As a means to stimulate the development and analysis of state data bases relevant to TSDQ, it was suggested that an annual TSDQ conference be held for key state representatives and TSDQ model developers and researchers.

Suggestion 25: Information Useful in Decision Making. Since the major purpose of generating information about TSDQ is to provide a factual basis for policy and administrative decisions in this area, TSDQ data base managers, model developers, and researchers need to understand better (a) the nature of current and emerging policy issues and (b) the attributes of information of practical value to education policy makers and others. NCES could convene focus groups on these topics periodically. A better understanding of information utilization is important as guidance for the production of technically sound but useful TSDQ data and analyses that minimize the risk of misinterpretation by consumers.

REFERENCES

American Association of Colleges of Teacher Education
1987 *Minority Teacher Recruitment and Retention: A Public Policy Issue.* Washington, D.C.: author.

Bobbitt, Sharon A., Elizabeth Faupel, and Shelley Burns
1991 Characteristics of Stayers, Movers, and Leavers: Results from the Teacher Followup Survey, 1988-89. June. NCES 91-128. Washington, D.C.: National Center for Education Statistics.

Chaney, Bradford
1991 *Teachers' Academic Preparation and its Connection to Teaching Methods and*

Student Outcomes in Science and Mathematics: NSF/NELS:88 Teacher Transcript Study. December. Prepared for the National Science Foundation, Washington, D.C.

Feistritzer, Emily
1990 *Alternative Teacher Certification: A State-by-State Analysis*. Washington, D.C.: National Center for Educational Information.

Freeman, Richard B.
1971 *The Market for College-Trained Manpower*. Cambridge, Massachusetts: Harvard University Press.

Gilford, Dorothy M., and Ellen Tenenbaum, eds.
1990 *Precollege Science and Mathematics Teachers: Monitoring Supply, Demand, and Quality*. Panel on Statistics on Supply and Demand for Precollege Science and Mathematics Teachers, Committee on National Statistics. Washington, D.C.: National Academy Press.

Grissmer, David W., and Sheila Nataraj Kirby
1991 Patterns of Attrition Among Indiana Teachers, 1965-1987. Santa Monica, California: The RAND Corporation.

Hammer, Charles H., and Elizabeth Gerald
1990 *Selected Characteristics of Public and Private School Teachers: 1987-88*. July. NCES 90-087. Washington, D.C.: National Center for Education Statistics.

Hanushek, Eric
1986 The economics of schooling: Production and efficiency in public schools. *Journal of Economic Literature* 26:1141-1177.

Kirby, S.N., D.W. Grissmer, and L. Hudson
1991 Entering and Reentering Teachers in Indiana: Source of Supply. R-4049-LE. October. The RAND Corporation.

Lanier, Judith
1986 Research on teacher education. Pp. 527-569 in M.C. Wittrock, ed., *Handbook of Research on Teacher Education, 3rd edition*. New York: Macmillan.

Manski, Charles F.
1987 Academic ability, earnings, and the decision to become a teacher: Evidence from the National Longitudinal Study of the High School Class of 1972. In David A. Wise, ed., *Public Sector Payrolls*. Chicago: University of Chicago Press.

Metz, A. Stafford, and H.L. Fleischman
1974 Teacher Turnover in Public Schools, Fall 1968 to Fall 1969. DHEW Publication No. (OE) 74-1115. Washington, D.C.: U.S. Department of Health, Education, and Welfare.

Murnane, Richard J., and Randall J. Olsen
1989 The effects of salaries and opportunity costs on duration in teaching: Evidence from Michigan. *The Review of Economics and Statistics* 71:347-352.
1990 The effects of salaries and opportunity costs on length of stay in teaching. *Journal of Human Resources* 25(Winter):106-124.

Murnane, Richard J., and Michael Schwinden
1989 Race, gender, and opportunity: Supply and demand for new teachers in North Carolina, 1975-1985. *Educational Evaluation and Policy Analysis* 11(2)(Summer):93-108.

Murnane, Richard J., Judith D. Singer, and John B. Willett
1989 The influences of salaries and "opportunity costs" on teachers' career choices: Evidence from North Carolina. *Harvard Educational Review* 59(3)(August):325-46.

National Center for Education Statistics

1991a *Digest of Education Statistics 1990.* Washington, D.C.: U.S. Department of Education.

1991b *E.D. TABS: Aspects of Teacher Supply and Demand in Public School Districts and Private Schools: 1987-88.* August. Charles H. Hammer, and Elizabeth Gerald. NCES 91-133. Washington, D.C.: U.S. Department of Education, Office of Educational Research and Improvement.

Oakes, Jeannie

1990 *Multiplying Inequalities: The Effects of Race, Social Class, and Tracking on Opportunities to Learn Mathematics and Science.* July. R-3928-NSF. With Tor Ormseth, Robert Bell, and Patricia Camp. Santa Monica, California: RAND.

Rollefson, Mary R.

1992 Sources of Newly Hired Teachers in the U.S.: Results of the 1987-88 Schools and Staffing Survey. Paper presented at the NCES Annual Data Conference, Washington, D.C. July. National Center for Education Statistics, Washington, D.C.

Schmidt, Peter

1992 Shortage of trained bilingual teachers is focus of both concern and attention. *Education Week* February 12:14.

NOTES

1. While the same assertion can be made about private education, these conference proceedings focus on public education at the elementary and secondary levels.

2. As used here, the expression *teaching force* always means the active, employed teaching force at any given time, as distinguished from all qualified teachers whether or not employed.

3. Much of the material presented in the remainder of this section has been adapted from an unpublished manuscript by David W. Grissmer of RAND and is used here with his permission. However, the editors of these proceedings are responsible for the content as presented.

4. The one exception to the relevance of tested ability is that some research evidence has demonstrated a positive, though not large, association between the general verbal ability of teachers and teaching success. However, even the significance of this evidence is contested by different reviewers.

5. Interest in forming regional data bases for teacher supply-demand analyses has recently appeared in the Southern region and in the North Central region.

III

POLICY ISSUES

Part III addresses policy issues in teacher supply, demand, and quality. The focus is on issues entailed in forming effective federal and state policies designed to ensure a sufficient supply of teachers who are fully qualified in their primary teaching assignment. The main purpose for addressing such policy issues is to identify specific data and research needed to provide a useful empirical base supportive of effective policy making in the future.

The Problem of Improving Teacher Quality While Balancing Supply and Demand

MARY M. KENNEDY

INTRODUCTION

At the same time improvements in education contribute to improvements in the social and economic well-being of the country, these social and economic improvements place further demands on the education system. Consequently, the history of education is in part a history of continuing efforts to improve both the quantity and quality of education provided to American youth. The reform effort we face today could be interpreted as one further step in this continuing effort.

Yet, while similar to previous reform efforts in its broad purposes, this reform also carries its own unique features, and these need to be taken into account. The problem of supply and demand of qualified teachers, for instance, is one that regularly confronts U.S. policy makers, but it takes on a special cast in the current reform in two different ways. First, the concerns about *supply* that we face today are not a function of an increase in the number of students we want to serve, as has often been the case in the past, but instead are a function of changes in the attractiveness of a teaching career relative to other careers. Moreover, problems of supply are uneven. In some regions and some subject areas, we have an oversupply, while in other regions and other subjects, we face an undersupply. Second, the problem of teacher *quality* is not one of increasing the required credential, as has often been the case in the past. Virtually all teachers now hold a bachelor's degree, and a great majority hold a master's degree as well. Yet we are still not satisfied with the quality of classroom teaching practices.

Before examining policy strategies of the current reform, I want to examine each of these unique problems.

The Contemporary Version of Teacher Supply and Demand

With the exception of the past two or three decades, education has almost always faced a problem of teacher shortages, in large part because the population of students needing an education was continually growing. Shortages in the past have largely been filled by women and minorities who had few other career opportunities (Sedlak and Schlossman, 1986). However, the past two decades have seen an increase in the career opportunities for these populations that have traditionally filled teaching positions. Thus, the supply problem we now face derives more from competition from other professions than it does from an increase in the actual number of teachers needed. This fact has led policy makers and scholars to attend more than they have in the past to such issues as the attractiveness of the profession as a whole, the extrinsic and intrinsic rewards of teaching, and the quality of teachers' working conditions.

At the same time, there has been an increase in the amount and quality of data available to assist in policy formulation. Longitudinal data bases have increased our understanding of the career paths of teachers, giving us more information about the length of time teachers tend to stay in teaching positions and more information about the source of new teachers. We now know, for instance, that many people who are prepared to teach never enter the profession, that many of those who do teach leave the profession after only a few years, and that only about 25 to 30 percent of leavers are likely to return after a career interruption. These returning teachers are often referred to as a reserve pool of teacher supply that augments the pool of new college graduates available for teaching. And we know that attrition rates are higher in chemistry and physics than in other subject areas (Murnane et al., 1988, 1989). Finally, we know that the reasons for leaving are often not the reasons presumed by policy makers. For instance, even though young women are more likely to leave than other groups, they are not necessarily leaving to rear children, and they are not necessarily leaving schools that are considered to present more difficult teaching assignments (Heyns, 1988). Most important, we now know that the most important predictor of teacher demand is teacher attrition (Haggstrom et al., 1988), and that the most unknown factor in predicting teacher supply is the size and character of the reserve pool (Gilford and Tenenbaum, 1990).

Since schools have a fixed clientele and must provide services to all those who are eligible for them, they must necessarily fill every classroom position with someone. Before teacher unions began negotiating class size, school districts often adjusted their services by expanding class sizes. As this strategy becomes less feasible, districts have resorted to other options, in particular assigning teachers to subjects they are not certified to teach or hiring new teachers who do not have the formal credentials required. States tacitly approve of these strategies by granting emergency credentials for these teachers. Thus, even though most states have steadily increased their requirements for teaching credentials, they have, at the same time, continually permitted teachers who do not have the requisite credentials to enter the profession through the back door, so to speak. These practices have become criticized recently, both because they threaten the quality of classroom practices and because they diminish the status of the profession as a whole.

Finally, much of the evidence currently available regarding teacher supply and demand suggests that the issue is not a universal one, but instead the ratio of supply to demand varies by school, subject matter, and grade level. That is, urban schools have more difficulty filling positions than suburban schools do, secondary schools have more difficulty filling physics positions than math positions, and so forth. That such patterns exist suggests that perhaps projections of teacher supply and demand would be more fruitful if they included particular school and job characteristics in their models.

The Contemporary Version of High-Quality Classroom Practice

Contemporary reform demands also differ from past demands in that they are based more heavily on empirical examinations of teaching and the outcomes of teaching than they have been in the past. Findings of recent research have contributed heavily to contemporary dissatisfaction with classroom practice and have seriously complicated the problem of maintaining an adequate supply of teachers. Let us review some of the evidence.

First, national assessments in virtually every subject indicate that, although U.S. students can perform basic skills pretty well, they are not doing well on thinking and reasoning. U.S. students can compute but they cannot reason through complex mathematical problems (McKnight et al., 1987). They can write complete and correct sentences but cannot prepare arguments (Applebee et al., 1990). They cannot reason through scientific problems very well (International Association for the Evaluation of Educational Achievement, 1988). Moreover, in international comparisons, U.S. students are falling behind not only students in European countries, but also those in many Third World countries as well, particularly in those areas that require higher-order thinking, problem solving, or conceptual work.

The second research finding gives us a clue as to why we have the first: textbooks in this country typically give no attention to big ideas, offer no analysis, and pose no challenging questions. Instead, they provide a tremendous array of information or "factlets" and pose questions that require nothing more than the ability to recite back the same empty list of facts. In fact, our textbooks often don't even provide much in the way of organization or coherence for these facts (Tyson and Woodward, 1989). So whatever real understanding students get about the subjects, whatever intellectual challenge they get, must come from their teachers.

The third finding from research is that most teachers teach content only for exposure, not for understanding (Porter, 1989). That is, their aim is not to ensure that students really understand the concepts they present, but rather only that they have been *exposed* to them. And the fourth finding is that teachers tend to avoid thought-provoking work and activities and stick to predictable routines. Why? Because students are easier to manage, and student outcomes easier to control, when the tasks are routine (Doyle, 1983, 1986; Doyle and Carter, 1984). So if we were to describe our current K-12 education system, we would have to say it provides very little intellectually stimulating work for students and that it produces students who are not capable of intellectual work. These problems are not, of course, all due to bad teaching. I have already pointed out that U.S. textbooks often don't provide intellectually defensible material, and I should add now that many features of school organization and school policy can yield these results as well. Still, these findings about what happens in U.S. classrooms help explain the findings from national and international assessments, and they demonstrate why policy makers care about the quality of classroom teaching practices.

Yet classroom practice is highly influenced by teachers' a priori ideas about what counts as good teaching. Teachers acquire seemingly indelible imprints of teaching from their own experiences as students, and these imprints are tremendously difficult to shake. The dominant impulse in any new teacher is to imitate the behaviors of his or her own former teachers. And this impulse will remain strong unless teachers are offered an equally strong and compelling alternative approach to teaching and are provided with a great deal of help learning to adopt this new approach.

And this is the fifth relevant finding from research: people who teach are highly likely to teach in the way they themselves were taught (Haberman, 1985; Lortie, 1975; Nemser, 1983). All of us, whether we choose to enter teaching or not, learn about teaching throughout our lives. From kindergarten through twelfth grade, we observe teachers. Those of us who go on to college observe even more teachers, and these teachers are not necessarily any better or different that those we observed when we were younger (McDiarmid, 1990). By the time we receive our bachelor's degree, we have observed teachers for over 3,000 days. For those of us who choose to enter teaching, the pervasiveness of this "apprenticeship of observation," both across grade levels and across subject areas, coupled with the sheer volume of time spent observing, yields a deeply entrenched *and tacit* set of beliefs about what can and should happen in schools: about the nature of intellectual work and the nature of school subjects, about the teachers' role in facilitating learning, and about the pedagogical implications of student diversity.

So, for instance, if your elementary school teacher presented mathematics to you as a set of procedural rules with no substantive rationale, you are likely to think that this is what mathematics is and that this is how mathematics should be studied. And you are likely to teach it this way. If you studied writing as a set of grammar rules rather than as a way to organize your thoughts and to communicate ideas to others, then this is what you will think writing is and this is how you will think it should be taught and learned.

Moreover, these beliefs are highly likely to be accompanied by an emotional commitment. People who choose teaching as a career not only have ingrained beliefs about what the enterprise is all about, but also have chosen it as a career precisely because this is what it is all about. They are not committed to the enterprise in the abstract; they are committed to it *as they understand it.*

POLICY EFFORTS TO IMPROVE THE SUPPLY OF QUALITY TEACHERS

The special problem facing contemporary policy makers is that of, at one and the same time, increasing the supply of teachers available and improving the quality of their classroom teaching practices. Certain features of the teaching population bear notice when considering either supply and demand or quality. One is that the teaching force in the public sector consists of some 2.3 million teachers. Any efforts to improve the quality of this large teaching force will be labor-intensive and therefore expensive. Second, some 15 percent of U.S. adults now have at least a baccalaureate degree, as do almost all teachers. And some 20 percent of all baccalaureate degree holders received their degrees in education, even though less than half of those who received such degrees are currently teaching (National Center for Education Statistics, 1989). Moreover, the number of college-educated adults is rising, so that the fraction is much higher among younger adults who are likely to be enrolling children in schools in the next decade or two.

The size of the college-educated population has two implications for policy makers concerned about balancing supply and demand and improving quality. First, as consumers of education, these segments of population—bachelor's degrees in general or education degrees in particular—form an increasing fraction of education's clientele. And clients of education have more direct knowledge of teachers' practices than clients of other professions have. Parents see their children's homework and often visit classrooms and they form judgments about quality from these observations. To the extent that their own education levels lead them to hold greater expectations for quality in teaching, or greater demands for teaching of the subjects they studied in college, we can expect public demands for improvements in teacher quality to continue or to increase over time, rather than to subside. Indeed, we expect that questions about the quality of teaching will necessarily continue to exist, given the educational levels of parents and given their direct knowledge of their children's teachers.

A second implication of these facts is that this entire population constitutes a potential reserve pool that could be recruited into teaching. Indeed, the current teaching force represents only 43 percent of the those who received degrees in education, and only 10 percent of those who have received degrees in all fields. If one assumes that even those who did not receive degrees in education could still teach, the reserve pool expands to include over 25 million adults.

Since actual teaching practices cannot be efficiently monitored, policy makers tend to work toward improving the supply of other aspects of teachers or teaching that are presumed to lead to improvements in practice. For purposes of this discussion I would like to distinguish five dimensions of quality that form the basis of most policy activities. The first two dimensions, *quality of credential* and *tested ability*, refer to characteristics of individual teachers: policy makers want to ensure that those who enter teaching hold credentials that are appropriate to their task, that they have acquired the subject matter knowledge and pedagogical training needed, or that they have some minimal level of intellectual ability deemed appropriate for teaching. The third dimension, *quality of demographic representation*, refers to the mix of teachers working in individual schools: policy makers want a population of teachers that roughly matches the racial and ethnic backgrounds represented in the student body. And as the composition of the student body changes, the demand for different types of teachers will also change. The fourth and fifth dimensions refer to the character of practices that occur within individual schools. The fourth dimension, *quality of professionalism* in schools, refers to the extent to which teachers are given real responsibility for their work and the extent to which they are able to make sound professional decisions in their work.[1] Many policy makers want to change the character of teaching practice so that teachers have the kind of independent responsibility for managing their work that other professionals have, believing either that sound educational practices cannot be dictated from afar or that teaching will be a more attractive line of work if teachers have more professional autonomy. Finally, the fifth dimension is the *quality of classroom teaching practice*: even if policy makers find ways to bring people into teaching who have the proper credentials, the right demographic characteristics, and higher tested ability, they need assurance that the actual classroom teaching practices of these teachers matches some level of acceptable practice.

Although nearly all policy makers recognize nearly all of these dimensions of quality, many assume the fifth dimension will be solved automatically by solving one or a combination of the first four. Indeed, much of the current policy debate in the area of teacher supply and demand has to do with which of the first four dimensions of quality is most likely to ensure the fifth. This is not to say, however, that the fifth dimension is the only one that matters. Arguments have been made for the independent value of most of the other dimensions, even if they do not necessarily yield improvements in classroom practice. The ethnic mix of teachers, for instance, may have positive benefits on both student motivation and learning that will not be easily discerned from observations of teachers' classroom practices, and changes in the professionalism of teaching may alter teachers' regard for their work in ways that influence both their retention in the job and the tacit messages they communicate to students about the importance of school and of learning to a variety of life's endeavors. The problem for policy makers is one of sorting out these several dimensions and recognizing each as a separate issue that warrants its own attention.

In this paper, I argue that these several dimensions of quality are not the same, and that improving quality on any one dimension will not necessarily improve quality on any of the others. The argument has two implications for policy. First, we cannot assume that we can improve classroom practice, the dimension of most importance to most policy makers, simply by improving any of the other dimensions. And second, to the extent that policy makers wish to alter any of the other dimensions of quality, they need to address them separately.

The remainder of this paper is divided into five sections, one addressing each of these five dimensions of quality. In each main section, I address three questions: how important this dimension of quality is to contemporary education policy, what policy activities are currently under way or under consideration to increase supply and quality within this dimension, and what are the measurement and data collection implications of these issues and activities for generating useful policy information about supply and demand within this dimension of quality.

SUPPLY OF QUALITY CREDENTIALS

Much of the contemporary work on measuring teacher supply and demand defines quality in terms of the teachers' credentials. That is, a teacher is qualified to teach if he or she is certified in the area in which he or she is teaching. So if, for instance, a history major is *certified* to teach history and political science, but not sociology, that teacher is considered *qualified* when teaching history or political science but not when teaching sociology. If such a teacher is found teaching all three of these subjects—a likely event in a small high school—it is difficult to know whether to count the teacher as qualified or not. The confusing array of assignments, misassignments, and joint assignments, combined with the variety of combinations of certification offered by different states and taken by different teachers, make it extremely difficult to define the supply or the demand of credential-qualified teachers.

How Important are Credentials?

One argument for emphasizing teaching credentials has to do with their symbolic function. If teachers are to maintain a professional standing, there should be some indication that they are entitled to teach, and formal credentials can play an important role in entitling teachers as professionals. Yet the empirical evidence of a relationship between formal credentials and student achievement is remarkably weak. Several aspects of teachers' formal education have been presumed important indicators of teacher quality. Three popular measures are: (a) whether the teacher is formally credentialed to teach the subject or grade being taught, (b) whether the teacher majored in the subject being taught, and (c) whether the teacher has taken courses beyond the bachelor's degree.

Researchers who have tried to connect these measures of teachers' education and certification to gains in student achievement have been unable to find any clear or meaningful relationship (Gilford and Tenenbaum, 1990; Hanushek, 1986). Particularly discouraging is research on teachers' subject matter majors, which has found very little relationship between subject matter major and teaching ability (e.g., Begle and Geeslin, 1972). Even college majors who have reasonably high grade points in their majors are often unable to explain important concepts from their disciplines or to illustrate them accurately (see, eg., Ball, 1990). The lack of convincing evidence has motivated Richard Murnane and others (Murnane et al., 1991) to argue for abandoning state program requirements that guide teachers' credentials, so that the field can experiment with a wider array of ideas for preparing teachers to teach. If there is no evidence that these program requirements yield better teachers, these authors argue, there is no reason to constrain teacher education programs.

On the other hand, the lack of association between credentials and student achievement gains may be an artifact of the wide range of educational backgrounds that can lead to a credential. Since each state defines its own credentialing system, the possession of a credential can mean that a teacher has either a bachelor's or a master's degree, depending on the state; that a teacher has taken an exam or not, depending on the state; that a teacher has participated in an induction program or not; that the teacher's classroom practices have been assessed or not; that the teacher has majored in an academic subject or not; or that a teacher has participated in a university-based preservice program or an alternative route. Given this variation, it should not be surprising that the presence of a credential per se does not correlate strongly with measures of student achievement growth.

Policy Activity in This Area

Typically, a formal credential means that a teacher has received both the requisite courses in teacher education and the requisite courses from the arts and sciences departments. Some colleges and universities—notably those that are members of Project 30—are working on courses that combine these two sides of teacher knowledge into integrated courses. However, the structure of most colleges and universities is such that these two sides of teachers' formal course work exist in a zero-sum relationship, such that additional courses in pedagogy are perceived to mean fewer courses in the subject areas. This means that, when policy makers want to improve the quality of the initial credential, they must choose which kind of courses they want to increase and which they will decrease.

The current trend is to reduce the emphasis on pedagogy courses and to increase the emphasis on subject matter courses, although policy makers and others are far from agreeing on what the exact nature of these subject matter courses should be, particularly at the elementary school level. Three states—Virginia, Texas, and New Jersey—have recently made such changes in their teacher education requirements. In addition, the Southern Regional Educational Board has recommended that Southern states try to reduce the number of credits teacher candidates take in their professional sequence.

These policies, however, manipulate only the supply of new graduates who might enter teaching. They do not address the large reserve pool of teachers, from whom many new hires are drawn. I should mention here, as an aside, that most states also have a mechanism for recognizing credentials from other states. That is, if a teacher moves from state A to state B, the teacher can apply to the state to have his or her original credential recognized. Though many states have such procedures in place, the criteria used to accept credentials from other states are often not synchronized with current policies for new graduates. In addition, states rarely keep track of the number of applicants for out-of-state credential recognition, nor do they know how many such applicants have been turned away. These immigrant teachers themselves could constitute a substantial reserve pool of teachers if their credentials were accepted. Moreover, despite policy makers' espoused interest in strengthening teachers' credentials, few states actually monitor teaching assignments. They often do not know how many teachers, or which teachers, actually have the required credentials to teach in their assigned area.[2] The nature of education is such that schools have a constant supply of students that must be taught; since they cannot turn away students when they have teaching vacancies, they always fill all their vacancies. Many states give emergency credentials to teachers who are hired to work in areas for which they do not have formal credentials, and some, such as Pennsylvania, maintain records on the number and location of such emergency-credentialed teachers. But advocates of improved credentialing argue that, as long as states permit easy entrance through the back door, improved requirements for entrance through the front door are virtually useless.

A related policy activity, often designed to influence both supply and quality, is the alternative route into teaching. Thirty-three states now have provisions for some form of alternative route to certification (Feistritzer, 1990). What this means is that the state drops its normal requirements for obtaining a teaching credential and permits certain individuals to enter teaching through some alternative route. Although it may seem counterintuitive to argue that providing shortcuts into the profession would enhance teacher's credentials, states offering alternative routes generally hope to attract into teaching people who have stronger subject matter knowledge and stronger liberal arts educations. Their reasoning is that such people were, as college students, either deterred from teaching by its curriculum requirements, or attracted to higher salaries in other career lines. In either case, they may have second thoughts later in life. So the state offers a way to become certified without having to go back to college and take a lot of teacher education courses (Adelman, 1986; Carey et al., 1988).

Many alternative routes are based on the same assumption as those policies that limit the number of courses candidates can take in education, namely that the quality of teaching will improve if teachers have more courses in academic subjects. Others are based on the assumption that such ad hoc training programs are an improvement over the emergency credentialing approach to filling new vacancies. In New Jersey, for instance, as more teachers are hired through alternative certification, the number of teachers hired on emergency credentials has dropped to nearly zero.

We are starting to get some evidence now about who enters teaching through alternative routes. Many of the people who acquire certification through these sanctioned loopholes have been teaching already in private schools, in which certification is not needed, and are now seeking more lucrative positions in public schools. Others are new college graduates with roughly comparable grades and academic backgrounds as graduates who are already certified. Even those who move into teaching from other career lines are moving from lower-status technical and clerical jobs more often than from higher-status business and science jobs (see Darling-Hammond et al., 1989, for a summary of 64 such programs).

Finally, one of the most controversial recent policy moves with respect to formal credentials was made by the National Board of Professional Teaching Standards (NBPTS), which decided not to require state credentials for teachers who wish to take the NBPTS and become board-certified as master teachers. The board's reasoning was based in part on the lack of evidence that such initial credentials were relevant to good teaching and in part on the recognition that their task was to directly assess the quality of applicants anyway, so that they did not, in principle, need any other indicators of quality to guide their decisions. The decision has been criticized by others who argue that credentials provide an important symbolic function in the formation of a profession and that they are important for that reason, even if empirical evidence of their value is missing.

At the same time these various policy initiatives are reducing the requirements for formal course work in pedagogy, the Holmes Group, a consortium of deans of research universities, has been pressing for a more demanding credential for teachers. They argue that the road to quality in teaching is through a master's degree, for this degree enables candidates to obtain the volume of subject matter they need and to still obtain the volume of pedagogical knowledge they need. In addition, they argue that schools need to be restructured to differentiate between teaching staff who are highly qualified and those who are really intending to teach for a few years and then move on to other careers (The Holmes Group, 1986). Their efforts have been criticized by some educators on the grounds that there is little demand in school districts for the more expensive master's degree candidates and that there is little cost-benefit advantage for the teacher candidates, given the current salary structure of schools, to invest in a master's degree in teaching (e.g., Hawley, 1986). In fact, however, close to half of all teachers now hold a master's degree anyway, obtaining it within their first few years of teaching.

In sum, then, states have been quite active in manipulating the educational requirements associated with teachers' initial credentials, and this activity has been geared largely toward improving the subject matter side of teachers' undergraduate course work. At the same time, they have initiated quite different policies regarding the reserve pool of teachers. Most states readily provide emergency credentials for misassignments, few monitor the appropriateness of teachers' assignments, and many promote alternative routes into teaching as a means of increasing the number of teachers who have specifically not obtained formal credentials.

Implications for Data Collection

We already have a relatively strong empirical basis for doubting the significance of formal credentials per se to teaching practice. My first recommendation is that we do not pursue this line of inquiry any further. Coding teachers on the subject they majored in, or on whether they have the correct credential for their teaching area, provides too little knowledge of the actual courses teachers took and of what they actually learned in these courses. Even transcript studies are unlikely to reveal the detail we need about teachers' formal education, for courses with similar titles can be remarkably different from one another.[3] If researchers wish to pursue further the relationship between credentials or formal course work and teaching practices, they need to invest in more carefully designed studies, studies that follow candidates over time and that examine the actual content they are taught rather than the number of credits they have taken.

Still, there are symbolic reasons for caring about teachers' credentials. Given the increasing level of education among parents, the demand for highly educated teachers, and for teachers who have majored in the subjects they teach, will increase. Two data collection strategies would be helpful here. First, states should be encouraged to improve the quality of data they maintain on the subject matter certifications of all their teachers, and in particular the certifications of those teachers who are teaching with emergency or provisional credentials and the certifications of those who have applied to have out-of-state certificates recognized. It would be useful to know, for instance, how many out-of-state credentials were rejected and why, and how many secondary teachers are teaching subjects for which they were certified to teach. And since many secondary teachers teach more than one subject, it would be useful to know how many different subjects such teachers are currently teaching and the proportion of their teaching load that is in the subject(s) for which they are certified and how many are misassigned. More detailed data on the relationship between teaching credentials and teaching assignments can help states determine the need for, for instance, targeted alternative route programs to fill particular shortage areas, and they could help them better determine the relationship between initial credentials and likely teaching assignments.

Second, the range of educational packages that can lead to a credential is worth documenting in itself. One way that national data bases might facilitate state policy makers would be by documenting the variety of educational backgrounds that certified teachers have, so that state policy makers can gain a better understanding of their own requirements in relation to others. That is, what college curricula are required to become certified to teach secondary math, for instance, in each of the states, and how different are these requirements from state to state? If these data were available, together with data on the number of teachers teaching out of field and the number of emergency credentialed teachers teaching in each area, we may begin to get a handle on the relationship between college course-taking requirements, actual teaching assignments, and teaching vacancies.

SUPPLY OF TEACHERS WITH HIGH TESTED ABILITY

There is evidence that those who enter teacher education, generally speaking, score lower on tests of academic achievement than those who enter other career tracks. Moreover, there is evidence that, among those who become certified, those with lower scores are more likely to take teaching positions. And finally, there is evidence that those who continue in the profession tend to have lower academic achievement scores than those who leave after a few years. Throughout the pipeline, then, we have created a system that systematically favors the lower scoring of all possible teaching candidates (Kerr, 1983; Murnane et al., 1989; Schlechty and Vance, 1983; Robertson et al. 1983).

Tested ability is the dimension of quality that most policy makers assume is related to classroom teaching practice, and consequently it has received more attention from policy makers than any of the other dimensions of quality. They fear that, by permitting low-achieving adults to teach, we are creating a bad situation. The statistics are reminiscent of the old George Bernard Shaw line, "Those who can, do; those who can't, teach."

How Important is Tested Ability?

The seriousness of the tested ability problem is hard to estimate, for to some extent, we do decide, as a society, how to allocate our talent. It is also complicated by the sheer size of the teaching population. Our society now employs about 10 percent of its college-educated women and 4 percent of college-educated men as teachers; no other profession draws such a large proportion of educated adults (Lanier, 1986). One implication is that if we were so successful in solving this problem that all, or even most, of our best and brightest went into teaching, we would soon be worrying about a similar problem in business, law, medicine, and several other fields as well. The size of the teaching force is simply too large to expect it to be filled entirely from the uppermost ranges of tested ability.

To gauge how serious the tested ability problem is in education, we would need to decide the level and range of tested abilities we are willing to tolerate, given the tradeoffs. We would need to be honest about how many high-scoring people we will want to bring into teaching when moving them into teaching means moving them out of business, computer science, medicine, law, and so forth. How many high-scoring teachers do we need, and how low we are willing to permit the bottom end of the achievement score distribution to go?

Even aside from the problem of allocating talent among different occupations, we face a difficult problem in arguing that tested ability is relevant to the tasks of teaching. Tests measure a particular kind of intellectual ability, one that some have argued is far too narrow. The achievement tests that are typically used to assess teachers really measure only their ability to choose the right answer when several possible answers are provided for them. Obtaining a high score on such a test does not necessarily mean a teacher could solve such problems if the right answer were not available there for them to recognize. Neither does it mean they could solve more complicated or open-ended problems for which no answer is clearly best. Nor does it mean they can explain to someone else how to solve such problems, as teachers must do. And, finally, it doesn't mean they can create problems for someone else to learn from, as teachers must do. Consequently, we don't know whether moderate-scoring adults actually teach less well than higher-scoring adults, nor do we know whether moderate-scoring adults have a less adequate understanding of the material they would actually teach in elementary or secondary classrooms.

I don't mean to suggest that tests don't measure anything useful. Obviously they do. We know that differences in test scores are relevant to a number of academic pursuits, and there is some evidence that scores on verbal ability are relevant to teaching. Nor do I mean to suggest that we can get away with a population of teachers who come from the bottom of the test score distribution. What I am saying, though, is that we don't know how low a score has to be before it makes a difference to teaching.

The only aspect of tested ability that has been found to relate to teaching is general verbal ability. Several researchers have found that tests of verbal ability are associated with teaching success. It seems reasonable to suppose that general verbal ability would be relevant to teaching. After all, teaching is largely an art of communication. However, even this finding has been contested, and the evidence is far from clear.[4]

So it is hard to say how serious the tested ability problem really is. It is conceivable that, if we took into account the other occupations that need to draw high-scoring individuals, and if we knew more about the relationship between test scores and teaching performance, we would conclude that the problem is not so grave as we have been supposing. It is also conceivable that tests that were structured to target more specifically on teaching valid content, rather than recognizing it when it is presented, would demonstrate a stronger relationship to classroom practice.

Policy Activity in This Area

The most popular approach to enhancing the tested ability of teachers is to build some form of test into state requirements for certification. Virtually every state now includes some form of teacher assessment in its certification requirements (Council of Chief State School Officers, 1988). These assessments vary considerably from state to state but, regardless of their particular features, most are intended to improve the tested ability of the teaching population.

Some of these assessments may accomplish that goal, but most probably won't. In order for a state assessment to really raise the tested ability of teachers entering the work force, it would have to satisfy three conditions. First, the test would have to include the kind of intellectually rigorous content we think teachers need to be able to handle. If the content of these tests rests mainly on the ability to recall simple facts, as much of the teacher assessment content does, the test will not raise anyone's confidence in the tested ability of teachers. Second, the test would have to be designed so that a lot of people failed it. If no one fails the test, then it can't, by definition, be *raising* the tested ability of new teachers. Yet many state teacher assessments are designed to ensure very low fail rates.

And finally, the test would have to pass legal criteria for job relevance, for as soon as very many people fail an entrance test, the state will face a lawsuit challenging the relevance of both the content and the cutoff score to the tasks of teaching. So far, no state has been able to demonstrate job relevance.[5] And to avoid these lawsuits, most states design their assessments so that very few teachers will fail. That is, they adopt relatively low cutoff scores and they provide ample opportunities for those who fail to try again. Consequently, no state assessment system really contributes to solving the tested ability problem. In the end, these programs serve more of a symbolic than a real function.

Even if such testing programs could be shown to improve the tested ability of new teachers, they would make only a small impact on this dimension of quality, since most of them affect only new college graduates. The existing population of teachers are usually exempted from such testing requirements—and so too presumably are those certified teachers in the reserve pool.

A second popular strategy for improving tested ability is the alternative route. Just as policy makers believe that college students with strong interest in the liberal arts might be repelled from vocationally oriented teacher education programs, many also believe that students with higher tested ability tend to avoid the presumably less rigorous teacher education curriculum. However, the evidence suggests that the new recruits who enter teaching through alternative routes do not differ substantially from conventional teacher education graduates in their tested ability.[6]

One surprising finding, however, is that alternative routes are attracting a more diverse population into teaching. Some alternative routes, for instance, are bringing more males and minorities into teaching than traditional teacher education programs do (Darling-Hammond et al., 1989). So even if this solution doesn't work well for improving tested ability, it may help improve demographic representation. This is one of the reasons why I emphasize the need to think about each dimension of quality separately.

My main reason for insisting on thinking about these dimensions separately, though, is that policy makers often assume that, if they improve tested ability, they also automatically improve classroom teaching practice. There are several reasons for doubting this assumption. First, evidence for a relationship between tested ability and teaching practice is remarkably scarce. Second, the dominant method for attracting higher-scoring people into teaching (i.e., alternative route programs) is rarely designed to challenge the conventional wisdom that teachers arrive with; instead they are designed to capitalize on this "wisdom." That is, these programs try to recruit teachers who are smarter than traditional teacher education graduates and give them only brief pedagogical training, presumably on the assumption that these smart future teachers can use their native intelligence to figure out how to teach. One result of this is that alternative route candidates might be even more likely than fully prepared teachers to emulate the practices they observed as children and less likely to develop new approaches to teaching. They receive virtually no preparation that would lead them to rethink the assumptions they bring with them. So even if alternative routes do raise the tested ability of teachers, or bring more minority teachers into teaching, they are not likely to improve teaching practice significantly.

Finally, high tested ability may actually impede a teachers' ability to teach. Have you ever heard someone say: "He is so smart, I don't understand a word he says." Surely that is not the kind of high-ability person we want in our classrooms. Knowing a lot, or being smart, is not enough for teaching, for the main job of the teacher is to get someone else to know a lot and to be smart.

Two policy efforts are currently under way to devise better tests for teachers. One is sponsored by the National Board of Professional Teaching Standards (NBPTS), an organization that eventually hopes to provide experienced, high-quality teachers with a special credential that certifies them as experts in their area. The other is that of the Educational Testing Service, which is developing a new version of its widely used National Teacher Examination (NTE) in the hope of providing a more valid assessment of beginning teachers. Both organizations are working to move beyond the multiple-choice format into items that require teachers to demonstrate how their knowledge of subject matter and of pedagogy actually influences their teaching decisions and teaching practices.

The research we have been doing at the National Center for Research on Teacher Education (NCRTE) offers some potentially useful new directions for learning about teachers' and prospective teachers' subject matter knowledge. We have relied heavily on interviews in the belief that teacher knowledge must be sufficiently explicit (i.e., not tacit), that they can articulate it. This is, after all, their task as teachers. So we ask them questions such as these:

• Suppose a student asks you whether to use *is* or *are* in the following sentence: "None of the books _______ in the library."

How would you respond and why?

• Imagine that you are teaching division with fractions. One of your students raises his hand and says, "I am very confused. This doesn't make sense. The answer I am getting is greater than the numbers I start with! What am I doing wrong?" And he hands you one of the examples he has done:

$1\ 3/4 \div 1/2 = 3\ 1/2$

What is going on here?

These questions have proved to be very difficult for our respondents to answer. English majors have almost as much trouble as elementary teacher candidates articulating the principles that should be used to select a verb for the first problem, and math majors have nearly as much difficulty explaining what is going on in the second problem. In fact, even math majors who have high grade point averages often provide erroneous story problems to illustrate this equation. Many of them generate story problems that divide by 2, rather than by 1/2.[7] This should not be surprising: the content that these two problems address is not college-level content. Verb usage is usually addressed in high school and division with fractions is usually addressed in middle school. And most teacher candidates have not thought about these content issues since they first learned them themselves, when they were students in high school or middle school.

The significance of questions of this sort is more apparent when these questions are contrasted with state assessments that focus on the content teachers will teach. Although many states employ some form of subject matter knowledge tests, these tests do not assess teachers' ability to explain subject matter, to generate illustrations of it, or to generate problems that will help students learn it. Instead, they tend to present teachers with multiple-choice questions that require no more than recall and that focus on less important aspects of the content. A question that asks, for instance, "Which of the following five authors wrote *Moby Dick*?" will not tell us much about subject matter knowledge that is relevant to teaching.

Implications for Data Collection

The question of the relationship between test scores and teaching performance is clearly one that needs further examination. But rather than continuing to conduct correlational studies that rely on existing tests, I would recommend that the greatest research effort be placed in the area of test development. At present, we really have no efficient, standardized way to test the pedagogical subject matter knowledge that is relevant to teaching. Interviewing teachers in the way my colleagues and I did at Michigan State would be far too costly a strategy to implement on a broad scale. The examples I describe, though, do provide some alternative ways of thinking about tested ability and about the kinds of questions we need to be asking teachers.

My second recommendation, though, is that this test development activity should not be undertaken by the National Center for Education Statistics (NCES), but instead should continue under the auspices of the NBPTS and the ETS, organizations whose primary reason for being is to develop such assessments, or through research centers such as the new Center for Research on Educational Accountability and Teacher Evaluation. This is not to say that there is no role for the NCES, however, for the validity of these alternative assessments still needs to be assessed. One useful contribution that could be made by the NCES would be to attach some items such as those devised by my research center, or those devised by ETS or the NBPTS, to its future National Assessment of Educational Progress (NAEP) studies, so that teachers' responses to these items could be correlated to the skills and abilities demonstrated in students.

There is probably also little value in maintaining, at a national level, records on the scores of teachers who take state-specific tests, for the content and character of these tests vary widely from state to state. And, since only those teachers who pass the test are permitted to teach, the data would not be very useful for testing relationships between test scores and teacher performance. Moreover, since most state testing systems are relatively new, data will not be available for most practicing teachers. However, within particular states, there might be some value in tracking the relationship between test scores and teaching careers. For instance, are teachers in certain subject areas more likely to pass or to fail these tests, or are teachers who pass with high scores more likely to be hired in certain locations?

SUPPLY OF DEMOGRAPHICALLY REPRESENTATIVE TEACHERS

Whereas the first two dimensions of quality refer to characteristics of individual teachers, this third dimension refers to the characteristics of groups of teachers. By now the demographic projections for the next several decades are well known. The student population is changing dramatically. In the near future, Hispanics will replace blacks as the dominant minority in this country; the total minority population will become a substantial portion of the total population; and in some states, Caucasians will become a minority group.

Yet, despite these changes in the student population, our teaching population is still largely white, suburban, middle class, and female. Our teaching force no longer represents the population at large and will represent it even less in the future unless we work actively to change it. By the mid-1980s, whites represented only 71 percent of the student body but 90 percent of the teaching force. Moreover, minority enrollment in teacher education programs decreased from 17 percent in 1980-81 to 10 percent in 1984-85.[8] Several authors have argued that we need to recruit into teaching people who better represent the students being taught.

How Important is Demographic Representation?

Is demographic mix really a valid measure of quality? How serious a problem is it, really, if we have mainly white, working-class suburban women teaching high-income students, low-income students, urban students, rural students, whites, blacks, Hispanics, and a host of immigrants? After all, we have allowed, for decades, both girls and boys to be taught mainly by women. One could argue that it shouldn't matter whether the teacher and student come from culturally similar or dissimilar backgrounds *provided that the teacher can actively engage students with important content.* In principle, you shouldn't need to be the same sort of person as your students to have an impact on them.

Furthermore, as a practical matter, we can never completely match students and teachers by their demographic characteristics. Any given student is likely to encounter some 30-35 teachers by the time he or she has finished 13 years of school. Simply from the standpoint of probabilities, many, if not most, of these teachers will be demographically different from the student even if the overall population of teachers is perfectly representative of the student population. So even if we successfully meet all our goals regarding demographic representation in the teaching work force, we would still have numerous individual teaching situations in which teacher and student come from different demographic backgrounds.

Given all of this, one could argue that, if our main concern is that minority students be able to learn school material, we should worry as much or more about measuring the dimension of *quality of classroom practice* as we do about measuring the demography of the work force, for no matter how representative the total population of teachers is, individual teachers will still need to serve students from a variety of backgrounds.

Yet students are aware of the full population of teachers in their schools, not just the teachers they encounter in their own classrooms. And this population as a whole does much more than literally teach content. They also personify content. They stand as models for what it is like to be an educated person, to be a member of the community of scientists, writers, mathematicians, or political scientists. They also serve as ex-officio parents, guides, and mentors to young people. And if we want students to believe that they themselves might one day be scientists, writers, or mathematicians or that they might be mentors, guides, and educated people, then we need them to see diverse examples of such people, including at least one who looks like they, the students, look. Moreover, diversity among teachers may increase both the students' and the teachers' knowledge and understanding of different cultural groups, thereby enhancing the abilities of all involved to interact with different cultural groups. For students, such diversity among teachers may improve their future chances of interacting successfully with the different groups they will encounter in their own work. For teachers, such diversity may enhance their ability to interact successfully with their own students, thereby improving the quality of their classroom practices.

This suggests, then, that even if better representation does not always, or even often, yield matched teachers and students, it is still important that we solve the representation problem, for students need role models.

Policy Activity in this Area

Demographic quality can be thought of as a "pipeline" problem. To get more minorities into teaching, policy makers want to help more minorities get into college in the first place.One popular solution for increasing minority enrollments in college is to offer financial assistance to minorities and low-income students. Financial assistance alone, of course, cannot ensure that any of its beneficiaries will actually enter teaching, for just as new employment opportunities have opened up for women, so have they opened up for minorities. But it can increase the pool of graduates available who might consider teaching as a career.

Another idea, currently being considered by Congress, is to revive some form of the Teacher Corps program. The original Teacher Corps, initiated in the 1960s, provided financial assistance during college to encourage students to teach in low-income areas for some period of time after graduation.[9] The idea is analogous to the Peace Corps: you don't assume these teachers will remain in these schools forever, but you give them an incentive to work there at least for a short time. Some Teacher Corps programs funded students while they were in college and encouraged them to go into teaching; some solicited liberal arts graduates and gave them graduate preparation in teaching. All sought candidates who came from low-income neighborhoods in the hope that they would return to those neighborhoods. Whether a new Teacher Corps program could accomplish this outcome, given the new job opportunities for minorities, is not clear.

Interestingly, very few policies move further back in the pipeline and strive to improve the quality of high school programs for these students. Yet if high school minority students aren't receiving a good education in the first place, financial aid will be inadequate, for the most it can do is help them get into less prestigious colleges. It won't make them eligible, or capable of responding to, more demanding colleges and universities. Many colleges and universities now have special remedial programs to assist their less qualified students, but their success rates often are not very good. If we really want to ensure a larger pool of qualified college students, one strategy we should attend more to is increasing the number of minority high school graduates who are qualified for college.

A significant weakness in all of these strategies for altering the demography of the teaching population is that they attend largely to new college graduates. To the extent that new teachers are actually hired from a reserve pool rather than from a pool of new graduates, these policies will not influence the demographic mix of teachers for many years. Indeed, the fact that the current teaching force is so short of minority teachers suggests that, if we were to redress this imbalance, we would need to be preparing far more than a proportionately representative group of new teachers. And, given the size of the teaching force and the continually changing student body, the problem of altering the demographic representation of teachers within schools is doubly challenging.

Implications for Data Collection

Of the five dimensions of quality that I have defined here, the demographic dimension is easiest to document. My first recommendation, therefore, is that any system for measuring supply and demand for teachers should include demographic variables as indicators of quality. Most universities already keep records of the gender, ethnicity, and language origin of their students, including those who are prospective teachers, and therefore could report the demographic characteristics of graduates who are credentialed to teach. Many school districts also keep such records both on their students and on their practicing teachers, and so could report on the makeup of their current teaching force and the similarities between their teaching populations and their student populations. And many NCES data bases include data on demographic characteristics. These data can give us a good sense for the match between the demographic characteristics of prospective and practicing teachers and characteristics of the population of students we project will fill our schools in the next several years.

Of course, demographic data can be made more complicated rather quickly if we also want to know how these different groups are dispersed across subject matter areas within the secondary level. Whether such fine-grained distinctions matter is not clear. We have known for years that most math and science teachers are males, and that female students tend to move away from these courses. However, we also have evidence to suggest that the reason for girls avoiding science courses may not be a lack of female role models in these particular content areas, but instead may be due to the teaching practices employed by these male teachers.[10] If that is the case, it is difficult to know whether we really need representativeness within each field of study or whether, instead, we might be satisfied with representativeness among teachers as a whole, provided that we also address the improvement of teaching practices within particular subject areas.

My second recommendation is that predictions of the number of potential minority college graduates should become part of NCES's routine projections. Because the supply of ethnically diverse teachers is a pipeline problem, policy makers need access to long-term projections in this area. To project the possible supply of minorities entering teaching, we will need first to estimate the size of the potential hiring pool, that is, the number of minority college graduates who have at least majored in teachable subjects, even if they did not obtain teaching credentials. Better still would be to step back yet another level and estimate the number of college-bound minorities as they graduate from high school. Although high school transcripts and Scholastic Aptitude Test scores are rarely used to project potential future teachers, data on the academic status of minorities while in high school could prove to be quite useful in estimating the total pool of minorities who are eligible for college and who therefore could become teachers if the appropriate incentives were provided. I am not sure what would be involved in gathering such data on minority students, but I think that some efforts in this area would be useful both in making projections and in helping policy makers recognize that the progress of minorities through college and into teaching does not begin once they are in college, but instead years earlier.

My third recommendation moves to the demand side of the equation. I think we should measure demand at two levels: the individual teacher level and the school composition level. At the individual teacher level, it would not be too difficult to portray the total number of students served from each racial/ethnic category and the total number of teachers from each group. More difficult, though, would be an index of the dispersion of these teachers that would indicate the relative overlap between teaching populations and student populations. I do not propose a quota-system for hiring teachers, but I do suggest a system for monitoring *schools* to determine how many have attained various levels of demographic mix and how well their mixes of teachers match their mixes of students. Such a system would enable us to identify and locate those schools that are most or least successful in matching their teacher demography with their student demography and thereby providing role models for their students.

SUPPLY AS A FUNCTION OF THE QUALITY OF PROFESSIONAL LIVES OF TEACHERS

The fourth dimension of quality that is of interest to policy makers today is the quality of professional lives of teachers. After a period in the 1960s and 1970s when curricula were designed to be "teacher proof," and a period in the 1980s when policies were designed to dictate the teaching behaviors in classrooms, policy makers are now turning to the belief that teachers should have the same professional responsibilities, and associated autonomy, that professionals in other areas have. Arguments for "empowering" teachers stem in part from a recognition that teaching is too complicated and context-specific to regulate centrally, and in part from a recognition that such central regulation may be an important contributor to teacher attrition.

At the same time, there are those who would argue that the quality of teaching and of teachers is so low that we cannot possibly entrust them with more autonomy and responsibility, for they are not prepared to handle these responsibilities well. Thus, even though there is a tremendous amount of rhetoric within this reform about empowering teachers and converting teaching to a True Profession, there is, at the same time, some countervailing pressure against this rhetoric.

How Important is Quality of Professional Life?

Arguments for improving the quality of teachers' professional lives are numerous. Some people advocate professionalism simply because teachers deserve to be treated better. Compared with other college graduates, for instance, teachers lack such basic amenities as private office space, telephones, and access to photocopying machines. Others advocate professionalism as a means to stem attrition by making the job more attractive. They extend the argument from telephones and private space to professional control over work and the work environment. Finally, some advocate professionalism as an avenue toward improved quality of classroom practice. These people believe that teachers are more qualified than central administrators to make decisions that will improve classroom practice, and that teachers should learn to examine and improve their own practices. The arguments are so diverse that it is difficult to assess the real potential of professionalism for improving either teaching quality or teacher supply. In addition, the arguments are still mainly at the stage of speculation, with few data available to test the merits of any of these propositions. At a minimum, we can separate their potential for reducing attrition from their potential for improving the quality of classroom practice.

With respect to professionalization as a means of improving the attractiveness of teaching as a career, we need to be more clear about what aspects of teaching make the job attractive in the first place, and what aspects of it are most responsible for decisions to leave it. Certain patterns of attrition could be interpreted as indicating that the quality of work life is not a major reason for leaving. For instance, young single women are more likely to leave teaching than are older women or men (Heyns, 1988; Murnane et al., 1988), a pattern that suggests the reasons for attrition may differ across subgroups of teachers. Moreover, leavers are not leaving those schools that might be considered "difficult" schools.

In fact, the pattern of entering and leaving teaching suggests that there is a subgroup of people are simply dabbling with teaching, who perhaps never really considered it as a long-term career option. Of those who were prepared to teach, 25 percent never entered the profession in the first place, a finding I take to mean that they were probably not seriously interested in teaching to begin with, but perhaps picked up a credential as a fallback career option. And those who take teaching jobs but leave them relatively soon tend to come from higher socioeconomic backgrounds, to have higher test scores, and to be teaching in private or suburban schools rather than urban schools. They are not leaving because they are less capable, nor because they have difficult teaching assignments. Perhaps they might not have taught at all if they couldn't find these more comfortable teaching assignments to start with. I suspect that, for this group, teaching is more of an avocation than a career.

This casual approach to teaching may account for the unevenness of supply across schools and teaching positions. The supply of teachers available to a particular school, for instance, depends, among other things, on how far the school is from a teacher's college,[11] the proportion of the student body which is nonwhite (and therefore more difficult to teach for the typical white teacher), and the safety of the school. Within schools, the supply available for particular teaching positions depends in part on the number of preparations required per day, whether the position is itinerant or includes a home room, and the proportion of classes taught outside the primary subject. These are aspects of the quality of work life may be more relevant to dabblers than aspects of professionalism that entail greater commitment to the task. If professionalizing the job requires more commitment from teachers, it is possible that this population of dabblers may be discouraged, rather than encouraged, to take teaching positions even for short periods of time.

With respect to professionalization as a means of improving the quality of classroom practice, we also have reason to be skeptical. If it is true that teachers teach as they were taught, then there is no particular reason to believe that, left to their own devices, teachers would be very likely to make radical changes in their own practices. Even if there were ample opportunities for teachers to observe one another and to discuss and compare their ideas about teaching, they may be more likely to reinforce traditional methods than to devise new ones. Houston's (1988) description of restructuring efforts in two schools illustrates this point: one group of teachers tried to devise new structures for educating their children but were overwhelmed with the difficulty of achieving the goals they had set for themselves, largely because their students were so diverse. They were unable to teach the students in whole groups, did not have the time to individualize their instruction, and did not have the wherewithall to devise new classroom structures that could accommodate their students. Eventually, they limited enrollments in this special program so that their student body was more homogeneous, thereby defeating at least one important goal of restructuring, that of improving education for the difficult-to-serve students.

One aspect of professionalism argues not merely to give teachers more responsibility for their own practices, but to convert teachers to researchers or self-examiners who can engage in critical analyses of their own practices, test new ideas, and improve their practices based on these examinations. In this context, one often hears the term *reflective practitioner.* Whether teachers can be rendered capable of such self-examination remains to be seen, particularly given the current workloads and time constraints most of them face. The only reflective practitioners I have met are working in highly unusual situations, characterized in part by severely restricted teaching loads and in part by extensive access to university colleagues. Unless policy makers are willing to provide the finances necessary to make such conditions commonplace, the concept of professionalism may never yield more than rhetoric.

Policy Activity Promoting Quality Professional Life

Most policies enacted in the last decade have increased, rather than decreased, regulation of teachers and teaching (Darling-Hammond, 1988; Darling-Hammond and Berry, 1988; McDonnell, 1989). Ideas promoting professionalism that have generated the most attention are school-based management and restructured schools, career ladders, merit pay, and peer evaluation.

School-based management programs are intended to release schools from strong district regulation and to encourage teachers to work together within each school to decide such matters as what areas they want to improve, what curricula they will use, how they want to allocate themselves and their students to classrooms, how they will coordinate their activities, and how they will evaluate their progress. While the idea is popular, and many districts are implementing some sort of program that presumably gives schools more autonomy, the degree to which these programs make a real difference in the quality of teachers' professional lives is highly variable. In some districts, teachers may simply be asked to fill out numerous forms listing their evaluation data, objectives, and plans. In others, teachers may be given resources such as released time or consultant services to help them plan and may be given responsibilities for their own budgets.

A related idea, restructured schools, is the central focus of the Coalition for Essential Schools. The goal of the coalition is not teacher empowerment per se, but instead improved teaching and learning. However, in the process of establishing these improvements, teachers become heavily involved in deciding how their respective schools will be organized, what it will be trying to accomplish for students, and what the teachers themselves will be doing to achieve these goals.

Programs that establish merit pay, career ladders, and/or peer evaluation focus more on individual teachers than on teams of teachers in schools. They are intended to recognize differences in teacher quality and to reward those differences in some formal way. In the case of peer evaluation, they are also intended to give teachers more voice in judging their professional colleagues. Like school-wide programs, these programs exist in only a few states or school districts, and have not existed long enough to have a noticeable impact on teachers. Or, if they do persist, it is often because they have been altered to the point that they are not so radical a change as reformers might have hoped for.[12]

Moreover, many of these empowerment activities are extremely difficult and time-consuming and are not necessarily embraced by teachers. Teamwork requires a tremendous commitment of time, time which many teachers do not have. In addition, plans that require teachers to observe and comment on one another's classroom practices fly in the face of the culture of teaching, in which teachers are very careful never to comment on one another's work (Little, 1988). Similarly, ideas that differentiate among teachers, either through staffing arrangements or through career ladders or merit pay, are generally distasteful to teachers. The evidence to date does not suggest that teachers perceive clear benefits from efforts to professionalize their work and that, moreover, these efforts increase their burdens.

Ironically, although the aim of these policies is to increase teachers' professional authority, most of these new policies are not originated by teachers themselves but instead by state or school district administrators. Thus, even though their rhetoric is that of teacher empowerment, the strategy continues to be that of establishing new rules for teachers to comply with. To the extent that these policies are viewed by teachers as burdensome new requirements, rather than opportunities, they are likely not to have their intended effect (see, e.g., Johnson, 1990). The Coalition for Essential Schools offers an alternative to the top-down strategy for school reform, as do some of the district-level devices that have been designed through negotiation between the district administration and the teachers' union.

There are at least two reasons, then, to be pessimistic about these proposals. First, the vision of professionalism espoused by researchers and policy makers is somewhat at odds with teachers' own vision of their work. Whereas the advocates of professionalism want to recognize the differential abilities of teachers and want teachers to strive to improve their own practices by engaging in research, making their own decisions about what to teach and how, engaging in critical reflection about their own practices and interacting with one another about all of these issues, teachers themselves prefer not to distinguish among themselves, not to discuss their practices with one another, not to examine one another's practices, and often not to make difficult curriculum decisions.[13] Second, even if we were to achieve this radical alteration in the character and quality of the teaching profession, we have no evidence that such changes will in fact improve the quality of classroom practices. The notion that teachers will somehow, simply by virtue of having the opportunity to make their own decisions, discover better practices, is weak at best, and no clear model has yet been articulated regarding where the better teaching practices are to come from when the existing population of teachers are committed to practices that derive from their own childhood experiences.

Implications for Data Collection

The problem with policies aiming for professionalism is that they are tremendously various. If we begin gathering data on the presence or absence of a particular idea, such as school-based management or merit pay, and then look for evidence that such programs have altered teacher attrition or improved classroom practices, we may easily find the same result we have found when studying the role of credentials. And the finding would be similarly difficult to interpret, for we cannot know whether such programs *could* make a difference, if done in such a way that teachers really feel more professional responsibility. Perhaps, instead of documenting the presence or absence of particular policy practices, NCES might contribute more to policy by documenting teachers' perceptions of their professional control over different aspects of their work, and see whether these perceptions are related to, say, attrition. These data might shed more light on what teachers really want in their jobs.

One thing that makes teacher attrition difficult to measure is that we often don't know, when a teacher leaves a particular position, whether that teacher is leaving the field or is leaving that particular position. Certainly improvements could be made in our knowledge of teachers who leave particular teaching jobs. I recommend that such data should not be limited to teachers' perceptions of their job satisfaction but include data on the job itself. For instance, how far it is from the teacher's home town or alma mater, what fraction of the teacher's courses are in his or her subject matter major, how many different preparations are required of the teacher each day, and how many students the teacher comes into contact with weekly. Such data, combined with data on the teachers' perception of job-related working conditions, responsibilities, and constraints, could be used to begin developing a predictive model of teacher attrition.

SUPPLY OF HIGH-QUALITY CLASSROOM TEACHING PRACTICE

Virtually all of the blue ribbon commissions that have studied education in the last decade have argued that we need a new and better kind of teaching: one that challenges students more than current methods do, that expects more of students, that demands higher-order thinking from them, that prepares them for the work place of tomorrow.[14] More than previous generations, today's students must learn to work collaboratively in teams, to solve problems, to be flexible and adaptable. Yet traditional teaching practices encourage students to work in isolation and compete with one another, to learn discrete facts and skills rather than to solve complex problems, and to follow fixed routines rather than experiment with novel tasks. Preparing students for tomorrow's work place requires a different kind of teaching, so policy makers face the task of finding ways to improve classroom teaching practices.

But improving the quality of classroom teaching entails more than merely a change in substantive orientation. I mentioned earlier that the student body itself is changing rapidly, and that even a good solution to the representation problem would not yield a complete match between teachers and students. This means not only that teachers must learn to teach different content, but also that they must learn to teach a different kind of student, one that has traditionally been alienated from schools and from academic subjects, and one that differs substantially, in most cases, from those the teacher grew up with. Schools have always served diverse groups of students and have never been able to serve them all equally well. As a society, we have vacillated in the degree to which we tolerate this problem. But as our population changes so that a larger fraction of students represent those that schools have been unable to serve, the problem of school failure becomes much more severe.

How Important is the Quality of Classroom Teaching Practice?

I have already discussed the importance of classroom teaching practice. My main argument here is that the importance of this dimension of quality stems from a recognition that the content being taught to students is at a far lower level than we want to see. If our educational goals were limited to basic skills and the memorization of specific facts, we might not be worried about the quality of classroom practice. But we have, as a nation, set much higher goals for education than we are now able to achieve.

The quality of classroom practice problem boils down to this: If we know that teachers are highly likely to teach as they were taught, and if we are not satisfied with the way they were taught, how, then, can we help them develop different teaching strategies? And how can we create schools and policies that support their use of these alternative strategies?

Of the five quality issues I have described, the improvement-of-practice problem is the most serious. We are caught in a vicious cycle of mediocre practice modeled after mediocre practice, of trivialized knowledge begetting more trivialized knowledge. Unless we find a way out of this cycle, we will continue to recreate generations of teachers who in turn recreate generations of students whom we already know are not prepared for the kind of information/technology society we are entering.

The heart of the problem is that if teachers and prospective teachers are driven to emulate the teachers they observed when they themselves were students, they will not quickly adopt new ideas. In our work at Michigan State, for instance, we have found that undergraduates who plan to enter teaching almost universally hold a limited view of their role as teacher, thinking that teaching entails little more than telling students what they know and assessing students' recall of that knowledge (see, e.g., Ball, 1988b; Feiman-Nemser et al., in press). When asked what they might do if their students did not understand a particular concept, their sole recourse was to "go over it again." They simply could not envision any alternative teaching strategies. They do not even imagine that the telling itself must be done with care. Their tacit view of the teacher's role limits their ability to envision, let alone enact, any more demanding forms of teaching. Having witnessed teaching throughout their lives, and having been successful students when their teachers taught mainly by telling students and then testing students, teachers cannot imagine the effort that is implied by the current demands for improvement.

More than any other aspect of instruction, the role teachers adopt in their classrooms is critical to the improvement of practice. Moreover, helping novices conceive of a new role may be the most difficult challenge facing teacher educators. Teachers cannot follow procedural manuals defining a list of new activities; they must adopt a role and make it their own. A role is an abstract concept to grasp, and the roles envisioned by education reformers must be adopted cognitively, affectively, and kinesthetically by teachers. A teacher's ability to adopt a new, more demanding role depends not only on his or her understanding of that role, but also on emotional acceptance of and commitment to that role.

Policy Activity in This Area

The traditional strategy of inservice teacher education continues to be a popular one for improving the quality of classroom teaching practices. Although most current efforts at inservice teacher education fall remarkably short of having any real impact, inservice programs are still one of the few policy options that can be expected to alter the practices of existing teachers or alter the practices of those hired from the reserve pool.

Moreover, some two decades of research into strategies for influencing teaching practices have given us a reasonable basis for designing inservice programs. Research on teaching meaningful content, for instance, suggests that the key to teaching lies in subject-specific pedagogy rather than generic pedagogy, and research on promoting changes in teaching practice suggests that changes are more likely to occur when they are introduced at the school building level, rather than to individual teachers working in isolation, and when the desired changes are promoted over a long period of time with ongoing classroom support.

Yet all of these features are absent from most state and locally supported inservice programs. Interestingly, one of the strongest inservice systems now in existence, the National Writing Project, is sponsored almost exclusively by teachers rather than by policy makers. Three weaknesses are particularly salient to state- and district-supported inservice programs. First, most inservice activities are not really full-blown programs, but instead are brief workshops. School districts typically build into their budgets one or two workshops each year, with each workshop consisting of a half-day to a two-day session on a particular issue. Given the depth of teachers' commitments to their current practices, it is highly unlikely that such brief exposures to new ideas will substantially alter their classroom practices. Second, the content of these workshops often changes from one to the next, so that teachers receive inconsistent messages regarding what counts as good practice. One may promote assertive discipline while another promotes teaching higher-order skills and a third promotes increases in time on task.

Because these workshops are independent of one another, teachers not only receive mixed messages regarding the relative importance of these ideas, but also receive no assistance in rectifying philosophical discrepancies among the different ideas. Finally, very few inservice programs provide follow-up assistance in the classroom to help teachers implement the ideas they have learned about. Consequently, teachers are left with only the general idea and with no specific means for implementing these ideas.

Some teacher educators are also investigating ways to help teacher candidates learn more from teacher education than they have tended to learn from it in the past. We now know more than we did even 10 years ago about what is involved in teaching higher-order thinking, and we know more about the nature of the knowledge teachers need.[15] Teacher educators are now experimenting with ways of getting more out of their candidates' formal classroom learning time (e.g., Schramm et al., 1988; Feiman-Nemser et al., in press; Ball, 1988a). One way they do this is through assignments that force their candidates to be more analytic about what they see in classrooms—to raise questions about what is being taught and what is being learned and to generate hypotheses about better ways to do it. Teacher educators are also experimenting with ways of helping candidate teachers develop alternative teaching strategies.

A popular new strategy designed to improve the classroom practices of new teachers is the inclusion of on-the-job assessments in hiring policies, such that teachers are placed on probation for the first year or two and their practices are assessed during this probationary period. The most visible systems, those in Virginia and Florida, focus on discrete teaching skills that are correlated with standardized test scores in early elementary grades, in which the content is heavily oriented toward basic skills. The research on which these assessments are based, often referred to as process-product research, has relied on measures of student outcomes that are themselves limited: standardized achievement tests that tend to measure students' acquisition of basic knowledge and skills. Moreover, this research has been conducted for the most part in the early elementary grades, in which students are learning largely basic skills.

Since the original research addressed the way teaching is currently done, most of its findings about pedagogical practices are valid only for the teaching of routine skills, not for teaching higher-level thinking, nor for adequately representing subject matter to diverse learners. Thus, the teaching behaviors identified through this research are not necessarily those that will yield the kind of improvements in practice that we now seek. Indeed, some reformers argue that these are the very skills that hinder higher-order reasoning in the classroom. Perhaps the most remarkable evidence of the limitation of this basic skills orientation appears in a response by Barak Rosenshine (1986) to a high school history lecture given by then-Secretary of Education William Bennett. Rosenshine confesses that he doesn't know what to make of the secretary's lesson because research on teaching has focused on teaching skills, not on teaching content. As Rosenshine tries to evaluate the secretary's lesson, using his own knowledge of teaching skills, he assumes that the goal of the lesson is to get students to recite the knowledge as opposed to getting them to understand it, interpret it, or use it to interpret current events. These performance assessment systems, then, are not likely to yield the kind of improvements in classroom practice that most reformers seek.

Another popular strategy for improving the classroom practices of beginning teachers is the *induction program*. Thirteen states now require some form of induction program beyond student teaching. In most cases, a state-level requirement for induction means that school districts must provide first-year teachers with some sort of guidance or assistance as they struggle through their first year or two of learning to teach (see Schlechty, 1985, for a discussion of induction rationales). Often this assistance appears in the form of an experienced teacher who serves as a mentor to the new teacher. There are numerous variations on this theme. Mentors can work independently in one-on-one relationships or they can provide a standardized orientation to all newcomers. Districts may release their mentors from full-time teaching while they serve as mentors, or they may require them to help novices in the cracks between classes. Given the range of strategies for providing assistance, it would be reasonable to expect these programs also to differ in the benefits that novices gain from them.

Gauging the benefits of induction programs forces us to face the difference between efforts to increase the supply of teachers and efforts to improve the quality of teaching practices. One strong argument for induction programs is that they may decrease the attrition rates among novice teachers. Yet, like alternative route programs, induction programs will probably not improve the quality of classroom practice. They may help new teachers learn what the current population of teachers already knows, and may help them over the difficult adjustments into teaching, but they will not help them learn new or different approaches to teaching. If anything, induction programs further reinforce the same kind of teaching we already have—the kind that emphasizes facts and skills rather than reasoning and analysis and that encourages student passivity and compliance rather than active engagement with subject matter. This is the kind of teaching that has led to the assessment results we are unhappy about.

Yet another proposal often put forward to improve classroom teaching practices is the professional development school, or PDS (The Holmes Group, 1986; Levine, 1988; Lieberman, 1989). There was a time when most colleges of education operated lab schools—schools located on or near university campuses where student teachers received their practical experience. It might be easy to think that professional development schools are a newer version of the same thing, and in many respects they are. But in one important respect they are not. The lab school was operated by the university, not by the community, and its students tended to be faculty offspring. Lab schools prepared teachers in a sort of ivory tower environment—no poverty, no uneducated parents, few children from culturally different backgrounds, and often plenty of resources.

Professional development schools, in contrast, are genuine collaborations between the university and the school. They serve the children who attend public schools, not those who attend private schools. Moreover, their reason for being is not just to provide a context for new teachers to learn to teach, but to allow all teachers to learn more about teaching. In that sense, they are truly laboratories.

Not many full-blown professional development schools exist now, so I can describe here only their idealized features. Modeled after the teaching hospital, one feature of the PDS is that university faculty would regularly teach there, and that teachers from these schools would regularly teach at the university. Another feature is that virtually everyone associated with a PDS—faculty, teachers, and student teachers—would be experimenting with new ways to teach children. And finally, the staffing patterns and the physical layout of PDSs would look different from regular schools. They would contain private places for teachers to plan and design new strategies and materials, conference rooms where teachers could work together on new ideas, and observation rooms connected to classrooms so that teachers, teacher candidates, and other visitors could observe these teaching practices without disrupting the activity itself.

Getting a sense of the layout and the kind of work that occurs in these places should indicate some of the staffing changes that would have to occur as well, for we cannot have genuine experimentation in the typical egg-carton school organization, where each teacher is tied to one or another group of children almost every hour of every day. Yet someone must be with these children, and the children must be learning throughout the day. To get a professional development school going, then, districts would need either to double the existing staff and be very creative in grouping students and teachers, or to develop a new cadre of teaching assistants who would free teachers to do the kind of experimentation and development that is needed.

The PDS proposal is clearly designed to contribute to the improvement of practice. It does nothing for credentials, demographic representation, or tested ability. Moreover, PDSs are intended to improve the practices of the existing teaching force as well as to provide a better preparation for new teachers. But while there is a tremendous amount of activity in this area, we are hardly at a point at which we can say that this strategy has clear potential. Moreover, most proposals for PDSs, even though they recognize the need to improve the practices of existing teachers, still take their main task as that of preparing new teachers. Existing practices are only improved in PDS schools themselves, not in the rest of the schools.

Implications for Data Collection

When it comes to data collection, the quality of classroom practice is the most muddy. Though nearly everyone believes they can distinguish good teaching from bad, we still face tremendous conceptual problems in defining ordinary teaching, bad teaching, and good teaching and even more problems in trying to measure these things. Add to all of this the problem of measuring changes in classroom practices—and we have a real soup.

Gathering data on practice itself offers us both the advantage of directly measuring the thing we are ultimately interested in, and the disadvantage that we have no clear methods for doing this. Performance assessments such as those described above, even if altered to capture more important aspects of teaching, still are susceptible to corruption if teachers learn what they are supposed to do while they are being observed. The work of the Educational Testing Service on a new version of the NTE, and the work of the National Board of Professional Teaching Standards on a certification assessment for teachers, will contribute to our understanding of teacher knowledge and perhaps to our understanding of their pedagogical subject matter knowledge. Both are intended to yield more valid and meaningful measures of teacher quality. And, although neither of these new devices will be ready in the near future, they will probably be ready before we could come up with any other alternative independently.

What these measures will not yield is evidence of teachers' inclinations to regularly engage in the practices that are advocated by the assessors. The more we recognize the importance of teachers' commitments to different teaching ideals, the more imperative it becomes to find ways to measure these commitments and to incorporate them in our estimates of the number of teachers available whose classroom practices approach those we are aiming toward. The research being done at the National Center for Research on Teacher Education includes a number of questions designed to tap teachers' beliefs and values as they are expressed in the context of particular kinds of teaching situations. Recognizing the importance of teachers' beliefs about what should be taught and about their role in facilitating learning, we ask several questions designed to learn more about these aspects of their teaching. Such questions, if added to, say, an NAEP assessment, might yield important findings regarding the relationship between these teacher characteristics and student outcomes in higher-order areas. Consider, for instance, the finding from the NAEP assessment that students can manage basic writing skills, but cannot develop coherent arguments. A likely reason for this outcome may be that teachers of writing emphasize basic skills more than coherence. Here is an item we asked teachers in our study that reveals their tendencies to emphasize different aspects of writing:

> I'd like you to imagine that your third grade students are writing stories. Jessie, one of your students hands you the following story.
>
> *One day my frend mary asked me. Do you want to have a picnik? When we got ther we started playing. At the picnik pepol said. Where's your puppy? He is at home? We went home happy. My mother said. I'm glad you had a picnik.*
>
> What do you think of Jessie's story?
> How would you respond to Jessie? Why?
> What grade would you give this paper? Why?

Responses to this question have been particularly telling with respect to teachers' assumptions about their role in helping students learn to write. Teachers can choose to focus on the content and coherence of the story or on its technical correctness. Even when focusing on its technical aspects, they may either identify one or two main problems or can enumerate every problem they see. What Jessie has done here is invent a way to indicate quoted material. Not knowing the convention of using quotation marks, Jessie indicates a new speaker by inserting a period.[16] In fact, three of the errors in this story derive from this one writing decision, and three others derive from an inability to spell the word *picnic*. So a teacher who focuses on technical correctness may count these as two errors, while another may count them as six errors. The former is diagnosing the student's writing and concentrating instruction on general skills, while the latter is not really teaching but instead only counting errors.

When responding to student work, teachers have enormous latitude in deciding what role they want to play in helping their students learn. Questions such as these may prove to be highly useful indicators of teaching practice and may be more efficient than direct observation. If such questions were embedded into NAEP surveys, they could improve our understanding of the relationship between teachers' fundamental orientations toward teaching and the kinds of outcomes they promote in their students.

SUMMARY

I have tried in this paper to distinguish among several different dimensions of quality, to review the kinds of policy alternatives that are generally under consideration with respect to each of these dimensions, and to consider data collection strategies that might be relevant to each. The dimensions of quality that I reviewed here differ in their attention to individual teachers and groups of teachers and in their attention to characteristics of teachers versus characteristics of teaching.

These dimensions also differ with respect to how easy they are to study. The dimensions of credentials and demographic characteristics are easier to define; consequently, supply and demand within these dimensions is easier to measure. The dimension of tested ability is somewhat more difficult to define, and consequently more difficult to measure as well. And in the absence of a handy measure of tested ability, it will be difficult to gauge supply and demand within this dimension of quality. The dimensions focusing on teaching behaviors—the professionalism of their work or their classroom teaching practices—are the most difficult to define, the most difficult to influence, and the most difficult to measure. Although we all believe we can recognize professional attitudes and good classroom teaching when we see it, we do not have ready indicators of it. Moreover, to the extent that we want data that can indicate whether teaching practice is improving, especially data that indicate whether we have an adequate supply of teachers who can promote substantive reasoning in their classrooms, we need ways of recognizing and documenting progress toward practices that are not well understood and are only occasionally available for examination. Change in practice will prove difficult not only for teachers, but also for researchers and policy makers, for all of us are more at home with teaching as we knew it when we were young.

I have also argued that solving any one of these aspects of quality would not necessarily solve any of the others and that, in particular, improving the supply of teachers who meet any of the first four dimensions of quality may not lead to improvements in the supply of teachers whose actual classroom teaching practice is better than current practice is. Improving the match between teachers' credentials and their teaching assignments won't necessarily lead to improved practice; getting a more demographically representative population of teachers won't do it; increasing tested ability won't; and neither, necessarily, will efforts to professionalize teaching. But it is also true that improving classroom teaching practices will not necessarily improve credentials or demographic representation or tested ability or teacher professionalism. So to the extent that we want all of these things, perhaps each for a different reason, each of these dimensions of quality must be considered in any estimates or projections of supply and demand.

My recommendations for improving data on supply and demand within these dimensions of quality are as follows:

With respect to credentials, states should be encouraged to maintain more and better data on the number of teachers who apply to have out-of-state credentials recognized and the number accepted and rejected, on the number of emergency-certified teachers in each teaching category, and on the actual teaching assignments of teachers with different credentials. In addition, NCES could facilitate state policy by documenting the variety of college curricula that lead to credentials in different states. Such data would enable state policy makers to examine their own policies in relation to those of other states.

With respect to tested ability, existing state tests are too various to warrant cross-state data collection systems. And since two major efforts are currently under way to improve the quality of national-level data on teachers' tested ability, it would not make sense for NCES to do so. However, NCES could play an important role in testing the validity of some of the alternative assessments currently being developed by attaching portions of them to future NAEP studies, so that teachers' responses to these items could be correlated with the different kinds of skills and abilities demonstrated in students.

With respect to demographic quality, NCES should capitalize on university data bases to predict the number of potential minority college graduates and, if possible, should step back yet another level and use secondary school data to estimate the number of college-bound minorities as they graduate from high school. When measuring demand for minority teachers, NCES should devise a metric that enables them to document teacher demography as a variable of *school composition*. An index of the demographic mix of teachers within schools could indicate the relative overlap between teaching populations and student populations. Such a system would enable us define the supply of schools available that offer students a locally representative teaching force and to identify and locate those schools that are most or least successful in matching their teacher demography with their student demography.

With respect to professionalism in teaching, the programs designed to promote professionalism are so various that documentation of programs per se will probably not yield much. Instead, NCES might try to develop better models for predicting teacher attrition—models that incorporate relevant features of teaching jobs and that incorporate teachers' perceptions of control over various aspects of their work.

With respect to classroom teaching practices, the nature of programs designed to promote improvements in classroom practices are extremely various, even though many of them share the same names. Moreover, direct measures of classroom teaching practices would be too costly to implement on a wide scale. Instead of documenting the presence or absence of such programs, NCES might better facilitate policy making by experimenting with measures of teachers' beliefs about what should be taught and about their role in facilitating learning. Such experimentation could be done by embedding context-specific questions about teachers' beliefs and values into NAEP or other NCES surveys. Such questions could improve our understanding of teachers' fundamental orientations toward teaching and the kinds of outcomes these orientations promote in students.

I have also argued that two particular features of the teaching force make policy efforts especially perplexing. One of these features is the sheer size of the teaching force. Numbering over 2 million, teachers represent the largest fraction of college graduates in this country—yet they represent less than half of all college graduates who have been prepared to teach. These facts have implications for all dimensions of quality, and for virtually any policy effort to influence quality and supply. Size has implications for credentialing, especially in light of the large number of people who obtain credentials but do not use them or use them only for a year or two. The data suggest that policy makers need to increase the supply of credentialed teachers at substantially greater rates than are actually needed if they want to ensure that credentialed teachers will actually be available to schools that need them. That is, projections of credential supply need to take into account the fact that a sizeable fraction of people with credentials never enter teaching or will teach for only a year or two.

Size also has implications for altering the demographic composition of the work force. If policy makers tried to encourage an equal proportion of each racial or ethnic group of college students to enter teaching, they would find that they still did not have enough new minority teachers to balance the proportion of minority students in schools. This result would occur in part because the production of new teachers will not alter the current teaching population, which is substantially out of balance with the racial and ethnic composition of the student population, and in part because the student population is changing so rapidly toward nonwhite students that even the most concerted minority recruiting programs are likely to lag considerably behind the student body changes.

The size of the teaching force also has implications for tested ability, for schools must compete with other industries for employees and cannot expect to take a substantial fraction of adults with high tested ability from other professions and businesses. Finally, the size of the teaching force has implications for virtually any efforts to alter teaching behaviors and norms, either through professionalization or through efforts to improve classroom practices, for the kinds of changes that are being sought. They would necessarily entail substantial labor costs, both for teachers, who need more time to develop new teaching strategies, and for consultants and other support services that would be needed to help teachers make these changes.

The second aspect of teaching that makes policy efforts more perplexing is that many of these issues of teacher quality and supply are differentially salient across different types of schools, so that nationally aggregated data will not capture the policy-relevant issues. Problems of supply are uneven across schools and types of teaching positions, so that data on supply and demand should be defined in terms of the particular school contexts, rather than through national averages. This admonition is relevant to all dimensions of quality and to all methods of measuring supply and demand within these dimensions. Schools differ, for instance, in their reliance on emergency credentials, so that data on the supply and demand of credentialed teachers will be more useful when they take schools into account. Problems of demography are also relevant at the school level, where discrepancies between populations of teachers and of students are most visible.

Tested ability is also likely to vary by schools. If brighter teachers tend to marry brighter spouses, they will live in communities that have jobs for their spouses. That is, we might find tested ability higher in communities that employ more highly educated people in general, rather than in communities in which the dominant employment is unskilled or skilled labor. Attrition is also uneven across types of schools and types of teaching positions within schools. Therefore, rather than measuring national variations, data bases should be constructed to indicate numbers and types of schools that exhibit different mixes of teachers and different mixes of teaching assignments. For all of these reasons, then, it would behoove the NCES to consider methods of measuring both quality and supply and demand through school units rather than through national aggregates of individual teachers.

REFERENCES

Adleman, Nancy

1986 *An Exploratory Study of Teacher Alternative Certification and Retraining Programs.* Washington, D.C.: Policy Studies Associates.

American Association of Colleges for Teacher Education

1987a *Teachers and Teaching: Facts and Figures.* Washington, D.C.: Author.

1987b *Minority Teacher Recruitment and Retention: A Public Policy Issue.* Washington, D.C.: author.

American Federation of Teachers

1985 *Making Do in the Classroom: A Report on the Misassignment of Teachers.* Washington, D.C.: Council for Basic Education.

Applebee, A.N., J.A. Langer, I.V.S. Mullis, and L.B. Jenkins

1990 The Writing Report Card, 1984-88. Princeton, New Jersey: Educational Testing Service.

Ball, Deborah L.

1988a Unlearning to teach mathematics. *For the Learning of Mathematics* 8(1):40-48.

1988b Knowledge and Reasoning in Mathematical Pedagogy: Examining What Prospective Teachers Bring to Teacher Education. Unpublished doctoral dissertation, Michigan State University.

1990 Research on teaching mathematics: Making subject matter knowledge part of the equation. In Jere Brophy, ed., *Advances in Research on Teaching, Volume 2: Teachers' Subject Matter Knowledge and Classroom Instruction.* Greenwich, Connecticut: JAI Press.

Begle, E.G., and W. Geeslin

1972 *Teacher Effectiveness in Mathematics Instruction.* Washington, D.C.: Mathematics Association of America and National Council of Teachers of Mathematics.

Carey, Neil, B.S. Mittman, and L. Darling-Hammond
1988 *Recruiting Mathematics and Science Teachers Through Nontraditional Programs: A Survey.* Washington, D.C.: The RAND Corporation.

Carnegie Forum on Education and the Economy
1986 *A Nation Prepared: Teachers for the 21st Century.* Washington, D.C.: Author.

Cohen, D.K., and R.J. Murnane
1985 The merits of merit pay. *The Public Interest* 80(Summer):3-30.

Council of Chief State School Officers
1988 *State Education Indicators, 1988.* Washington, D.C.: Author.

Darling-Hammond, Linda
1988 Policy and professionalism. Pp. 55-77 in A. Lieberman, ed., *Building a Professional Culture in Schools.* New York: Teachers College Press.

Darling-Hammond, L. and B. Berry
1988 *The Evolution of Teacher Policy.* Washington, D.C.: The RAND Corporation.

Darling-Hammond, Linda, Lisa Hudson, and Shiela N. Kirby
1989 *Redesigning Teacher Education: Opening the Door for New Recruits to Science and Mathematics Teaching.* Washington, D.C.: The RAND Corporation.

Doyle, Walter
1983 Academic work. *Review of Educational Research* 53(2):159-199.
1986 Content representation in teachers' definitions of academic work. *Journal of Curriculum Studies* 18(4):365-379.

Doyle, Walter, and K. Carter
1984 Academic tasks in classrooms. *Curriculum Inquiry* 14:129-149.

Feiman-Nemser, S., G.W. McDiarmid, S. Melnick, and M. Parker
in press Changing conceptions of beginning teacher education students: A description of an introductory course. *Journal of Education for Teaching.*

Feistritzer, Emily
1990 *Alternative Teacher Certification: A State-by-State Analysis.* Washington, D.C.: National Center for Educational Information.

Gallagher, James J.
1989 Research on Secondary School Science Teachers' Practices, Knowledge and Beliefs: A Basis for Restructuring. Paper presented at the American Association for the Advancement of Science, San Francisco.

Gilford, Dorothy M., and Ellen Tenenbaum, eds.
1990 Precollege Science and Mathematics Teachers: Monitoring Supply, Demand, and Quality. Panel on Statistics on Supply and Demand for Precollege Science and Mathematics Teachers, Committee on National Statistics. Washington, D.C.: National Academy Press.

Haberman, Martin
1985 Can common sense effectively guide the behavior of beginning teachers? *Journal of Teacher Education* 36(6):32-35.

Haggstrom, G.W., L. Darling-Hammond, and D.W. Grissmer
1988 *Assessing Teacher Supply and Demand.* Washington, D.C.: The RAND Corporation.

Haney, Walter, G. Madaus, and A. Kreitzer
1987 Charms talismanic: Testing teachers for the improvement of American educa-

tion. In E.Z. Rothkopf, ed., *Review of Research in Education, Volume 14*. Washington, D.C.: American Educational Research Association.

Hanushek, Eric
1986 The economics of schooling: Production and efficiency in public schools. *Journal of Economic Literature* 26:1141-1177.

Hawley, Willis D.
1986 The risks and inadequacy of extended programs. In Eva C. Galambos, ed., *Improving Teacher Education: New Directions for Teaching and Learning* 27:27-36. San Francisco: Jossey Bass.

Heyns, Barbara
1988 Educational defectors: A first look at teacher attrition in the NLS-72. *Educational Researcher* April:24-32.

The Holmes Group
1986 *Tomorrow's Teachers*. East Lansing, Michigan: The Holmes Group.

Horner, B., and J. Sammons
1987 *A NYPIRG Report: The Test That Fails*. New York: New York Public Interest Research Group, Inc.

Houston, Holly
1988 Restructuring secondary schools. Pp. 109-128 in A. Lieberman, ed., *Building a Professional Culture in Schools*. New York: Teachers College Press.

International Association for the Evaluation of Educational Achievement
1988 *Science Achievement in Seventeen Countries: A Preliminary Report*. New York: Pergamon.

Johnson, Susan M.
1990 Redesigning teachers' work. Pp. 125-151 in R.F. Elmore and Associates, eds., *Restructuring Schools: The Next Generation of Educational Reform*. San Francisco: Jossey Bass.

Kennedy, M., ed.
1989 *Competing Visions of Teacher Knowledge*. East Lansing, Michigan: National Center for Research on Teacher Education.

Kerr, Donna H.
1983 Teaching competence and teacher education in the United States. Pp. 126-149 in L.S. Shulman and G. Sykes, eds., *Handbook of Teaching and Policy*.

Lanier, Judith
1986 Research on teacher education. Pp. 527-569 in M.C. Wittrock, ed., *Handbook of Research on Teacher Education, 3rd edition*. New York: Macmillan.

Levine, Marsha, ed.
1988 Professional Practice Schools: Building a Model. Washington, D.C.: American Federation of Teachers.

Lieberman, Ann, ed.
1988 *Building Professional Cultures in Schools*. New York: Teachers College Press.

Little, Judith W.
1988 Assessing the prospects for expanding leadership. Pp. 78-106 in A. Lieberman, ed., *Building a Professional Culture in Schools*. New York: Teachers College Press.

Lortie, Daniel
1975 *Schoolteacher*. Chicago: University of Chicago Press.

McDiarmid, G. Williamson
1990 The liberal arts: Will more result in better subject matter understanding? *Theory into Practice* 29:21-29.

McDiarmid, G. Williamson, D.L. Ball, and C.W. Anderson
1989 Why staying ahead one chapter doesn't really work: Subject-specific pedagogy. In M. Reynolds, ed., *The Knowledge Base for Beginning Teachers.* New York: Pergamon.

McDonnell, Lorraine M.
1989 *The Dilemma of Teacher Policy.* Washington, D.C.: The RAND Corporation.

McDonough, M.W., Jr., and W.C. Wolfe, Jr.
1988 Court actions which helped define the direction of the competency-based testing movement. *Journal of Research and Development in Education* 2(3)37-43.

McKnight, C.C., F.J. Crosswhite, J.A. Dossey, E. Kifer, J.O. Swafford, K.J. Travers, and T.J. Cooney
1987 *The Under-achieving Curriculum: Assessing U.S. School Mathematics from an International Perspective.* Champaign, Illinois: Stipes Press.

Murnane, Richard J., J.D. Singer, and J.B. Willett
1988 The career paths of teachers: Implications for teacher supply and methodological lessons for research. *Educational Researcher* 17(6)22-30.
1989 The influence of salaries and "opportunity costs" on teachers' career choices: Evidence from North Carolina. *Harvard Educational Review* 59(3):325-346.

Murnane, R.J., J.D. Singer, J.B. Willett, J.J. Kemple, and R.J. Olsen
1991 *Who Will Teach? Policies That Matter.* Cambridge: Harvard University Press.

National Center for Education Statistics
1989 *Digest of Education Statistics.* Washington, D.C.: U.S. Department of Education.

National Commission on Excellence in Education
1983 *A Nation at Risk.* Washington, D.C.: U.S. Department of Education.

National Research Council
1989 *Everybody Counts: A Report on the Future of Mathematics Education.* Mathematical Sciences Education Board. Washington, D.C.: National Academy Press.

Nemser, Sharon Feiman
1983 Learning to teach. Pp. 150-170 in L.S. Shulman and G. Sykes, eds., *Handbook of Teaching and Policy.* New York: Longman.

Porter, Andrew C.
1989 A curriculum out of balance: The case of elementary school mathematics. *Educational Researcher* 18(5):9-15.

Robertson, S.D., T.Z. Keith, and E.B. Page
1983 Now who aspires to teach? *Educational Researcher* 12(3):13-21.

Rosenshine, Barak
1986 Unsolved issues in teaching content: A critique of a lesson on Federalist Paper No. 10. *Teachers and Teacher Education* 2:301-308.

Schlechty, Phillip C.
1985 A framework for evaluating induction into teaching. *Journal of Teacher Education* 36(1)37-41.

Schlechty, Phillip C., and V.S. Vance
1983 Recruitment, selection and retention: The shape of the teaching force. *The Elementary School Journal* 83:469-487.

Schramm, Pam, S. Wilcox, P. Lanier, and G. Lappan
1988 *Changing Mathematical Conceptions of Preservice Teachers: A Content and Pedagogical Intervention.* Research Report 88-4. East Lansing, Michigan: National Center for Research on Teacher Education, Michigan State University.

Sedlak, Michael, and Steven Schlossman
1986 *Who Will Teach? Historical Perspectives on the Changing Appeal of Teaching as a Profession.* Santa Monica, California: The RAND Corporation.
Shulman, L.S.
1987 Knowledge and teaching: Foundations of the new reform. *Harvard Educational Review* 57:1-22.
Stoddart, Trish
1987 Who is Entering Alternate Routes into Teaching and What Views Do They Bring with Them? Paper presented at the Annual Meeting of the American Educational Research Association, San Francisco. March.
Tobin, Kenneth
1987 Forces which shape the implemented curriculum in high school science and mathematics. *Teaching and Teacher Education* 3:287-298.
Tobin, Kenneth, and James J. Gallagher
1987 What happens in high school science classrooms? *Journal of Curriculum Studies* 19(6):549-560.
Tyson, H., and A. Woodward
1989 Why students aren't learning very much from textbooks. *Educational Leadership* 3(11):14-17.
Wilson, S., L.S. Shulman, and A.E. Richert
1987 "150 different ways" of knowing: Representations of knowledge in teaching. Pp. 104-124 in J. Calderhead, ed., *Exploring Teacher Thinking.* London: Cassell.
Zumwalt, Karen, G. Natriello, A. Hansen, and A. Frisch
1987 Everybody into the Pool: Characteristics of Entering Teachers in New Jersey. Paper presented at the Annual Meeting of the American Educational Research Association, San Francisco. March.

NOTES

1. I am indebted to James Stedman for suggesting this dimension of quality as relevant to issues of supply and demand.

2. A recent report from the American Federation of Teachers (1985) and the Council of Basic Education indicates that, even though virtually all states have requirements about who can teach in various areas, almost none has any methods for checking on local compliance with these rules.

3. Some unpublished work done by the National Center for Research on Teacher education is relevant to this point. We found, for instance, that one of the staples of teacher education, the educational psychology course, can look remarkably different in different programs. We have also found that, when states change their curriculum requirements for undergraduate teacher education, programs are likely to simply rename their courses rather than actually change the content to match new requirements.

4. Hanushek's work tends to support the idea that verbal ability is relevant to teaching; however, other reviewers have questioned this finding. See, for instance, Haney et al. (1987).

5. For a history of the legal precedents in this area, see McDonough and Wolfe (1988). For an example of a report questioning the validity of such assessments, see Horner and Sammons (1987).

6. Few studies actually examine the premises of these programs; most look instead at the number and biographical backgrounds of recruits. Two studies sponsored by the National Center for Research on Teacher Education, however, did examine the test scores and grade point averages (GPAs) of alternative route candidates. One is Zumwalt et al. (1987). The other is Stoddart (1987). Stoddart found that grade point averages, for instance, were rela-

tively high among alternative route English teachers but were relatively low among alternative route mathematics teachers. Based on data from the American Association of Colleges for Teacher Education, I would guess that these English teachers have grade point averages a bit above those of traditional teacher education graduates, whereas the math teachers have grade point averages a bit below those of traditional teacher education graduates. See American Association of Colleges for Teacher Education (1987a).

7. A problem using 2 as the divisor, for instance, might be: "My roommate and I have 1 3/4 pizzas and we want to divide them equally between us. How much pizza can we each have?" A problem that uses 1/2 as a divisor would be: "I have 1 3/4 yards of cloth to make tutus for the ballerinas. Each tutu requires 1/2 yard of cloth. How many tutus can I make?"

8. The American Association of Colleges for Teacher Education (1987a) has documented these trends and has developed a strong set of policy initiatives (1987b) related to it.

9. For purposes of this discussion, I am describing a few general ideas. For a more detailed discussion of a variety of other approaches to the representation problem, see the American Association of Colleges for Teacher Education (1987b).

10. For instance, Tobin and Gallagher (Gallagher, 1989; Tobin, 1987) have shown that science teachers often do not include all students in their lessons and call on only a few students whom they believe to be most capable. They have also argued that teacher's beliefs about their role in promoting learning can severely limit their practices.

11. There is considerable evidence that college students who intend to teach enroll in colleges within roughly 50 miles from their home town, and that they intend to return to this same region when they take teaching positions. Since most teacher's colleges, by design, are scattered through the less populous regions of states, this pattern means that few teacher candidates are drawn from, and intend to return to, urban areas.

12. See, for instance, Cohen and Murnane (1985). The districts they examined, which had been operating merit pay systems for at least six years, had altered the concept in one or more important ways: they made the system voluntary rather than universal; they made the size of financial rewards small or distributed rewards widely; they defined merit in terms of *extra* work rather than *better* work; or they allowed teachers to define their own criteria for effectiveness. These authors argue that merit pay will probably not have an impact on classroom teaching practices and may not be feasible in those districts that are most in need of improvement.

13. Aspects of this argument can be found in a wide range of places. For instance, the Carnegie Forum on Education and the Economy (1986) specifically addresses the problem of teacher quality; the National Commission on Excellence in Education (1983) addresses mainly the quality and rigor of U.S. secondary education; the National Research Council (1989) addresses the issue of mathematics education in particular; and The Holmes Group (1987) addresses both teacher education and the attractiveness of the workplace to teachers.

14. Much of this development has occurred through the work of Lee Shulman and his colleagues at Stanford University and the work of the National Center for Research on Teacher Education at Michigan State University. And some professional associations, such as the National Council for Teachers of Mathematics and the National Council of Teachers of English, are now incorporating these new ideas into their teaching standards. Some illustrative work from Stanford include Shulman (1987) and Wilson et al. (1987). From the NCRTE are Kennedy (1989); McDiarmid et al. (1989); and Ball (1990).

15. A good book on some of the dilemmas of professionalizing teaching is Lieberman (1988). Several of the chapters, both empirical works and general analyses, are relevant to this point.

16. The story is taken from a real teaching situation, and when Jessie's teacher asked Jessie why the periods were put into these sentences, Jessie said that they indicated a pause, and that when a new speaker was mentioned in a story, there was always a pause to indicate this new speaker.

Discussion

JAMES B. STEDMAN

Mary M. Kennedy has fashioned a thought-provoking and well-reasoned analysis of several of the dimensions of teacher quality. Those that she addresses are salient for the development of policy to address our current and future teaching force needs. There is no question that each of the dimensions she considers is, or should be, part of the policy debates at the local, state, and federal levels. In my comments, I focus first on three of these quality dimensions. I then consider how policy making at the federal level, the level with which I am most familiar, relates to Kennedy's conceptualization of quality. Finally, I comment briefly on data gathering relative to quality, as well as Kennedy's recommendations to the U.S. Department of Education.

At the outset, let me say that I agree with one of the paper's overall conclusions: in policy making, the issue of the quality of the teaching force has been too easily divorced from the supply and demand issue, or sacrificed in efforts to balance supply and demand. Furthermore, our understanding of quality has been relatively narrow. Unless we view quality broadly, as Kennedy does, and as intimately related to supply and demand questions, policy making and data gathering are likely to remain largely focused on the filling of teaching positions, and the relatively easily measured characteristics and qualifications of teachers filling those positions. Kennedy's analysis is a strong statement that, if we are serious about as-

---

The author is a specialist in social legislation for the Congressional Research Service of the Library of Congress. These comments do not necessarily reflect the views of the Congressional Research Service or the Library of Congress.

sessing teacher quality, then our data-gathering efforts have to get inside the classroom in much more substantial ways than before, with more sophisticated ways of assessing classroom practice. She correctly reminds us that, although quality remains an elusive concept, what we are most often searching for are those attributes or factors that positively affect student outcomes.

Finally, Kennedy identifies a key context for any analysis of addressing supply, demand, and quality issues: the size of the teaching force. The dilemma is how to fashion policies to improve teacher quality when the target population is one of such magnitude. When one considers what it will take in resources and time to change the classroom practice of any substantial portion of the teaching force, the generic applicability of the size issue is clear.

DEMOGRAPHIC QUALITY

The demographic characteristics of current and prospective teachers are of major concern at many levels and will become even more critical as we move toward the twenty-first century. The mismatch between the racial and ethnic characteristics of the teaching force and those of the public school student population is stark, as Kennedy notes.

Nevertheless, some analysts and policy makers may struggle with a treatment of the racial and ethnic characteristics of teachers as an indicator of quality. The logic is as follows: a function that teachers can fill is that of offering role models for students; as Kennedy puts it, teachers can "*personify* content." It is a critical issue for the teaching force and one that involves not just race and ethnicity, but mixes gender in as well. For example, the demographic mismatch of teachers and students has sparked an important policy debate over instructional programs directed specifically at blacks, particularly black males (Leake, 1990; Southern Education Foundation, 1990; Stevens, 1990). One issue such efforts are intended to address is the absence of black male teachers. Arguments abound on either side of this particular kind of program but, in the final analysis, the demographic mismatch is fertile ground for more policy debates such as this.

A consequence of thinking about demographic characteristics as a dimension of quality is that, when shaping policy in this area, one may be better equipped to articulate pedagogical reasons for seeking minority teachers. Another result is that, as Kennedy observes, the movement of minorities through the entire educational pipeline becomes of critical concern. Ultimately, I think, attention to demographic characteristics of teachers is a policy-relevant approach to consideration of quality.

PROFESSIONALISM DIMENSION

Kennedy draws an important distinction between high-quality classroom practice and the behavior and attitudes of teachers that are increasingly discussed in the context of school restructuring. As a consequence, she offers *quality of professionalism* as a dimension of teacher quality, separate from classroom practice. I think this dimension is important and real because it offers a vision of what some policy makers and analysts believe constitute the attributes of a quality teacher. That vision is being articulated in many of the school restructuring or site-based management efforts under way in various places around the country, and among the calls for reform of teacher education. According to this vision, teachers should be: researchers into their own practice; decision makers about the nature, content, and direction of practice; critical observers of their practice; members of collegial teams considering and acting on practice; and occupiers of a stratified career track (The Holmes Group, 1991).

Perhaps only time will tell if efforts to imbue teachers with these characteristics and offer them these opportunities will improve actual classroom practice or improve students' performance. Nevertheless, these are the characteristics that are being used by many to define teacher quality; there should be efforts to measure them. Kennedy's analysis is helpful in suggesting that teacher retention is among the possible reasons for attending to the professionalism dimension. Importantly, she identifies the policy issue of providing the necessary resources to change conditions in schools so that teaching professionals can in fact improve the quality of their classroom practice.

CLASSROOM PRACTICE

As I read Kennedy's analysis, all of the quality dimensions she identifies are secondary to the last dimension—classroom practice. Thus, given the critical nature of classroom practice for the definition of quality, we have some distance to travel to define what that *high-quality* practice is, much less identify how to achieve it. Through her analysis of the classroom practice dimension, Kennedy weaves a recurrent theme—this country "needs a new and better kind of teaching." We need to implement efforts to generate new practice at the same time that the population in our schools is changing, becoming composed increasingly of the very kinds of children and youth with which our schools have been least successful.

This kind of dilemma—*matching practice to a moving target*—is not, I think, restricted to the composition of the student population. It permeates the classroom practice dimension. Can we define high-quality practice, not only in terms of a sound understanding of the characteristics of the students to be served, but also in the absence of what will in fact be demanded of these students in their future educational or employment endeavors? Furthermore, the curriculum we expect teachers to teach also constitutes a moving target, particularly so in subjects such as mathematics and science. This counsels us to design policy and indicators of quality that are capable of change and redirection.

According to Kennedy, few of the techniques for improving classroom practice—such as inservice training and induction programs—pass muster. Professional development schools do appear to be among the few approaches offering a prospect for improving practice. Her comments on induction programs raise a concern. The critical flaw in these efforts, she asserts, is that they become a means of passing on traditional practice, the traditional teaching role. This analysis may be correct, in general. But, in painting the current teaching force in such broadly negative terms, to the point that we wouldn't want any of today's teachers to mentor tomorrow's teachers, might the analysis be unnecessarily pessimistic? Is it not possible to structure induction programs that carefully and sensitively select mentors for novice teachers? Furthermore, and somewhat ironically, if we do a better job of instilling more teachers with a conception of their new role and a grasp of high-quality classroom practice, induction programs involving those very teachers would be a sound investment.

TEACHER QUALITY ISSUES AT THE FEDERAL LEVEL

The quality question, as it relates to supply and demand, is important at all policy levels, including the federal. Kennedy's analysis directly relates to debate over federal policy and programs for teachers, as it is occurring in the U.S. Congress. Let me focus on activity by the 101st and 102nd Congresses.

101st Congress

Although the 101st Congress ultimately did not approve the major teacher legislation that it had under consideration, the debate in the Senate on that legislation showed some of the difficulties for policy making inherent in quality issues.

The bill drafted by the Senate Labor and Human Resources Committee had two broad objectives: recruitment of teachers in particular fields and with particular demographic characteristics and enhancement of the skills of new and currently practicing teachers (U.S. Congress, Senate Committee on Labor and Human Resources, 1990a). As the committee deliberated on this bill, it heard testimony from a wide variety of witnesses, including the U.S. Department of Education.

The testimony from the department brought aspects of the policy problems into focus (U.S. Congress, Senate Committee on Labor and Human Resources, 1990b:474-501). The department characterized the bill as a package of old and tired ideas, which was based on the belief that there was a general shortage of teachers. The department asserted that it already administered a broad array of programs that addressed the needs articulated in this legislation. What was required, it argued, were carefully tailored efforts to address specific needs, as well as a vision of what should be occurring in classrooms.

The committee responded that its bill was "not premised on the belief that there will be an absence of people to occupy teaching positions. As a result, this legislation focuses on the caliber and preparation of the individuals . . . hired by school districts across the country to teach. . . . These new teachers must be well trained, knowledgeable, and capable. There must be no shortcuts to filling teaching positions and no lowering of standards." Furthermore, the committee noted that the bill took steps to provide practicing teachers "with access to the best scholars, in-service training, and research in designated fields" (U.S. Congress, Senate Committee on Labor and Human Resources, 1990a:4).

In this debate, there was a significant absence of supply side data and data on teacher quality. As a result, much of the discussion involved assertions using fragmented data, resulting in antagonism rather than any agreement about these issues and appropriate policy responses.

Significantly, these congressional efforts were much more attuned to Kennedy's concerns than not. Credentials and tested ability were not the focus of the legislation and not being given serious consideration; rather, recruitment of minority teachers and improvement of teachers' mastery of subject matter and classroom practice were.

102nd Congress[1]

The 102nd Congress has revisited much of this territory. With the expiration of the legislative authority for the programs of the Higher Education Act, the 102nd Congress has drafted legislation that amends and extends many of that act's programs. As of early spring 1992, the House and Senate had passed different versions of legislation to reauthorize the Higher Education Act. Both versions contain substantial amendments and extensions to Title V of the Higher Education Act, which currently authorizes such teacher programs as the Paul Douglas Teacher Scholarships and the Christa McAuliffe Fellowships. Both houses have approved similar new teacher programs that would, among other activities, establish state-level academies for inservice teacher training, create professional development schools, and provide short-term support for development of alternative routes to teacher certification (U.S. Congress, 1992a; U.S. Congress, 1992b).

The two proposals differ in some areas. The Senate proposal would support a number of new, discrete programs. Among these programs is a new Teacher Corps program to help students meet the costs of teacher education in exchange for teaching service involving structured induction. It would also authorize the establishment of inservice teaching academies at the national level. In contrast, rather than authorizing all of its professional development activities in separate programs, the House proposes a broad framework under which state educational agencies, local school districts, and higher education institutions can address the preservice and professional development needs of teachers. Among its new initiatives, the House creates a program to support a national job bank to link teachers to jobs.

Concurrent with this legislative action is heightened attention by the 102nd Congress to the question of setting national curriculum content standards, student performance standards, and criteria for a system of national assessments. This question sparks additional concern about improving teacher quality. *Raising Standards for American Education*, the report of the congressionally mandated National Council on Education Standards and Testing, has called for federal statutory language establishing a process to certify content and performance standards, as well as criteria for national assessments of student performance (National Council on Education Standards and Testing, 1992). Significantly, that report and congressional debate over its recommendations focus in part on the critical role to be played by the professional development of teachers to ensure that all children have an "opportunity to learn" what is embodied in any new curriculum content standards. Clearly, as I have already noted, the definition of what is a "qualified" teacher is elusive. In particular, as educational standards are raised and new assessments are implemented to measure progress against those standards, our entire teaching force will be expected to understand subject matter more deeply than is generally true now, and to have mastered a wider range of pedagogical skills in order to teach all children. As a result, issues of teacher quality are likely to remain at the center of education policy debates.

FEDERAL DATA GATHERING

What is the task for data gathering by the federal government? Kennedy calls for consideration of quality primarily from the dimension of classroom practice. The task is one of measuring beliefs, behaviors, and other aspects of the teaching culture. This is a herculean endeavor on even a small scale. Although it is not clear to me what the prospects are of successfully doing this on a national level through current data-gathering efforts, we should not retreat from the challenge.

A critical step, as I see it, is to engage in more sustained research on the attributes of teacher quality and how indicators of those attributes might be integrated into ongoing national surveys conducted by the National Center for Education Statistics (NCES), among others.

As the National Education Statistics Agenda Committee of the National Forum on Educational Statistics concluded in its assessment of national data gathering: "[T]here are no regularly collected national measures of instructional quality, chiefly because there is neither a consensus on what constitutes valid 'indicators' of such quality nor agreement on how such indicators should be measured. Even efforts to collect seemingly straightforward measures such as teacher qualifications have been hampered by similar conceptual and technical concerns (e.g., how do you define a qualified teacher?)" (National Education Statistics Agenda Committee, 1990:71).

The committee made some useful recommendations and identified a number of points at which NCES surveys touch on the teacher quality issues, particularly classroom practice or instructional strategies. For example, the National Education Longitudinal Study of 1988 eighth graders (NELS:88) has focused partly on the link between teacher quality and student outcomes, asking questions about teaching strategies. The National Assessment of Educational Progress (NAEP) includes teacher background questions that ask about broad teaching practices and the use of time in the classroom. I would add that the Schools and Staffing Survey (SASS) offers some avenues for exploring some aspects of quality.

Kennedy notes the usefulness of longitudinal studies of teachers to capture some of aspects of teachers and teaching under analysis. Efforts to do some longitudinal surveys of teachers through the SASS should continue.

With regard to the demographic issues raised in the paper, particularly the usefulness of linking teachers' racial and ethnic characteristics to those of the classes they actually teach, the SASS might be the appropriate source. Perhaps some thought should also be given to adding questions about teachers' race and ethnicity to the 101/102 surveys funded by the department's Office for Civil Rights. This would permit the gathering of data on teachers' racial and ethnic characteristics matched to those of their particular students.

Finally, as a concluding observation and one that may be only indirectly a federal concern, I agree with Kennedy that the assessments of the National Board for Professional Teaching Standards and the new National Teachers Examination (NTE) from the Educational Testing Service will potentially help our understanding of teacher quality. But, I think that we have to recognize that these two assessments are intended to act as levers to change teachers' preparation and behavior. As such, they are not neutral instruments for measuring change in teacher quality in general. Ultimately, we need both kinds of assessments of teacher quality—ones that seek to change behavior and instill quality practice, and ones that seek to measure the system's progress in improving quality.

REFERENCES

The Holmes Group

1991 *Toward a Community of Learning: The Preparation and Continuing Education of Teachers.* The Holmes Group Occasional Paper No. 5. East Lansing, Michigan: The Holmes Group.

Leake, Donald O.

1990 Averting a lifetime of segregation. *Education Week* 10(13):20.

National Council on Education Standards and Testing

1992 *Raising Standards for American Education.* A report to Congress, the Secretary of Education, the National Education Goals Panel, and the American People. Washington, D.C.: The National Council on Education Standards and Testing.

National Education Statistics Agenda Committee

1990 A Guide to Improving the National Education Data System. A report by the National Education Statistics Agenda Committee of the National Forum on Educational Statistics.

Southern Education Foundation

1990 Finding more black male teachers for America's classrooms. *Pipeline* 1(spring/summer):7.

Stevens, Leonard B.

1990 'Separate but equal' has no place. *Education Week* 10(9):32.

U.S. Congress

1992a Higher education amendments of 1991 (S. 1150). *Congressional Record* February 26:S2397-S2415. Washington, D.C.: U.S. Government Printing Office.

1992b Higher education amendments of 1992 (H.R. 3553). *Congressional Record* March 26:H1916-H1931. Washington, D.C.: U.S. Government Printing Office.

U.S. Congress, Senate Committee on Labor and Human Resources

1990a *National Teacher Act of 1990.* Report 101-360 to Accompany S. 1676. 101st Congress, 2nd Session. July 10. Washington, D.C.: U.S. Government Printing Office.

1990b Teacher excellence: Recruitment and training. Pp. 474-501 in *Senate Hearing 101-824.* 101st Congress, 2nd session. Washington, D.C.: U.S. Government Printing Office.

NOTE

1. This section was added at the time the proceedings went to press to provide a current picture of proposed legislation related to teachers.

Discussion

ARTHUR E. WISE

I will take a slightly different perspective on teacher quality, or maybe even a radically different perspective; I leave that for you to judge.

I read the Kennedy analysis with considerable interest. Certainly she identified the significant dimensions of teacher quality about which we need to be concerned; I think her treatment of them is excellent.

But in thinking about these dimensions one at a time, I was puzzled about why it is necessary to go down this path when talking about teachers, when in fact we go down a quite different path when we talk about other professionals, i.e., doctors, lawyers, architects, engineers, accountants, and perhaps nurses. It became clear to me that the definition of a teacher is everything. That is, our culture has no difficulty counting lawyers, doctors, architects, nurses, and engineers. The fact of the matter is that we allow these professions to determine who will be counted. The job of the government is then relatively easy. It simply has to count the number of people who meet the definition that the profession has set.

So when we count doctors, we count an artifact or construct. What is our construct of a doctor? Among other things, a doctor is the product of a process of education and assessment that results ultimately in the designation of an individual as a doctor. In fact, the medical profession itself creates the minimum standards for awarding the title of doctor. It means, among other things, that a person has completed successfully four years of college, indicating some approximate facts (crude, to be sure) about that individual, i.e., that he or she has successfully completed a four-year liberal arts program having certain characteristics. He or she persisted through that program, learned some material, was graded 120 times in the course of the four-year experience, and so on. The individual applied to a medical school, an accredited medical school, in fact. Thus, the issue of school accreditation is part of the process of quality determination in other professions. Once admitted to a professional medical school, the doctor candidate must successfully negotiate his or her way through it. Along the way, the candidate must pass a series of examinations, one on basic medical science, one on clinical medical science, and ultimately one on the ability to apply clinical knowledge to practical settings, a step that is not allowed until the person has completed a year of practical experience under supervision—what used to be called the internship but is increasingly called the first year of residency.

So we know what a doctor is. It has been defined for us by the medical profession. It is the result of an educational process associated with a licensing process that applies to the individual and an accreditation process that applies to the school through which the individual has gone. To a greater or lesser degree, the same can be said of the other professions mentioned earlier. The point is simply this—our ability to count professionals nationally in a number of professions other than teaching is based on our acceptance of a set of constructs of what a member of each profession is.

Since such a definition of the teaching profession is not yet widely accepted, we are plagued with a variety of problems. The anomalous situation in education is that some people become teachers by completing accredited teacher education programs; others attend programs that are not accredited. Some have been through a testing process; others have not. Some have had their teaching assessed in their first year.

Most teachers hired in a state have been through whatever the state has prescribed as the process for determining whether a person qualifies as a teacher. This is so unless the state cannot find enough people who have been through that process, in which case whoever was interviewed on Labor Day, administered the breath test, hired by a school district, and made a member of the relevant labor union is now also regarded as a teacher, basically indistinguishable from the former in function.

I believe that we will never get out of the conundrum of defining a teacher until we have a teacher education accreditation and teacher licensing process that specifies the requirements for qualifying as a fully qualified teacher. When we have a real teacher licensing process and a real teacher certification process, we will be able to count the number of people who meet the minimum standards for licensure and the minimum standards for advanced certification.

The National Board for Professional Teaching Standards (NBPTS) will present a defining construct for advanced certification. For example, a board-certified teacher of secondary school mathematics will be a person who meets a set of requirements that the board will ultimately prescribe.

I think there is very little else we can do to move beyond where we are right now. Indeed, I think I might differ with my colleagues on this panel by suggesting that we cannot get into classroom practice as a way of judging quality, except insofar as that is incorporated into the initial teacher licensing process or into NBPTS's advanced certification process.

Here is an illustration of how classroom practice can be incorporated into the initial teacher licensing process. Before I joined the National Council for Accreditation of Teacher Education, I had the opportunity, along with some of my colleagues at the RAND Corporation, to work with the state of Minnesota in defining for that state the direction in which teacher licensing should move. We laid out a set of expectations in concert with the Minnesota Board of Teaching. It included among other things the notion that a teacher candidate would first graduate from an accredited program of teacher preparation, and that the individual would then take an examination that assessed pedagogical and professional knowledge. While we can discuss the characteristics of that test, it is really not important at this juncture to articulate what they are, except to say that the notion was that the test would really assess the underlying professional and pedagogical knowledge base.

The teacher candidate would then have a year-long internship. In the course of that internship, one hopes in something that resembles a professional development school, the individual would be instructed in educational practice and would, in the course of a year or so, have the opportunity both to develop as a practicing teacher and to be assessed as a beginning teacher. In other words, what we did was to call on those who were responsible for the internship program at the local level to make a determination of whether the candidate was now ready to take the final exam. Essentially, this meant that a number of senior personnel in a school district would have had to make a judgment about whether a particular teacher candidate had successfully mastered the minimum teaching skills necessary for licensure.

This process of course is fraught with problems of reliability and validity. That is why it is not the final point for entry into the profession. By analogy, the medical internship has exactly the same characteristics associated with it. Human beings must make a more or less subjective judgment that an individual is ready to take the final part of the National Board of Medical Examiners test.

That is the only way in my opinion that teaching performance can ever be assessed in a way that allows you to begin to make some national analyses. So at this point, the teacher candidate would take the final exam, which can be characterized as testing intellectual skills—not interactive teaching skill—that a new teacher should be able to demonstrate. That becomes the final exam on which the awarding of a teaching license is based.

You do not have to accept the particular licensing system that I just outlined. But we must have some kind of system for licensing teachers. Otherwise, we will not get out of the current conundrum with respect to teacher credentialing.

In my opinion, there is no way, other than superficially, that classroom teaching practice can be sampled for purposes of judging teacher quality. Nor is it feasible to carry out the serious, national studies that would be necessary to connect teaching behavior, or teaching performance, with student outcomes very frequently. Perhaps it can be done in a research sense, but doing large-scale national studies would be extremely difficult, unless the scope of educational outcomes examined is so narrow that little of what a teacher does is connected to what students learn—as past studies have regularly demonstrated. I will soon return to this point more specifically.

In teaching, we pose for ourselves problems that those in other professions would never dream of. For instance, what research suggested that lawyers need four years of college before they enter law school, or that law school should be a three-year experience rather than a two-year experience or a one-year experience, or that medical schools should be a four-year experience preceded by four years of college? I would like to see the longitudinal studies that demonstrated the connection between those practices and the outcomes that those practitioners secure with their clientele. I daresay that supportive studies cannot be found. Nonetheless, we in education, because we are so trained in empirical methods and are so beleaguered by the policy-making community, fight back with what we have.

After-the-fact studies are therefore conducted to examine the relationships between college majors and student outcomes, or the relationships among teacher credentials and student outcomes, knowing full well that when the research rises to a sufficiently high level of abstraction, we really do not know what we are talking about. To suggest, for example, that there is no connection between a teacher's tested knowledge, or a teacher's major, and a teacher's ability to teach; to suggest that there is research that supports such a bald conclusion is preposterous. In fact, it is impossible for me to imagine teaching Russian without having had a major in Russian, some linguistic facility in Russian, or certainly the ability to test out in Russian. Or do we really think that a person can teach physics in the way that it needs to be taught in school today, either to elementary school students or high school students, without knowing physics?

The idea that there is no connection between knowledge about physics, knowledge about mathematics, knowledge about Russian, and the ability to teach each of these subjects is just preposterous and an artifact of the peculiar kind of longitudinal research that we are disposed to do in the field of education. It begets a very curious kind of cynicism, because the results of our own studies are used against us by those who are already predisposed to be skeptical of the teacher education community.

Having damned such studies, I do want to point out that there is an omission in the Kennedy paper that could easily be rectified. The preponderance of research that assesses the efficacy of teachers who have had teacher education versus those so-called teachers who have not had teacher education is clear. These studies reveal an advantage for those teachers who have had teacher education.

A major review of that literature has recently been compiled. The evidence is persuasive. The fact that such findings are not well known in the research community—and even more broadly in education—is surprising to me. This research reveals that teacher education confers an advantage on those who have it in contrast with those who do not (Darling-Hammond, 1991).

I return now to the issue of testing because it deserves a few more comments. The testing of teachers that has been done is not great, and it is not well matched to the teacher education curriculum. One of the virtues of other professions, compared with teaching, is that professional education, professional education accreditation, and licensing examinations and procedures are all tied together conceptually, practically, theoretically, and empirically. The same organizations work together to design both the educational program and the licensing program.

The teaching profession today is quite imperfect in this regard. For example, it is forced to compare the Scholastic Aptitude Test scores of teachers and nonteachers when the real interest is in the teacher candidate's ability—to use one of Kennedy's examples—to divide fractions or perform other teaching tasks enumerated by Kennedy and her colleagues from the National Center for Research on Teacher Education.

The point is not whether some enterprising reporter can get a higher National Teacher Examinations (NTE) score than a teacher education major. The fault there lies entirely with the examination. The more important question is, what is it that a new teacher needs to know, and what is it therefore that we shall properly expect to assess on an examination?

So judgments made from past studies of teachers and comparisons with nonteachers are misleading. Involving the profession both in the design of the curriculum and in the assessment system is really very important.

Although I am not quite sure of what to make of it, I was recently struck by the results of an examination released by the state of Texas that was administered to teachers who volunteered to take it. It was designed to distinguish those who would be designated as high-level master teachers. Several thousand teachers volunteered to take the test, and ultimately 6 percent passed. The way this outcome was characterized by the *Washington*

Post, and I suspect nationwide, was as follows: there was a test developed for master teachers, and only two or three hundred people measured up. Therefore, the other 2,700 who took the test and failed it are deadbeats, and certainly all those who were afraid to try are also deadbeats. In considering such findings, no one ever stops for a minute to ask about the intellectual integrity of the examination, the extent to which it is appropriately tied to pedagogical and professional knowledge, and the extent to which it appropriately calls on teachers to apply what they know to practical situations.

Furthermore, the number of people who will pass any examination is predetermined by those who control it. It can be a 2 percent pass rate, a 6 percent pass rate, or a 50 percent pass rate, and that is decided by actors who may have various agendas to advance.

All this is critical because it determines the definition of teacher quality. Teacher quality is whatever those in legitimate authority say it is. For the moment, whoever is in charge of the Texas system is defining quality teaching in Texas. We need to be mindful of the fact that there is wide and ready acceptance of whatever it is that those in power decide.

The Texas authorities define teacher quality for the state of Texas, just as NBPTS ultimately will define high levels of teaching competence. With no alternative, the public will be forced to accept this definition of teaching competence. What we all need to learn from this is that unnecessary trouble will be created if we do not understand these issues and if we do not try to learn from the established professions.

Understanding teacher quality, as well as teacher supply and demand, is critical. One of the reasons is that teacher quality is maldistributed today and will, in all probability, continue to be maldistributed until minimum teacher competence or minimum teacher credentialing can be defined accurately.

We know where those who are not qualified actually teach. By and large, the largest groups of them are to be found in New York City, Los Angeles, and Houston. Those are the places that hire the largest numbers of people who are not certified through the traditional process. Furthermore, we know that unqualified teachers are not randomly assigned within cities. Instead, they are typically assigned to schools where parents are least likely to notice that their child is being taught by somebody who is not qualified. Therefore, getting a fix on teacher quality is extraordinarily important because it will then allow us to track the distribution of teacher talent and ultimately to adopt policies that will help foster equal educational opportunity.

REFERENCE

Darling-Hammond, Linda

1991 Are our teachers ready to teach? Teacher education results in better student learning. *NCATE Quality Teaching* 1(1):6-7, 10.

General Discussion

The general discussion covered the following topics: (a) dimensions of teacher quality; (b) licensure as an indicator of teacher quality; (c) modeling the teacher quality-quantity tradeoff; (d) variability of teacher quality; and (e) data gathering of teacher qualifications. These are summarized in the paragraphs that follow.

Since facets of the concept of teacher quality, in relation to teacher supply and demand, was the central topic in the Kennedy paper and subsequent discussions, much of the general discussion addressed the meaning and significance of the concept of quality in this context. There was considerable agreement that quality is multidimensional and difficult to specify. In this regard, one participant quoted from Robert M. Peirsig's book titled *Zen and the Art of Motorcycle Maintenance* as follows: "Quality. You know what it is, yet you don't know what it is. That's self contradictory, but some things are better than others. That is, they have more quality. When you try to say what quality is apart from the things that have it, it all goes poof. There's nothing to talk about. If you can't say what quality is, how do you know what it is or how do you know that it even exists? If no one knows what it is, then for all practical purposes it doesn't exist at all."

One approach to dealing with the elusive concept of teaching quality, broadly conceived, is to specify its dimensions (as Kennedy did), each of which will be more concrete and therefore amenable to measurement and empirical research. The main dimensions raised in the general discussion (closely paralleling those of Kennedy) were (a) teacher characteristics, such as training, tested ability, and race; (b) the teaching environment, such as the degree to which the teaching role is professionalized; and (c) teaching practices in the classroom.

While it was asserted that the relationship of all these dimensions of quality should be explored further, it was noted that past research has found little relationship between measures of teacher characteristics, professionalism, and practices on one hand, and student performance outcomes on the other. However, at least for some of these dimensions, such as teacher professionalization, the relationship might not be immediate and direct. For example, creating a more professionalized role for teachers might make the profession more attractive to more able teacher candidates and therefore in the long run lead to better student outcomes through the development of a higher-quality teaching force.

A second approach to dealing with the concept of quality teaching is to establish substantial and uniform requirements across the nation for teacher licensure, and to restrict teacher hiring to individuals who are fully qualified for the teaching license. At the present time, such requirements vary widely from state to state and are widely disregarded by school districts and states when an insufficient supply of regularly licensed applicants exists for particular teaching positions. Furthermore, school systems and teachers' unions routinely consider all persons hired into teaching positions to be teachers, regardless of their qualifications. Consequently, students in many schools are instructed by teachers lacking formal qualifications. However, a representative of one national teachers' union indicated that if a national licensure system existed, membership would be limited to those who qualify under it.

While the solution to the problem of defining a quality teacher could be operationalized as a person qualifying for a teaching license under a rigorous, uniform national system, several concerns were raised. One concern is the likelihood of an insufficient supply of licensed teachers for many teaching positions, particularly those located in schools serving disadvantaged groups of students.

Another concern is that qualifying for a license does not ensure success in teaching, and the lack of a license does not ensure failure. For example, an unlicensed individual might perform poorly while teaching in a disadvantaged public school, while the same individual might perform adequately while teaching in an elite private school. Although research was cited that consistently shows an overall advantage (sometimes marginal) for teachers with formal training over those without it, this research should be scrutinized more carefully. While there may be an overall advantage for trained teachers, the distributions of effectiveness of trained and untrained teachers no doubt overlap a great deal—thereby indicating that training is not an overriding factor in determining teacher quality.

The third concern involved professional liability of a teacher if a rigorous, uniform teacher licensure system were in place, and if teacher hiring were restricted to licensed individuals. One view was expressed that, indeed, not only the teacher, but also the school district that hires the teacher, could be held liable for unsatisfactory student performance and sued for malpractice, since the education of students is a joint responsibility.

The concern raised above about a sufficient supply of qualified teachers for staffing all teaching positions focuses attention on the question of teacher quantity in contrast with the prior discussion of teacher quality. In reality, there is a tradeoff between the quantity and quality of teachers, since many, if not most, school districts experience an insufficient supply of "quality teachers." However, there are no models of supply and demand that address either the quantity-quality or the quality distribution tradeoff problems. If there were such models, it was hypothesized that they would show that the poorer, less advantaged districts would end up with teachers drawn from the lower end of the quality distribution. Also, if rigorous licensure standards were adopted, these disadvantaged districts would end up with fewer teachers than needed to fill open positions.

Since the teaching force in the nation is very large (on the order of 2.5 million), the characteristics in such a large population will vary widely. Therefore, regardless of the credentialing system that is in place, the lower end of the quality distribution of this large population also will be a large number. And because the number of teachers from the lower end of the quality distribution is large, they will be very visible, especially to the well-educated adults in our population who hold degrees at approximately the same level as those held by teachers.

It was observed that one of the reasons poorly qualified teachers are retained in the profession is that there is no process for winnowing them out, after licensure, as there is in other professions such as law and medicine, in which clients choose which professionals to patronize. In public education, parents are locked into the system and have little opportunity to choose teachers for their children.

In conclusion, the view was expressed that it is important for the National Center for Education Statistics (NCES) to collect statistics on teacher qualifications, such as licensure status and certification by the National Board for Professional Teaching Standards (when available), and tabulate these data by the types of schools and communities in which they teach. Since it would be prohibitively expensive for NCES to employ independent in-depth measures of teacher qualifications, it will necessarily have to rely on definitions of teacher qualifications set by licensure systems and the profession. Nonetheless, data on the distribution (actually, maldistribution) of teacher credentials, by type of school and community, will reveal serious inequities among school districts in the quality of teachers they can hire. These data will strengthen equity litigation brought by disadvantaged districts and should stimulate efforts to upgrade the quality of the profession further—even though the qualifications recorded will not necessarily be indicative of the quality of teaching practice.

IV

MODELS

Part IV addresses issues involved in the modeling of teacher supply, demand, and quality phenomena. The focus is on models developed to project teacher supply and demand variables for use in estimating prospective teacher shortages and surpluses. One purpose is to identify, review, analyze, and compare the most promising of such models that have been developed at the state, regional, and national levels, as well as to review research relevant to modeling teacher supply and demand variables. The range of alternative approaches is described, and the strengths and limitations of the best examples of alternative types are analyzed. Another purpose is to relate the models to information needs of policy makers in dealing with teacher work force issues and to analyze the potential of these models to yield useful information about such issues.

Models for Projecting Teacher Supply, Demand, and Quality: An Assessment of the State of the Art

STEPHEN M. BARRO

INTRODUCTION

Although concerns about future teacher supply and demand seem to be perennial, their content changes to suit the times. The alarms heard not so long ago about an imminent general teacher shortage have receded, to be replaced by increasing attention to the adequacy of prospective supply in science, mathematics, special education, and other particular teaching fields. Discussions of adequacy are now at least as likely to focus on teacher quality as on teacher numbers. The lesson seems to have been absorbed, after much contention over whether there will be "enough" teachers, that quantity per se is not the central problem. Given the willingness to pay and/or sufficient flexibility about standards, we can always hire enough people—and usually enough nominally qualified people—to fill the classrooms. But whether we can find teachers good enough to produce the educational performance gains the nation so urgently needs or to reach the ambitious national education goals that high officials have recently proclaimed are quite different matters. In these respects, the adequacy of the teacher supply is very much in question, and the future supply-demand balance is a major policy concern.

Policy makers' questions about prospects for staffing the schools have stimulated efforts over the years to generate better information on the outlook for teacher supply and demand. Many of these efforts have focused on creating the data bases on which supply and demand analysis necessarily depends—data on the size and makeup of the teaching force, on teacher assignments and career patterns, on persons trained and certificated to teach, on teacher training institutions and programs, and on the agencies (mainly local school districts) that recruit, employ, and seek to retain teachers. At the same time, other efforts have focused on creating, and then applying, the analytical tools needed to make the data meaningful and to provide policy makers and other users with the information they need—not just the facts, but estimates, inferences, and judgments as to what the facts imply. Prominent among these tools are the teacher supply-demand projection models reviewed in this paper. Ideally, state and federal officials, equipped with such projection models, should be able to monitor and assess developments in the teacher market, estimate trends, and anticipate imbalances or deficiencies (whether quantitative or qualitative) in time to take remedial action. How well these functions can be accomplished with current supply-demand models and how models can be improved to accomplish them better are the principal questions addressed in this assessment.[1]

Teacher Supply-Demand Models and Their Characteristics

A teacher supply-demand projection model consists of a set of mathematical relationships with which future levels of supply, demand, and (in principle) quality can be estimated and (ideally) linked to future economic and educational conditions and policies. Such models have been constructed for particular states by state education agencies and various research organizations; a regional model covering the New England states and New York is under development; and different types of national models have been introduced over the years by the National Center for Education Statistics (NCES). Although these models differ in important respects, all share a common basic structure. A complete teacher supply-demand model consists of three main components or submodels: (1) a submodel for projecting the demand for teachers, (2) a submodel for projecting the supply of continuing or retained teachers (or, equivalently, a model of teacher attrition), and (3) a submodel of the supply of potential entrants into teaching. The latter two components, taken together, should yield projections of the total teacher supply, which one should be able to juxtapose to, and compare with, projections of total demand.[2] As will be seen, however, many current models offer incomplete treatments, or no treatments at all, of the supply of potential entrants, a situation that seriously limits their usefulness for assessing the overall supply-demand balance.

The types of questions that can be addressed and the types of information that can be generated with a teacher supply-demand projection model depend on several key model characteristics. One is the extent of *disaggregation* of teachers by teaching field or subject specialty. Some models deal only with teachers in the aggregate (or only with such broad subgroups as elementary teachers and secondary teachers) and consequently are of no use for assessing the prospective supply-demand balance in particular subject areas. Other models disaggregate in different ways and to different degrees, making it possible to respond to correspondingly more or less detailed policy questions.

A second key characteristic is whether the model is *mechanical* or *behavioral*. Mechanical or "demographic" models are capable only of estimating what will happen in the future if established patterns or trends continue. For example, a mechanical model of teacher demand yields estimates of the numbers of teachers that will be required in the future if teacher-pupil ratios (or trends therein) remain constant, and a mechanical model of teacher retention predicts how many teachers will remain in the teaching force if the attrition rate for each type of teacher remains unchanged. Behavioral models, in contrast, link the demand and supply estimates to pertinent conditions and policies. Only behavioral models can be used to address what-if questions about the effects of hypothetical changes in circumstances on teacher supply and demand.

A third critical attribute is whether and how the models deal with teacher *quality*. In fact, nearly all the current projection models focus on numbers of teachers only, avoiding the quality dimension entirely. This makes them at best only peripherally relevant for addressing the quality-related teacher supply and demand issues referred to above. Because of the growing urgency of quality concerns, this assessment places special emphasis on the initial tentative steps that have been taken, and the further steps that may be feasible, to take teacher quality into account.

Models also differ in many characteristics of a more technical nature, including explicit and implicit behavioral assumptions, definitions of variables, statistical methods, types of data used, and length of the projection period. The assessment considers how all of the above affect the validity and usefulness of the supply and demand projections.

Purpose and Scope

The general purpose of this assessment is to determine whether the current teacher supply-demand projection models and methods (and some now under development) are well conceived, technically sound, and—most important—capable of satisfying policy makers' information needs. More specifically, the assessment addresses the following issues:

- How adequate are the present models and methods for estimating future levels of teacher supply, demand, and quality?
- How adequate are they for analyzing the effects on teacher supply, demand, and quality of changes in pertinent conditions and policies?

• Which current approaches to supply-demand projection modeling appear to be the most promising?

• What new or modified models, methods, and data bases might improve the quality of projections and the usefulness of teacher supply-demand analyses?

The assessment covers national models and a selection of models developed by or for individual states. The national models in question are mainly those produced by or for NCES. The state-level models to be examined were chosen semisystematically from among models cited in the literature, models submitted by states to the National Research Council in response to a general request for teacher supply-demand studies, and models suggested by experts in the field. The coverage of state models is neither comprehensive nor necessarily representative; almost certainly, it is skewed in favor of the more elaborate and sophisticated modeling efforts. The specific state models discussed in this report are those for Connecticut, Indiana, Maryland, Massachusetts, Michigan, Nebraska, New York, North Carolina, Ohio, South Carolina, and Wisconsin. In some instances, however, the available state studies present only certain model components (e.g., only models of teacher attrition for Michigan and North Carolina) rather than complete supply-demand models.

Organization

The main body of this paper is organized around the three model components defined above. Thus, the next sections assess models of the demand for teachers, the supply of retained teachers, and the supply of potential entrants into teaching, respectively. The section on the supply of entrants also covers the approach taken within each model (if any) to analyzing the supply-demand balance. Each section includes a discussion of general issues pertaining to the model component in question; a series of descriptions and evaluations of individual state and national models; and a general assessment of the current state of the art, unresolved problems, and possible avenues of improvement. A final brief section provides an overview of the current state of the art and prospects for improved supply-demand projections in the future.

MODELS OF THE DEMAND FOR TEACHERS

The size of the teaching force in a state or in the nation is determined primarily by how many teachers school systems are able and willing to maintain on their payrolls—that is, by how many teachers the employers demand. Projections of demand are the logical starting points for assessing the future supply-demand balance. Taken together with estimates of future attrition (discussed in the next section), demand projections indicate how many entrants into the teaching profession will have to be found to replace those who leave, to adjust to changes in enrollment, and to respond to new education policies. Likewise, disaggregated projections of demand by field or subject specialty provide some of the basic information needed to judge whether serious problems are likely to arise, as some have alleged, in finding enough teachers in such areas as science, mathematics, and special and bilingual education. Ideally, demand projection models should also be instruments for assessing the effects of future economic, fiscal, and demographic changes on the size and makeup of the teaching force; examining connections between teacher staffing and teacher compensation; and even exploring tradeoffs between numbers of teachers and teacher quality; but as will be seen, major advances in the state of the modeling art will be needed before any of these broader ambitions can begin to be realized.

Unlike research on teacher attrition, which has progressed rapidly in the last few years, research on the demand for teachers has been minimal. Methods of projecting demand are little changed from what they were when the National Research Council last undertook reviews of teacher supply and demand models (Barro, 1986; Cavin, 1986; Popkin and Atrostic, 1986). The main noticeable advance is that demand estimates now seem more often to be disaggregated, and disaggregated in greater detail, by grade level and subject specialty; however, methods of projecting subject-specific demand are still rudimentary. Some of the more fundamental improvements called for in earlier reviews—most notably, a shift toward behavioral modeling—have been slow in coming. The importance of making models behavioral is regularly reaffirmed (see, e.g., Gilford and Tenenbaum, 1990), but real behavioral modeling remains, as it was five years ago, a hoped-for future development rather than a reality.

Considerations in Modeling Demand

Before reviewing specific projection models, I discuss briefly some of the major generic issues that arise in modeling the demand for teachers and certain key considerations in assessing present and proposed projection methods.

The Definition of Demand

The number of teachers demanded in a state or in the nation refers, both in standard English and in economics, to the number that school systems want to employ and are prepared to pay for at a given time. The everyday and economic definitions differ, however, in that the former is usually framed in terms of fixed requirements (e.g., predetermined teacher-pupil ratios), whereas the economic definition treats the number of teachers demanded as contingent on such things as how much teachers cost and how much money the employers (school systems) have to spend. The economist, therefore, thinks of demand as a mathematical relationship or schedule—i.e., as a function rather than a number. A demand function relates the number of teachers that employers seek to hire—the quantity demanded—to such factors as the size and composition of enrollment, the level of education funding, and the prices that must be paid for teachers of various types and qualities. According to the everyday definition, a demand projection is an estimate of the number of teachers that will be "required" in the future (e.g., to maintain some stipulated teacher-pupil ratio), but, according to the economic definition, it is an estimate of how many teachers school systems will seek to employ, contingent on certain projected values of an array of underlying determinants of demand.

The significance of this definitional difference is that the two concepts lead to different models and modeling strategies. The requirements notion of demand translates into mechanical (sometimes termed demographic) projection models, in which, typically, ratios of teachers to pupils (or trends therein) are assumed to be fixed and projections of numbers of teachers are driven by enrollment forecasts. In contrast, the economic definition points to behavioral models, in which projections derive from multivariate equations linking the number of teachers demanded to various economic, fiscal, and demographic causal factors. Thus far, the mechanical models dominate the field. As a result, the only demands that can now be projected are those that will materialize if no significant changes occur in any of the factors that influence school systems' ability and willingness to employ teachers.

The Relationship Between Demand and Employment

A crucial but often unappreciated consideration bearing on the validity of demand projections is the relationship between the number of teachers demanded and the number actually employed. In principle, both the economic concept and the requirements concept of demand allow for the possibility that the former could exceed the latter—that is, school systems might fail to find the numbers of teachers they are able and willing to pay for.[3] In practice, however, analysts have almost always assumed (usually implicitly) that the number of teachers demanded is currently the same, and has been the same in the past, as the number actually employed. That is, the prevailing assumption is that the teacher market is characterized by supply-demand balance or excess supply—that there is and has been no excess or unfulfilled demand.[4]

The validity of demand projections depends strongly on whether the assumption of excess supply is correct. Invariably, the quantities referred to as demand projections in teacher supply-demand studies are projections of employment rather than demand per se. The implicit assumption is that school systems were able, historically, to find as many teachers as they wanted, and hence a projection of employment and a projection of the number of teachers demanded are one and the same thing. If this were not true—if past levels of employment were determined by numbers of teachers available (supply) rather than by demand—then projections of employment would be supply rather than demand projections. It would become meaningless, then, to speak of the projected supply-demand balance. The distinction between numbers of teachers demanded and numbers actually employed is especially critical when it comes to projecting disaggregated demand by teaching field, for reasons spelled out below.

Disaggregation by Field of Teaching

Recently, concerns about general teacher shortages have receded, and attention has focused instead on the supply-demand balance in particular fields of teaching, especially fields in which difficulty is anticipated in finding enough qualified teachers. To respond to these concerns, many state models offer disaggregated, subject-specific demand projections. The standard approach to disaggregation is to apply to each subject area exactly the same method as is used to project demand in the aggregate: namely, to multiply projected enrollment in the subject area by an extrapolated, subject-specific teacher-pupil ratio. However, this approach suffers from two serious but often unappreciated conceptual limitations.

First, it presumes that the excess-supply assumption holds for each subject area separately—i.e., that the number of teachers demanded in each field is the same as the number actually employed. This assumption, even if approximately correct for teachers in the aggregate, is less likely to hold for teachers in particular fields. We have been hearing for some time, for example, that there are "not enough" teachers in such fields as physics, chemistry, mathematics, and special education. If this is true, it cannot be correct to project future demands for such teachers on the basis of current and past employment. For example, if the number of physics teachers currently demanded were 2 per 1,000 high school students but the number actually employed were only 1.5 per 1,000 because too few qualified applicants were available, then it is logically the former ratio rather than the latter that should be used to project future demand. This is admittedly a difficult prescription to implement because the actual teacher-pupil ratio is observable, while unfilled demand is neither observable nor readily inferred. Nevertheless, the issue is unavoidable: it would be logically inconsistent to say that there is excess demand for physics teachers today but then to project the future demand for physics teachers from the number currently employed.

Similarly, subject-specific demand projections based on historical patterns of course enrollment rest implicitly on the assumption that past course enrollment patterns were wholly demand-determined rather than jointly determined by both demand and supply. It is quite likely, however, that past levels of enrollment in some subjects were constrained by limited course offerings, which in turn reflected the limited availability of teachers. At the high school level, in particular, the pattern of course taking gives the appearance of being largely demand-determined, in the sense that it reflects the pupils' own choices, but pupils can choose only among courses that are offered and for which teachers exist. Consider, for example, what would happen if one attempted to project the demand for teachers of Japanese from data on the number of such teachers currently employed. The estimate obtained from such a projection would undoubtedly be very low, but this would reflect the limited present availability of Japanese teachers and the consequent rarity of Japanese as a curricular offering. It seems quite likely that if teachers of Japanese were abundant, many more Japanese courses would be offered, more teachers would be employed, and projected demand would be considerably higher than in the present supply-constrained situation.

A further obstacle to producing valid disaggregated projections of demand is that neither data bases nor methods have been developed for projecting future rates of course taking by subject. The present models merely reflect the assumption that current or recent distributions of course enrollments by subject area will remain unchanged for the indefinite future—an assumption that is often demonstrably false, given the changes that have been taking place in state curricula and graduation requirements. To my knowledge, no methods of projecting changes in subject-specific course enrollment rates have yet been demonstrated. It appears, however, that some data bases are now available that would make such projections possible. Certain states (e.g., California and Florida) maintain detailed pupil-level data bases that include information on enrollment by subject and could be used to study changes in course taking over time. National studies of course-taking behavior based on samples of high school transcripts may also be useful for projecting subject-specific demands.[5] This particular unexplored area of demand modeling appears to be ripe for substantial progress.

The Demand for Teacher Quality

Even the most sophisticated projections of numbers of teachers likely to be wanted in the future would not meet the needs of those concerned with issues of teacher quality. The quality dimension of demand has received very little attention (apart from acknowledgments of its omission) in supply-demand studies. No demand projection model, to my knowledge, takes any quality-related attribute of teachers into account. This situation is unlikely to be rectified soon. Nevertheless, certain aspects of the quality issue are worth addressing, even if for no other reason than to indicate what is missing from, and may be misleading about, projections that do not take teacher quality into account.

States and school districts are clearly not indifferent between teachers of higher and lower quality—however quality might be defined—and there is good reason to believe that districts are willing to pay more to acquire teachers with the quality-related attributes they value. For example, some school systems (usually the more affluent ones) generally do not hire inexperienced teachers but instead recruit higher-priced teachers who already have taught elsewhere. Some districts (again, usually the more affluent) appear to offer higher salary schedules than neighboring districts specifically to attract large pools of applicants among whom they can choose. The fact that teacher salary schedules almost universally reward teaching experience and training is evidence in itself that qualifications matter to employers, and that all teachers are not viewed as essentially interchangeable labor. Thus, it is clearly meaningful to speak of a demand for teacher quality, just as one normally speaks of a demand for quantity.

Two related aspects of the demand for teacher quality that merit investigation (and that could conceivably be reflected in a future generation of demand projection models) are (1) the nature of the quality-price relationship (how much extra are school systems willing to pay for valued attributes of teachers?) and (2) the nature of quantity-quality tradeoffs (to what extent would school systems be willing to accept lower teacher-pupil ratios to get higher-quality but presumably more expensive teachers). The possibility of quantity-quality tradeoffs raises serious concerns about projections of numbers of teachers. For instance, a state that has been shifting its emphasis toward higher teacher quality may be employing fewer teachers (but better ones) than would have been projected on the basis of earlier data. With a demand model that takes no account of quality or price, such a development would either be missed or misconstrued. Moreover, even a behavioral demand model would yield misleading results if it lacked a quality dimension; for example, a tradeoff of quantity for quality could be misinterpreted as a reduction in the number of teachers demanded in response to rising cost. Interstate comparisons of teacher demand also remain problematic without methods of taking quality differentials into account.

Ideally, one can envision a model that projects both the number of teachers and the quality of teachers demanded in a state, but the obstacles to creating such an analytical tool are formidable. Quality measurement is only one major problem. It is actually less of a problem in connection with demand projections than in other contexts because what counts in a demand analysis is only whether employers are willing to pay for a given teacher characteristic, not whether that characteristic is truly educationally valuable. For example, if districts are willing to pay extra for teachers with master's degrees, then having a master's is an appropriate element of quality to include in a demand model regardless of whether master's degrees translate into improved learning for pupils. But even assuming that teacher quality can be measured, there are still difficulties in characterizing, much less projecting, the quality of a teaching force. One is that states employ mixes of teachers with different characteristics and quality, not teachers of uniform quality, which makes it difficult to characterize any particular state's quality or to compare quality levels among states. Another is that each state's teaching force was accumulated over a period of many years, which means that the average quality of today's teaching force reflects both the demand for and the supply of teacher quality in many past periods. The value that the state currently places on quality is reflected only in hiring new teachers. Moreover, the quality of retained teachers reflects demand-side influences but also such supply-side phenomena as the relative rates at which lower-quality and higher-quality teachers leave the profession and the propensities of teachers to improve their own quality through education and on-the-job learning. Thus, there is much to sort out before even beginning to model or project the demand for teacher quality.

National and State Demand Projection Models

The Standard Demand Projection Model

With few exceptions, projections of the demand for teachers are made according to a simple, mechanical, standard model. Each version of this standard model projects the future demand for teachers (either in the aggregate or in a particular category) as:

$$\text{Projected number of teachers demanded in year } t = \text{Projected enrollment in year } t \times \text{Projected teacher-pupil ratio in year } t$$

where the projected number of teachers demanded refers either to all teachers or to teachers at a particular level (elementary or secondary) and/or in a particular subject area; the projected teacher-pupil ratio refers to the same level and/or subject category; and projected enrollment is either aggregate enrollment, enrollment at the specified level, or course enrollment in the specified subject area, as the case may be.

The enrollment projections that enter into these models are generally produced separately and treated as inputs into the teacher demand calculations.[6] Many state education agencies routinely maintain and operate enrollment projection models for reasons unrelated to concerns about teacher supply and demand (e.g., to develop and justify budget requests), and NCES provides regularly updated national enrollment projections and, of late, enrollment projections by state.[7] The accuracy of demand projections naturally depends on the accuracy of the underlying projections of enrollment. Whether the enrollment projection methods deal adequately with migration, dropping out, and private school enrollment are particularly sensitive concerns. To cover these issues adequately, however, would require a specialized review of enrollment projection methodology—a task beyond the scope of this paper. From here on, I simply take enrollment projections as given, leaving it to others to assess their quality.

Projections of future teacher-pupil ratios are generated, in the standard model, by one or a combination of the following methods:

- Method 1: Assume that teacher-pupil ratios in future years will be the same as in the most recent year for which data are available.
- Method 2: Assume that teacher-pupil ratios in the future will be equal to the averages of the corresponding ratios in several recent years.
- Method 3: Estimate future teacher-pupil ratios by extrapolating the trends of recent years.
- Method 4: Set the projected teacher-pupil ratios to reflect adopted or anticipated future staffing norms or staffing policies.

There is little scope for creativity within the framework of the standard model. The principal choices to be made by each model developer concern (1) the number and type of teacher categories for which separate demand projections will be developed, (2) which of the four methods listed above will be used to project teacher-pupil ratios, and (3) the number of future years for which projections will be made and the number of past years on which the projections will be based.

Variations on a Theme

The following are brief descriptions of how several states have implemented the standard model and how NCES used it to make national projections prior to introducing a new methodology in 1988. The descriptions are followed by remarks on the limitations of this general approach to projecting teacher demand.

Nebraska A Nebraska model (Ostrander et al., 1988) illustrates the standard model in its simplest form. It projects demands for elementary and secondary teachers (grades K-6 and 7-12, respectively) for the years 1988-

89 to 1993-94 by multiplying projected enrollment for each level in each year by the corresponding teacher-pupil ratio in the most recent year, 1987-88, for which data were available. In essence, this model simply assumes that the number of teachers wanted at each level will increase each year in proportion to the annual increase in the number of pupils to be served.

Wisconsin A Wisconsin analysis (Lauritzen and Friedman, 1991) projects demand for the three-year period 1991-92 to 1993-94 on the basis of enrollment projections prepared by the Wisconsin Department of Public Instruction. It then extends the projections two additional years into the future (i.e., past the period for which enrollment projections are available) by making broad assumptions about rates at which enrollments will continue to grow. The model uses fixed teacher-pupil ratios (actual ratios in the 1990-91 base year) to project demands for elementary, secondary, and special education teachers. Thus, like the Nebraska model, it reflects the assumption of simple proportionality between the number of teachers at each level and the number of pupils enrolled. (Interestingly, the same Wisconsin study also offers more detailed projections of future numbers of *newly hired* teachers, covering 16 subject-area categories of regular education teachers and 8 categories of special education teachers, but these are not based on projections of numbers of teachers demanded but rather on direct extrapolations of numbers of new hires in previous years.)

New York A model developed by the New York State Education Department (1990) projects demand for teachers in 15 subject specialties grouped into elementary (K-6), secondary (7-12), and combined elementary-secondary (K-12) levels. The projected demand for each type of teacher for each year from 1989-90 to 1993-94 is determined by multiplying projected enrollment for the appropriate level by the projected teacher-pupil ratio for the subject area in question. Separate projections are prepared for New York City and for the remainder of the state, and the two sets of figures are summed to produce estimates for the state as a whole. According to the New York report, most teacher-pupil ratios were assumed to remain constant at their base-year (1988-89) values throughout the projection period, but "for a few high-growth subjects, the ratios were allowed to [increase] slightly for a year, and then held constant." Note that this method allows for no changes in the enrollment mix by subject area—that is, enrollments in secondary mathematics, secondary English, secondary occupational education, etc., are all assumed to change over the years in the same proportion as total secondary enrollment.

South Carolina The South Carolina Department of Education (1990) projects the 1995 demand for teachers in 36 different subject specialties on the basis of teacher-pupil ratios prevailing in 1990. (For some reason, projections for the intermediate years are not provided.) The model is driven by enrollment projections for each of six levels: child development, kindergarten, other early childhood, elementary, junior high, and high school. Specifically, the projected 1995 demand for teachers in each subject category is determined for each level by multiplying the actual number of teachers in the category in 1990 by the ratio of projected 1995 enrollment to actual 1990 enrollment at the level in question. The results are then summed over levels to determine the total demand for teachers of each subject. This procedure is mathematically equivalent to assuming that all teacher-pupil ratios will remain fixed and that course enrollments in all subjects offered at a given level will increase in proportion to the increase in that level's enrollment. In other words, this model, like the New York model, imposes the rigid assumption that no change will occur during the projection period in the mix of subjects taken by the pupils at each level.

Ohio An Ohio model (Ohio Department of Education, 1988) differs from the models outlined above in that it projects the teacher-pupil ratio in each subject area according to a trend extrapolation. The model uses data for school years 1982-83 to 1986-87 to project demands for teachers in 29 subject areas over the five-year period 1987-88 to 1991-92. The teacher-pupil ratio for a particular subject area is projected, in most instances, by fitting a least-squares regression line to data for the five-year base period. In a few cases, time-trend extrapolations are deemed inappropriate, and teacher-pupil ratios are set at base-period averages or other stipulated values. These projected teacher-pupil ratios are then applied to projected enrollments for the appropriate grade levels. As in the models described previously, no allowance is made for the possibility that the mix of courses taken by pupils at a given grade level will change during the projection period.

Massachusetts A teacher supply and demand analysis and projection model for Massachusetts has been produced by a group at the Massachusetts Institute for Social and Economic Research (MISER), based at the University of Massachusetts (Coelen and Wilson, 1987). Unlike the other modeling efforts described above, this one seeks to provide a simulation tool rather than a single set of numerical projections. In pursuit of this goal but faced with severe data constraints, Coelen and Wilson have created a more complex conceptual structure than they have been able to implement empirically. On the demand side, the model features a full matrix of course enrollment rates by grade level in each of 20 subject areas, which would allow, in principle, for varied and flexible assumptions about trends in subject-area enrollments. But the available course-taking data for Massachusetts, unfortunately, are so skimpy that Coelen and Wilson could do no better than to assume the same fixed-proportion course enrollment patterns as underlie more modest models.[8] Also on the demand side, the part of the model that deals with teacher-pupil ratios reflects no particular theory about how those ratios will be determined in the future but rather is intended to answer what-if questions about alternative possibilities. Consequently, the model's base-case assumption becomes, by default, essentially the same as underlies many other states' projections—namely, that the teacher-pupil ratio in each subject area will stay constant in the future at its current or recent value.[9] In these respects, the Massachusetts demand model, though more elaborate than the others, remains in the standard model category.

The analysts at MISER have been engaged for some time in a much more ambitious project intended to produce teacher supply and demand information, including projections, for a multistate region encompassing the New England states and New York. This project, known as the Northeast Educator Supply and Demand study (NEDSAD), has amassed large, multiyear data bases for each participating state, and efforts to develop the supply and demand projection models are now under way. Coelen and Wilson have said that they intend these models to be "econometric," or behavioral (as contrasted with the "demographic," or mechanical, models presented in the Massachusetts study), but it appears, at this point, that this applies to the supply side of the models and not to the projections of demand. My understanding, based on preliminary model specifications (Coelen and Wilson, 1991a) and a discussion with Coelen, is that demand projections in the new model, as in the earlier Massachusetts model, will continue to be driven exclusively by projected enrollment and course-taking patterns. Moreover, the present MISER plan apparently is to develop demand models using only data aggregated to the state level, whereas a district-level analysis would be needed to capture relationships between the demand for teachers and multiple economic, fiscal, and demographic factors. (Note: remarks on the supply components of the NEDSAD model appear in later sections.)

Connecticut Connecticut's approach to projecting demand (Connecticut Board of Education, 1988) conforms in most respects to the standard model but also includes two useful extensions: (1) a mechanism to allow for nonproportional responses of the demand for teachers to changes in enrollment and (2) an explicit provision for adjusting demand projections for changes in staffing policies. The model projects demands for three grade-level groupings (elementary, middle/junior high, and high school) and eight staff categories: six subject-area categories of classroom teachers plus a support staff category and an administrator category.[10] It provides projections for the 14-year period from 1988-89 to 2000-2001, based on data for the years 1986-87 and 1987-88.

The Connecticut model calculates the projected year-to-year *change* in the demand for staff in each category and at each level as the mathematical product of (a) the projected enrollment change for the level in question, (b) the applicable teacher-pupil ratio, and (c) a response rate, which represents the rate at which Connecticut school systems tend to increase their staffs in response to each unit increase in enrollment. The set of response rates is a distinctive feature of the Connecticut model. These rates vary by staff category and level, but generally have values less than 1.0, signifying that, although staff hiring responds to changes in enrollment, it responds less than in proportion. Moreover, the response rates take on higher values for increases in enrollment than for decreases, reflecting evidence that district hiring responds more strongly to enrollment increases than to enrollment declines. The values of all the response rates were determined by comparing rates of staff change with rates of enrollment change between the years 1986-87 and 1987-88.

The model also allows explicitly, as noted above, for changes in staffing due to changes in education policies, but these are determined on an ad hoc basis. For instance, the Connecticut analysis allows for phasing in of anticipated staffing increases attributable to expected increases in the number of Connecticut districts offering full-day kindergarten programs.

The computations of projected changes in demand are repeated year by year for each year of the projection period. Because of both the response-rate factors and the allowances for effects of policy changes, the teacher-pupil ratios used in the projections change from one year to the next. Were it not for the enrollment and policy changes, however, the ratios would remain constant; that is, there is no assumption of any underlying trend.

The response-rate feature of the Connecticut model reflects the findings of a research paper (Murnane et al., 1985) on district responses to upward and downward changes in enrollment. It should be noted, however, that the projection model does not take into account one important finding of that research—namely, that there is a significant difference between short-run and long-run responses of staffing levels to enrollment changes, especially in the case of falling enrollment. The distinction between immediate responses and long-term adjustments could be important, especially following a period of enrollment decline, and projections might be more accurate if it were taken into account.

The NCES Pre-1988 National Model NCES has produced projections of the demand for teachers for many years, but its projection method changed drastically in 1988. The current model, described later, uses a regression equation to relate projected demand to several causal factors (Gerald and Hussar, 1990). The pre-1988 model is a version of the standard model outlined above—that is, it projects demand as the mathematical product of projected enrollments and projected teacher-pupil ratios. Specifically, NCES, as of 1985, produced so-called low, intermediate, and high projections of numbers of elementary and secondary teachers by multiplying the projected enrollment at each level by teacher-pupil ratios determined as follows:

- For the low projection, assuming that the teacher-pupil ratio would remain constant at its value in the most recent year for which data were available;

• For the high projection, extrapolating the trend in the teacher-pupil ratio according to an exponential smoothing technique, wherein the historical data are weighted according to an exponential function so that more recent observations receive greater weight; and

• For the intermediate projection, setting the teacher-pupil ratio at the average of the high and low projections (Gerald, 1985).

Thus, the former NCES approach actually blended two variants of the standard model: one reflecting the assumption of a constant teacher-pupil ratio; the other, the assumption of a continuing trend.

NCES Projections of Numbers of Teachers by State Although NCES has shifted to a regression-based model for its national demand projections, it has adhered to the standard model in producing a set of teacher demand projections by state (Gerald et al., 1989b). The state-level projection model is essentially the same as the pre-1988 NCES national projection model: the number of public classroom teachers in a state (elementary and secondary combined) is projected for fall 1988 to fall 1993 by multiplying the state's projected K-12 enrollment by a projected teacher-pupil ratio. The latter is obtained by extrapolating the trend in the state's teacher-pupil ratio from 1970 to 1987 according to the aforementioned exponential smoothing technique.

General Assessment of Projections Based on the Standard Model

The limitations of the demand projections described above are for the most part self-evident and have been discussed in earlier reviews, so I summarize them only briefly here.

First, although the mechanical projection models reflect no explicit assumptions about future conditions affecting teacher demand, they implicitly reflect the assumption that all major influences on demand will either remain constant or continue to change at the rates at which they have been changing in the past. If anything substantially different were to happen—for instance, if state or local fiscal conditions were to change or if the relative salaries of teachers were to rise or fall sharply—the projections obtained from such models would probably be incorrect.

Second, although the projection models can produce teacher demand estimates corresponding to different stipulated teacher-pupil ratios and different patterns of enrollment by subject, the models themselves have no capability to predict how these ratios or patterns would be affected by policy changes or other external developments. Consequently, they cannot be used (except in conjunction with ad hoc outside analyses) to respond to what-if questions about the effects of such changes on teacher demand.

Third, although some models break down projections of teacher demand by subject area, they do so only by assuming that the mix of course enrollments by subject area will remain the same in the future as it is today. They make no allowances for disparate trends in course taking in different fields or for specific developments, such as changes in curricula and graduation requirements, that are causing course-taking patterns to change.

Fourth, an implicit assumption underlying the projections of teacher demand by subject area is that the market for each type of teacher is and has been in a condition of excess supply. Although this assumption is realistic for teachers in the aggregate, it may not be valid for certain specific fields, such as chemistry, physics, and special education. If it is not, projected demands for teachers in those fields would be understated.

Fifth, an assumption built into the standard model is that the demand for each type of teacher responds proportionately to any increase or decrease in the corresponding category of enrollment. Evidence has shown, however, that the actual response is likely to be less than proportional, especially in the short run. Of the models examined, only that of Connecticut allows for these nonproportional responses.

Finally, even taking the models on their own terms—that is, accepting their mechanical nature and assuming that the built-in assumptions are valid—there are still certain possibilities for improvement. The models that base projections only on data for the most recent year might benefit from using multiyear data to quantify trends in the teacher-pupil ratio. Similarly, models that assume permanently fixed patterns of course taking by subject might be upgraded by projecting separate trends in enrollment by subject area.

An NCES Venture into Econometric Modeling

In 1988, NCES switched from the standard projection model described earlier to a new econometric approach. In the three most recent editions of its *Projections of Education Statistics*, the agency has used regression equations fitted to national time series data to predict future numbers of public elementary and secondary teachers (Gerald et al., 1988, 1989a; Gerald and Hussar, 1990). This regression model, as it now stands, is a very simple one with some serious conceptual and technical flaws; yet it represents an important first step, and one to be encouraged, away from the traditional mechanical projections and in the direction of behavioral models.

Model Description

The NCES regression equations for elementary and secondary teachers both relate the number of teachers demanded to enrollment, per capita income, and state education aid per pupil. The equation for elementary teachers, as presented in Gerald and Hussar (1990) is:

$$ELTCH = b_0 + b_1PCI_{-2} + b_2SGRANT + b_3ELENR$$

and the equation used to project the number of secondary teachers is:

$$SCTCH = b_0 + b_1PCI_{-2} + b_2SGRANT_{-3} + b_3SCENR$$

where ELTCH and SCTCH are the numbers of public elementary and secondary teachers, respectively; PCI_{-2} is disposable income per capita (adjusted for inflation), lagged 2 years; SGRANT is local education revenue receipts from state sources per capita (adjusted for inflation); $SGRANT_{-3}$ is the same variable lagged 3 years; and ELENR and SCENR are public elementary and secondary enrollment, respectively. NCES used ordinary least-squares regression to fit these equations to 30 sets of annual observations. The particular functional form and the different data lags were arrived at, apparently, by trying various specifications and selecting the one with the best statistical properties. The regression equations presented in the immediately preceding edition of *Projections* (Gerald et al., 1989a) resemble the foregoing equations very closely, differing only in the time lags in the PCI and SGRANT variables.[11]

To use such equations for projecting numbers of teachers, one must, of course, have projections of all the independent variables. Projections of the two enrollment variables, ELENR and SCENR, are obtained from the NCES enrollment projection models described in the same annual *Projections* volumes. Projections of disposable per capita income (PCI) are derived from a macroeconomic model created by Data Resources, Inc. (DRI). The projections of the state grant variable (SGRANT) are produced simply by assuming that state grants per pupil will continue to increase at the same percentage rate as during the three most recent years, namely, by 3.1 percent per year. Using these inputs, NCES generates estimates of numbers of public elementary and secondary teachers for each year of the projection period (1989-90 to 2000-2001, in the case of the most recent NCES report). In addition, NCES projects private school teacher demand simply by assuming that the numbers of private elementary and secondary teachers will increase at the same rates as estimated for their public school counterparts.

Assessment

At this point, the new NCES regression method is less valuable for what it is than for what it may bring forth. In the hope that further development of the econometric approach will occur, I offer the following critique and suggestions for improvement.

From a theoretical perspective, the regression equations presented by NCES represent only part of a model of the demand for teachers rather than a complete theory-based specification. For example, although the models do allow for the effect of per capita income on demand, they leave out the effects of the pupil-population ratio and the price (relative salary) of teachers, even though the relevance of both is well established in the literature. A full theoretical model could be specified in either of two ways, depending on which economic and fiscal variables are to be taken as given for the purpose of projecting demand. One approach is to treat the level of education expenditure per pupil as the major fiscal determinant of the demand for teachers and, accordingly, to express demand as a function mainly of expenditure level and price. Per-pupil expenditure itself would have to be projected first, presumably as a function of per capita income, the pupil-population ratio, some indicator of the relative price of educational services, and perhaps other factors. The second approach is to merge the two stages of the aforesaid model into one, as Gerald and Hussar (1990) apparently intended to do with their regression equations. In the merged version, the demand for teachers would be expressed as a function of per capita income (or some other fiscal capacity indicator), the pupil-population ratio, the relative price of teachers, and possibly some additional factors.

An important conceptual shortening of the present Gerald-Hussar formulation is that it treats state aid to local school systems (SGRANT) as an exogenous variable instead of as a factor that itself needs to be explained. Although it is certainly true that state aid is a major determinant of spending by local school districts, the objective in this instance is to explain the overall level of spending, and hence teacher demand, in the nation. Treating the largest component of school spending, state aid, as exogenous and projecting it mechanically merely avoids the issue. If state aid does need to appear in the teacher demand function (or in the equation for estimating per pupil spending), then it too should be projected as a function of underlying economic and demographic variables.

Turning to modeling strategy, I question for several reasons whether fitting the teacher demand equations to a 30-year set of national time-series data is reasonable. First, 30 data points would be too few to fit fully specified teacher demand or expenditure models. Second, the assumption of a stable relationship between the education and fiscal variables extending over 30 year is difficult to accept, especially considering that good measures are not available of changes in the relative price of education over that extended period. Third, it seems to me that there is a better alternative: the model can be fitted to pooled time-series, cross-section data for states. There is no reason why the demand equations, even though they are to be used for making national projections, need to be estimated with national-aggregate data. Using state-level data (for, say, the last 5 to 10 years) would permit development of a more detailed model, while avoiding the strained assumption of stable public tastes for education over three decades. Although a state-level analysis would, admittedly, be a much larger endeavor than the present national time-series analysis, it would also yield richer, more useful, and probably more valid results.

On the technical level, I believe that it is misleading to express the dependent variables of the equations in absolute terms (i.e., actual number of teachers) and to use enrollment as one of the explanatory variables. Doing so creates the illusion of high explanatory power (high R^2) simply because of the correlation between number of teachers and number of pupils; at the same time, it obscures the roles of the other explanatory variables. I would treat the teacher-pupil ratio as the dependent variable and express all the righthand side variables in per-pupil or per capita terms. I also believe that the price deflators in the model need to be reconsidered. Assuming that a relative price variable appears in the model, as it should, the appropriate specification would be to deflate the education variables (spending and state aid per pupil) by a measure of education cost and to deflate per capita income by a general price index.

In sum, a great deal can be done to develop the strategy of econometric projection modeling opened up in the 1988 to 1990 editions of the NCES projections. If similar models could be developed for a few individual states, so much the better. This is the general approach that needs to be followed if we are ever to have behavioral models for assessing teacher supply and demand.

MODELS OF THE SUPPLY OF RETAINED TEACHERS

The preponderant share of a state's teaching force in any school year—typically, 92 to 96 percent of the total—consists of teachers retained from the previous year. The ability to estimate the future numbers of these continuing teachers, and hence the number of new teachers to be hired, depends on the accuracy with which retention or attrition rates can be measured and predicted. Even a small percentage error in projecting retention translates into a large error in the estimated demand for new hires. For example, a change in a state's teacher retention rate from 96 to 95 percent corresponds to an increase in attrition from 4 percent to 5 percent and hence a 25 percent increase in the number of entrants needed to maintain the size of the state's teaching staff. There is considerable practical motivation, therefore, for efforts to improve and refine teacher attrition/retention models.

When I and others reviewed teacher supply and demand projection methods for the National Research Council in 1986 (Barro, 1986; Cavin, 1986; Popkin and Atrostic, 1986), we found attrition models generally to be crude. Many states projected the supply of retained teachers simply by applying undifferentiated statewide-average attrition rates to all categories of teachers in all future years. NCES did the same thing in making its national projections. The states of New York and Connecticut, however, had made the major leap forward of basing projections on disaggregated age-specific and subject-specific attrition rates. That, in 1986, was the leading-edge methodology. There were at that time no behavioral models of attrition, no models of change in attrition rates over time, and, of course, no models dealing with the quality as well as the numbers of retained teachers.

Has much has the state of the art advanced? The answer differs sharply depending on whether one considers practical supply-demand projection models only or also takes into account the recent academic research on teacher attrition. Judging only by the explicit projection models, one would have to conclude that little progress has been made. Some states still use a single, undifferentiated, average attrition rate to estimate numbers of continuing teachers. NCES, in its national model, has advanced only from using a single average rate to using separate average rates for elementary and secondary teachers. New York and Connecticut, now joined by Massachusetts and possibly others, disaggregate attrition rates by age and subject specialty as they did before. Otherwise, no major new features are apparent, at least not in the less-than-representative sample of state models I have examined.

In sharp contrast, progress in research on teacher attrition has been dramatic. Several scholars, most notably Richard Murnane of Harvard University and his colleagues and David Grissmer and his associates at the RAND Corporation, have developed far more sophisticated models of teacher attrition and other aspects of teachers' career paths than existed just a few years ago. Using large-scale, multiyear state data bases and the statistical tools of survival or hazard modeling, they have been able to address some of the major hitherto unresolved issues of teacher attrition. Thus, we now have multivariate behavioral analyses of attrition, some initial analyses of changes in attrition patterns over time, and even, in Murnane's work, an analysis of the relationship of attrition to an indicator of teacher quality. Although these analyses were not conducted specifically to develop projection models, some of the key research findings and methods seem eminently suitable for that purpose. Accordingly, I deal in this review with selected research on teacher attrition as well as with explicit state and national projection models. First, however, I comment on some general considerations pertaining to attrition rates and their uses in projecting the supply of retained teachers.

Considerations in Modeling Attrition

The following issues must all be dealt with, explicitly or implicitly, in constructing a projection model, and all should be kept in mind in assessing the specific attrition models described later in this chapter.

Defining and Measuring Attrition Rates

An attrition rate is the fraction or percentage of teachers employed in one period (either in some specified teacher category or in all categories combined) who are not employed as teachers in a subsequent period. A retention rate is the complement of the corresponding attrition rate—that is, retention rate = 1 – attrition rate or, in percentage terms, retention percentage = 100 – attrition percentage. But although the basic definition is clear, at least two of its aspects require attention: (1) the unit of analysis or level of aggregation and (2) the treatment of individuals who leave teaching for a time but not permanently. (A third aspect, the degree of disaggregation of teachers by level and subject specialty, is discussed separately below.)

The unit-of-analysis issue is significant because teachers often transfer among jurisdictions. The average attrition rate experienced by the local school districts in a state is greater than the statewide attrition rate because some teachers leaving particular districts are hired by other districts in the same state and are not lost to the state as a whole.[12] Similarly, the average state attrition rate is greater than the national rate because some teachers leave one state to teach in another. The fact that some local and state attrition reflects interjurisdictional transfers has implications for both measurement and modeling. The implication for measurement is that one cannot determine a state's attrition rate accurately simply by adding up the numbers of teachers that the state's individual districts or schools have lost. Districts usually are not well equipped to distinguish between teachers transferring and teachers leaving the profession.[13] Statewide data on individual teachers are generally required to measure a state's attrition rate properly. For the same reason, one cannot measure national attrition correctly by adding up attrition reported by states; a national data base is required, such as that provided by the NCES Schools and Staffing Survey (SASS), applications of which are discussed later.

Transfers between public and private schools also complicate the task of quantifying attrition. Because some teachers leave private schools to take jobs in public school districts (and vice versa), the total number of teachers leaving a state's teaching force in a given year is less than the sum of leavers from the public and private sectors. An analysis of total statewide attrition (public and private combined) would have to be based, therefore, on a data file that includes both public school and private school teachers. In practice, however, most teacher supply-demand models pertain only to the public schools, which means that attrition from private schools is not taken into account and transfers from private to public schools are treated as a component of the supply of "new" public school teachers.

The implications of the transfer phenomenon for modeling are that (1) it is important to distinguish, in modeling attrition, between teachers who transfer and teachers who leave the profession and (2) it may be equally important, in modeling the supply of entrants, to distinguish between transferring teachers and other new hires. Each teacher who transfers from one state (or district) to another counts not only in the former state's (or district's) attrition but also in the latter's new teacher supply. Projecting this component of supply is important wherever there is significant importation of teachers into a state. It is particularly important in constructing a multistate model of teacher supply and demand, such as the NEDSAD model now being developed by the MISER group in Massachusetts. But developing importation projections, it turns out, is one of the more difficult and least explored tasks in modeling teacher supply.

The distinction between temporary and permanent (or between short-term and long-term) attrition is of considerable importance both to policy makers and to those attempting to project teacher supply. On the policy side, a state's decisions about such things as how many new teachers to train and what measures to take to attract teachers from other sources could be affected by information about the rate at which departing teachers are likely to return. Several recent studies have shown that substantial percentages of each year's entering teachers (i.e., teachers employed in a given year who were not teaching in the previous year) are, in fact, former teachers reentering the profession (Grissmer and Kirby, 1987, 1991; Coelen and Wilson, 1987; Connecticut Board of Education, 1988).

The question of how reentering teachers should be treated in modeling attrition is not yet resolved. Grissmer and Kirby (1987, 1991) distinguish between "annual" and "permanent" attrition. The annual attrition rate is the fraction of teachers employed at the beginning of one year who are not employed at the beginning of the next, including teachers who eventually return; the permanent attrition rate is the (significantly lower) fraction of teachers who leave and do not return, at least during the period for which data are available. Grissmer and Kirby (1991) present separate analyses of attrition patterns and determinants of attrition corresponding to the two definitions. In contrast, most other analysts deal with the reentry problem by analyzing only what Grissmer and Kirby call annual attrition but then modeling the reentry rate as a separate phenomenon (e.g., Murnane et al., 1988, 1989; Connecticut Board of Education, 1988; Coelen and Wilson, 1987). Each approach, thus far, seems to have significant limitations. The notion of permanent attrition is flawed in that (1) it lumps together in the nonpermanent category teachers who leave for only 1 year with teachers who leave for as much as 5 or 10 years and (2) it requires, as a practical matter, either an arbitrary cutoff (e.g., teachers who do not return within 5 years) or retrospective longitudinal data that cannot be collected in time to be useful for projections. The alternative of treating all leavers alike and then modeling reentry separately has the potential weakness of lumping together persons who may be leaving teaching for very different reasons—e.g., teachers going on one-year leaves with the intention of returning and teachers leaving permanently for higher-paying occupations. Thus, it remains unclear at this time how the dual phenomena of short-term attrition and reentry might best be quantified and modeled.

Voluntary versus Involuntary Attrition

In most supply-demand modeling efforts, the supply of retained teachers is taken as synonymous with the number who actually remain in their jobs from one year to the next, the implicit assumption being that all prior-year teachers who want to continue teaching are retained by their employers. The possibility that the supply of would-be retainees might be *greater* than the number actually employed is rarely, if ever, allowed for in projections, even though the number supplied and the number employed are two different concepts. The former might exceed the latter for two reasons. First, sharp cuts in demand (due, e.g., to enrollment declines and/or budget cuts) might lead local LEAs to lay off teachers who want to continue working. (Cuts must be quite sharp to have this effect, considering that some teachers leave on their own each year.) Second, some prior-year teachers might be discharged for other reasons (e.g., incompetence) and replaced with new hires, even though they want to continue teaching. The latter is very rare (although not unheard of) and probably would have little effect on state or national projections. Statewide reductions-in-force have definitely occurred in response to both demographic and fiscal developments, however, and may recur in the future. For instance, Coelen and Wilson (1987) cite sharp staff cutbacks following the enactment of Proposition 2-1/2 (a statewide tax limitation provision) in Massachusetts in 1981. Therefore, although it is reasonable to assume in most instances that the number of prior-year teachers actually employed in a given year is roughly the same in the aggregate as the number willing to supply their services, this assumption is sometimes violated, and projections based on it may confound supply-side and demand-side effects on teacher retention.

In principle, a clear distinction should be made between voluntary and involuntary attrition in modeling the supply of retained teachers. Voluntary attrition is a supply-side phenomenon that reflects the decisions of individual teachers. It makes sense, therefore, to project voluntary attrition as a function of individual teacher characteristics and variables that may affect teachers' decisions (salaries, working conditions, etc.), as is done in some of the attrition models discussed later. Involuntary attrition is a demand-side phenomenon that reflects decisions by employers. Mixing together teachers who decide to leave on their own with teachers who are laid off or fired can lead to incorrect inferences about patterns of, and influences on, attrition and hence to incorrect projections of future attrition rates.

Although most model developers are aware of the problem, none has yet invented a method of dealing with it. The prevailing approach seems to be to rely as little as possible on data for periods in which involuntary terminations are believed to have been numerous. Coelen and Wilson (1987), for instance, do not allow data for the period when Proposition 2-1/2 took effect to influence their attrition projections, and Murnane and Olsen (1990), in their analysis of North Carolina, place more emphasis on years of growing enrollment and demand for teachers (1975-79) than on years of contracting demand (1980-84). Thus far, the issue remains unresolved of whether it is feasible to distinguish analytically between demand-side and supply-side influences on attrition.

Disaggregation by Subject Specialty

Projections of the supply of retained teachers must be disaggregated into the same categories as projections of demand to produce the subject-specific assessments of the future supply-demand balance that policy makers want, but disaggregation creates additional problems for attrition modeling and adds to some of the problems already discussed. Among the principal complications are the following.

First, measuring attrition rates and numbers of teachers by field is not a straightforward matter because many teachers have certificates in multiple fields. According to Coelen and Wilson (1991b), the average Massachusetts teacher holds 3.3 certifications.[14] To the extent that teachers are multiply certificated or multiply qualified, the sum of teacher supply by field will exceed teacher supply in the aggregate. For instance, an LEA might have 100 mathematics and science teachers, of whom 40 are certificated to teach mathematics only, 35 to teach science only, and 25 to teach both mathematics and science. It could be misleading, then, to project the retained supply of, say, science teachers by applying a retention rate to the number of teachers actually teaching science in a particular year. Such a projection would understate the supply (or potential supply) of science teachers because some individuals teaching mathematics are in the supply of science teachers as well. Although most developers of supply and demand models recognize this problem, the usual response is to circumvent it by such expedients as classifying teachers only according to the main subject that they actually teach in the base year of the attrition calculations. The actual supply of teachers in any given field is likely to be considerably larger than such calculations indicate. Also, the overall teacher supply is likely to be considerably more flexible than is implied by a method that rigidly assigns each teacher to one and only one field.

Second, disaggregation by subject creates a major new category of transferring teachers: those who change subject areas between one school year and the next. An individual who transfers from teaching mathematics to teaching science within the same LEA (or state) presumably counts as a departing mathematics teacher for the purpose of measuring the attrition rate in mathematics and, at the same time, as an entering science teacher. In the aggregate, however, such a teacher is a retainee. Some special treatment of intersubject transfers is required, not only to reconcile the aggregate attrition rate with the subject-specific attrition rates but also, more importantly, because different causal factors are undoubtedly associated with shifts among subject fields than with exits from the teaching force. Very little is said in the reports I have seen about how such transfers are handled; the topic appears to qualify, at present, as one of the loose ends in projection methodology.

Third, disaggregation by subject has the effects of (1) amplifying the importance of distinguishing between voluntary and involuntary attrition and (2) undercutting the key assumption of attrition modeling that the number of retained teachers in each category is less than the number of teachers demanded. Although the latter assumption may be only infrequently violated in the aggregate, it is likely to be violated much more often in individual subject fields. Even when enrollments and education budgets are stable, changes in curricula and graduation requirements or in the makeup of the pupil population may cause the demands for course enrollments in particular fields to decline while demands for other fields are rising. Thus, there may be too little demand for teaching in a particular field to justify retaining all the prior-year teachers in that field who want to continue working. As academic requirements for high school graduation are strengthened, for example, the demand for vocational education courses may decline, and hence vocational teachers may have to be laid off or transferred to other fields even though total high school enrollment is rising. Under such conditions, conventional methods of quantifying attrition would confound voluntary with involuntary attrition, and supply projections based on the resulting attrition rates would be misleading. Again, the major unresolved issue—this time in the context of field-specific rather than aggregate attrition—is whether it is possible to distinguish analytically between demand-side and supply-side determinants of the attrition rate.

Attrition Rates in Relation to Attributes of Teachers

A major characteristic that distinguishes more refined projections of the supply of retained teachers from crude ones is disaggregation of attrition rates by age, subject specialty, and perhaps other attributes of teachers. Several aspects of the pattern of these disaggregated rates are now firmly established in the literature (the specific studies on which these findings are based are described later in this section.

First, the relationship between attrition rate and age is U-shaped. Young (or new) teachers and older teachers (age 55 and over) leave at high rates; those in between (especially in the 35 to 55 age range) leave at much lower rates. The key implication for projection modeling is that the overall rate of teacher attrition in a state, or in the nation, is likely to change over time simply because of the changing age composition of the teaching force, even if there is no change in the propensity to leave of the teachers in each age bracket. Models that neglect this age-composition effect on attrition are unlikely to yield accurate estimates of numbers of future retainees.

Second, there are substantial differences in attrition rates among subject specialties. Several studies have shown that secondary teachers tend to leave sooner than elementary teachers and that teachers of chemistry and physics tend to leave sooner than teachers of other subjects. Any model that purports to offer subject-specific supply and demand projections must take these subject-area differences in attrition into account. Applying an undifferentiated average attrition rate to all categories of teachers is unsatisfactory. Incidentally, one of the unexpected findings of the recent attrition research, in light of concerns about possible shortages of mathematics and science teachers, is that mathematics teachers are not among those with shorter-than-average lengths of stay in teaching. Moreover, even within the science category, the attrition patterns of biology teachers are quite different from those of chemistry and physics teachers. It appears, therefore, that "mathematics and science" is not a good category to use in assessing subject-specific attrition.

Third, male and female attrition patterns differ. Women appear to have higher attrition rates early in their careers, but male and female rates converge later on (Grissmer and Kirby, 1987, 1991). There is also evidence of an age-gender interaction effect, wherein the early attrition rates of young women are higher than those of young men, but attrition patterns of older male and female entrants are essentially the same (Murnane et al., 1988, 1989; Murnane and Olsen, 1989). Other things being equal, jurisdictions that hire different mixes of male and female teachers are likely to experience different rates of attrition—a finding that has not yet been reflected in supply projection models.

Fourth, it appears that attrition patterns may also differ significantly by race, although this is not as well established as the findings about other personal attributes. Racial differences would be important because of some policy makers' concerns about the future racial balance of the teaching force, and so there could be reason to bring this variable, too, into the attrition models.

Projection modelers up to now have produced disaggregated attrition rates simply by computing separate attrition rates for the teachers in each subcategory, but as more teacher attributes are taken into account, the proliferation of subcategories makes this method infeasible. Analyses that go much beyond breakdowns by age and subject need to use multivariate methods to sort out the relationships of the different teacher characteristics to attrition. Multivariate methods are also better suited for estimating the effects on attrition rates of hypothetical or projected changes in particular teacher attributes. For example, the high early attrition rates of chemistry teachers may be due partly to some aspect of the field of chemistry as such (e.g., attractive employment opportunities outside teaching) and partly to age and gender differences between chemistry teachers and teachers in other fields. With a multivariate model, one can hold constant the effects of age and gender in order to estimate the marginal effect of subject specialty. Moreover, it is only with multivariate models that one can progress from mechanical projection models to behavioral models that allow, for example, for the effects of salaries, working conditions, and other policy variables on teacher attrition.

Variations in Attrition Rates Over Time

Even if all the difficulties of measuring and disaggregating attrition rates were overcome, the problem would remain of projecting attrition rates into the future. As will be seen, the prevailing approach in recent national and state models is to assume that attrition rates in future years will be the same as in the recent past. More specifically, the standard practice is to assume that attrition rates throughout the projection period (which may extend 10 or more years into the future) will remain fixed at the rates observed in the most recent year for which data are available. Yet ample evidence is now available that rates of teacher attrition, both in the aggregate and by subject field, have varied substantially in the past (Grissmer and Kirby, 1987; Coelen and Wilson, 1987) and, moreover, that such variations can be explained only partly by the changing age structure of the teaching force (Murnane and Olsen, 1990; Grissmer and Kirby, 1991). The assumption that age-specific, subject-specific attrition rates will remain constant is therefore, to say the least, questionable, yet it is embedded in most of the recent projection models that have come to my attention. How one might project changes or trends in the rates is one of the major unresolved issues of attrition modeling.

The Quality of Retained Teachers

Finally, just as it would be desirable to project the demand for teacher quality, it would be valuable to be able to estimate the quality of future retainees. A major concern of policy makers, unfortunately borne out by some research (Murnane et al., 1989; Murnane and Olsen, 1990), is that teachers' propensities to leave may be adversely selective in relation to quality—that is, better or "smarter" teachers are likely to leave sooner. Although the same problems of quality measurement arise in analyzing the quality dimension of attrition as in dealing with the quality dimension of demand, the modeling task is easier in the case of attrition because there is no need to estimate what the quality of teachers would have been under hypothetical conditions. Murnane and his associates, in the two studies just cited, have shown how a quality indicator (in their case, National Teacher Examination scores) can be included in an analysis of determinants of attrition along with other teacher characteristics. Thus far, however, no distinction by quality has been made, to my knowledge, in any attrition projection model. Introducing this element, in some state where test scores or other quality indicators are included in statewide teacher data files, would be a significant methodological advance.

National Projection Models and Attrition Estimates

In reviewing specific attrition models and studies, I distinguish first between explicit projection models and other research on attrition and second between national-level and state-level analyses. The review is in three parts. This part deals with national-level projection models and attrition estimates; the following part covers state-level projection models; and the third part examines selected studies of teacher attrition, which, although not intended to yield projections, do provide findings directly relevant to the development of projection methodology.

The NCES Projection Model

The NCES national projection model uses extrapolated national-average attrition rates to project numbers of retained teachers in the future. The projection methodology has evolved but remains very simple, as the following comparison of the method circa 1985 and the method today will indicate.

Until recently, NCES estimated attrition by applying a single, national-average, estimated attrition rate to all categories of teachers. It was assumed that this rate, set for many years at 6.0 percent, would remain constant over a projection period extending up to 12 years into the future (see, e.g., NCES, 1985). The estimates obtained by applying the 6.0 percent rate were said (in 1985) to represent "medium" projections. Alternative "high" and "low" projections, corresponding to assumed attrition rates of 8.0 percent and 4.8 percent, were also provided. The 8.0 percent high estimate derived from a study of teacher turnover between 1968 and 1969 (Metz and

Fleischman, 1974). The 6.0 percent medium rate—frequently cited as *the* NCES estimate—was a downward revision of that number based on an NCES assessment (nature unknown) of altered market conditions (Cavin, 1986). The 4.8 percent figure was characterized as a theoretical minimum for reasons that I have not been able to discover. These rates, coupled with alternative projections of demand, yielded a wide range of estimates of the net demand for entering teachers during the projection period.

The present method (Gerald and Hussar, 1990) differs from the earlier method in several respects. First, the projections are now based on separate attrition rates for elementary teachers and secondary teachers rather than on a single average rate for elementary and secondary teachers combined. Second, the attrition rates that NCES now uses are derived from a broad study of separation rates by occupation in the U.S. economy conducted by the Bureau of Labor Statistics (BLS).[15] Third, NCES no longer assumes that attrition rates will remain constant in all future years but instead projects that they will follow a slowly rising trend. This trend projection comes from a rough model of retirement rates in the teaching force, based on age distribution data developed by BLS (for details, see Gerald and Hussar, 1990). Fourth, NCES still provides three sets of projections (low, middle, and high), based on alternative assumptions about how rapidly separations other than retirements will grow relative to projected retirements. According to the middle set of projections, the attrition rate for elementary teachers will rise from 5.5 percent in 1989 to 6.4 percent by the year 2001, while the secondary rate will rise from 6.9 to 8.0 percent over the same interval. The underlying BLS estimates of the separation rate, which are for 1983-84, are 4.9 and 5.6 percent for elementary and secondary teachers, respectively, employed full time in public schools. Apart from the elementary-secondary distinction, there is no differentiation of attrition rates by subject or by any teacher characteristic.

Although the present NCES attrition projection method is an improvement over the previous one, its limitations are evident. It yields only highly aggregative projections; it rests on a series of more or less arbitrary assumptions; and it depends on BLS attrition data collected seven years before the start of the projection period. However, it is pointless for two reasons to focus on these shortcomings today. One is that NCES has had very few options. Given the almost total lack of pertinent data, there is no way that a more sophisticated model could have been constructed. The other is that inquiry into the previous NCES approach has been rendered moot by the emergence of a major new data source, the NCES Schools and Staffing Survey (SASS), which will support much more detailed and sophisticated national attrition modeling than has previously been feasible. Although it is not yet clear precisely what form the new SASS-based models will take, I comment briefly on some possibilities below.

Attrition Estimates from the Schools and Staffing Survey

NCES has completed the first round (1987-88) of SASS data collection and processing and is now carrying out the second round (1990-91) of what is henceforth supposed to be a regular periodic survey. The 1987-88 SASS system collects data from linked samples of public and private teachers, administrators, schools, and LEAs. Also, of special significance for attrition modeling, it includes a follow-up survey, administered one year later (in 1988-89) to a subsample of the original sample of teachers, designed specifically to obtain information on patterns of teacher turnover.

The SASS surveys provide two types of data that can be used to estimate attrition rates. First, the public and private school surveys ask each school to report the number of teachers employed on October 1, 1986, who were no longer employed at that school on October 1, 1987, and then to indicate how many of the departed teachers were employed in another school at the latter date or engaged in various other enumerated activities. Second and more important, the SASS individual-teacher surveys (the 1987-88 baseline survey and the 1988-89 follow-up) provide the wherewithal for a much more detailed analysis of attrition patterns and behavior. The baseline survey provides information on most of the personal characteristics of teachers that have been identified in previous research as major determinants of attrition. These include but are not limited to age, experience, gender, race, marital status, full-time/part-time status, subject specialty, and salary. In addition, other SASS questionnaires provide data on school-level and district-level variables that may be associated with attrition, including pupil composition, locational factors, and certain working conditions. The teacher follow-up survey asks each respondent no longer employed at his or her original school to indicate, among many other things, whether he or she is still teaching and, if so, whether he or she is employed in another school in the same district, a school of a different district in the same state, or a school in a different state and if he or she has switched from a public to a private school or vice versa. Respondents no longer teaching are asked about their current activities. The follow-up sample is designed so that comparisons can be made among teachers who left the profession, teachers who switched schools, and teachers who remained at their original schools.

In an analysis of the school-level data, Rollefson (1990) estimated that the overall rate of attrition of public school teachers from the profession was 4.1 percent between fall 1986 and fall 1987 (4.2 percent among elementary teachers and 4.0 percent among secondary teachers). The estimated rates of attrition of private school teachers from the profession were much higher—9.3 percent for elementary teachers, 6.8 percent for secondary teachers, and 8.7 percent for elementary and secondary combined. The 4.2 and 4.0 percent estimates for public elementary and secondary teachers are considerably lower than the BLS figures of 4.9 and 5.6 percent, respectively, that NCES has been using in its recent projection work. The difference may be partly due to timing, as the BLS figures are based on data for 1983-84.[16] However, the fact that the SASS data yield an elementary attrition rate higher than the secondary rate is suspicious, considering that the opposite is true according to not only the BLS estimates but also most other attrition research.

The salient issue concerning the validity of Rollefson's figures is whether schools (i.e., school principals) are able to report with acceptable accuracy how many of their departing teachers have taken other teaching jobs. According to the SASS school-level data, the rate of attrition from the profession is less than half the rate of attrition from individual schools; that is, the majority of teachers who leave a particular school take jobs in other schools (Rollefson, 1990). Therefore, errors in reporting the leavers' destinations could easily distort the attrition rate estimates. An analysis of attrition rates based on the SASS individual-teacher data should give some indication of whether these errors are substantial.

Just before this review was completed, NCES released a report (Bobbitt et al., 1991) containing initial attrition rate estimates based on the aforementioned SASS individual teacher baseline and follow-up surveys. According to this report, 5.6 percent of public school teachers left the profession between 1987-88 and 1988-89 (5.5 percent of public elementary teachers and 5.6 percent of public secondary teachers). The corresponding rates for private school teachers were 12.6 percent at the elementary level, 12.9 percent at the secondary level, and 12.7 percent for both levels combined. The report also confirms the U-shaped form of the age-attrition profile, shows a higher attrition rate for women than for men (5.8 percent versus 5.1 percent among public school teachers), and provides disaggregated estimates of attrition by teacher experience, degree level, race/ethnicity, and subject specialty.

The overall public school attrition rate of 5.6 percent reported in Bobbitt et al. (1991) is sharply higher than the 4.1 percent rate reported by Rollefson (1990). Part of the difference may reflect the different time periods to which the two sets of estimates pertain (i.e., the estimates based on the school-level data are for leavers between 1986-87 and 1987-88, while the estimates based on the individual-teacher data are for the interval 1987-88 to 1988-89). Another part may stem from the fact that the 4.1 percent figure is for full-time teachers only, whereas the 5.6 percent figure includes part-time teachers as well. It is also quite possible, of course, that the 4.1 percent figure is understated because of principals' inability to distinguish teachers leaving the profession from teachers transferring to other teaching jobs. A full analysis of the discrepancies has not yet been undertaken. The estimates based on the individual-teacher data have the stronger a priori claim to validity, provided that it is kept in mind that they reflect rates of attrition of full-time and part-time teachers combined.

A more extensive attrition study based on the SASS individual-teacher data is now being conducted under a contract from NCES by MPR Associates, Inc., of Berkeley, California. The MPR work will include not only tabulations of attrition rates, such as those produced by NCES, but also multivariate analysis, using discrete-choice models, of influences on teachers' decisions to stay or leave. Results are expected in the latter half of 1992.

State Attrition Models

State models of teacher attrition (as of teacher supply and demand in general) vary widely in scope, detail, and analytical sophistication. The simplest attrition models merely apply an undifferentiated, statewide-average, time-invariant attrition rate to all categories of teachers. The more advanced models break down the attrition rate by age and subject specialty and apply the differentiated rates to numbers of teachers in each age-subject subcategory. The simpler models are of little methodological interest and are mentioned here only briefly. The bulk of this discussion focuses on the more elaborate methods.

Selected Simple Models

The simple, aggregative state attrition models are very similar to the models NCES has used to make national projections. A Nebraska study (Ostrander et al., 1988), for example, projects numbers of retainees by assuming a constant attrition rate of 9.0 percent for the period 1988-1994. An earlier California study (Cagampang et al., 1985) provides two alternative projections, one based on the assumption that the state's average attrition rate in the future will remain fixed at its base-year value, the other based on a time-trend extrapolation of average attrition rates of the 10 most recent years. Neither of these studies projects numbers of retainees by subject area, and neither takes into account the effect on the attrition rate of the changing age composition of the teaching force.

Perhaps also worth mentioning under the heading of simple models is one that circumvents attrition projections altogether. A study of teacher supply and demand in Maryland (Maryland State Department of Education, 1988) deals with the supply of new entrants in some detail but bypasses an analysis of retention by relying on reports from local school districts on expected numbers of continuing teachers and vacancies. Setting aside the question of how well local districts can project their own numbers of retainees, it should be noted that this procedure seems to neglect the important point that teachers who leave a particular district do not necessarily stop teaching in the state.

A model developed in South Carolina (South Carolina Department of Education, 1990) is one level more advanced than the simple models described above in that it breaks down attrition rates by subject area but not by age. In this model, state data files on individual teachers for the years 1985 and 1990 are used to determine net attrition rates during that five-year period for teachers in each of approximately 35 subject areas, and the resulting subject-specific rates are then used to project numbers of retainees by subject area five years into the future—that is, to 1995. (Net attrition is defined as the percentage of teachers who leave less the percentage who return during the five-year period.) The implicit assumption is that the net attrition rate in each subject area will remain fixed during the five-year projection period at the average rate observed during the five-year base period. The state's data base, it turns out, contains information on every teacher in the state from 1981-82 to the present, which means that annual attrition estimates could have been developed; also, the data base would apparently support breakdowns by age and, presumably, other teacher characteristics.[17] However, these features have not yet been incorporated into the South Carolina analysis.

Two other state studies, those for Ohio (Ohio Department of Education, 1988) and Wisconsin (Lauritzen and Friedman, 1991) produce subject-specific projections of numbers of entering teachers (new hires) but avoid having to project attrition by instead projecting numbers of entrants directly. In the Ohio analysis, this is accomplished by making the assumption that the percentage of all teachers who are new hires in each subject area will follow its historical trend. That is, the model first projects teacher employment by subject area (demand) on the basis of projected enrollment and extrapolated teacher-pupil ratios and then applies extrapolated new-hire percentages to the results to obtain estimates of future numbers of entrants. In most cases, the extrapolations are produced by fitting simple linear regression equations to the historical data, but in some instances, the new-hire percentages are estimated simply as averages of the actual percentages in a few recent years. Clearly, if numbers of new hires can be estimated independently, then projections of attrition are not needed to derive them. However, the Ohio method rests on the hard-to-defend premise that the number of new hires in each field—which, after all, reflects not only attrition but also changes in enrollment patterns and staffing ratios—will remain in a stable relationship over time to total teacher employment in the field.

Similarly, in the Wisconsin analysis (Lauritzen and Friedman, 1991), future numbers of new hires are projected by extrapolating from numbers of entrants in the past. The Wisconsin approach differs from Ohio's, however, in that the projections are not based on a statistical trend extrapolation method. Instead, the Wisconsin analysts apparently have assumed that certain ratios will remain constant over time—e.g., the ratio of the number of newly hired, inexperienced Wisconsin-trained teachers in a particular subject specialty to the number trained in that specialty in the previous year—and have projected future new hires on the basis of past averages of such ratios. Unfortunately, the specifics of the projection methodology are too vaguely described in the Wisconsin report to permit a more detailed explanation here. In any event, the key point is that the Wisconsin study does not use explicit attrition estimates (in conjunction with demand estimates) to estimate numbers of new hires needed in future years.

The absence from the Wisconsin study of attrition projections and estimates of the demand for new hires based on them is surprising because the same group of analysts examined attrition patterns in some detail in earlier studies. For example, a report issued one year earlier by Lauritzen and Friedman (1990) presents not only attrition rates by certification category but also age-attrition profiles for particular subject fields. With such information, the Wisconsin group should have been able to produce the same kinds of detailed retention estimates as in the more advanced models that I describe below.

More Advanced Models

Three state models that I have had the opportunity to review—those for Massachusetts, New York, and Connecticut—project the supply of retained teachers on the basis of detailed attrition rates, disaggregated both by the teacher's age and the teacher's subject specialty or field of certification. I provide brief explanations of how each state model develops and uses the disaggregated attrition-rate figures as well as comments on selected methodological points.

New York The New York teacher retention model (New York State Education Department, 1990) projects numbers of retained classroom teachers on the basis of separate retention rates for 15 subject areas and 7 age brackets: under 35, 35-39, 40-44, 45-49, 50-54, 55-59, and 60 and older. The retention rate for each age-subject subcategory is derived by comparing individual teacher records for the two most recent years for which data are available and determining the percentage of teachers present in the earlier year who were present in the later year as well. To project numbers of retained teachers, the New York analysts assume (implicitly) that the retention rate for teachers in each subject area and age bracket will remain constant at its base-year value over a five-year projection period. Accordingly, they apply the aforesaid retention rates to the base-year (1988-89) teaching force to project 1989-90 retainees; then apply the same rates to the projected 1989-90 teaching force to project 1990-91 retainees; and so forth for years through 1993-94.

In addition to the attrition estimates themselves, a logically necessary element of such a model is a set of assumptions concerning the age distribution of newly hired teachers in each subject area. That is, in each year after the base year, the teaching force consists partly of retained teachers and partly of newly hired teachers, which means that information on the age distribution of the latter as well as the former is needed to project retention in subsequent years.[18] The New York report says nothing about these assumptions. However, data tables provided to me separately by the New York State Department of Education include breakdowns of new hires by age for the base year, which suggests that the age distribution of newly hired teachers in years 1989-90 to 1992-93 was probably assumed to be the same as the distribution in 1988-89.

An important limiting feature of the New York model is the assumption that the attrition rate for each subject area and age will remain constant for the whole five-year projection period. (As will be seen, this assumption is not peculiar to the New York analysis but is shared by the Connecticut and Massachusetts models as well.) Several studies have shown that attrition rates vary substantially over time and have suggested that the rates are sensitive to market conditions prevailing in different periods (Grissmer and Kirby, 1987, 1991; Murnane and Olsen, 1990). With the multiyear teacher data files available to New York, it would be feasible to determine empirically whether the assumption of constant rates is warranted and, if not, to use some method—even if nothing more than trend extrapolation—to allow for changes in the age-specific, subject-specific attrition rates over time.

A more specialized feature of the New York model that deserves scrutiny is that its age strata are defined in a way that masks the attrition rates of young, recently trained teachers. The lowest age stratum considered in the model, teachers younger than 35, includes, without differentiation, teachers in their first year of service and teachers with as much as 10 to 12 years of experience. Yet research has shown that attrition rates are much higher during the initial years of teaching than just a few years later (see, e.g., Grissmer and Kirby, 1987). Combining new teachers—those in the first 3 to 5 years of teaching—with teachers with 10 or more years of experience seems on its face to be an unpromising idea. The New York data base would certainly support finer disaggregation at the low end of the teacher age scale.

Connecticut The Connecticut model (Connecticut Board of Education, 1988) projects the supply of retained teachers on the basis of age-specific attrition rates for six subject-area categories of classroom teachers plus two categories of staff other than classroom teachers. The classroom-teacher categories are labeled (1) elementary, (2) special education and bilingual education, (3) mathematics, chemistry, physics, and computer science, (4) teachers of required secondary subjects other than those in category 3 (i.e., teachers of English, social studies, biology, and earth science), (5) teachers of elective secondary subjects (foreign language, business and office practices, industrial arts, and other vocational fields), and (6) teachers described as "K-12 specials" (art, music, and physical education). The two nonteacher categories are "support staff, librarians, and media specialists," and "administration" (the latter including district-level as well as building-level administrators and supervisors). Age-specific attrition rates within each category are computed for the base year 1986-87 by determining how many teachers employed at the beginning of the prior year did not return at the beginning of the 1986-87 school year.

The Connecticut model projects numbers of retained teachers for all school years through 2000-2001 by applying the aforesaid attrition rates, year by year, to data on the composition of the teaching force by category and age. (There is some ambiguity in the Connecticut report as to whether the attrition rates used for this purpose pertain to individual years of age or to five-year age brackets; however, the latter seems more likely because tables in the report present attrition rates for five-year intervals from 20-24 to 65-69.[19]) The very strong implicit assumption underlying these projections is that the attrition rates of teachers in each staff category and age bracket will remain constant over the whole 14-year projection period.

Assumptions about the age composition of newly hired teachers are particularly important in the Connecticut model because of the unusually long period for which projections are offered. At the average annual attrition rate of 5.8 percent cited in the Connecticut report, only about 43 percent of the initial teaching force would remain after 14 years, while the other 57 percent of the force would consist of teachers hired during the period. Therefore, estimates of the number of retained teachers, especially for the later years, depend strongly on whether new hires are assumed to be young, inexperienced teachers (presumably with high attrition rates) or older, more experienced teachers (presumably with lower attrition rates). According to the report, the Connecticut projections rest on the assumption that the age distribution of future entrants will be the same as that of entrants in the base year (1986-87). The report also refers, however, to an alternative "theoretical" age distribution for new hires derived from certain assumptions about future changes in the mix of sources of entering teachers. Exactly how this alternative distribution was derived is not explained, however, and, in any case, it does not seem to have been used in the projections. Nevertheless, the discussion of such a distribution does raise the important issue of whether analysts can do better than simply to assume that the composition of new hires will be the same in the future as in the past.

The Connecticut report also contains, in an appendix, a more detailed analysis of attrition that takes into account gender and part-time status as well as age and subject and examines attrition patterns in 24 staff categories rather than the 8 described above. This analysis apparently uses multivariate techniques to sort out the effects of different teacher attributes on the propensity to leave teaching, but the specific multivariate statistical method is not explained. The extended analysis makes it possible, among other things, to distinguish differences in attrition rates associated with subject specialty per se from differences due to the varying age and gender composition of different fields. In addition, it demonstrates significant male-female differences in attrition patterns, confirming a finding that has emerged in recent econometric studies of teacher attrition. Thus far, however, it appears that the results of this interesting part of the Connecticut work have not been reflected in supply projections.

The Connecticut model shares with the New York model the dubious assumption that all the age-specific, subject-specific attrition rates will remain constant at their base-year values over all years for which projections are made. If anything, that assumption is less tenable in the Connecticut case because of the unusually lengthy projection period. Connecticut, like New York, has multiyear data on individual teachers and has been in the business of calculating disaggregated attrition rates for some time. In fact, an earlier study (Prowda and Grissmer, 1986), generated the same types of age-specific, subject-area-specific attrition rates for 1983-84 as are described here for 1986-87. The information would seem to be available, therefore, to determine whether the disaggregated attrition rates have changed systematically over time and, if so, to make some allowance for changes in the future.

A more specific question concerning the design of the Connecticut model is why teachers are grouped into only six categories and, especially, why into the six categories listed above. Some of the subject-area groupings combine teacher categories that are (1) known to have different attrition rates and (2) unlikely to experience similar changes in demand in the future. For example, special education teachers are combined with bilingual teachers; physics and chemistry teachers are grouped together with mathematics teachers; teachers of biology and earth sciences are grouped with teachers of English and social studies; and foreign language teachers are combined with teachers of vocational education. Some realignment of these categories seems desirable. Moreover, the availability of a more detailed breakdown of teachers into 24 categories, as mentioned above, indicates that both realignment and further disaggregation are feasible.

Massachusetts The MISER model for Massachusetts (Coelen and Wilson, 1987, 1991a) disaggregates retention rates by age (five-year age brackets) and into 20 staff categories. The latter include 17 subject-area categories plus administration, counseling, and media/librarian. The task of estimating age-specific retention rates for each category appears to have been considerably more complicated for Massachusetts than for New York or Connecticut because of serious limitations of the available data files. Without attempting to go into detail, the basic problem seems to be that data on actual subject-area assignments of individual teachers were not available, making it necessary to draw on teacher certification files and aggregate staffing data rather than teacher assignment data and to rely on various assumptions and imputations to disaggregate the teaching force by both age and subject.[20] But in principle, if not in practice, the method of measuring retention is the same as in New York and Connecticut: annual retention rates are obtained by determining what percentage of teachers in each age-subject category employed in a given year are still employed in the following year.

The Massachusetts study differs from the New York and Connecticut analyses in that its attrition rate estimates are based on multiyear attrition data rather than only on data for a single base year but, unfortunately, the potential advantages of having multiyear data seem not to have been realized. Data on Massachusetts teachers were available for the 13 school years from 1973-74 to 1985-86, making it possible to compute 12 sets of year-to-year retention rates. According to Coelen and Wilson (1991a), the retention rates actually used to project numbers of retainees in each staff category and age bracket are historical averages of the past rates. Based on further inquiry, however, it appears that the projections reflect only the last few years of subject-specific attrition data and only the most recent age profiles of attrition. There is considerable ambiguity about exactly how the rates used in the projection models were derived (the MISER report itself is not forthcoming on this matter), but two points do seem clear: (1) the rates used in the projections do not reflect an analysis of how attrition rates are likely to change over time, and (2) the rates used are assumed to remain constant throughout the 10-year period, 1986-87 to 1995-96, for which projections are offered.

The rationale for assuming that attrition rates will remain fixed in the future at their recent historical levels is, according to Coelen and Wilson (1991a), that there has been little variability in Massachusetts attrition rates over the years. It seems, however, that this contention is not well supported by the data. Both a table of retention rates by five-year age brackets (Coelen and Wilson, 1987:Table 12) and a set of time-trend regression equations (Table 14) show upward trends in attrition (declining rates of retention) during the period for which data are available.[21] Therefore, unless rates stabilize or the historical trend reverses itself, the likely effect of basing projections on fixed historical rates will be to overestimate retention and consequently to underestimate the number of new teachers to be hired.

Like the New York and Connecticut models, the Massachusetts model also relies on the assumption that the age composition of new hires by subject area will be the same throughout the projection period as in the base period. Although multiyear data on these age distributions are available, they are not used to explain or project trends (if any) in the ages of entrants. The Massachusetts model does go beyond the New York and Connecticut models, however, in that it breaks down new hires into three categories—reentering teachers, new entrants with certification, and new entrants hired under waivers of certification—and attributes separate age distributions to each. This makes sense because the new teachers and the reentering teachers are likely to have quite different age distributions. Whether this form of disaggregation improves the projections also depends, however, on whether the future mix of new and reentering teachers can be estimated satisfactorily—a question taken up in the following major section.

The MISER Multistate Model

As explained earlier, the analysts at MISER who developed the Massachusetts model are now engaged in a larger-scale effort to construct the NEDSAD (Northeast Educator Supply and Demand) model for the New England states and New York. According to preliminary model specifications (Coelen and Wilson, 1991b), the treatment of teacher retention in this multistate analysis will be behavioral. Specifically, retention rates are to be estimated and projected as functions of teacher age, sex, and assignment; the female fertility rate by age (included because of a presumed relationship to the differential female rate of "stopping out"); and the relative teacher salary by assignment (subject) category. Successful empirical implementation of such a model would represent an important step forward in the state of the art.

One aspect of the proposed model design is very disappointing, however, and seems to merit reconsideration. According to the preliminary model specifications (Coelen and Wilson, 1991b), only state-aggregate data on attrition rates within teacher categories (defined by age, sex, and subject specialty) will be used to model attrition behavior and then to project the future supply of retained teachers. If this is indeed to be the NEDSAD approach, a valuable opportunity will have been lost or deferred. The individual-teacher data bases, assembled by MISER at great effort and expense, would support detailed and sophisticated attrition models, similar to those developed by Murnane and his associates and by Grissmer and Kirby at RAND (and which are discussed below). In fact, such models could deal with many more individual-teacher, district-level, and state-level influences on attrition than those mentioned in MISER's preliminary specifications. A model based only on aggregated data would be unlikely to yield satisfactory estimates of the effects of salaries and other causal factors on rates of attrition. Whether the potential benefits of the MISER effort will be realized depends to a considerable degree, therefore, on how this issue of level of aggregation is resolved.

Assessment of National and State Models

Although the foregoing review is not comprehensive, it does provide a reasonably good basis for assessing the present state of the art in projecting the supply of retained teachers at the national and state levels. In the following remarks, I confine myself to assessing the models on their own terms; that is, I take as given that the objective is limited to projecting numbers of retained teachers and refrain from criticizing models because they are nonbehavioral and do not deal with teacher quality.

The main attribute that now distinguishes relatively respectable attrition models from crude ones is disaggregation of attrition rates by age. Such disaggregation is essential to take into account the changes in overall attrition rates (in the aggregate and by field) that occur naturally, without any change in teacher or employer behavior, simply as a result of the changing age composition of the teaching force. Disaggregation by age requires data at the individual teacher level, but not all states with individual-teacher files have made the transition to working with age-specific attrition rates. For instance, both Ohio and South Carolina seem to have the data needed to measure attrition by age, but both rely on average attrition rates (by subject area) to make projections. The most important step forward that they and other similarly situated states could take would be to shift to the types of disaggregated models developed for New York, Connecticut, and Massachusetts. States without statewide individual teacher data files would, of course, have to develop such data bases to be able to compete in the same league.

A serious limitation of the models that do disaggregate by age is adherence to the assumption that age-specific attrition rates will be the same in the future as in the period for which data are available. This assumption is not supported by the historical data, and there is little reason to believe that it will prove valid in the future. The developers of the New York, Connecticut, and Massachusetts models all had multiyear data to work with and could have tried to model changes in age-specific, subject-specific rates over time, but the New York and Connecticut analyses do not draw on the multiyear data at all, and the Massachusetts analysis does not use the longitudinal information effectively. Even relatively simple trend extrapolations of the detailed attrition rates would seem preferable to the currently prevailing constant-rate assumption.

The same criticism applies to the practice of assuming that the age distribution of new hires will remain fixed, even when multiyear data are available that could show whether and how those distributions have been changing. Moreover, the failure to distinguish (except in the Massachusetts model) between new entrants and returning teachers in characterizing the age distribution of new hires is an easily correctable flaw.

There seem to be some major weaknesses in the methods used to disaggregate the supply of retained teachers by subject, but I say this hesitantly because these methods often go unexplained. One question is how teachers are categorized by subject for the purpose of modeling attrition. I suspect that they are often classified only by primary subject taught, which, if true, raises concerns about whether turnover rates are being measured correctly, especially in fields that teachers are likely to teach as sidelines. A related question is how teachers with multiple certifications are treated. Ideally, the projections would take into account the subjects that retained teachers are qualified to teach as well as the subjects they actually taught in the prior year, but no extant model, to my knowledge, has this capability. Consequently, the models may stimulate undue alarm about inadequate supply in particular subject areas. A third related question is how the models deal with teachers who transfer among fields. The logic of a subject-specific model would seem to require treating each such teacher as a leaver from one field and an entrant into the other, but there is no indication in the reports I have reviewed that this is actually done. The usual approach, I suspect, is to categorize teachers only according to the subject they taught initially, and then to ask only whether they return in the following year, not whether they return to teach the same subject. If my suspicion is correct, both the projections of subject-specific retainees and subject-specific entrants may be distorted.

Finally, although the strong connection between age and attrition has been taken into account in some state projection models, there has been no such recognition of the relationships of attrition rates to other personal characteristics of teachers. In particular, none of the models that I have examined reflects the now well-established findings that attrition rates vary by gender and race and perhaps by marital status and full-time or part-time employment. The Connecticut report (Connecticut Board of Education, 1988) is unique in that it includes a supplementary analysis of the relationship of attrition to age, gender, and full-time/part-time status, but the results have not yet been used for projections. Bringing some of the additional factors into the models would be an improvement. However, to deal with additional variables would probably require switching from simply computing average attrition rates for different subcategories of teachers to inferring the rates from a multivariate statistical model. Such models have already been developed in research on attrition (see below). Applying them to supply projections is likely to be the next major advance in the state of the art.

Research on Patterns and Determinants of Attrition

Apart from efforts to project national and state supplies of retained teachers, major progress has been made during the last few years in research on the patterns and determinants of teacher attrition. The key to these efforts is the exploitation of large-scale state data files, especially longitudinal files, on individual teachers. Using such data, researchers have been able both to characterize teacher attrition (and reentry) rates in considerable detail and to construct multivariate behavioral models that link attrition rates to economic and policy variables as well as to the teachers' own characteristics. The most important efforts along this line are those of Richard Murnane and his associates at Harvard and David Grissmer and his colleagues at the RAND Corporation, and it is mainly their work that I report on here.

The empirical research on teacher attrition has been conducted with two types of data bases: cross-sectional and longitudinal. Each supports different types of analyses and different analytical methods. A cross-sectional data set contains observations at a single point in time of all teachers, or a sample of teachers, teaching in a state or in the nation. A longitudinal data base provides repeated (time-series) observations on members of particular cohorts of teachers—e.g., all teachers who began teaching in a state in 1975. The individuals represented in each cohort are homogeneous with respect to time of entry and, in some cases, age as well, and the longitudinal data make it possible to follow their careers over some period of years.[22] It is possible, by collecting longitudinal data on enough different cohorts or, alternatively, collecting cross-sectional data for many years, to have the best of both worlds—that is, to be able to carry out both cross-sectional and longitudinal analyses with the same data base. Thus far, only an Indiana study by Grissmer and Kirby (1991), which has assembled 24 sets of annual observations on all teachers in the state, is in this enviable position.

Cross-Sectional Analyses

The disaggregated state modeling efforts described above are all cross-sectional attrition analyses of a sort, in that they yield information on how teacher attrition rates vary with age and subject specialty, but they are very limited analyses in several respects. They do not take into account other factors associated with differences in attrition rates, do not examine the dynamics of attrition, and do not apply the multivariate tools needed to sort out the marginal effects of, and interactions among, the various determinants of attrition. Much more could be learned about attrition by analyzing in greater depth the data bases that some of these states have already used to project numbers of retained teachers.

The Connecticut report (Connecticut Board of Education, 1988) is somewhat more advanced than its counterparts in this regard because it supplements its projections with a more complete analysis of the determinants of attrition (found in an appendix and separate from the projection model). The main purpose of this analysis is to estimate the differences in attrition rates among subject areas that remain after controlling statistically for the age, gender, and full-time or part-time status of the teachers in each field. Unfortunately, no details on the analytical method are provided—not even whether the multivariate analysis was conducted with individual-level or aggregated data, so there is no way to judge whether the analysis provides a prototype potentially useful to other states.

The most important cross-sectional attrition studies of which I am aware are the 1987 and 1991 RAND Corporation contributions by Grissmer and Kirby.[23] The 1987 Grissmer-Kirby report, *Teacher Attrition: The Uphill Climb to Staff the Nation's Schools*, contributes to understanding teacher turnover by bringing together and comparing attrition data (mainly cross-sectional) for several states and providing a detailed theoretical framework within which the empirical evidence can be interpreted. The study also offers a set of proposals for improving data on teacher attrition, some of which are now reflected in the NCES Schools and Staffing Survey.

The Grissmer-Kirby theoretical framework draws on theories of human capital, career progression, and imperfect information in the labor market. It explains, among other things:

- The many factors that produce U-shaped age-attrition profiles—high attrition rates for the youngest and oldest teachers and much lower attrition rates for those in between;
- Why the U-shaped curves are likely to have different shapes for men and women, with higher attrition rates for women in the early years of teaching;
- How differences in opportunities outside teaching (opportunity costs) for teachers trained in different disciplines lead to differences in attrition rates among subject areas;
- Why the influence of salaries and working conditions on attrition is likely to diminish as teachers progress in their teaching careers; and
- How changing economic and demographic conditions may cause the whole attrition profile (i.e., the U-shaped age-attrition curves) to be higher in some periods than in others.

Grissmer and Kirby (1987) use cross-sectional data for six states (cross-sections for multiple years in most instances) to support their theoretical hypotheses. By comparing the U-shaped age-attrition profiles for different groups, they are able to confirm that attrition patterns differ for men and women, for elementary and secondary teachers, and for teachers specializing in different subject areas. Then, using time-trend data from several states, they are able to demonstrate that overall attrition rates declined substantially from the 1960s and 1970s to the 1980s. They also present evidence that these declines are explainable only in part by the changing age composition (i.e., the aging) of the teaching force during the period in question and that attrition rates declined as well among teachers within specific age groups.

The 1987 Grissmer-Kirby analysis is not statistically elaborate. Its empirical contribution consists mainly of presenting and comparing age-attrition profiles. It offers no multivariate analysis of attrition, much less any behavioral model. Nevertheless, it has played an important role as catalyst and precursor by focusing attention on two central aspects of attrition analysis: (1) the underlying demographic determinants of attrition and (2) the dramatic but as yet inadequately explained changes in attrition patterns that have occurred over the years.

In their new study of Indiana, Grissmer and Kirby (1991) are able to explore the same and other aspects of attrition with a larger and richer data base—one containing data on all teachers employed in that state (about 50,000 at any one time) in each of 24 years. The cross-sectional, descriptive portion of this analysis reconfirms that age-attrition profiles conform to the classic U-shaped pattern, but, in addition, the availability of 24 years of data makes it possible to examine in detail how the level and shape of these U-shaped curves vary over time. Grissmer and Kirby are able to show a continuing decline in these curves from 1965 to 1987. They also report that the dynamics of attrition have been different for women and men: the level of the attrition curve for women has declined more rapidly than the level of the curve for men, to the extent that male and female departure rates nearly converged by the mid-1980s. These findings reinforce the conclusion that using a fixed set of attrition rates to project numbers of retained teachers 5 or 10 years into the future is not a satisfactory procedure. The most important contribution of the Grissmer-Kirby work on Indiana is not this cross-sectional analysis, however, but rather a multivariate analysis of longitudinal data on entering cohorts, described separately below.

The only multivariate attrition analysis based on cross-sectional data that has come to my attention is a study of teachers in Washington State by Theobald (1990). This study uses three sets of annual data on all certificated teachers in Washington (for school years 1984-85, 1985-86, and 1986-87) to investigate variations in, and determinants of, the rates at which teachers left their districts (i.e., the study is of district-level rather than state-level attrition). Theobald presents a multivariate, discrete-choice model in which each teacher's decision to leave or stay is represented as a function of (1) an array of individual teacher characteristics, including age, sex, race, years of experience, degree level, assignment (elementary or secondary), and, notably, the teacher's projected next-year salary and (2) a set of school district characteristics, including racial/ethnic composition of the student body, staff/pupil ratio, per-pupil spending, per-pupil tax base (assessed property value), enrollment, and the county unemployment rate (the last taken as an indicator of employment opportunities outside teaching). Using a maximum-likelihood probit estimation procedure, Theobald is able to derive estimates of the degree to which each of the aforesaid variables adds to or subtracts from the probability that a teacher will leave his or her district in a given year.

Theobald's findings are compatible in most respects with those of the Grissmer-Kirby studies (and of the longitudinal analyses reported later). Theobald captures the U-shaped form of the age-attrition relationship by representing attrition as a quadratic function of age. He shows that the attrition curves differ for men and women and that age and gender interact—that is, attrition rates are higher for young women than for young men but lower for older women than for older men. He also finds that teachers with higher degrees (men) tend to leave sooner than teachers without them (although some of the former "leave" by becoming administrators). Of special interest, he demonstrates that higher-salaried teachers (again, especially men) are more likely to stay. He also shows influences on attrition rates of both district wealth and staff/pupil ratios, although the proper interpretations of these results seem to be uncertain.

Apart from the particular findings, Theobald's work is significant for demonstrating that a useful analysis of attrition patterns can be conducted with cross-sectional data. This demonstration is important in connection with national-level modeling based on the SASS teacher survey data. The previously mentioned multivariate analysis of the SASS data by MPR Associates, Inc. is likely to rely on techniques similar to those used by Theobald (logit or probit modeling with multilevel data), and thus the Theobald work may provide a helpful prototype.

Longitudinal Analyses of Entering Teacher Cohorts

By following cohorts of entering teachers over time, it becomes possible to move from snapshot studies of attrition during a particular year to longitudinal analysis of teacher career paths. With longitudinal data, one can focus on the *duration* of each entering teacher's employment and on the factors associated with differences in length of stay. Moreover, one can consider not only whether teachers leave teaching at some point in their careers but also whether they return later (and, if so, when) and how long they remain in the teaching force the second time, or subsequent times, around. The combination of longitudinal data bases with the recently developed statistical techniques of survival and hazard modeling (see below) creates favorable conditions for developing useful behavioral models of the supply of retained teachers.

In a series of recent articles, Richard Murnane and his colleagues have analyzed the career paths of entering teacher cohorts in detail, considering both attrition after initial entry into teaching and the likelihood of commencing and continuing subsequent teaching spells. Working primarily with data from Michigan and North Carolina, they have been able to relate teacher entry, persistence, and exit behaviors not only to the teachers' own characteristics but also to salaries, opportunity costs, and various school district characteristics. Although the findings in their present form are not directly usable for projections, this line of work could eventually lead to a new class of behavioral projection models.

In a study of Michigan public school teachers who entered teaching in 1972 or 1973, Murnane et al. (1988) use the statistical technique of *proportional hazards modeling* to relate the length of stay in teaching to the teacher's age, sex, and subject specialty. They find, as expected, that younger teachers leave sooner than older teachers and women leave sooner than men; but they also report a strong interaction effect between age and sex—namely, that the male-female difference in the attrition rate exists for younger (under 30) entrants only. They also find important differences in attrition patterns by subject field.[24] Controlling for age and gender, teachers of chemistry and physics are likely to leave teaching the soonest (i.e., their attrition rates in the early years are the highest); teachers of English are the next most likely to leave; and teachers of other subjects tend to remain longer. Interestingly, teachers of mathematics, often lumped together with science teachers in discussions of "shortage," are not among those with particularly high attrition rates—a finding that has since been corroborated by other studies.

In a farther-reaching study of entering Michigan teachers (entrants between 1972 and 1975) Murnane and Olsen (1989) examine the relationship of attrition not only to age, gender, and subject specialty but also to salaries in teaching, salaries in occupations outside teaching, and a variety of school district characteristics. The inclusion of these additional variables puts the analysis into a different class from the analyses described previously, as it introduces the possibility of linking attrition to economic conditions and policy variables as well as to characteristics of the teachers themselves. In this study, Murnane and Olsen use an analytical method known as *waiting time regression* to relate the duration of each teacher's stay in teaching (and hence, the rate of attrition) to the aforesaid set of explanatory variables. In addition to confirming the same general age, gender, and subject-field effects on attrition as in the Michigan study cited just above, they show that (1) higher-paid teachers are likely to remain in teaching longer and (2) teachers prepared in fields that offer higher salaries outside teaching (especially chemistry and physics) are likely to leave sooner. These findings support the views that teacher supply is sensitive to the relative salary level in teaching and that salary movements can play the same role in equilibrating supply and demand in teaching as they do in labor markets generally.

Murnane and his associates have also worked extensively with data on entering teacher cohorts in North Carolina. In Murnane et al. (1989), hazard models are used to analyze attrition/retention patterns among individuals in that state who entered teaching in 1976 and 1978.[25] These models, which are constructed separately for elementary and secondary teachers, relate each teacher's length of stay to age, gender, the age-gender interaction, subject specialty, selected district characteristics, salary, and—a unique feature—the teacher's score on the National Teacher Examination (NTE). As in the Michigan study, attrition is higher in the initial years of teaching than in later years; there are significant differences in median duration among subject specialties; and higher salaries are associated with higher retention rates, but with the influence of salary on retention diminishing over time. In addition, the North Carolina analysis yields the striking finding that teachers who score higher on the NTE tend to leave sooner—that is, higher-quality teachers (to the extent that NTE score signifies quality) are less likely to remain in the retained teaching force.[26] This demonstration, in a multivariate framework, that NTE scores are negatively associated with retention rates appears to be the closest that anyone has yet come to dealing with teacher quality in an analysis of teacher supply.

In another North Carolina study, Murnane and Olsen (1990) use the aforementioned waiting-time regression technique to analyze attrition patterns among teachers who began their careers in the years 1979 to 1984. The principal findings, this time reflecting data on a larger number of entering cohorts, reinforce those of the study mentioned just above: (1) there are important differences in expected duration among subject areas, with teachers of chemistry and physics likely to leave soonest, teachers of English likely to leave somewhat later, and elementary teachers and—again—mathematics teachers likely to remain the longest; (2) better-paid teachers are likely to remain in the profession longer than lower-paid teachers; and (3) teachers with relatively high NTE scores are likely to leave sooner than their lower-scoring colleagues. In addition, this study demonstrates that attrition rates depend on certain characteristics of local school districts, such as size, income, and socioeconomic composition, as well as on characteristics of the teachers themselves. Differences in these characteristics, according to the authors, may serve as proxies for differences in teachers' working conditions, which, in theory, should affect attrition in much the same way as differences in salaries. Finally, the study demonstrates that intercohort differences in attrition patterns persist even when all the other factors mentioned above are held constant, confirming that the standard projection-model assumption of constant rates is unfounded.

The Grissmer and Kirby (1991) study of Indiana, described earlier, offers two different longitudinal analyses of the attrition behavior of entering cohorts. In the first analysis, all individuals who began teaching in years 1965-66 to 1982-83 (18 successive cohorts) are followed through the year 1988. Using a proportional hazards model, Grissmer and Kirby relate each individual's duration in teaching to the individual's age, gender, subject specialty, and year of entry. The findings fit closely with others reported above: the age profiles have the usual shape; similar male-female differences appear; and the differences in attrition patterns among subject areas resemble those found in other states. In addition, year of entry clearly matters, reinforcing the point that it is inappropriate to assume constancy of attrition rates over time.

In their second analysis, Grissmer and Kirby again use proportional hazards modeling but, in this instance, they focus exclusively on attrition during the first four years of teaching among those who entered the profession between 1965-66 and 1985-86 (21 entering cohorts). The models, estimated separately for men and women, relate duration in teaching not only to age and subject specialty but also to each individual's starting salary, the teacher-pupil ratio in the individual's district, and, as options, the general labor force participation rate in the economy and the median income of full-time workers. The rationales for the last two factors are, respectively, that the labor force participation rate is an indicator of alternative economic opportunities, especially for women, and that the median income of workers is a proxy for the level of compensation outside teaching. With these models, Grissmer and Kirby are able to show that early attrition rates are (1) highly sensitive to salary, corroborating the findings of Murnane's Michigan and North Carolina studies, and (2) sensitive to working conditions as well, insofar as these are represented by the teacher-pupil ratio. They also find that declining female attrition rates are associated with the increasing labor market participation rate for women. They are not able, however, to demonstrate an effect of earnings outside teaching, possibly because their median income variable is too crude an indicator of the opportunity wage.

Assessment and Implications

Teacher attrition is a field in which research seems to be playing just the right roles in relation to practice—opening up new issues, generating new knowledge, and yielding both analytical methods and substantive findings that can be put to practical use. The attrition studies described above have already produced important information that we can expect to see reflected, sooner rather than later, in state and national models for projecting the supply of retained teachers. Moreover, this line of research is relatively new, and its potential has only begun to be explored; if it continues, more practical applications are likely to follow. In particular, the possibility seems well within reach of developing a new class of research-based, behavioral, attrition projection models.

Among the potential direct and immediate contributions of the research to projection modeling, I would cite the following:

• Findings about the U-shaped age-attrition profiles are so compelling that they should convince any state or local model developer who does not already disaggregate attrition rates by age (and who has individual-teacher data) that such disaggregation is essential.

• Research findings concerning attrition-rate differences among categories of teachers should guide model developers in disaggregating their projections by subject specialty and grade level.

• Findings about male-female differences in attrition patterns, which are not currently reflected in projection models, can easily be incorporated into models based on individual-teacher data.

• The strong indications from the research that attrition rates vary over time should help convince model developers to abandon the assumption that rates will remain constant and to introduce time-varying rates into their projections, even if, initially, these are based on nothing more than trend extrapolations.

I would place in a different category research findings pertaining to the effects on attrition of such factors as teacher salaries, opportunity wages outside teaching, working conditions, and other characteristics of schools and school systems. Although the findings to date demonstrate that such factors influence attrition, the model specifications and measures on which they are based are not yet well enough developed to yield good estimates of the magnitudes of the effects. As examples, measures of opportunity wages are crude; only a few rough indicators of working conditions have been tested (and those may not be measured at the appropriate level of aggregation); and the effects of such other factors as pupil composition, size of school, and type of community have not been examined systematically. Also, models that allow for both time-varying factors and time-varying effects of each factor apparently have not yet been applied to the attrition problem. Thus, although the relevance of behavioral attrition models has been established, considerably more work on model design will be needed before such models can be developed for practical use.

MODELS OF THE SUPPLY OF ENTERING TEACHERS AND THE SUPPLY-DEMAND BALANCE

According to the conceptual scheme underlying, or implicit in, most efforts to model teacher supply and demand, projections of the supply of entering teachers should provide the third and final ingredient needed to assess the future supply-demand balance. The two model components discussed in previous sections, projections of demand and projections of numbers of retained teachers, taken together, yield estimates of future demands for new hires, and comparisons between the projected numbers of new hires and the projected supply of entrants should lead to conclusions about the adequacy of supply and the likelihood of future shortages or surpluses. This implicit modeling strategy is only slightly closer to accomplishment today, however, than it was five years ago—the principal reason being that projecting the supply of entrants has remained an intractable problem. I would adhere today to the conclusions I expressed in my earlier review (Barro, 1986):

> Projecting the supply of [entering] teachers, and hence the total teacher supply, is beyond the capacity of all the current models. The methods that have been proposed for making such projections have fatal conceptual flaws, and the results—though perhaps useful for some purposes—cannot legitimately be labeled supply projections. Little credence should be given, therefore, to any findings of "shortage" or "surplus" based on comparisons between projections of demand and purported projections of supply.

This negative general conclusion notwithstanding, there is some positive news to report. Some modest steps toward improved teacher supply modeling have been taken in recent years. More state studies now take account of multiple sources of teacher supply, including the supply of returning former teachers and other hires from the "reserve pool"; fewer focus solely on the flow of new graduates from teacher training institutions, as most studies did in the past. There seems to be heightened awareness of key conceptual problems in modeling the supply of entrants—for instance, that past rates of entry into teaching were determined more by demand than by supply—even though methods for dealing satisfactorily with these problems have not yet been developed. Perhaps most encouraging, researchers have begun to deal analytically and behaviorally with certain pieces of the supply problem and to create the large-scale data bases needed to support further analytical efforts. Thus, although the basic problem remains unsolved, it does not follow that nothing worthwhile has been accomplished.

Considerations in Modeling the Supply of Entrants

Given the present undeveloped state of models for projecting the supply of entering teachers, it is at least as important to focus on conceptual issues and general approaches as on specific modeling techniques. The following are some of the key issues and considerations.

Definitions and Concepts of Supply

The supply of entering teachers in a state or in the nation is the number of persons (not already teaching) who are available and willing to take teaching jobs. Like the demand for teachers, the supply of teachers is contingent on multiple factors, including the standards that an individual must meet to be deemed eligible to teach and the salaries, benefits, and working conditions that prospective employers are offering. Thus, it is meaningful to speak of the current or projected supply of entrants under currently prevailing conditions (current certification standards, salary schedules, etc.) and the altered levels of supply that would correspond to alternative sets of conditions. Ideally, a projection model would yield a mathematical relationship between the supply of entrants and all the aforesaid factors. Thus far, however, we have yet to achieve even the more modest goal of projecting supply under the assumption that all pertinent factors will remain fixed at their current values.

The key conceptual problem in projecting supply (or even in measuring the current supply) is inherent in defining supply in terms of the availability and willingness of eligible persons to take teaching jobs. Availability and willingness are unobservable mental states. What one does observe with the personnel data normally obtainable are the numbers of persons actually hired as entering teachers, not the numbers who would have taken positions had they been offered. The number of persons willing to supply their services as teachers in a state might be 10 percent, 50 percent, 100 percent, or 500 percent greater than the number actually hired; there is no way to determine the supply of would-be entrants from employment or hiring data alone.

But, one might object, the same holds true of demand. The demand for teachers is defined as the number that school systems are able and willing to pay for (of specified quality, at specified salaries, etc.), but all one can observe is how many teachers districts actually employ, not the possibly larger number that they might employ if more qualified applicants were available. This apparent symmetry is misleading, however. Generally speaking, the teacher market in the nation and in the states, albeit with local and subject-specific exceptions, is characterized by excess supply—more trained and eligible applicants than there are teaching jobs. States and school systems, for the most part, can obtain the aggregate numbers of teachers (if not the precise characteristics of teachers) that they want. If they attract too few applicants, they can relax their hiring standards. In other words, setting aside the quality issue, the number of teachers actually employed closely approximates the number demanded. In contrast, not all applicants for teaching jobs are able to obtain them. The number of teachers employed is smaller than total teacher supply, and the number of entering teachers hired each year usually falls short of the number seeking teaching positions.

The implication for projection modeling is that, although one can approximate future demand by projecting employment, one cannot estimate the future supply of entrants by projecting the number of teachers hired. The number hired ordinarily reflects only a fraction of the supply—namely, teachers actually selected for employment. Consequently, no analog of the previously described mechanical approach to projecting demand and attrition is available for projecting the supply of would-be entrants into teaching. The supply of entering teachers must be inferred indirectly rather than merely extrapolated, but such inference requires methods more sophisticated and demanding of data than any currently employed.

Faced with uncertainty about what one should project under the heading "supply of entering teachers," model developers have generally fallen back on one or the other of two unsatisfactory conceptions of supply. One notion is that the future supply of potential entrants into teaching can be represented by projecting the number of persons with teaching certificates and/or the annual increment therein. The other is that the supply of entrants can be projected by applying projected entry rates, based on actual entry rates observed in the past, to the numbers of persons in various pools from which teachers are drawn. Neither is logically sound. The details are spelled out later. Suffice it to say that the first approach, projecting future numbers of certificated persons, falls short because certification is only tenuously linked to supply, while the second approach, projecting numbers of entrants, fails because entry rates, both past and future, are more likely to be determined by how many teachers school districts want than by how many are in the supply. The upshot, therefore, is that there have been no valid projections of the supply of entrants and, consequently, no meaningful assessments of the supply-demand balance.

Sources and Categories of Entrants

Apart from the underlying conceptual problems discussed above, an important complicating factor in modeling the supply of entrants is that entering teachers come in different categories and from multiple sources. The propensities of individuals to enter teaching vary greatly among these categories, as do the factors that influence supply behavior. Instead of focusing on a single supply projection model, therefore, it is more realistic to think in terms of a set of submodels, each pertaining to supply from a different class of potential teachers.

There is no one generally accepted taxonomy of sources or categories.

The most commonly encountered distinction is that between the flow of newly produced teachers (recent graduates of teacher training programs and/or persons recently certificated to teach) and the flow of teachers from the so-called reserve pool. This important concept, the reserve pool, is defined narrowly by some analysts and broadly by others. According to the most common narrow definition, the reserve pool is the stock of persons not currently teaching but certificated to teach in a state. More broadly conceived, the reserve pool encompasses all persons eligible to become teachers or even, in some versions, a state's (or the nation's) entire college-educated population. It has become apparent, .however, that the two-way distinction between newly produced teachers and reserve-pool members is inadequate for modeling supply. For instance, the supply behavior of teachers who have recently left teaching jobs is very different from that of certificated persons who have never taught, even though both groups are considered to be in the reserve pool. In practice, most state studies of the supply of teachers to the public schools classify potential entrants into finer categories, based on various combinations of the following distinctions:

- Entrants with and without previous teaching experience (i.e., new or entry-level teachers versus experienced teachers). Note that the latter may or may not be defined to include teachers with experience in private schools.
- Newly trained teachers (new graduates of teacher training programs) versus teachers who graduated in earlier years,
- Teachers who have never taught in the state versus teachers previously employed in the same state (the latter usually described as reentering teachers),
- Teachers resident in the state versus immigrants from other states,
- Teachers trained in a state's own teacher training institutions versus teachers trained out of state, and
- Teachers with and without full certification (or with different levels of certification, where applicable).

Different model developers seem to have come to different conclusions about which sources and categories need to be analyzed separately in projecting the supply of entering teachers. For example, the basic distinction in the Connecticut analysis (Connecticut Board of Education, 1988) is between first-time certificated persons and certificated persons in the reserve pool; the main distinction in the Massachusetts model (Coelen and Wilson, 1987) is between first-time entrants (persons who have not previously taught in the state) and reentrants; and the two key distinctions in the Maryland study (Maryland State Department of Education, 1988) are between in-state versus out-of-state and experienced versus inexperienced teachers.

Disaggregation by Subject Specialty

To analyze the supply-demand balance by field of teaching, one needs disaggregated projections of the supply of entrants as well as of teacher demand and the supply of retainees. This need to disaggregate complicates the supply models, just as it complicates models of attrition, and raises certain conceptual problems that appear not to have been addressed in the modeling literature.

One issue that arises is how one should deal with potential entrants who hold certificates in multiple fields. If an applicant is certificated as both a physics teacher and a mathematics teacher, for example, should that person be counted in the supply of potential entrants to both fields, or should he or she only be counted once (if so, in which field?) or somehow prorated between fields. How multiply credentialed teachers are treated obviously can affect subject-specific assessments of the supply-demand balance. Much the same issue was raised earlier in connection with the supply of retained teachers, but the appropriate answer is more elusive in the case of entrants because retained teachers can be categorized according to the subjects they have actually been teaching, but potential new teachers cannot.

Although the classification issue may seem like a matter of bookkeeping, it can have substantive implications—that is, it can affect supply projections and the subsequent assessments of supply-demand balance. An arbitrary method of fitting each prospective teacher into a single subject field, for example, or of assigning hypothetical fractions of such individuals to different fields, can generate findings of shortage where none actually exists. It seems important not to make the teacher supply seem less flexible than it is, which means that the capability of teachers and prospective teachers to teach multiple subjects should not be ignored. Thus far, however, none of the models I have seen takes the possibilities of substitution and mobility across fields adequately into account. How these possibilities can be accommodated is an interesting unsolved problem in model design.

Disaggregation by subject also creates a new category of entrant not mentioned in the foregoing taxonomy of supply categories and sources—namely, entrants into a particular subject area who are transferring from another subject area in the same state or school system. Because such persons are entrants in one sense but retained teachers in another, it would seem unreasonable to lump them together with other entrants for the purpose of modeling or projecting subject-specific supply. Yet they must be taken into account somehow to make assessments of the supply-demand balance come out correctly. The handling of such transferees is currently one of the loose ends in supply-demand modeling. It is not clear how such persons are counted or whether they are included in entry rates or, if so, whether they are treated as new or experienced teachers. Certainly, no theory has been offered of the supply behavior underlying transfer decisions.

The Quality Dimension of the Supply of Entrants

Changing the quality standards applicable to entrants is the principal strategy available to a school system or state for eventually altering the quality of its teaching force. Both the feasibility of improving quality and the rate at which quality can be improved depend on the distribution of quality in the supply of prospective new hires. In principle, and assuming the availability of suitable quality indicators, prospective entrants (both newly trained teachers and members of the reserve pool) could be classified by quality, and separate entry rates or propensities to apply for or accept positions could be determined for persons in the different quality strata. Alternatively, quality could be taken into account in a multivariate analysis of determinants of entry into teaching. The latter approach has, in fact, been implemented in a recent study of new teachers in North Carolina (Murnane and Schwinden, 1989), but the results are not directly transferable, for reasons to be explained, to teacher supply projection models. At present, the unsolved basic conceptual problems of supply modeling are so severe that taking the quality dimension into account seems at best a remote prospect.

State Projection Models

Given what has been said thus far about the conceptual obstacles to projecting the supply of entrants, it should not be surprising that the so-called supply projections presented in state supply-demand studies are, almost invariably, something other than true projections of supply. Mostly, these projections are of the two types mentioned earlier: (1) estimates of the future flow of persons into certificated status and/or the stock of certificate holders or (2) estimates of future numbers of entrants into teaching of various types and/or from various sources. Such projections are not necessarily uninformative. They may, in fact, be of considerable value either for reassuring policy makers that future supplies of teachers will be adequate or for identifying areas in which recruitment may become difficult. But neither type answers the question that one would hope to have answered by a supply projection: How many teachers (of specified qualifications or quality) are likely to be available and willing (under specified conditions) to enter the teaching force in the future?

The following descriptions of selected state models cover both the methods used to project the supply of entering teachers and the corresponding approaches (if any) used to assess the supply-demand balance.[27] The sequence of descriptions is arranged to emphasize the different concepts and modeling strategies now in use. An overall assessment of the models is provided at the end.

Projections of Numbers of Certificated Teachers

Two models that I have examined, those for Nebraska and South Carolina, reflect the notion that the stock or flow of persons with teaching certificates constitutes a state's teacher supply.

Nebraska The Nebraska analysis (Ostrander et al., 1988) equates supply (of new entrants) to the number of persons added annually to the ranks of Nebraska certificated teachers. In principle, the analysis recognizes three sources of potential new hires: (1) newly certificated Nebraska graduates, (2) out-of-state teachers who become eligible to teach in the state, and (3) persons in the reserve pool—defined as the stock of persons holding certificates but not currently teaching. Entrants from the reserve pool are excluded from the supply projections, however, because of lack of information on how many reserve pool members might actually be available to teach. The projection method applied to the two new-flow categories is simple trend extrapolation. The number of new graduates from Nebraska teacher training programs is projected to follow its historical downward trend (a decline of about 3 percent per year); the same trend is assumed for new graduates in fields other than teacher training who obtain teaching certificates; and the number of newly certificated teachers from other states is also extrapolated on the basis of a continued declining trend (in this case, a 4 percent decline per year). No attention is given in this analysis to the rates at which newly certificated persons actually enter teaching, nor to the rate at which former teachers return (the latter is part of the unanalyzed supply from the reserve pool). Thus, the model is seriously incomplete. Nevertheless, the Nebraska report proceeds to compare the projected demand for new hires (projected demand less projected number of retainees) against projected supply of new certificants, as defined above, and, finding the latter greater than the former, declares that the state will be enjoying a teacher surplus.

South Carolina A model developed in South Carolina (South Carolina Department of Education, 1990) also equates the supply of entrants to the number of new certificates issued annually. A distinction is made between new certificate holders trained in South Carolina institutions and those trained outside the state (the latter accounting for almost half the newly certificated individuals in recent years), but the same projection method is applied to both categories. This method consists simply of assuming that the annual number of new certificate holders in each subject area will be the same in the projection period (1990-1995) as it was, on average, during the five-year base period, 1985-1990.

The South Carolina report acknowledges the importance of returning teachers as a source of supply (30 percent of leavers return) but does not project their numbers explicitly. Instead, it deals with returning teachers on the demand side of the model by measuring and projecting attrition in terms of the *net* number of leavers (i.e., the number of leavers net of returnees) rather than according to the usual concept of gross annual attrition. No mention is made of any hires of certificated persons from the reserve pool other than these returnees.

Based on this model, the South Carolina analysts characterize the future supply-demand balance in each subject area in terms of the annual projected gain or loss of teachers—that is, the difference between the projected number of new certificate holders and the projected demand for new hires. A loss is said to signify increasing future difficulty in finding enough teachers. This projection-based assessment is supplemented by separate assessments based on district-reported shortages and numbers of vacant positions. Overall rankings of subject fields according to degree or severity of shortage are then constructed by combining rankings of losses based on the projections with rankings based on the survey data. Special education, science, foreign language, library science, and mathematics turn out to be the principal fields of shortage.

Projections of Entrants by Category

Two other state analyses, those for Maryland and Wisconsin, present relatively simple models based on the premise that one can estimate the future supply of entering teachers by projecting numbers of entrants or rates of entry from various pools of potential teachers. The MISER study of Massachusetts presents a more elaborate model founded on essentially the same proposition.

Maryland The Maryland model of teacher supply (Maryland State Department of Education, 1988) recognizes four categories of entrants: (1) in-state returning experienced teachers (i.e., teachers formerly employed in Maryland schools), (2) beginning teachers who are graduates of Maryland teacher training programs, (3) beginning teachers who are graduates of out-of-state teacher training programs, and (4) out-of-state experienced teachers. The number of new Maryland graduates who will enter teaching in each subject area is projected by applying a projected entry rate to an estimate of the future number of graduates with that subject specialty who will emerge from the state's teacher training programs. The estimated numbers of graduates by field are compiled from data supplied by individual

Maryland institutions of higher education. The projected entry rates appear to be the actual rates in the most recent year for which data are available, but whether these rates are subject-specific is not clear from the Maryland report. Numbers of entrants (by subject specialty) from the other three sources of supply are projected, it appears, by assuming either that they will be the same as in the most recent year for which data are available or that recent trends in the numbers will continue. No explanations are provided of the specific assumptions applicable to each category.

As to the supply-demand balance, the Maryland study reports a "projected discrepancy" for each subject specialty—the difference, whether positive or negative, between the projected supply of and demand for entrants—and also the projected supply of entrants as a percentage of the projected demand. These percentages are as low as 60 to 70 percent for some subjects (referred to as fields of "critical shortage"), but the fact that such large shortfalls are anticipated seems not to be taken as cause for alarm. Instead, the report merely notes that Maryland school systems can expect to fill only some of their vacancies from "normal sources of supply" in the years for which the deficiencies are projected.

Wisconsin The Wisconsin report on teacher supply and demand (Lauritzen and Friedman, 1991) presents unusually detailed descriptive information on numbers and characteristics of entrants into teaching but only a rudimentary and incomplete model for projecting the entrant component of supply. The projection method consists, in essence, of calculating the number of new Wisconsin-trained teachers who would be hired in each subject specialty if the same percentages of new graduates were hired in the future as in the recent past. The study does not explicitly project rates of entry from other sources (e.g., returning former teachers and teachers imported from other states) but seems to assume implicitly that such entrants will account for the same percentage of total entrants as in prior years. Lauritzen and Friedman give special attention to two phenomena neglected in many other state studies: (1) that the entry of newly trained teachers into the profession is distributed over time, not all concentrated in the year following certification, and (2) that expected entry rates for persons holding multiple certification are higher than for persons certificated in only a single subject specialty.[28] In general, however, their study is more useful for (and oriented toward) assessing the employment prospects for persons trained, or in training, in different teaching fields than for projecting the future supply-demand balance in the state.

Massachusetts The MISER model for Massachusetts (Coelen and Wilson, 1987, 1991a), defines supply as, in essence, a weighted sum of numbers of potential teachers in multiple categories; the weights are historically determined probabilities of entry. The model recognizes three broad types of entering teachers: (1) reentering teachers—teachers who have taught previously in the state but have interrupted their careers (also referred to as stop-outs); (2) new entrants with certification—a category that mixes together (a) teachers who have just graduated and been certificated in Massachusetts, (b) persons certificated in earlier years but who have never taught in Massachusetts, and (c) certificated teachers immigrating from other states; and (3) entrants hired under waivers of certification.

The supply of reentering teachers is projected by applying historical transition rates to the numbers of teachers who left in each prior time period. These rates (probabilities of reentry) vary with the length of time since leaving active teaching, reflecting the well-established finding that recent leavers are more likely to return than those who left many years ago. The transition rates are derived from a regression procedure, in which numbers of reentrants in a given year are related to numbers of leavers in past years, but the specifics of the regression methodology are unclear. It does appear, however, that year of departure is the only attribute considered in estimating the probability that former teachers in the reserve pool will return to teaching; such other factors as the teacher's age, gender, and subject specialty are not taken into account.[29]

The supply of new entrants with certification is also estimated by applying a set of estimated transition rates to numbers of persons in the pool of certificate holders who have never taught. In this case, the transition rates vary according to the time elapsed since certification was obtained. Individuals recently certificated are likely to enter in relatively large percentages; those who received their certification five or more years ago have much lower entry probabilities. Note that new graduates of teacher training programs—a category singled out for special attention in most other analyses—are here treated merely as certificate holders of the most recent vintage. Coelen and Wilson (1987) indicate that a regression model was used to estimate the set of transition rates, but the details of the modeling technique are not laid out. Again, it appears that no characteristics of certificated persons other than time since certification are taken into account in estimating the entry probabilities; that is, the projected entry rates are not differentiated by age, sex, or subject specialty.

The number of entrants in the final category, teachers hired under waivers of certification, is projected as a fixed percentage of the combined number of teachers hired in the previous two categories. The rationale for this specification is difficult to discern. It would seem more natural to treat the noncertificated group as a residual category, hired in such numbers as necessary to fill out the ranks of the teaching force. Such treatment would imply an inverse relationship rather than a proportional relationship between numbers of certificated and noncertificated entrants (holding the total number of new hires constant). It would be interesting to know which approach is more consistent with the empirical evidence.

Two other aspects of the treatment of the supply of entering teachers in the Massachusetts model are noteworthy. First, in addition to modeling rates of entry of certificated persons into active teaching, Coelen and Wilson also seek to explain the rate at which teachers obtain certification. They report what they characterize as a myopic pattern of behavior, whereby the number of new certificates issued in a year appears to depend mainly on the number of teachers hired in the immediately preceding year (Coelen and Wilson, 1991a). It is not clear how this pattern relates to the flow of potential new teachers through the training pipeline, nor whether it is largely explained by a phenomenon alluded to in the 1987 Massachusetts report—namely, that some teachers obtain certification at or after the time they are hired.

Second, Coelen and Wilson impose on their supply-of-entrants model a hierarchical structure, wherein the demand for new hires is assumed to be satisfied with reentering teachers, if enough are available, and only then with new entrants if unfilled vacancies still remain. It is not clear what the empirical basis is for this assumed order of precedence nor how the formulation holds up in practice, particularly in years in which relatively few teachers were hired. Moreover, the fact that the number of noncertificated new entrants is projected as a constant percentage of all new hires raises the possibility that such persons could be given priority over persons with certificates, according to the model, in the teacher hiring process.

Finally, a word is needed on the treatment of the supply-demand balance in the Massachusetts analysis. The Coelen-Wilson model differs from other state models in that it does not yield separate demand and supply estimates but instead offers projections of teacher hiring and employment that are supposed to reflect both demand and supply factors. The employment projections depend, however, on the simplistic assumption that the number of teachers employed in each future year will be the *lesser* of the projected number demanded or the projected number supplied.[30] Specifically, if the supply projections, based on the previously described sets of projected entry rates, fall short of the demand projections, the model "adjusts" by resetting teacher-pupil ratios at levels consistent with projected supply. The need for such an adjustment could easily have been avoided simply by assuming, not unrealistically, that the number of noncertificated entrants will expand or contract as needed to balance supply and demand. Alternatively, it could have been assumed that salaries and/or certification standards would adjust as needed to compensate for any supply-demand imbalance. The present assumption, taking the number of teachers in the supply as literally fixed at a level consistent with past entry rates, seems far too artificial and mechanical to be an acceptable representation of how the teacher market operates.

The MISER Multistate Model

According to preliminary specifications for the MISER NEDSAD model (Coelen and Wilson, 1991b), the supply of entrants will be projected, as in the 1987 Massachusetts analysis, by applying estimated transition rates to numbers of certificated persons in various supply pools. These transition rates will be differentiated primarily according to the durations of such persons in their respective pools—that is, the number of years since certification, in the case of persons who have never taught, and the number of years since leaving teaching, in the case of persons who have previously taught in the state in question. The specifications do not allow for entry rates to vary in relation to such other characteristics of potential teachers as age, sex, and subject specialty. Coelen and Wilson say that they will allow for effects of relative salaries on rates of entry and reentry into teaching (this is the only explicit behavioral element of the model), but their proposed treatment of the salary variable is both unusual and restrictive. They postulate that relative salaries affect entry rates only in periods of "supply shortage" and, moreover, that such periods can be identified from data on the percentage of entrants who have no teaching experience (the premise seems to be that inexperienced teachers are hired only as a last resort). They propose, therefore, to construct a model in which entry rates are determined by relative salaries in so-called shortage periods and by total hiring rates in so-called demand-dominated periods. This approach, they believe, will allow them to distinguish between supply-side and demand-side influences on hiring of teachers. They also indicate that the model will deal with interstate flows of teachers, but the details are not spelled out. Finally, although the NEDSAD data base consists of multiyear files on individual teachers, Coelen and Wilson intend not to use these individual-level data sets to analyze entry patterns but rather to limit themselves to estimating entry-duration relationships from aggregated data on average entry rates of persons in the various duration categories.

These model specifications are problematic in multiple respects, but it is not feasible at this preimplementation stage (nor would it be fair) to offer a detailed critique. I confine myself to noting some major concerns. First, at the conceptual level, the MISER framework does not distinguish clearly between influences on teacher supply and influences on entry into teaching. Although Coelen and Wilson recognize that the effects of demographic factors, salary levels, and other influences on supply behavior may or may not be reflected in entry rates, depending on what is happening on the demand side of the market, this awareness is not reflected in the proposed modeling technique. Second, the suggested method of sorting out demand-side and supply-side effects on hiring is difficult to reconcile with labor-market economics. The either-or, surplus-or-shortage characterization of the teacher market is untenable; shortage cannot be defined meaningfully without reference to teacher quality; and the mix of entrants per se bears no necessary relationship to the tightness of supply (for instance, even with no experienced teachers to hire, there could be more than enough newly trained teachers to staff the schools). Third, it is especially troubling that Coelen and Wilson seem to have decided in advance not to include potentially important influences on entry rates in their model. Specifically, the decision to model entry rates solely as functions of duration in the supply pool is hard to defend in the face of evidence that such rates also vary by age, sex, and subject specialty (see "research on the supply of entrants," below). Finally, MISER's decision to construct only relatively crude aggregative models of hiring seems inexplicable, considering that large-scale individual-level data bases are available and that Murnane, Grissmer, and others have convincingly demonstrated both the feasibility and the value of modeling supply behavior at the individual teacher level.

Survey-Based Supply Projections: The Connecticut Approach

The Connecticut teacher supply-demand study (Connecticut Board of Education, 1988) provides an unusually rich body of descriptive information on sources and characteristics of entering teachers but offers only a simple and incomplete set of projections of future supply. What makes these projections noteworthy, however, is the method used to determine how many persons in a particular category should be considered "in the supply." Instead of calculating historical entry rates, the Connecticut analysts chose to base their estimates of each group's participation rate on survey findings concerning potential teachers' job-seeking behavior and intentions. The Connecticut method, therefore, constitutes a third approach to projections, distinct from the two methods described previously.

The Connecticut definition of supply is linked to certification but, unlike the Nebraska and South Carolina models described earlier, the Connecticut model does not equate numbers of cetificate holders with numbers in the supply; instead, it focuses on the propensities of different categories of certificated persons to seek teaching positions. The analysis focuses primarily on two broad categories of prospective teachers: new certificants and members of the reserve pool. The latter is defined simply as the stock of persons certificated in earlier years but not currently teaching. It includes both former Connecticut teachers (including some on leave from school districts) and persons previously certificated who have never taught. The new-certificant category includes potential teachers of four types: new Connecticut college graduates who have just obtained certification, earlier Connecticut graduates now applying for certification, individuals newly trained in other states and immigrating to Connecticut, and experienced immigrating teachers. (In recent years, only about 30 percent of entrants have come from the new certificant category; the remainder are from the reserve pool.)

In separate surveys of samples of new certificants and former Connecticut teachers, respondents were asked about their actual job market behavior and the results (whether they had applied for Connecticut teaching positions, whether they had been accepted, and why, if accepted, they had not taken jobs) as well as about the likelihood of their applying for teaching jobs in the forthcoming year and within the next five years. The details of how the survey results are used to project the future supply of entrants are hazy, but what is clear is that the reported rates of applying for jobs are the basis for short-range (one year) projections of likely numbers of applicants from the two groups covered by the survey.[31] It is not clear to what degree these rates are differentiated by subject specialty. The sample sizes, except in the large area of elementary education, appear too small to support subject-specific estimates. The rates at which respondents expressed interest in applying in the future are reported, but it is not indicated that these rates were used to make longer-range projections. No complete projection model is presented. For instance, no method is described for estimating the future size of the new certificant pool, even though a relatively simple trend analysis would probably suffice for that purpose. Also, no projections are offered for members of the certificated reserve pool who are not in the former-teacher category. Given all these gaps, the Connecticut analysis cannot be offered as an example of a complete projection model. Nevertheless, the notion of using survey data to estimate participation rates merits further attention and development, especially considering the present lack of viable alternatives.

Assessment of Projection Methods

All the models described above clearly have major conceptual and technical shortcomings. None qualifies, in its present form, as an acceptable method of estimating the future supply of new entrants. The question is what, if anything, might be made of each approach in the future. I comment here on the problems with each type of model and the possibilities for further development.

Attempting to measure or project supply solely in terms of numbers of persons with teaching certificates is a conceptual dead end. The problem is that certification is only weakly and indirectly related to teacher supply. The connection between the two breaks down in two respects: first, many people with teaching certificates are not in the supply—that is, they are not interested in applying for or accepting teaching positions. This applies both to newly trained, newly certificated individuals, some of whom demonstrate no interest in actually becoming teachers, and especially to certificate holders in the reserve pool, many of whom could not be induced to enter or reenter teaching under anything resembling current salaries and job conditions in teaching. Second, the supply of teachers is not necessarily limited to certificated persons. In many states, significant percentages of new teachers enter with provisional or emergency credentials or under waivers of certification. Some states have lateral entry, or "alternative certification" provisions, under which people without traditional teacher training can be hired as teachers with little delay. Even where regular certificates are required, it is only in the very short run that the supply is limited to persons who already hold them. The potential supply of certificated teachers two years from now includes not only current certificate holders but also all the people who could obtain certificates within a two-year period—and who might do so if salaries and other job conditions were sufficiently appealing. Thus certification is, in one sense, too broad a criterion and, in another sense, too narrow a criterion for determining who is in the supply.

Projections of numbers of certificate holders might be useful in conjunction with a model that also projects the rates at which different types of certificated persons apply to teach. Such projections would be needed, for instance, to implement the approach reflected in the Connecticut analysis described above. But comparisons between projected demands for new hires and projected stocks or flows of certificate holders, such as those provided in the aforementioned Nebraska and South Carolina studies, yield very little useful information about the future supply-demand balance.

Analyses and projections of the rates at which various class of potential entrants actually enter teaching are useful for a variety of purposes, but as projections of supply they are gravely flawed. Such projections rest on the unwarranted assumption that the observed rates of entry depend only, or mainly, on the choices of the prospective entrants themselves (supply-side behavior) and not on the hiring decisions of school systems (demand-side behavior). But as explained earlier, under a regime of excess supply, such as probably prevails most of the time in all but a few "critical shortage" fields of teaching, the opposite is closer to the truth. Typically, only a fraction of those who seek teaching jobs are hired; the remainder end up in nonteaching activities (or perhaps in teaching jobs in other states). Under normal circumstances, therefore, entry rates per se convey little information about teacher supply. That only 30 percent of the new graduates of a state's teacher training program actually enter teaching, for example, does not signify that only 30 percent were in the supply. A much larger fraction—perhaps 50 percent or even 90 percent—may have been willing to supply their services. There is no way to find out from data on numbers of new hires alone. Similarly, there may be 1,000 members of the reserve pool ready and willing to enter teaching this year, but if school systems want only 200, only 200 will be hired. The true supply is not observable directly and cannot be estimated from data on the actual number of entrants. In general, therefore, a projection of entrants, either in the aggregate or by category, does not constitute a projection of teacher supply.[32] Consequently, it is normally not correct to assume (as is done, e.g., in the previously described Massachusetts analysis) that the supply of entrants in the future will be limited to numbers consistent with entry rates in the past.

The problem of disentangling supply and demand econometrically is very difficult but not necessarily insuperable. In a recent paper prepared for MISER, Ballou and Podgursky (1991) sketch out a preliminary theoretical framework showing how, and under what conditions, a separate teacher supply function might be estimated statistically. Significantly, their work seems to imply that bringing the quality dimension of teacher supply into the model is critical—that is, the possibility of estimating a supply function hinges on being able to observe the quality-related characteristics of the teachers hired at different times or in different places. Thus, two key deficiencies of existing models, the lack of a sound method of quantifying teacher supply and neglect of teacher quality, prove to be logically related. It appears that both will have to be dealt with together if either is to be dealt with at all.

What of the survey-based approach represented, in embryonic form, in the Connecticut model? In general, economists tend to resist using such kinds of survey data on the grounds that statements of intent and responses to hypothetical choices are poor substitutes for, or predictors of, actual behavior. In this instance, however, the alternatives are unpromising. The other methods now used in projection models are inadequate for reasons already explained. The standard techniques of econometric supply-demand modeling that one would bring to bear in an analysis of a private labor market seem inapplicable because an essential analytical assumption—supply-demand equilibrium—seems inappropriate to make about the teacher market. Without that assumption, there is no way to estimate supply behavior from information on quantity (number of hires) and price. Using "soft" data, such as survey responses, may be, under the circumstances, a reasonable default option.

One other possibility suggested by the Connecticut survey approach is to base supply projections on more systematically collected data on numbers of applicants for teaching positions. The rates at which members of various pools of eligibles apply to teach is certainly more closely related to supply than are the rates at which they are hired. It is possible, as in the Connecticut approach, to collect application data from individuals, but it may also be feasible, and perhaps preferable, to collect such data from local school systems. Doing so would have the advantage that the data would not be limited to particular predefined categories of applicants—for instance, out-of-state as well as in-state applicants would be covered. An important practical problem is that individuals often submit multiple applications, which means that screening for duplication would be required. A more important problem is the conceptual one that application behavior is partly demand determined. Such actions by employers as announcing and advertising vacancies (or simply the fact that hiring is taking place) generate applications, while other behaviors, such as making known that no teachers are needed, discourages them. Therefore, estimates based on application rates are likely to understate supply. Even so, they are likely to come much closer to the truth than would estimates based on the rates at which teachers are actually hired.

Research on the Supply of Entrants

I concluded in a previous section that the most promising work on patterns of teacher attrition and retention has come from academic research rather than from efforts to project the future supply of retained teachers. The same is true, although to a lesser degree, of work on the supply of entering teachers. In fact, the same body of research as is summarized in the attrition section yields, often as a by-product, some interesting findings about entry behavior and some useful suggestions as to how future research on entry into teaching might proceed.

The component of the supply of entering teachers that is easiest to model is reentry by individuals who have temporarily left teaching jobs. The same longitudinal data on cohorts of entering teachers and the same hazard modeling techniques as are useful for studying attrition can be used to analyze reentry as well. In both their Michigan and North Carolina studies, Murnane et al. (1988, 1989) use these data and methods to relate the probability of reentry to teacher characteristics. With respect to Michigan teachers (entering cohorts of 1972 and 1973), they find that one-fourth to one-third of all leavers return. The probability of entry varies with age and gender—young women, in particular, being both the most likely to leave and the most likely to return. Reentry rates also vary significantly among subject fields, with chemistry and physics teachers the least likely to return, elementary teachers the most likely, and teachers of other subjects (including mathematics) falling in between. Similarly, in their analysis of North Carolina teachers (entering cohorts of 1976 and 1978), the same authors find that 30 percent of all leavers during the first five years of teaching eventually return, with women twice as likely to return as men, elementary teachers more likely to return than secondary teachers, and teachers of mathematics less likely to return than teachers of other subjects. In addition, they report that the likelihood of returning is significantly lower for teachers with high NTE scores than for teachers with low NTE scores—one of the few findings yet presented on the quality dimension of the supply of entering teachers.

In the only multivariate study of new entrants into a state's teaching force that has come to my attention, Murnane and Schwinden (1989) use North Carolina data to analyze the rates at which newly certificated individuals enter teaching jobs. This analysis, which covers persons with no prior teaching experience who obtained certificates between 1975 and 1985, uses a logit model to relate the probability of entry to characteristics of the certificants. Among the principal findings are that (1) entry rates were once much higher for women than for men, but the male and female rates have since converged, (2) entry rates vary among subject areas, being highest in special education, lowest in business education, and in-between in mathematics and science, and (3) entry rates in certain subject areas, including mathematics, chemistry, physics, and English, tend to be lower (among whites only) for persons with high NTE scores than for persons with low NTE scores.[33] Also, Murnane and Schwinden cite evidence, albeit less rigorous, showing that both numbers of certificants and certificants' choices of subject specialty appear to be sensitive to demand.

An important implication of these findings for projections of rates of entry into teaching is that both the rates at which newly trained teachers enter and the rates at which former teachers reenter need to be differentiated by subject specialty and in relation to certain teacher characteristics. Applying the same entry or reentry probabilities to everyone is no more reasonable than applying undifferentiated attrition rates to all categories of teachers. Similarly, it appears (although the evidence thus far is limited) that entry and reentry rates vary over time, just as do attrition rates, and therefore that projections based on fixed rates are likely to be unsound.

It should also be recognized, however, that although multivariate models of entry behavior are preferable in several respects, the estimates of entry and reentry rates from such models are no more indicative of supply behavior than are the average entry and reentry rates used in state projection models. In both cases, rates of entry and reentry into teaching may be determined more by school systems' hiring decisions than by the supply behavior of potential teachers. Murnane and his colleagues are, of course, fully aware of this problem and warn explicitly that their models cannot be interpreted as representing supply behavior. Whether anything more can be done in the multivariate framework to reduce the confounding of demand and supply factors is not yet clear. One possibility is to estimate models that contain explicit demand factors (e.g., measures of enrollment or expenditure growth or even aggregate measures of hiring), with a view to controlling for demand-side influences on entry rates. To implement such models properly is likely to require a particularly data-intensive form of modeling, in which entry behavior is studied with multiyear files of both employment and certification data.

Prospects for National Projections of the Supply of Entrants

There are currently no national models for projecting the supply of entering teachers. Formerly, NCES offered projections of one element of that supply, the flow of new graduates from teacher training programs, but these have been abandoned as unreliable and, in any event, did not yield estimates of how many new graduates (much less any other potential teachers) would actually enter teaching jobs. Today, however, two other types of national data are available that have some potential to provide information about the future supply of new teachers: (1) the Schools and Staffing Survey (SASS), discussed in connection with teacher attrition, and (2) the National Longitudinal Study (NLS) of the high school class of 1972 and, eventually, other longitudinal surveys of later cohorts. I comment here on the earlier NCES projections and on potential applications of these other data sets.

The Former NCES Supply Projections

The classroom teacher sections of NCES's annual *Projections of Education Statistics* included, as of 1985, not only projections of teacher demand and teacher attrition but also projections of one element of teacher supply, the annual production of new graduates of teacher training programs. These projections were linked to the NCES projections of numbers of recipients of bachelor's degrees. Specifically, this was accomplished by extrapolating the ratio of new-teacher graduates to all new bachelor's degrees according to a log-linear trend equation. The resulting estimates of numbers of newly trained teachers were referred to, in years prior to 1985, as supply projections and compared with projections of the demand for new entrants. If the projected demand for new hires exceeded the projected number of new graduates, the difference was referred to as an anticipated shortage.

NCES eventually ceased comparing projections of new teacher graduates against projections of demand after recognizing that the number of new teacher graduates (1) overstated the supply of newly trained teachers because not all graduates actually sought to become teachers and (2) neglected entirely all other sources of teacher supply—i.e., all reentering teachers and other reserve pool members. It then dropped the projections of new teacher graduates entirely, possibly because of findings that such projections were proving highly inaccurate (Cavin, 1986). Currently, the agency offers no projections of any component of the supply of entering teachers.

Data from the NCES Schools and Staffing Survey

The NCES Schools and Staffing Survey provides considerably richer national data than have hitherto been available on the sources from which entering teachers have been obtained. Using these data, it should be possible to carry out a detailed descriptive analysis of sources of supply, showing, among other things, how the mix of entrants by source varies among types of places and among subject fields. Such information, though not directly indicative of future supply prospects, is of considerable value in its own right.

Two features of the SASS data base limit its usefulness for developing projections of the supply of entering teachers. One limitation is that SASS is a cross-sectional data base, now applicable to only the single year 1987-88. It cannot yet be used, therefore, to establish or project trends. As subsequent rounds of data collection are conducted (the round now under way covers 1990-91), SASS will begin to provide some time-trend data. The second limitation is that SASS provides data on actual teachers but not on nonteaching members of the groups from which teachers are drawn. Thus, the SASS data base, by itself, cannot be used to estimate the rates as which members of particular groups enter teaching or to relate entry rates to particular characteristics of individuals. Combined with information from other sources, however, the SASS data could shed some light on these matters. For example, the SASS data on the educational backgrounds of new entrants (degrees and majors), combined with external data on degrees granted, could be used to estimate entry rates for recent college graduates, broken down by race, sex, and perhaps other characteristics. These rates could then be used to project numbers of entering college graduates in the future. Like other such projections, however, these would confound the effects of supply and demand factors on numbers of entrants and would not constitute true projections of supply.

The usefulness of SASS for analyzing teacher supply from the reserve pool is particularly limited because neither SASS itself nor any other national data base provides data on the size or composition of the pool. However, one aspect of supply from the reserve pool, namely the rate at which teachers who leave teaching subsequently return, may eventually become analyzable. It is now planned, I understand, that teachers in the 1990-91 SASS sample who leave their jobs will be followed up several times, rather than just once as in 1987-88. The multiple follow-ups will make it possible to identify returners and to establish the rates at which leavers resume teaching. Other flows from the reserve pool will be observable with SASS data, but it will not be possible to translate them into rates or to project them for lack of data on the size of the pool itself.

Data from Longitudinal Surveys

Data from NCES's National Longitudinal Study of the high school class of 1972 (NLS-72) have already been used to study certain aspects of teacher supply, and other longitudinal data sets, including High School and Beyond, should also be useful for that purpose in the future. An analysis by Manski (1985), using only the NLS-72 data accumulated through 1979, examines, among other things, factors associated with the choice of teaching as an occupation. A more recent analysis by Heyns (1988), using data from the 1986 NLS-72 follow-up survey, examines the rates of entry into teaching of individuals who had completed teacher training as well as subsequent rates of attrition and return to the profession. These analyses are preliminary, aggregative, and descriptive, but the same data base has the potential to support more complex multivariate analyses of factors associated with individuals' entry and reentry decisions. Moreover, when similar analyses are undertaken with the High School and Beyond data (high school classes of 1980 and 1982), it will become possible to say something about changes in entry and reentry patterns over time. Thus, considerable potential resides in the longitudinal data sets to gain new insights into national teacher supply.

OVERVIEW: THE STATE OF THE ART AND PROSPECTS FOR IMPROVEMENT

The State of the Art in General

The main attributes, capabilities, and limitations of current models for projecting teacher supply, demand, and quality can be summarized, in capsule form, as follows:

1. Teacher supply-demand projection models remain mechanical rather than behavioral, which means that they can project future teacher employment and future numbers of new hires only under the implicit assumption that all influences on demand and attrition (or on trends therein) will remain unchanged.
2. Because the models do not link estimates of teacher supply and demand to budgets, salary levels, and other underlying causal variables, they cannot be used to predict how teacher markets will adjust or to answer what-if questions about the effects of changing conditions and policies.
3. The better models now yield much more accurate and detailed projections than in the past of the supply of retained teachers, but projecting the supply of potential entrants (other than reentrants) into teaching remains beyond their capabilities. With the supply side incomplete, the models are of limited use for assessing the future supply-demand balance.
4. It is now common for models to disaggregate projections by level of education and subject specialty, but the current methods of disaggregating demand are too crude and inflexible to capture the effects of changing curricula and patterns of course enrollment.

5. The models deal only with numbers of teachers and not with teacher quality and thus cannot be used to address concerns about the future quality of the teaching force.

The following paragraphs deal in more detail with the state of the art in projecting the demand for teachers, the supply of retained teachers, and the supply of potential new entrants and with the prospects for improvement in each area.

Projections of Demand

The prevailing method of projecting demand is still simply to multiply projected enrollments by current or extrapolated teacher-pupil ratios. This method yields no information on how the teacher-pupil ratios themselves, and hence the numbers of teachers demanded, can be expected to change in the future in response to changing economic, demographic, or fiscal conditions. The fact that teacher-pupil ratios are merely stipulated or extrapolated rather than linked to underlying causal factors does not necessarily mean that the models will predict future teacher employment inaccurately, but it does render them only minimally useful as policy analysis tools. There seem to have been no recent state-level efforts to create behavioral demand models, but NCES has moved to develop such a model at the national level by shifting from a mechanical to a regression-based projection method. Although the present NCES model falls short in many respects, it represents an important step in the right direction and a point of departure for further national and state-level modeling efforts.

Models offering disaggregated projections of teacher demand by level of education and subject specialty have now become relatively common, but the methods used to disaggregate by subject are extremely crude. The standard approach is simply to assume that the distribution of enrollment among subjects at each level of education will be the same in the future as it is today. None of the models reviewed for this report is designed to project changes in enrollment by subject (except on an ad hoc basis), not even by so simple a method as extrapolating recent course-enrollment trends.

An important implicit assumption built into all the current demand projection models is that the teacher market, both in the aggregate and in each subject specialty, is and has been in a condition of excess supply. This assumption is reasonable in the aggregate and for most subject areas, but it may be wrong for certain critical fields, such as science, mathematics, and special education, that are of particular interest to policy makers. Wherever the excess-supply assumption is violated (i.e., where unmet demand exists), projections based on actual numbers of teachers employed in the past will understate the numbers of teachers likely to be wanted in the future. Although some model developers recognize this problem, none has yet offered a solution.

Although the key to making the demand models more useful is to make them behavioral, a number of lesser improvements can be made within the existing mechanical projection framework. These include, for example, developing disaggregated trend projections of enrollment by subject; taking into account that numbers of teachers do not adjust necessarily adjust immediately or in direct proportion to changes in enrollment and that responses to enrollment growth and enrollment decline may be asymmetrical; and perhaps taking into account additional aspects of student body composition, such as changing numbers of handicapped, disadvantaged, and other special-need enrollees. However, although such additions might improve the accuracy of demand estimates, they would not do much to improve the models' usefulness for policy analysis.

Making demand models behavioral means, concretely, basing demand projections on multivariate econometric models relating numbers of teachers to the fiscal, economic, and demographic factors that ultimately determine how many teachers school systems are able and willing to employ. The pertinent variables include such things as per-pupil expenditure, per capita income or fiscal capacity, the pupil/population ratio, the makeup of the pupil population, and salary levels both inside and outside teaching. It appears that such models will have to be constructed at a level of aggregation one rung below the level at which they are to be used; that is, state-level demand models will have to be constructed with district-level data, and a national model with state-level data. The necessary data appear to be available nationally and for at least some states. Such modeling seems eminently feasible and could proceed if the necessary resources were made available.

Projections of the Supply of Retained Teachers

Attrition/retention modeling has become the bright spot in the supply-demand projection field. The more sophisticated state retention models now project numbers of continuing teachers by applying age-specific attrition rates to age distributions of teachers, differentiating also by level of education and subject specialty. Moreover, recent research on teacher attrition, although undertaken separately from supply projection efforts, has yielded findings that may soon translate into further improvements in models for projecting numbers of retainees. Among these are findings about male-female differences in attrition patterns, changes in attrition rates over time, and, perhaps most important, effects of salary levels, working conditions, and other economic factors on exit rates from teaching. Further work on these economic factors is required, but if the estimates of effects of salaries, working conditions, etc., can be refined, taking them into account would transform the present mechanical (albeit sophisticated) models into behavioral models of teacher attrition.

At the national level, the most recently published NCES projections still rely on crudely estimated aggregative attrition rates, but this is about to change because of the availability of more accurate and detailed estimates from the SASS individual-teacher surveys. It will soon be possible to project national as well as state teacher retention on the basis of disaggregated age-specific and subject-specific attrition rates. Research now under way may also lead to the incorporation of certain behavioral elements (e.g., responses to salary changes) into the national models.

In sum, attrition/retention models are already the most advanced elements of teacher supply-demand models, and further progress (and a widening sophistication gap between attrition models and the other components) appears to be imminent.

Projections of the Supply of Entering Teachers

The lack of adequate methods, or even a sound conceptual framework, for projecting the supply of potential entrants into teaching continues to prevent the development of complete supply-demand models that can be used to assess the supply-demand balance. Although several extant models do offer so-called supply-of-entrant projections, the projection methods and the premises underlying them are all gravely flawed and the results are invariably projections of something other than supply. It follows, therefore, that little credence should be given to such projections or, especially, to reports of teacher shortage or surplus based on them.

Many current models offer no projections at all of the supply of potential entrants into teaching. Those that do rely on one or the other of two unsatisfactory approaches. The first approach, equating the projected supply to the projected stock of persons certificated to teach in a state, is easily dismissed. Many certificated persons are not in the supply (i.e., willing to teach under current conditions), and many persons in the supply may not (yet) be certificated. The second approach, projecting so-called supply by applying past entry rates to numbers of persons in various supply pools, is invalid because past entry rates are more likely to have been determined by numbers of teachers wanted (demand) than by numbers available (supply). The fundamental problem, with which most model developers have not yet come to grips, is that if past hiring mainly reflects demand, then supply is not directly observable. Consequently, the current teacher supply cannot be measured, and the future supply cannot be projected, from data on employment and hiring. Additional information is needed to estimate how many teachers would be available to take teaching jobs if hiring were not limited by demand.

A possible exception to the above is that it may be reasonable to construe entry rates for one category of entering teachers, those reentering teaching after having left temporarily, as indicators of the magnitude of that element of supply. Some progress has been made recently in modeling reentry behavior, using essentially the same methods as have been used to model teacher attrition. Similar methods may prove acceptable for projecting the supply of reentering teachers. These methods do not apply, however, to the other major categories of potential entrants—newly trained teachers, members of the reserve pool (other than the temporary leavers), and teachers immigrating from other states.

Satisfactory methods of projecting the supplies of these other categories of entrants are unlikely to be developed soon, but several strategies do seem worth pursuing. One is to attempt to estimate supply from information on numbers of applicants for teaching positions. Such information is collectable either from individuals or school districts. Serious problems would arise in interpreting it, but the resulting estimates, even if flawed, might be substantially better than what is now available. A related approach is to derive supply estimates from survey data on the job-seeking behavior and intentions of persons in selected groups. The surveys could be freestanding or linked to such major longitudinal survey efforts as the NCES High School and Beyond. This method would be subject to all the usual problems of using responses to hypothetical questions to infer labor market behavior, but again, the question is whether substantial gains could be made, compared with the present unsatisfactory situation. A third approach is to attempt to distinguish econometrically between the effects on employment and hiring of demand and supply behavior, but as has been shown (Ballou and Podgursky, 1991), this strategy seems to hinge on solving the teacher quality at the same time. This complication places it firmly in the category of long-term (and long-shot) possibilities.

REFERENCES

Ballou, Dale, and Michael Podgursky

1991 Estimating Teacher Supply in a Demand-Constrained Regime. Draft paper. January. Economics Department, University of Massachusetts.

Barro, Stephen M.

1986 *The State of the Art in Projecting Teacher Supply and Demand.* Paper prepared for the Panel on Statistics on Supply and Demand for Precollege Science and Mathematics Teachers, Committee on National Statistics, National Research Council. Washington, D.C.: SMB Economic Research, Inc.

Bobbitt, Sharon A., Elizabeth Faupel, and Shelley Burns

1991 *Characteristics of Stayers, Movers, and Leavers: Results from the Teacher Followup Survey, 1988-89.* June. NCES 91-128. Washington, D.C.: National Center for Education Statistics.

Bureau of Labor Statistics

1986 *Occupational Projections and Training Data, 1986 Edition.* Bulletin 2251. Washington, D.C.: U.S. Department of Labor.

Cagampang, Helen, Walter I. Garms, Todd Greenspan, and James W. Guthrie

1985 *Teacher Supply and Demand in California: Is the Reserve Pool a Realistic Source of Supply?* September. Berkeley, California: Policy Analysis for California Education (PACE), University of California.

Cavin, Edward S.

1986 *A Review of Teacher Supply and Demand Projections by the U.S. Department of Education, Illinois, and New York.* Paper prepared for the Panel on Statistics on Supply and Demand for Precollege Science and Mathematics Teachers, Committee on National Statistics, National Academy of Sciences. Princeton, New Jersey: Mathematica Policy Research, Inc.

Coelen, Stephen P., and James M. Wilson III

1987 *Report on the Status of Teacher Supply and Demand in Massachusetts, Massachusetts Institute for Social and Economic Research (MISER).* June. Amherst, Massachusetts: University of Massachusetts.

1991a Preliminary Specifications of the Supply Side of State Teacher Supply and Demand Models. Memorandum. June 13.

1991b MISER Demographic Teacher Supply and Demand Model. Memorandum.

Connecticut Board of Education

1988 Teacher Supply and Demand in Connecticut: A Second Look. November.

Gerald, Debra E.

1985 *Projections of Education Statistics to 1992-93: Methodological Report with Detailed Projection Tables.* July. Washington, D.C.: National Center for Education Statistics.

Gerald, Debra E., Paul J. Horn, and William J. Hussar

1988 *Projections of Education Statistics to 1997-98.* CS 88-607. Washington, D.C.: National Center for Education Statistics.

1989a *Projections of Education Statistics to 2000.* NCES 89-648. Washington, D.C.: National Center for Education Statistics.

Gerald, Debra E., Paul J. Horn, Thomas D. Snyder, and William C. Sonnenberg

1989b *State Projections to 1993 for Public Elementary and Secondary Enrollment, Graduates, and Teachers.* CS 89-638. Washington, D.C.: National Center for Education Statistics.

Gerald, Debra E., and William J. Hussar

1990 *Projections of Education Statistics to 2001: An Update.* NCES 91-683. Washington, D.C.: National Center for Education Statistics.

Gilford, Dorothy M., and Ellen Tenenbaum, eds.

1990 *Precollege Science and Mathematics Teachers: Monitoring Supply, Demand, and Quality.* Panel on Statistics on Supply and Damand for Precollege Science and Mathematics Teachers, Committee on National Statistics. Washington, D.C.: National Academy Press.

Grissmer, David W., and Sheila Nataraj Kirby

1987 *Teacher Attrition: The Uphill Climb to Staff the Nation's Schools.* R-3512-CSTP. August. Santa Monica, California: The RAND Corporation.

1991 *Patterns of Attrition Among Indiana Teachers, 1965-1987.* Santa Monica, California: The RAND Corporation.

Haggstrom, Gus W., Linda Darling-Hammond, and David W. Grissmer

1988 *Assessing Teacher Supply and Demand.* R-3633-ED/CSTP. May. Santa Monica, California: The RAND Corporation.

Heyns, Barbara
1988 Educational defectors: A first look at teacher attrition in the NLS-72. *Educational Researcher* April:24-32.

Lauritzen, Paul, and Stephen Friedman
1990 *CSPD Technical Manual: Procedures for Comprehensive Assessment of Educational Personnel Supply/Demand.* CSPD [Comprehensive System of Personnel Development] Special Project. Whitewater, Wisconsin: University of Wisconsin-Whitewater.
1991 Wisconsin Teacher Supply and Demand: An Examination of Data Trends, 1991. Report prepared for the Wisconsin Department of Public Instruction, Wisconsin Teacher Supply and Demand Project.

Manski, Charles F.
1985 Academic Ability, Earnings, and the Decision to Become a Teacher: Evidence from the National Longitudinal Study of the High School Class of 1972. Working Paper No. 1539. January. National Bureau of Economic Research.

Maryland State Department of Education
1988 Teacher Supply and Demand in Maryland, 1988-1991. September.

Metz, A. Stafford, and H. L. Fleischman
1974 *Teacher Turnover in Public Schools, Fall 1968 to Fall 1969.* DHEW Publication No. (OE) 74-1115. Washington, D.C.: U.S. Department of Health, Education, and Welfare.

Murnane, Richard J., Edward S. Cavin, and Randall S. Brown
1985 School district responses to enrollment changes: The direction of the change matters! *Journal of Education Finance* 10(4)(Spring).

Murnane, Richard J., and Randall J. Olsen
1989 The effects of salaries and opportunity costs on duration in teaching: Evidence from Michigan. *The Review of Economics and Statistics* 71:347-352.
1990 The effects of salaries and opportunity costs on length of stay in teaching. *Journal of Human Resources* 25(Winter):106-124.

Murnane, Richard J., Judith D. Singer, and John B. Willett
1988 The career paths of teachers: Implications for teacher supply and methodological lessons for research. *Educational Researcher* August-September:22-30.
1989 The influences of salaries and "opportunity costs" on teachers' career choices: Evidence from North Carolina. *Harvard Educational Review* 59(3)(August):325-46.

Murnane, Richard J., and Michael Schwinden
1989 Race, gender, and opportunity: Supply and demand for new teachers in North Carolina, 1975-1985. *Educational Evaluation and Policy Analysis* 11(2)(Summer):93-108.

New York State Education Department
1990 Projections of Public School Classroom Teachers, New York State, 1989-90 to 1993-94. January. Albany, New York.

Ohio Department of Education
1988 Ohio Teacher Supply and Demand. March.

Ostrander, Ray, John Prasch, Robert Stalcup, Cy Yusten, and Linda Zech
1988 *Teacher Supply and Demand in Nebraska, 1988-1994.* March. Lincoln, Nebraska: Bureau of Education Research and Field Services, Department of Education Administration, Teachers College, University of Nebraska.

Popkin, Joel, and B.K. Atrostic
1986 *Evaluation of Models of the Supply and Demand for Teachers.* Paper prepared for the Panel on Statistics on Supply and Demand for Precollege Science and

Mathematics Teachers, Committee on National Statistics, National Academy of Sciences. Washington, D.C.: Joel Popkin and Company.

Prowda, Peter M., and David W. Grissmer
1986 Perspective on Teacher Supply and Demand: There is No General Shortage. Paper presented at the annual meeting of the American Educational Research Association. San Francisco, California.

Rollefson, Mary
1990 Teacher Turnover: Patterns of Entry to and Exit from Teaching. Paper presented at the annual meeting of the American Educational Research Association.

South Carolina Department of Education
1990 *Teacher Supply and Demand for South Carolina Public Schools, 1989-90 Update*. December. Columbia, South Carolina: Management Information Section, Office of Research, South Carolina Department of Education.

Theobald, Neil D.
1990 An examination of the influence of personal, professional, and school district characteristics on public school teacher retention. *Economics of Education Review* 9(3):241-250.

Tuma, John, Antoinette Gifford, Laura Horn, and E. Gareth Hoachlander
1989 *Enrollment Trends in Vocational and Academic Education in American Public High Schools, 1969-1987*. Berkeley, California: MPR Associates, Inc.

NOTES

1. The data base development work, although no less important than, and in fact, essential for, supply-demand modeling, is not covered here but is reviewed in several of the other papers in this volume.

2. A note on nomenclature: there are two different ways of characterizing the demand and supply sides of models in the teacher supply-demand literature. According to the scheme used here, *demand* refers to the total number of teachers wanted by employers (school systems), and *supply* refers to the sum of the supply of retained teachers and the supply of potential entrants into teaching. The alternative usage is to use *demand* to refer to the net demand for new hires (i.e., the total number of teachers wanted *less* the number of retained teachers) and to reserve the term *supply* for the supply of potential entrants. I prefer the former usage because the number of continuing teachers is determined mainly by supply side behavior—that is, by decisions of individual teachers as to whether to remain in teaching. In this paper, therefore, *demand* means total demand, except where I refer explicitly to the demand for new hires or entrants into teaching.

3. Conceivably, the demand for teachers could also be smaller than the number actually employed if, for example, there were impediments to reducing the teacher work force, such as state laws or collective bargaining agreements limiting layoffs or reductions in force. Presumably, any such disequilibria would be short-run phenomena, as the affected states and school systems would quickly be forced to take action to bring staffing and funding levels into alignment.

4. There are some exceptions. A RAND Corporation study of teacher supply and demand (Haggstrom et al., 1988) allows for the theoretical possibility that demand may exceed employment by defining demand as employment plus unfilled positions. The NCES School and Staffing Survey (SASS) implicitly allows for the same possibility by asking local education agencies how many of their authorized teaching positions have gone unfilled. However, no satisfactory method has yet been invented of quantifying, in practice, the gap between the number of teachers desired by employers and the number actually employed.

5. For example, a major study of transcripts for multiple high school graduating classes was completed in 1989 by MPR Associates, Inc., for the U.S. Department of Education's National Assessment of Vocational Education (see Tuma et al., 1989).

6. In a few instances, however, the development of enrollment projections has been an integral part of teacher supply-demand studies. Coelen and Wilson (1987), for example, present their own enrollment projections for Massachusetts.

7. The most recent NCES enrollment projections, both national and by state, appear together with national projections of teacher demand and attrition in Gerald and Hussar (1990). The NCES state-by-state enrollment projections made their first appearance only slightly earlier in Gerald et al. (1989b).

8. According to Coelen and Wilson (1987), the available course-taking data for Massachusetts were limited to results from a survey of 2,900 high school students conducted in 1985. Course-taking patterns below the high school level and even for parts of the high school curriculum had to be specified by assumption or, as Coelen and Wilson say, on the basis of anecdotal evidence.

9. Note, however, that the Coelen-Wilson formulation yields projections of employment rather than projections of demand per se. It does so by projecting the number of teachers in each subject area as the *lesser* of (1) the number implied by the specified teacher-pupil ratio or (2) the number projected to be "available" according to a very rigid model of the determinants of teacher supply (see below). Moreover, in the event that the projected number of retained teachers is greater than required to meet the specified teacher-pupil ratios, Coelen and Wilson assume that the "excess" retainees will remain employed and that teacher-pupil ratios will be allowed to fall accordingly. In these respects, the Massachusetts model deviates from the standard modeling approach, which is first to project the number of teachers required to maintain specified teacher-pupil ratios and then to ask separately whether the required numbers of teachers are likely to be available.

10. The Connecticut teacher categories are examined in greater detail in the discussion of teacher attrition below because of concerns about whether the eight staff categories are appropriately defined and sufficiently homogeneous to be used in attrition modeling.

11. Specifically, in Gerald et al. (1989a), the per capita income variable enters into the elementary teacher equation with a lag of two years and into the secondary teacher equation with a lag of one year, while the state aid variable enters into the elementary equation with no lag and the secondary equation with a lag of one year. These differences in lag structure can be construed as warning signals that the model structure has not been correctly or completely specified.

12. According to Grissmer and Kirby (1987), "the main reason teachers leave district teaching jobs is to teach in other districts; this accounts for between 15 and 40 percent of district attrition."

13. The SASS public and private school questionnaires do attempt to elicit information from school-level administrators about the whereabouts of teachers employed in fall 1986 who were no longer employed in fall 1987. In particular, respondents are asked whether such leavers are currently teaching in other schools. It would be interesting to determine the accuracy of the resulting data and hence the feasibility of assembling attrition data from school-level (or local education area-level) surveys, but unfortunately the timing of the SASS individual-teacher surveys does not allow comparisons between the individual and school-level reports (i.e., the individual results pertain to attrition between fall 1987 and fall 1988, whereas the school-level results pertain to attrition one year earlier).

14. The significance of the number of certificates per teacher depends strongly on how finely subjects of instruction are classified and how the certification categories correspond to the subject fields taken into account in projecting teacher supply. For instance, a teacher might hold certificates in three closely related subjects (e.g., three subfields of mathematics), but all

three might be included in a single subject-specialty category for the purpose of supply-demand analysis. Note in this regard that there are major differences among state teacher supply-demand models in the number of subject categories for which separate projections are developed.

15. The broad study (BLS, 1986) covers separation rates in many occupations, two of which are elementary teachers and secondary teachers. However, in addition to the general findings about teacher turnover reported in this published study, BLS also produced for NCES a special supplemental analysis that distinguishes public school teachers and, especially, full-time public school teachers from all other persons called teachers (and for whom separation rates are far higher). Both the general and the more disaggregated findings are based on Current Population Survey (CPS) data for 1983-84.

16. For its 1988 projections, NCES simply assumed that the BLS turnover figures for 1983-84 were still valid for the 1986-87 base year and would remain constant throughout the projection period. For the 1989 and 1990 projections, the NCES analysts used the previously mentioned trend extrapolation method to estimate future rates of attrition.

17. Personal communication from an official involved in preparing the South Carolina projections.

18. Strictly speaking, estimates of the age distribution of entering teachers should be among the outputs of models for projecting the supply of entrants rather than of the models of teacher attrition, but given the undeveloped state of models of entrants (see below), it appears necessary, for the time being, to deal with the topic as part of the analysis of attrition.

19. These data are presented in Appendix C of the Connecticut report. The ambiguity arises from a presentation of year-by-year attrition rates for elementary teachers in the main body of the report, which suggests that single-year as well as five-year interval data were available.

20. Massachusetts has since instituted a teacher census, which should provide more detailed data, including teacher assignment data, for future supply-demand analyses.

21. For example, according to Coelen and Wilson (1987:Table 12), the attrition rate for teachers 20-24 rose from about 11 or 12 percent in the early 1970s to about 20 percent by 1984; the rate in the 25-29 age bracket rose from about 11 percent at the beginning of the period to about 15 percent at the end; the rate for those ages 30-34 rose from less than 7 percent to about 9 percent; and the rate for the 35-39 age group rose from about 3.5 or 4 percent to slightly over 5 percent.

22. An important issue concerning longitudinal studies is whether cohorts should be defined to include all teachers who enter teaching in a state in a particular year or only new teachers—those with no prior experience. The studies by Murnane and his associates use the narrower definition in the interests of homogeneity but at the cost of narrowing the applicability of the findings to only a subset of each year's entrants.

23. The Grissmer and Kirby 1991 study of Indiana offers both cross-sectional and longitudinal analyses and so is discussed both here and under the "longitudinal analysis" subheading.

24. This study and other studies by Murnane and his associates cover only teachers in selected subject fields and therefore do not provide a complete picture of interfield differences in attrition patterns. In particular, they do not cover vocational education or special education teachers.

25. This study covers white North Carolina teachers only. Murnane and his associates determined that both personal characteristics and attrition behavior differed substantially between white and black teachers and, consequently, that pooling the data for the two groups would distort the results.

26. Murnane et al. offer careful disclaimers to the effect that NTE scores are not necessarily indicators of teacher quality (in the sense of teaching effectiveness), although they do characterize such scores as indicators of teachers' general ability.

27. Fewer state studies are discussed here than in the previous chapters. This is because some teacher supply-demand studies offer no projections of the supply of entering teachers. In particular, the Ohio and New York analyses circumvent the supply-of-entrants issue by projecting numbers of new hires as fixed or extrapolated percentages of the total number of teachers employed.

28. The Lauritzen-Friedman study also deals at length with a special situation affecting the teacher market in Wisconsin in the 1989-1991 period—namely, the creation of a one-time, apparently attractive, early retirement window for currently employed teachers. This window apparently has had a drastic, if temporary, impact on employment opportunities for new teachers in Wisconsin, and Lauritzen and Friedman devote large portions of their report to sorting out and quantifying the effects.

29. Based on discussions with the model developers, I understand that the various entry and reentry rates are not derived from analyses of individual-teacher data but rather from regression equations fitted to aggregative data for whole entering cohorts. Using the individual data would presumably make it possible not only to estimate the transition rates more accurately but also to determine how they vary in relation to age, gender, and perhaps other characteristics of teachers. However, the limitations of the Massachusetts data would apparently have precluded any individual-level analysis of variations in transition rates among teachers of different subjects.

30. As noted earlier, the Coelen-Wilson model also allows in some circumstances for a supply constraint in the opposite direction—namely, that school systems will be required to employ more teachers than they want and to adjust their teache-pupil ratios upward if the supply of retained teachers exceeds the number demanded. That is, Coelen and Wilson assume that Massachusetts school districts have no ability to eliminate already employed teachers who wish to continue teaching—an assumption that seems unrealistically rigid compared, say, with an assumption that districts must adjust gradually rather than instantly to an excess supply of retainees.

31. More specifically, the Connecticut report offers "high" and "low" estimates of supply for each group, corresponding, respectively, to the assumptions that nonrespondents to the survey behave like respondents and that all nonrespondents are not in the supply.

32. This statement should perhaps be qualified by noting that the supply of short-term temporary leavers—especially teachers who took one- or two-year leaves of absence—may be approximated reasonably well by the numbers who return. The premise is that many such temporary leavers retain official connections with their districts (formal leave status) and are accorded priority in hiring. It is unlikely, however, that the same can be said of former teachers who have been away longer and whose formal claims to jobs have lapsed.

33. The NTE scores of newly certificated white teachers in North Carolina are substantially higher than the scores of newly certificated black teachers. Murnane et al. speculate that the negative relationship between entry rate and NTE score for whites reflects the better nonteaching job opportunities available to high-scoring whites (a supply-side phenomenon), whereas the absence of such a relationship for blacks reflects the lack of job offers for low-scoring black applicants (a demand-side phenomenon).

Discussion

GUS HAGGSTROM

Stephen Barro has given us a comprehensive, informative, and thought-provoking review of conventional wisdom and practice for monitoring teacher supply, demand, and quality. His emphasis is on *models*, notably supply-demand projection models, that can be used to track the condition of teaching, identify trends, anticipate changes, and provide detailed projections of teacher supply and demand. Adopting an idealistic perspective, he downplays *mechanical* and *demographic* models that are "capable only of estimating what will happen in the future if established patterns or trends continue" in favor of *behavioral* models that can allow for the "effects of hypothetical changes in circumstances on teacher supply and demand." Since examples of the latter do not yet exist, Barro devotes most of his discussion to *modeling* desiderata laced with provocative critiques of recent efforts to provide the basic information about teachers needed to gauge the breadth and severity of school staffing problems today and in the future.

The italicized terms above are often controversial when used to advocate some methods and denounce others. The term *model*, coupled with adjectives such as *causal*, *econometric*, *utility-maximizing*, or *structural*, can incite reverence or raise a red flag. Noting that *model* refers to a wide variety of conceptual frameworks in the social sciences, David Freedman, a University of California statistician, called it the *m-word*. Thanks in part to Freedman's efforts to reveal the tenuous underpinnings of some time-honored models in psychology, econometrics, drug toxicity assessment, and census adjustment (e.g., see the summer 1987 issue of the *Journal of Educational Statistics* and the 31 May 1991 issue of *Science*), the word *model* has lost some of its mystique. So has the word *modeling*, which suggests *model-building*. But, to many data analysts, *modeling* is closer to *muddling* and refers to the use of largely atheoretical methods, perhaps including model-fitting, for converting raw data into more readily assimilated information in the form of tables, plots, regression equations, and so forth.

Unlike mathematical and statistical models, such as the models for graded social systems discussed in *Stochastic Models for Social Processes* (Bartholomew, 1973), Barro's review of supply-demand projection models reveals a collage of model fragments, statistical techniques, flow chart imagery, and generalities about relationships. Although Barro cites some studies that make use of mathematical and statistical models, his discussion is not a treatment of models per se, but rather a discourse on modeling considerations.

Despite his theoretical perspective, Barro's discussion of teacher supply and demand is down-to-earth and insightful. I especially liked his interesting and revelatory summary of existing studies of teacher demand and turnover. It shows that several states already have data systems that allow continual assessments of their teacher work forces along several dimensions. It also underscores the sorry state of information on teacher stocks and flows at the national level that existed prior to the fielding of the Schools and Staffing Survey. Much of Barro's discussion pertains to narrowly focused assessments, often just tabulations, of teacher attrition based on administrative records at the state level. As he observes, there are numerous definitional problems associated with the terms *turnover* and *mobility* depending on the teacher population under study, and there are several kinds of losses and status changes that need to be separated for some purposes. I found his discussions of teacher supply and quality less informative, but those topics present difficult conceptual and measurement issues that make them relatively intractable, except in the abstract.

Although this review of existing work is interesting and informative, the implications for forecasting or monitoring the condition of teaching are not clear. In particular, the paper provides little guidance for creating data bases to support educational planning models at any level of aggregation or for developing data systems on teachers to inform real-time decision making by school administrators.

While few would deny the desirability of having an overarching conceptual framework to guide thinking about the components of a data system and to facilitate bookkeeping associated with codifying data elements, maintaining linkages, and ensuring consistency across subsystems, the need for an all-encompassing model is debatable. With respect to Barro's interest in detailed projections of teacher supply and demand, I feel that the task is so highly dependent on the nature of the forecasts and data availability that generalities are academic. Full-blown manpower planning models have their place, but so do simple ad hoc data-gathering efforts. To support spring hiring decisions at the district level, for example, estimates of impending losses of current teachers derived from reports of principals are bound to be more credible and reliable than projections based on analyses of previous years' losses.

Insofar as long-term projections of teacher supply and demand are concerned, it seems plausible that the year-to-year flows into and out of narrowly defined teacher categories can be simulated using transition and entry rates estimated from flow data, so that the resulting "model" can be manipulated recursively to generate disaggregated projections several years into the future. However, as demographers have long known, projections of this type are extremely sensitive to shifts in the rates, and the errors build up multiplicatively over time (Keyfitz, 1972).

The main attractions of these models are that they build on irrefutable accounting equations and seem to afford unlimited possibilities for refinements. One way of expressing the accounting equations is in terms of the matrix identity

$$S(t) = P(t)\, S(t-1) + N(t)$$

relating the stocks of teachers in year t, denoted by $S(t)$, to the stocks in year $t - 1$ and the numbers of "new" teachers, $N(t)$, in year t. Here, $S(t)$ and $N(t)$ are n-dimensional vectors, such that the ith component $s(i;t)$ of $S(t)$ is the number of teachers in the ith teacher category; and $P(t)$ is an n-by-n matrix of flow rates between categories, i.e., $p(i,j;t)$ is the proportion of teachers in the ith category at time $t - 1$ moving to the jth category at time t.

Since the components of $S(t)$ and $S(t - 1)$ can be defined to include any number of teacher categories (e.g., by state, field, and years of service) as well as loss categories for nonreturning teachers, the components can be extended to fit any data system, real or imaginary. Alternatively, the equations can serve as overall constraints for sets of underlying relations, such as equations linking stocks of teachers to enrollment levels, or equations relating flow rates into certain loss categories as parametric functions of teacher characteristics, school attributes, and economic factors.

The realities of providing all the numbers and estimates needed to fill in the equations inevitably lead to simplifying assumptions about linkages in the flows over time or across teacher categories. In addition to structural simplifications, statistical pooling and smoothing techniques come into play, e.g., procedures for smoothing subsets of the transition and loss rates by logistic regression or survival analysis methodology. Given the variety of constraints, feedback mechanisms, statistical adjustments, and allowances for exogenous factors that can be imposed, it is impossible to generalize about the appropriateness of the models. But, as is clear from the limited successes of large-scale computer models of the economy, adding complexity and detail may not improve predictability or credibility. Complicated models of social processes are difficult to justify or explain, detracting from their utility for informing the public of the nature and quality of the data system supporting the projections.

It is easy to challenge some of the particulars in the methodology used by the National Center for Education Statistics (NCES) for generating the 10-year projections published in the *Projections of Education Statistics*. But Debra Gerald and her colleagues at NCES do more than just list extrapolations from a set of prediction equations. I salute NCES's long-standing practice of listing the time series that feed into the projection equations, documenting the data sources, and providing a full accounting of their methodology, often including three sets of projections (low, middle, and high) to reveal their sensitivity to key parameter specifications. Given the methodological warts and data gaps, including the dearth of information on private schools, readers can judge for themselves whether the information justifies saying, for example, that the demand for new teachers will greatly exceed the number of college graduates planning to enter teaching over the next several years.

In any case, national projections are almost devoid of content about local conditions, because the teacher labor market is fragmented into small segments by state, sector, and teaching field. Hefty salary increases in a large school district or the relaxation of state certification requirements can cause big swings in teacher supply and demand within a state by stimulating the mobility of current teachers or opening up new sources of supply. National projections at best whet the appetite for more definitive information about, say, the qualifications, backgrounds, and employment patterns of mathematics teachers in California public schools. Recognizing that many of them launched their teaching careers in private schools, other states, and other fields, and that some of them have taken breaks away from teaching, we see that monitoring the condition of teaching requires tracking alternate routes into teaching and examining the occupational mobility of teachers, not only across states, sectors, and fields, but also into and out of nonteaching activities. As Emily Feistritzer reports in her *Profile of Teachers in the U.S.—1990*, more than a third of current public school teachers have had at least one break from teaching, and nearly half of the "new" teachers hired since 1985 have had at least one break.

A number of other demographic and economic factors affect teacher flows at the district and state levels. On the demand side, the states differ markedly in their school-age population growth rates and their means for funding public education. In California, as a result of a severe budgetary crunch at the state level, some districts have laid off hundreds of teachers and resorted to substantial increases in class sizes. Uncertainties about the possible effects of "school choice" and voucher programs add another layer of unknowns. On the supply side, teacher preparation and certification policies seem to be in a continual state of flux. And little information exists about the dependence of teacher supply on economic conditions affecting other college-trained workers in the same area.

It was considerations like these that guided our NCES-sponsored work at RAND in redesigning the Schools and Staffing Survey to enhance their utility for making assessments of the condition of teaching across the nation. Our 1988 RAND report *Assessing Teacher Supply and Demand*, coauthored with Linda Darling-Hammond and David Grissmer, spells out our rationale for the linked surveys of districts, schools, principals, teachers, and former teachers that were subsequently implemented. Since NCES adopted the survey instruments that we devised almost without change, most of our specifications of data desiderata for a national data base on teachers can be inferred from an examination of the questionnaires themselves.

The district and private school questionnaires asked for detailed staffing breakdowns to permit estimating teacher stocks by state, sector, level, and field. The school surveys also elicited information on teacher turnover by field that can be aggregated to provide key turnover estimates at any level of aggregation or used to augment the individual data on samples of teachers in the same schools.

In addition to providing individual data for profiling teachers along numerous dimensions, the teacher surveys contained a sequence of items pertaining to the teachers' work histories to identify sources of entry into teaching and to pinpoint the nature and timing of subsequent transitions. Since the items include current and previous year's statuses (full-time, part-time, itinerant teacher, substitute, etc.), year of entry into full-time teaching, total years of service, years at present school, number of breaks in service, and main activity during the year prior to current teaching assignment, the items extract the key information needed to support analyses of employment patterns and their linkages to school policies, family characteristics, and economic factors.

As the first step in implementing a one-year follow-up survey of teachers and ex-teachers, we recommended going back to the school representatives in the SASS school sample and asking them to fill out a checklist encoding the current statuses of all teachers who participated in the base year survey, including their reported reasons for leaving and current main activities. In effect, this created polytomous outcome measures for updating the work histories of the base year participants to support detailed analyses of "competing risks" in teacher turnover.

Hence, the SASS surveys were specifically designed to allow analyses of teachers' career patterns along numerous dimensions—attrition, field-shifting, mobility, longevity, breaks in service, retirement, etc. For the most part, the individual data for these analyses are right-censored observations of continuing sojourns of teaching activity, i.e., most SASS participants will continue teaching for one or more years. The data can be analyzed by adapting standard procedures for fitting year-to-year transition rates (e.g., by logistic regression) or by using nonparametric or semiparametric procedures that have been especially tailored to handle censored failure-time or event-history data in demographic and biostatistical contexts (Elandt-Johnson and Johnson, 1980; Kalbfleisch and Prentice, 1980; Cox and Oakes, 1984; Tuma and Haanan, 1984).

It is also important to undertake the kinds of analyses of teacher stocks, flows, and utilization needed to assess the condition of teaching across the nation today and to pinpoint shortcomings, trouble spots, and signs of erosion that could worsen over the next few years. Here, I am not just referring to the basic information needed to fill in the blanks in manpower planning models, such as those discussed in Bartholomew and Forbes's *Statistical Techniques for Manpower Planning* (1979), but also the information about teachers' characteristics, qualifications, working conditions, family status, future plans, and attitudes that is needed to profile the teaching work force along many other dimensions that bear directly or indirectly on teacher supply, demand, and quality.

In my view, the SASS survey instruments were well designed to gather the necessary information to meet these objectives. But merely asking the right questions is not sufficient, because the surveys are restricted to probability samples of districts, schools, and teachers. The requisite statistical infrastructure has to be in place to allow extrapolations from SASS samples to the entire population and to permit linkages with other data bases. For the public schools, NCES's Common Core of Data, the repository of annual censuses of districts, is the main linkage between the SASS files and the population; it provides the sampling frame and subpopulation counts needed to support the sampling plan. The SASS files can be viewed as augmentations to the Common Core, which serves as the central data base on public schools. Since the state data systems and studies that Barro cites are also additions to the same data base, the linkages in the combined data base can be exploited provided that the data elements in the various segments are commensurate. Regrettably, there is no similar census or sampling frame for the private schools, so that statistical underpinnings of the SASS private school data are less firm.

By providing detailed information on the employment patterns of teachers and principals, the SASS files also provide data for examining flows into, within, and out of a sizable segment of the college-educated work force. Most teachers, especially those with science, mathematics, and business backgrounds, have highly marketable job skills. Analyses of the flows of college graduates into and out of teaching can shed light on the non-teaching opportunities for teachers, circumscribe pools of workers that have some propensity to enter teaching, and identify economic factors related to shifts into or out of teaching. The major vehicles for tracking the entire labor force are the Current Population Survey (CPS) and the decennial censuses. The Bureau of Labor Statistics (BLS) relies on CPS data to make the projections of demand by occupation that are cited in several publications, including its two series entitled *Occupational Outlook Handbook* and *Outlook 2000*. Perhaps because the complicated BLS projections methodology suffers from some of the expositional problems that I mentioned earlier, it is difficult to determine how the projections of teacher supply and demand were generated, and the information in the *Handbook* about the outlook for teachers is vague. Nevertheless, the CPS and SASS files provide the data and the linkages for extending examinations of teacher mobility into more general studies of employment decision making in the college-trained labor force, and this opportunity should be exploited.

REFERENCES

Bartholomew, D.J.
1973 *Stochastic Models for Social Processes.* Second edition. New York: John Wiley and Sons.

Bartholomew, D.J., and A.F. Forbes
1979 *Statistical Techniques for Manpower Planning.* New York: John Wiley and Sons.

Bureau of Labor Statistics
1989 *Outlook 2000.* Bulletin 2352, November. Washington, D.C.: U.S. Department of Labor, Bureau of Labor Statistics.
1990 *Occupational Outlook Handbook.* Bulletin 2350, April. Washington, D.C.: U.S. Department of Labor, Bureau of Labor Statistics.

Cox, D.R., and D. Oakes
1984 *Analysis of Survival Data.* London: Chapman and Hall.

Elandt-Johnson, R.C., and N.L. Johnson
1980 *Survival Models and Data Analysis.* New York: John Wiley and Sons.

Feistritzer, Emily
1990 *Profile of Teachers in the U.S.—1990.* Washington, D.C.: National Center for Education Information.

Freedman, David A.
1987 As others see us: A case study in path analysis. *Journal of Educational Statistics* 12(2)(Summer):101-128.
1991 Adjusting the 1990 census. *Science* 252(May):1233-1236.

Haggstrom, Gus W., Linda Darling-Hammond, and David W. Grissmer
1988 *Assessing Teacher Supply and Demand.* May. R-3633-ED/CSTP. Santa Monica, California: The RAND Corporation.

Kalbfleisch, J.D., and R.L. Prentice
1980 *The Statistical Analysis of Failure Time Data.* New York: John Wiley and Sons.

Keyfitz, Nathan
1972 On future population. *Journal of the American Statistical Association* 67(338)(June):347-363.

Tuma, Nancy B., and Michael Hannan
1984 *Social Dynamics: Models and Methods.* New York: Academic Press.

Discussion

RONALD E. KUTSCHER

The rose-colored glasses that my remarks will be filtered through are those of an economist specializing in the labor market and, in fact, most of my professional career has been devoted to projecting the labor market, so, what I say has been through that filter.

I really have no quarrel with the paper that Steve Barro has prepared. Most of what I hope to bring to you is explicitly or implicitly in his paper. Perhaps I will rephrase them in a somewhat different way, and by doing so provide some additional insights.

I would like to begin by asking a question. Why are supply and demand projections of teachers being developed? I think we must begin with that question because it is a very important issue in determining how much to invest in improving the models used in these projections. That is, if these supply and demand projections of teachers are to be used for information and indicative purposes only, then the cost to users of errors in the projections may be relatively low. If these projections are used to make very concrete decisions such as expanding teacher training programs or institutions, adding to or constructing new buildings, or adding or subtracting staff, then the cost of errors in these projections becomes much higher. If the cost of errors is very large, then we should be willing to spend more time, money, staff, and effort in exploring means of improving the projections.

The principal cost of improving projections is in defining the types of data needed and in collecting underlying data necessary for estimation of new or improved models. The model-building portion of the added cost is a relatively small part of the total cost. Once you determine what data are needed to develop the models, and you have collected those data, then the model builder's marginal or additional cost is relatively low. In the interim, however, the data development and the data collection phase will have taken considerable time.

If the cost of errors in the use of these projections is relatively low in terms of these decisions, simple models may be providing us with information that is not all that bad. We must judge which of these two costs is closer to reality. If, however, the costs are quite high and we decide it pays to develop more elaborate models, one has to be careful not to fall into a common trap. That trap is that use of a more sophisticated and theoretically elegant model does not ensure that the accuracy of the projections will be significantly improved.

A more sophisticated model may assist you in other ways, however, by explaining why you were wrong when your projections are in error. Secondly, it allows you to be a classical two-handed economist, because you can run what are labeled what-if simulations. For example, you can simulate what-if revenues drop by three percent, how will that affect the demand for teachers? Or, if demand increases for other professionals, what impact will that likely have on the supply of teachers? Answers to such simulations can be very useful to policy makers.

I am assuming the cost of errors is high and that therefore there is a desire to move to develop more detailed and sophisticated models. I say that because, otherwise, why are we here? Consequently, I will make observations that I think are very pertinent to consider in developing a more elaborate model. First, I am extremely skeptical of what I will label as isolated models. These are models that cover only a small segment of a larger entity. I believe there is considerable interaction within an economy. If I were asked to develop a model for Estonia or for Delaware, I believe it could not be done without taking into consideration everything else that is going on around those jurisdictions. Consequently, in developing better models for projecting teacher supply and demand, I urge that this be done in a broader context, which I will elaborate on in a moment. In addition, we must decide whether these models of teacher supply and demand are designed primarily for short-term or for long-term projections. This is an important distinction because the fundamental nature of how you build these two types of models is different.

How to proceed? I would urge that a teacher supply-demand model begin initially with a broad aggregate type model that describes the entire U.S. economy. From that starting point, the model would be disaggregated toward the subject matter of concern, in this case the teaching profession. To do so it certainly would be necessary to consider the educational industry, government revenues sources and uses, and public-private education distinctions—to name just a very few obvious inclusions.

There are two factors are important in any model building: national trends and local trends. In order to try to model any phenomenon, you must attempt to capture both the impact of overall national trends and the impact of local trends on this phenomenon. If you do one and not the other, you will likely increase your projection errors. Local trends can mean geography or they can mean more specific detail about the segment of the economy in which you have the greatest interest.

After this broad beginning, one can begin to disaggregate toward what you need. If ultimately you are concerned with the teaching profession, you start out overall, but then you begin to disaggregate the model by industry in order to capture other employment opportunities for those educated as teachers, by type of school, by geography and other important factors, which could affect teacher supply and demand. Although disaggregating the model by industry will yield more precision in its estimating equations, there is a concern, however, because you very likely will have more error in the underlying disaggregated data. The disaggregation should not proceed so far that the error in the underlying data overwhelms any additional forecasting power that you have gained by the disaggregation.

What other things would I want to see in this model? Well, Steve Barro and Gus Haggstrom both have talked about wages. I think it is very important that wages be in any model that considers supply and demand factors in teaching. According to the *Washington Post* of March 23, 1991, the average salary of players in the National Basketball Association is $950,000. Does anyone think this conference on teacher supply-demand problems would be held if the average teaching salary was $950,000? If the situation were reversed, maybe the National Research Council would be concerned about the supply and quality of players for the National Basketball Association. So wages are a very important determinant of both the supply and demand of future teachers. Wages are needed not only for teachers but also for other employment opportunities as well.

An additional aspect is the revenues that will be available. You cannot use some overall income variable to project the ability to hire teachers, because income is not necessarily a good proxy for the tax revenues of state and local governments or the share of those revenues that will be devoted to education. Furthermore, it can be important to look at nonwage aspects of working conditions—benefits, for example. We reviewed the supply and demand issues in nursing recently and it turned out that, while wages was one of the factors, working conditions may have been as important a determinant of supply problems in nursing as wages.

One needs to put all of this into a broader economic context. I think it has been noted a number of times that the supply and demand balance for an occupation in a state in which the unemployment rate is 8 percent is much different than it is in a state in which the unemployment rate is 4 percent. When you examine any occupational shortage, you are very unlikely to find shortages if the unemployment rate in the area is 8 or 9 percent. It is only when the unemployment rate drops and other alternative employment opportunities are available that shortages are much more likely to occur. Thus, it is very important to look at the overall economic situation. Of course, I am returning to a point I made earlier about whether the model was to be primarily of a short-term (1-3 years) or long-term (5 or more years) in orientation.

From my viewpoint, it is most important to look at other employment possibilities. That clearly is so since some persons educated as teachers can decide to teach or they can decide to go into other fields. Consequently, if you do not know what is happening in these other employment opportunity fields, then it is very hard to know what the supply and demand tradeoff is for teachers.

In commenting on Steve Barro's paper, someone noted that they were surprised that the retention rate for mathematicians was different than it was for other scientists. To me, that can be explained by the fact that the alternative employment opportunities for those educated in the other sciences are much greater than are the possibilities for pure mathematicians. Pure mathematicians have a much smaller scope of jobs that are open to them than do natural scientists. So they are more likely to stay on that job.

An additional point that I would think important to consider in model development is to take into account the types of pupils that are to be enrolled. Pupils with handicaps have different teacher requirements, as may pupils in rural areas. Size of the school and size of the community may be variables that are extremely important in terms of demand and even the supply of teachers. All these important factors should be built into a more sophisticated model of teacher supply and demand.

All of my points are made for consideration in improving models for *analyzing* teacher supply and demand. Even if these recommendations were followed, one could still not develop a model capable of projecting a *numerical* shortage or surplus of teachers. Techniques are simply not available to accomplish that and are not likely to be so in the foreseeable future.

I would like to close my remarks with one final observation that may only be related indirectly to the question of teacher supply and demand. There is one important trend that is dominant over the last 30 years in the labor market. Almost every professional group has developed a very large paraprofessional or technical group that goes along with the profession. This development of technicians and paraprofessionals exists for the medical, accounting, engineering, and legal professions.

It is interesting and ironic that this trend is not true in the education industry—at least not to any degree approaching that found in the other professional groups. This fact may have an important implication for supply and demand balance in teaching. We are at the point in the medical profession, for example, at which physicians and dentists are among the slowest-growing component of the health care delivery industry. It is the technician component that is growing very rapidly. A physician's office 40 years ago was staffed by a nurse and a receptionist. Today that same office may still have 1 or 2 physicians, but very likely will have 4 to 10 trained technicians and clerical assistants. By analogy, if the teaching profession had developed like other professions, a teacher would be responsible for 50 or 75 students. However, each teacher would have several paraprofessionals and clerical assistants in the classroom in order to teach such a large group. I think this may be another important dimension of the supply and demand balance that needs detailed examination.

General Discussion

The general discussion addressed the following topics: (a) theory underlying TSDQ projection models; (b) the reciprocal relationship of TSDQ modeling and data bases; (c) constraints on accuracy of TSD projections imposed by the quality of data used in projection equations; (d) equilibration mechanisms in teacher supply and demand; (e) problems in modeling the supply of graduates from teacher preparation programs; (f) the appropriateness of applying concepts from economics to modeling teacher supply and demand; and (g) the utility of TSDQ models and of state and national data bases for informing policy issues in education. The following paragraphs summarize each of these topics.

Since the Barro paper did not consider theory relevant to TSDQ projection models, a suggestion was made that explication of the theoretical underpinnings of these models would be useful for policy makers who are concerned about teacher supply and demand projections. Although Stephen Barro recognized that such theory was not brought out in the paper, he stated that there is a clear theoretical base for much projection modeling of the teacher force on both the supply side and on the demand side.

On the supply side, theoretical strands from human capital theory, labor market search theory, and labor market uncertainty theory pertain to factors that might influence the decisions of individual teachers to enter or to remain in the profession. On the demand side, economic theory of public fiscal behavior is relevant to decisions of state and local government on spending priorities, including the place of education in such priorities. In turn, the demand for teachers is a function of fiscal capacity and the relative price of teachers compared with alternative expenditures.

The reciprocal relationship of TSDQ models and data bases was noted. On one hand, models are useful in furthering the development of data bases. On the other hand, the development of models is constrained by limited availability of data, especially data of sufficient precision and relevance to determine whether the teacher labor market is supply- or demand-constrained.

The precision of teacher supply and demand projections, even with good models, is limited by the inaccuracy of estimates for key variables used in projection equations, when the variables themselves have to be projected. Since projections of variables such as teacher attrition rates and enrollment growth in public education are imprecise, so will be projections of teacher supply and demand derived from equations that use these variables.

In a world of limited resources, however, projection models will continue to be imperfect. The issue is how to handle this uncertainty. Either sufficient resources will have to be invested to develop projections of adequate precision, or the teacher market will be left to equilibrate on its own in accordance with decisions of individuals in the market based on information available to them at the time.

Equilibration mechanisms have been neglected in TSDQ models. In economics, the long-running equilibration mechanism is relative wage rates. While this mechanism is working out in the teacher labor market, shorter-term equilibration occurs through the mechanisms of adjustments in teacher quality requirements and in teacher-pupil ratios. The definition and measurement of teacher quality continues to be a problem. In teaching, a virtually unexplored, but potential equilibrating mechanism is the hiring of a given number of trained teachers versus the hiring of fewer teachers plus paraprofessional assistants. Good TSDQ models will explicate these equilibrating mechanisms and how they function under conditions of disequilibrium.

Since much of the entering supply of teachers comes directly from output of teacher preparation programs, difficulty in modeling this source was discussed. It was observed that undergraduate students contemplating teaching as a career can delay making a commitment to this profession much longer than students committing to other professions such as medicine and engineering. In essence, it was hypothesized that the pipeline for newly prepared teachers is much shorter than in many other professions and therefore more difficult to model accurately.

Although some doubt was expressed about the validity of this hypothesis, the presumed shortness of the pipeline was viewed as an advantage in that the teacher preparation process, including decisions by individuals to enter it, is very responsive to shifts in demand in the teacher labor market. With increased demand, however, there is the possibility that new supply might quickly overshoot the increase in demand. While the asserted shortness and flexibility of the new teacher pipeline might indeed be valid observations, wide variations in teacher preparation and certification regulations, by state, pose great difficulties in modeling this aspect of teacher supply. This modeling must be done on a state-by-state basis.

A question was raised about the utility of applying economic principles of supply and demand to modeling the teacher labor market, since hiring decisions in education typically are made by principals at the school level, and must be responsive to changes in curriculum policy such as increased requirements for mathematics courses. These hiring decisions are strongly affected by school variables such as size. Smaller secondary schools require many teachers who are capable of teaching in more than one field, such as in chemistry and physics, while very large high schools might be able to hire specialized mathematics teachers. Principals consider tradeoffs such as hiring a new teacher in a particular subject matter or reassigning a teacher already on the staff. Similarly, teachers who must instruct in two or more subject areas might be more likely to leave a school for one in which they can concentrate their instruction in their preferred subject. Rather than large-scale supply and demand modeling, it might be more productive to study and model teacher flows at the school level.

In the final analysis, the utility of TSDQ projection models depends on the degree to which they inform education policy issues. While there are many problems with models, state and national data independent of models can help clarify a number of policy issues. For example, state and national data can contribute significantly to understanding issues such as the role of minorities in teaching, the quality and preparation of science teachers, and the impact of changes in licensing requirements of teachers. Data can be organized to inform policy debate on such issues, even though such data may not fit well into TSDQ models.

V

DATA BASES

Part V addresses issues entailed in developing and maintaining data bases supportive of TSDQ modeling and research. Relevant data bases at the state, regional, and national levels are identified, reviewed, analyzed, and compared in terms of quality, comprehensiveness, timeliness, and inclusion of longitudinal information. Supplementary material describing relevant national data bases is contained in Appendix B, and the identification of variables relevant to TSDQ models and research contained in these national data bases is reported in Appendix C.

In addition, the paper by Murnane and the discussion by Grissmer illustrate the use of state data bases to investigate important TSDQ problems. The information contained in teacher data bases is also considered in relation to the information needs of policy makers concerned with teacher work force issues. Finally, the adequacy of existing data bases and the need for improved or additional data bases is examined.

State Data on Teacher Supply, Equity, and Qualifications

ROLF K. BLANK

State departments of education have been active in building and improving management information systems. An important part of most state systems is a data file of teachers and other professional educators in public elementary and secondary schools. States typically collect and report information on characteristics of teachers in response to a state law requiring such data. But state information systems are designed for a multitude of purposes, such as reporting data to federal agencies, monitoring the quality of teachers hired by local districts, and analyzing teacher supply and demand in the state.

The Council of Chief State School Officers (CCSSO), the national association of state superintendents and commissioners, has analyzed the types of data on teachers that are available from state education information systems. The CCSSO State Science/Mathematics Indicators Project has developed a system of indicators of the condition of science and mathematics education that are partly based on state-collected data, along with information about teacher characteristics (Blank, 1986; Blank and Dalkilic, 1990). The CCSSO Education Data Improvement Project has worked with states and the National Center for Education Statistics to standardize the definitions for state-collected teacher data and to improve the quality of state data (CCSSO, 1988). Information gathered from states through these two projects form the basis for this paper.

The characteristics of teachers that are included in state information systems vary widely, and the definitions used to collect these data also vary among states (Blank and Espenshade, 1988; CCSSO, 1988). The uses of state data on teachers for producing statistics on teacher supply and demand also vary widely (National Research Council, 1987). As of 1987, 34 states had developed state reports on teacher shortages or supply and demand, while 26 of them indicated that such a report is provided annually (Blank and Espenshade, 1988). If state data are to be considered as a source for national analyses of the teaching force or for projections of teacher supply and demand, it is important to consider the availability, quality, and utility of state teacher data.

This paper addresses the following four questions concerning state data on elementary and secondary teachers in public schools:

(1) What is the breadth of teacher data are available from state information systems?

(2) What is the quality and timeliness of the state data?

(3) To what extent are state data on teachers linked through one or more data files so that analyses can be conducted?

(4) How can state data be used for national-level analyses?

BREADTH OF STATE DATA ON TEACHERS

CCSSO conducted a survey of all state departments of education in 1987 to determine the availability of state-collected data on a variety of possible indicators of science and mathematics education (Blank and Espenshade, 1988). The results were used to select a small set of indicators that were subsequently developed as state-by-state and national indicators (Blank and Dalkilic, 1990). In 1988 the CCSSO Education Data Improvement Project collected information from state departments of education on the definitions used to collect and report on characteristics of education staff (CCSSO, 1988). The information was used to consider revisions in procedures and data elements reported to the National Center for Education Statistics in the Common Core of Data.

Information on availability of state data from the two CCSSO projects was integrated to produce a summary of the number of states that collect data on elements of teacher supply, demand, and quality. The delineation of these three categories of teacher data and the identification of desired variables for measuring supply, demand, and quality followed the analysis and recommendations of two National Research Council reports (1987, 1990). The results of the NRC survey on "availability of state data on public school professional personnel" (1991) were used to check the results of the CCSSO surveys.

Table 1 lists the number of states that collect data on demographic characteristics of teachers, measures of teacher quality, and elements of teacher supply and demand. CCSSO surveys indicate that 49 states have an automated data file on the characteristics of teachers (and other professional

TABLE 1 State Data on Teachers: Number of States that Collect Data on Elements of Teacher Supply, Demand, and Qualifications as of Spring 1987 (N = 50 states and District of Columbia)

	Number of States
Teacher Assignment by:	
District	49
School	48
Grade level of assignment	43
Subject of current assignment	48
Demographic Characteristics of Teachers:	
Date of birth (age)	40
Sex	47
Race/Ethnicity	44
Teacher Qualifications:	
Education attainment (degree status)	47
Academic major (bachelor's degree)	40
Certification type	41
Subject/field of certification	40
Years of professional experience:	40
Years of teaching experience	25
Years in current district	36
Years in other district	23
Years in current assignment	13
Teacher Demand:	
Pupil-teacher ratio	37
Pupil-teacher ratio by subject	22
Enrollment projections	36
Emergency/provisional certificates	41
Positions vacant or withdrawn, or filled with non-certified teacher or substitute	31
Teacher salary (contract or base)	47
Teacher Supply:	
New college graduates in education	33
New graduates with non-education majors and certified to teach	20
In-migration of teachers from other states	27
Re-entrants into teaching	21
Entrants from other occupations	17
Continuing teachers/teacher attrition	32
Continuing teachers in new subject/field	27
Teachers retiring	37
New Hires:	
Occupation prior year	10
Location of occupation prior year	7

SOURCE: State Science/Mathematics Indicators Project, 1987 (unpublished data). Council of Chief State School Officers, Washington, D.C.

education personnel). All of the variables listed in Table 1 are generally not included on the same data file. There are three kinds of data files on teachers in most states: (a) current teacher file (including demographics, district and school, current assignments, education attainment, contract salary, and experience); (b) certification file (including type of certification and subjects or fields of certification); and (c) state retirement system file (including year of birth and year entering the system). Most states can link the files through the teacher social security number or other identifier.

The items listed in Table 1 under Teacher Demand and Teacher Supply may be from several data sources at the state level, including student membership counts by grade and higher education data, as well as from computations or analyses of data on the current teacher file, such as identifying the source of new hires. In 1987, 34 states reported having developed estimates of teacher shortages or supply and demand, but states were not asked to identify which of the data elements were used in these estimates. Thus, the list of elements by number of states in Table 1 shows the *potential* of state data for analyses of teacher supply, demand, and quality.

Over 40 states collect data on teachers' demographic characteristics, education attainment, and certification status. Cross-tabulations of data on combinations of these variables are difficult to accomplish in some of the states. For example, the Science/Math Indicators Project found that only 30 of the 40 states could report the number of teachers assigned in mathematics and science by their certification status in the subject(s) they were teaching.

QUALITY AND TIMELINESS OF TEACHER DATA

State departments of education collect data on characteristics of teachers for their current teacher file through several different data collection approaches. One approach is an annual survey form developed by the state for each individual teacher in the state. This form asks for new or updated demographic information, current teaching assignments and student enrollments by school period, and information on education attainment and salary. This type of form is used by about 20 states, including California, New York, Connecticut, Ohio, Minnesota, South Carolina, Alabama, and Virginia.

A second approach is a district or school form that lists teachers on the current state file and asks the district or school to update the existing data or provide new data on teacher demographics, subject and grade assignments, and education attainment and salary. Over half the states use this method of collecting data on teachers.

A third approach is a student-based computerized information system in which information about teacher assignments and teacher characteristics is linked to a statewide data base on each student. Student records and schedules and teacher data are relayed on computer files from the school to the district to the state. This system is in place in Florida and Hawaii and is being developed in Georgia, Texas, North Carolina, and other states.

Certification information is collected and maintained in a separate certification file in most states. A majority of states have the current teacher file and certification file linked by social security number and annually check the certification status of each teacher. Some states have only recently computerized their certification file and some states do not cross-check assignments and certification.

There are a variety of issues in assessing the quality of state data on teachers. One issue is the response rate, i.e., the proportion of teachers in classrooms for which data are reported to the state. The Science/Math Indicators Project asked states to report on response rates and data editing procedures. About one-third of the states collect data directly from teachers, and response rates for those states were from 98 to 100 percent. However, both these states and states that collect data through schools and districts must depend on lists of current teachers and new teachers that are provided by schools or school districts.

A second issue is the reliability of the data that are reported by teachers and stored on state files. States reporting data on science and mathematics indicators were asked to report on data editing procedures in 1989-90. The large majority of states use computer edits, logic checks, and external validity comparisons. However, there are states that use few editing procedures and the quality of the data could be questioned.

Another issue is the comparability of teacher data between states due to differing definitions of teacher characteristics. The Education Data Improvement Project analyzed state definitions for 22 data elements concerning professional staff and found some variation for all the data elements. For example, variation in the definition of teacher age was very slight. The definitions and categories of types of teaching certificates are different in almost every state, although all but three states' definitions could be placed in three categories: regular/standard, probationary, and temporary/provisional/emergency. CCSSO worked with groups of state representatives to develop consensus definitions for data elements recommended to the Common Core of Data. Then, differences in definitions were reported to states so that data collection could be standardized, or, in some cases, a cross-walk could be designed for analyzing a state's data in relation to the consensus definition.

Another criterion of completeness of teacher data is the response rate for each requested data element. The 1989-90 data reported on science and mathematics indicators also provides information on this question. A total of 34 states reported on the age of teachers assigned in high school science and mathematics. Among these states, 1 percent of data on teacher age was missing. One state had 8 percent missing data on teacher age. A total of 32 states reported data on the race/ethnicity of science and mathematics teachers, and a total of 1 percent of these data were missing. One state (Hawaii) had 5 percent missing data on race/ethnicity.

All of the states with teacher files collect or update the data at least annually. Most states ask that data be reported early in the fall of each school year. The National Center for Education Statistics requests that Common Core of Data on education staff be reported as of October 1. States enter, edit, and clean the data between October and March. Some states do not have the data ready until June. For the CCSSO Science/Mathematics Indicators Project, 43 states reported data on teacher characteristics for the preceding school year by the end of July.

LINKED TEACHER DATA FROM STATES

Table 1 reports the number of states that collect and file data on elements of teacher quality, demand, and supply. An important question for any researcher or policy analyst is whether these data can be linked together for purposes of analysis. For many analyses, the ideal situation is to analyze teacher characteristics at the teacher level, such as teacher assignment by teacher age. Some analyses could be with data aggregated at the school, district, or state level. For example, in analyzing teacher demand and supply, it is useful to compare the number of new hires in a state who are first-time teachers with the previous year's number of college graduates who were certified to teach. If possible, however, it is most desirable to have data on teachers that can be analyzed at the teacher level.

To gain some perspective on the availability of state data on teachers that are linked at the teacher level, Table 2 shows a state-by-state listing of teacher characteristics and the extent to which the data are linked. The first column indicates that 44 states have data on teacher assignments by field or subject (e.g., subject=science, field=biology). Of these states, 36 states can analyze assignment by age, 40 states assignment by sex, and 33 states assignment by race/ethnicity. The second column shows that 30 states can determine the number of teachers assigned to a subject/field that are certified in the subject/field. The third column indicates that 35 states have data on student enrollments in secondary-level courses and 19 states (with links between teacher and student data) can analyze the proportion of students in a course taught by a teacher certified in their assigned field.

EXAMPLE OF USES OF STATE DATA FOR NATIONAL ANALYSES

The CCSSO Science/Mathematics Indicators Project gave high priority to developing three types of indicators of teacher work force: (a) supply,

TABLE 2 State Data Linked to Individual Teachers (Fall 1989)

State	Teacher Assignment by Field/Subject by Age (A), Sex (S), Race/Ethnicity (R)	Teacher Assignment by Certification Field	Secondary Course Enrollment
Alabama	Field by A,S,R	Yes	Yes, link
Alaska	No	No	No
Arizona	Subject by S,R	No	No
Arkansas	Field by A,S,R	Yes	Yes, link
California	Field by A,S,R	Yes	Yes, link
Colorado	Subject by A,S,R	Yes	No
Connecticut	Field by A,S,R	Yes	Yes, link
Delaware	Field by A,S,R	Yes	Yes
District of Columbia	No	No	Yes
Florida	Field	No	Yes, link
Georgia	No	No	No
Hawaii	Field by A,S,R	No	Yes, link
Idaho	Field by A,S,R	Yes	Yes
Illinois	Field by A,S,R	Yes	Yes, 5 yrs.
Indiana	Field by A,S,R	No	Yes
Iowa	Field by A,S,R	No	Yes, link
Kansas	Field by A,S,R	No	Yes
Kentucky	Field by A,S,R	Yes	Yes, link
Louisiana	Field	No	Yes
Maine	Field by A,S,R	No	No
Maryland	Subject by A,S,R	Yes	No
Massachusetts	Field	No	No
Michigan	Field by A,S,R	No	No
Minnesota	Field by A,S	Yes	Yes, link
Mississippi	Field by A,S,R	Yes	Yes, link
Missouri	Field by A,S,R	Yes	Yes, link
Montana	Field by A,S,R	Yes	Yes
Nebraska	No	No	Yes
Nevada	Field by A,S,R	Yes	Yes, link
New Hampshire	Field by S	No	No
New Jersey	Field by A,S,R	Yes	No
New Mexico	Field by A,S,R	Yes	Yes
New York	Field by A,S	Yes	Yes, link
North Carolina	Field by A,S,R	Yes	Yes, link
North Dakota	Field by A,S,R	Yes	Yes, link
Ohio	Field by A,S,R	Yes	Yes, link
Oklahoma	Field by A,S,R	Yes	Yes
Oregon	Field by A,S	Yes	No
Pennsylvania	Field by A,S,R	Yes	Yes
Rhode Island	Field by A,S,R	Yes	No
South Carolina	Field by A,S,R	Yes	Yes, link
South Dakota	Field by A,S	Yes	No
Tennessee	Field by A,S	Yes	Yes

continued on next page

TABLE 2 *Continued*

State	Teacher Assignment by Field/Subject by Age (A), Sex (S), Race/Ethnicity (R)	Teacher Assignment by Certification Field	Secondary Course Enrollment
Texas	Field by S,R	No	Yes, link
Utah	Field by A,S,R	Yes	No
Vermont	No	No	No
Virginia	Field by A,S,R	Yes	Yes, link
Washington	No	No	No
West Virginia	No	No	No
Wisconsin	Field by A,S,R	No	Yes, 3 yrs.
Wyoming	Field	Yes	Yes
Total	Field/subject = 44 Age = 36 Sex = 40 Race = 33	Yes = 30	Yes = 35

SOURCE: State Science/Mathematics Indicators Project, 1990 (unpublished data), Council of Chief State School Officers, Washington, D.C.

(b) equity, and (c) qualifications. Another priority area for state indicators of science and mathematics is school conditions that affect teaching and learning.

The CCSSO plan for state-by-state indicators of science and mathematics is based on cross-sectional data that can be compared by state and tracked over time. Some desirable indicators of teacher quality that require more complex data or qualitative measurement were not selected, such as state-by-state projections of teacher supply and demand and quality of instruction in the classroom. Other possible indicators of teacher quality, such as degree level and years of experience, were not selected because there is less evidence of a relationship to outcomes in science and mathematics.

States reported data on teachers using a common reporting system designed by the Science/Mathematics Indicators Project. CCSSO also conducted state-by-state analyses of the Schools and Staffing Survey of NCES. Some of the indicators are summarized in the following sections. A full report, entitled, *State Indicators of Science and Mathematics Education: 1990* is available (Blank and Dalkilic).

Indicators of Current Teacher Supply

States reported data on the total number of teachers assigned to teach science, math, and computer science in grades 9-12 as of October 1, 1989.

The state teacher numbers are universe counts based on data collected through state information systems.

Proportion of Teachers with Primary and Secondary Assignments

The CCSSO state data reporting plan requested the number of teachers with primary and secondary assignments in each of eight subjects. The operational definition of *primary assignment* is a teacher assigned to one subject for 50 percent or more of teaching periods; and *secondary assignment* is a teacher assigned to one subject less than 50 percent of teaching periods. The state data show that 89 percent of high school teachers of mathematics have their primary assignment in mathematics. Only slightly over half (53 percent) of all teachers of chemistry have their primary assignment in chemistry, and three-fourths of all teachers of physics have their primary assignment in another field (24 percent in physics). In many schools, physics is taught by a teacher with primary assignment in chemistry or earth science.

States vary in the proportion of teachers with primary assignments in science and math. For example, teachers of mathematics in Connecticut (95 percent) and Illinois (96 percent) are almost all teaching mathematics as their primary assignment, while California (68 percent primary assignment) and Utah (69 percent primary assignment) have about one-third of teachers of mathematics who have their primary assignment in another subject. Higher numbers of teachers with secondary assignments are probably due to population growth (such as in California) as well as increases in state course requirements. States with more small, rural districts, such as Arkansas, Oklahoma, and North Dakota had fewer teachers with primary assignments in any of the science fields, while states with a greater proportion of urban and suburban districts, such as Connecticut, New York, and Pennsylvania, have more teachers with primary assignments in the science fields.

Age of Science and Mathematics Teachers

Although the state science and mathematics indicators do not include detailed projections of teacher supply and demand, the age distributions of current science and mathematics teachers provide useful information on possible shortage fields as teachers near retirement age. The average percentage of teachers over age 50 is 20 percent in mathematics, 20 percent in biology, 23 percent in chemistry, and 23 percent in physics. The average percent of teachers under age 30 is 13 percent in mathematics, 12 percent in biology, 12 percent in chemistry, and 11 percent in physics.

The age distributions of mathematics and science teachers vary widely by state in all fields. The percentage of mathematics teachers over age 50 varies from 29 percent in Minnesota to 10 percent in Kentucky, compared with 10 percent under 30 in Minnesota and 19 percent under 30 in Kentucky. In chemistry, the percentage over 50 varies from 45 percent in Minnesota to 10 percent in Nevada, compared with 9 percent under 30 in Minnesota and 13 percent under 30 in Nevada.

The age distribution for mathematics and science teachers can be compared with the age statistics for *all high school teachers* as reported to the project from state data systems. A total of 21 percent of all high school teachers are over 50, and 10 percent are under 30. Only the fields of chemistry and physics have higher percentages of teachers over 50 than the average for high school teachers. There are slightly higher percentages of teachers under 30 in mathematics and science than the average for high school teachers.

One way of analyzing teacher age statistics by state is to note that states that have had flat or declining populations, particularly northeastern and midwestern states, have higher proportions of older science and mathematics teachers (e.g., Connecticut, Delaware, Illinois, Iowa, Minnesota, New York, Rhode Island, and Wisconsin). Many of the teachers over 50 in these states were hired in the 1960s, when school enrollments were increasing. These states may experience a shortage of such teachers in a few years as this group of teachers reaches retirement age.

Indicators of Equity in the Teaching Force

States reported data on two indicators of equity among current teachers in science and mathematics: sex and race/ethnicity. The distribution of science and mathematics teachers by sex and race/ethnicity provides a basis for states and the nation to compare the characteristics of the current teaching force with goals of improving the match between students and teachers in terms of sex and race/ethnic characteristics.

Gender of Science and Mathematics Teachers

The average percentage of female teachers by subject is 45 percent in mathematics, 37 percent in biology, 34 percent in chemistry, and 22 percent in physics. By comparison, 50 percent of *all high school teachers* are female, and 50 percent are male, as reported to the project from state data systems.

State-by-state statistics on the gender of mathematics and science teachers show that the distributions vary widely. In mathematics, the percent of female teachers varies from 21 percent in Minnesota to 66 percent in Virginia. (The data on all high school teachers shows 41 percent female in Minnesota and 62 percent female in Virginia.) Region is associated with the sex distribution of science and mathematics teachers (and high school teachers in general). Thirteen states have more female than male mathematics teachers, and eight of these states are in the Southeast. In biology, the percentage of female teachers varies from 15 percent in Iowa to 63 percent in Alabama. Four states have more female than male biology teachers (Alabama, Mississippi, South Carolina, Virginia). Chemistry and physics have fewer female teachers in most states, but five states have more female than male chemistry teachers (all but Hawaii in the Southeast). No state has a majority of physics teachers that are female.

Race/Ethnicity of Science and Mathematics Teachers

The second indicator of equity in the science and mathematics teaching force is the race/ethnicity of current teachers. Nationally, 30 percent of elementary and secondary students are minorities, and 70 percent are non-Hispanic whites (NCES, 1989).

As of the 1989-90 school year, state data on the race/ethnicity of science and mathematics teachers (grades 9-12) show the following percentages of minority teachers by subject: 11 percent in mathematics, 10 percent in biology, 7 percent in chemistry, and 5 percent in physics. By comparison, the statistics for *all high school teachers* show 11 percent minority and 89 percent white.

The proportion of minority science and mathematics teachers in each state can be compared with the proportion of minority students. Among the 32 states that reported teacher race/ethnicity by field and student race/ethnicity, only 11 states had over 10 percent minority teachers in any of the 3 fields. Of the 19 states with more than 20 percent minority students, only 5 states have even half as many minority teachers in mathematics, biology, or chemistry as the proportion of minority students (Virginia, Alabama, South Carolina, Mississippi, Hawaii). The states with the highest proportions of minority teachers (among science and mathematics as well as all high school teachers) are in the southeastern states and Hawaii. There is relatively little variation among mathematics, biology, and chemistry in the percentage of minority teachers, although chemistry has slightly fewer minorities in most states. The state data show that, except for Hawaii, no state has representation of minority teachers similar to the racial/ethnic background of students.

Indicators of Teacher Qualifications in Subject Area

A state-by-state indicator of teacher qualifications is the proportion of science and mathematics teachers who are not state certified in their field, i.e., teaching "out of field." State-collected data on teacher assignments by certification status as of October 1, 1989, were reported to CCSSO.

The proportion of teachers who are teaching out of field is a useful policy indicator because it is a quantifiable measure of the proportion of teachers in a district or state that do not meet basic qualifications (Shavelson et al., 1989). Certification has often been used as a working definition of *qualified* in the analysis of current teacher shortages in science, math, and other subjects (Darling-Hammond and Hudson, 1989; Oakes, 1990).

A major advantage of using state data on teacher assignments and certification is that the data can be computed from state administrative records and computerized data files, thereby alleviating the need for special surveys of teachers that require teachers' self-report of certification status. Since certification standards for each teaching field differ by state, it is important to report state-by-state information on state certification standards (see Blank and Dalkilic, 1990).

Thirty states reported results of cross-tabulating state data on teacher assignments by teacher certification status. The percentages of teachers assigned in high school mathematics and science that are not state certified are as follows: 9 percent of mathematics teachers, 8 percent of biology teachers, 8 percent of chemistry teachers, and 12 percent of physics teachers. These total percentages are based on 30 states (including four large states—California, New York, Illinois, and Pennsylvania) but do not include Florida and Texas (which are expected to report the data in the next reporting cycle).

In mathematics, the percentage of teachers not state certified varies by state from 52 percent in South Dakota and 31 percent in Colorado to 0 percent in Connecticut and North Dakota. In biology, the percentage out of field varies from 34 percent in Arkansas to 0 percent in several states, with the median state at 3 percent out of field. States with more than 15 percent of teachers out of field in chemistry and physics are Arkansas, California, Illinois, Mississippi, and South Dakota. Alabama, Delaware, and New York have more than 15 percent out of field in physics. The data show that some of the states with substantial numbers of science and mathematics teachers out of field have many small, rural districts (and thus many small high schools), such as South Dakota, Illinois, and Mississippi. States experiencing population growth such as California have high demand for teachers, and have more teachers out of field.

According to data from the Schools and Staffing Survey for 1987-88, less than 5 percent of teachers with primary assignments in science and math are assigned out of field (Bobbitt and McMillen, 1990). The state-by-state data from the CCSSO Project on certification status by teachers with primary *and* secondary assignments reveals that, in many states, a large proportion of chemistry and physics teaching is done by teachers with a secondary assignment in these fields (total for 28 states: chemistry—40 percent secondary assignment, physics—61 percent secondary assignment;

Blank and Dalkilic, 1990). Teachers with secondary assignments are less likely to be certified in the secondary field, particularly teachers of chemistry and physics.

Two-thirds of the states certify science teachers through "broad-field" certification as well as in specific fields of biology, chemistry, physics, etc. States reported teaching assignments by certification according to broad-field versus specific-field certification. Individual states may be able to increase the number of certified science teachers in more classrooms with a broad-field policy. However, as a group, states with broad-field science certification do not currently have lower percentages of science teachers out of field than states with only specific-field science certification (Blank, 1990).

School Conditions—Number of Teachers and Schools per State

National surveys have analyzed the proportion of schools that offer advanced science and mathematics courses (Weiss, 1987; Neuchatz and Covalt, 1988; Oakes, 1990). Neuchatz and Covalt found that 83 percent of high schools in the nation offer physics, and these schools include 96 percent of students. However, only 66 percent of schools offer physics each year.

The number of science and mathematics teachers in each teaching field can be compared with the number of high schools in a state to approximate the proportion of schools that are able to offer science and mathematics courses in each field. Accordingly, a state-level indicator of course coverage in science and mathematics is the ratio of high schools in a state to the number of teachers assigned in each teaching field.

This *school/teacher ratio* is particularly applicable to analyzing school conditions in each state for teaching chemistry and physics. In many states the number of teachers is close to the number of schools, and in states that have fewer teachers than schools it is likely that some schools are not offering chemistry or physics. However, one caveat in using the school/teacher ratio to identify shortages of teachers in a state is that chemistry and physics teachers may be shared among several schools, and this cooperative arrangement is not accounted for in the school/teacher ratio. Also, this ratio may understate the problem of shortages in states that have large high schools with more than one physics or chemistry teacher and small schools with none (the state average would show each school having a teacher).

The school/teacher ratios in chemistry and physics reveal that:

- 11 of 41 reporting states have more high schools than chemistry teachers,
- 28 of 41 reporting states have more high schools than physics teachers, and
- the number of high schools in Illinois, Iowa, Michigan, Mississippi, New Hampshire, Oklahoma, and Utah is more than twice the number of physics teachers.

Several of the states with more high schools than physics teachers reported few or no teachers teaching out of field, such as Idaho, Nevada, North Dakota, Ohio, and Utah. In these states, a state policy may prevent assignment of noncertified teachers to shortage fields, or school districts do not offer a course if there is not a certified teacher.

SUMMARY

This paper has summarized the breadth of available state data on teacher supply, equity, and qualifications. A high proportion of states collect and store data on many of the desired data elements. The quality and timeliness of state data are good in many states, while other states have fewer quality controls and edits. State teacher data are typically stored on several different files, which makes analyses more problematic. State-by-state comparisons depend upon development of a consensus definition used by states or development of a cross-walk for comparing data among states. The example of analyses with state data on science and mathematics teachers shows that some states cannot report cross-tabulated data even though the data are collected. The science/mathematics indicators illustrate how state data can be used to assess conditions of teacher supply, equity, and qualifications among the states and in the nation.

REFERENCES

Blank, Rolf K.

1986 *Science and Mathematics Indicators: Conceptual Framework for a State-Based Network.* Washington, D.C.: CCSSO, State Education Assessment Center.

1990 *Preliminary Report on State Indicators of Science and Mathematics Education: Course Enrollments and Teachers.* Washington, D.C.: CCSSO, State Education Assessment Center.

Blank, Rolf K., and M. Dalkilic

1990 *State Indicators of Science and Mathematics Education: 1990.* Washington, D.C.: CCSSO, State Education Assessment Center.

Blank, Rolf K., and P. Espenshade

1988 *Survey of States on Availability of Data on Science and Mathematics Education.* Washington, D.C.: CCSSO, State Education Assessment Center.

Bobbitt, Sharon A., and Marilyn M. McMillen

1990 *Teacher Training, Certification, and Assignment: A Presentation to the American Educational Research Association.* Washington, D.C.: National Center for Education Statistics, U.S. Department of Education.

Council of Chief State School Officers

1988 *Results of the Shuttle to Verify Staffing Data Elements.* Washington, D.C.: CCSSO, State Education Assessment Center.

Darling-Hammond, Linda, and Lisa Hudson

1989 *Teachers and Teaching Indicators for Monitoring Mathematics and Science Education: A Sourcebook.* Santa Monica, California: The RAND Corporation.

Gilford, Dorothy M., and Ellen Tenenbaum, eds.
1990 *Precollege Science and Mathematics Teachers: Monitoring Supply, Demand, and Quality*. Panel on Statistics on Supply and Demand for Precollege Science and Mathematics Teachers, Committee on National Statistics. Washington, D.C.: National Academy Press.

National Center for Education Statistics
1989 *Digest of Education Statistics*. Washington, D.C.: U.S. Department of Education.

National Research Council, Committee on National Statistics
1987 *Toward Understanding Teacher Supply and Demand: Priorities for Research and Development. Interim Report*. Panel on Statistics on Supply and Demand of Precollege Science and Mathematics Teachers. Washington, D.C.: National Academy Press.

Neuschatz, M., and M. Covalt
1988 *1986-87 Nationwide Survey of Secondary School Teachers of Physics*. New York: American Institute of Physics.

Oakes, J.
1990 *Multiplying Inequalities: The Effects of Race, Social Class, and Tracking on Opportunities to Learn Mathematics and Science*. Santa Monica, California: The RAND Corporation.

Shavelson, Richard, L. McDonnell, and J. Oakes., eds.
1989 *Indicators for Monitoring Mathematics and Science Education: A Sourcebook*. Santa Monica, California: The RAND Corporation.

Weiss, Iris R.
1987 *Report of the 1985-86 National Survey of Science and Mathematics Education*. Research Triangle Park, North Carolina: Research Triangle Institute.

Developing a Regional Data Base on Educators in the Northeast: Problems, Products, and Prospects

JAMES M. WILSON III AND DAVID QUINBY

INTRODUCTION

In 1988, seven states in the Northeast agreed to explore the benefits of configuring their region as a common market for educators.[1] In response to this possibility, the project reported here was initiated, in part, to collect data on educators in the region, to compile statistics on their migration within the region, to project educator supply and demand, and to develop policy simulation software.

The Massachusetts Institute for Social and Economic Research (MISER), having completed the study on educator supply and demand in Massachusetts in 1987, was selected to undertake work toward these objectives. Success of the project hinged on its endorsement by the education commissioners of the seven states in the region. Through this endorsement, the commissioners provided much-needed access to the sundry organizations and agencies that could provide relevant data.

Across the 7 states, more than 25 agencies and organizations were asked to provide data. They included certification bureaus, management information divisions of departments of education, departments of public health, teacher retirement boards, and private service bureaus. This information for the region was gathered on over 140 magnetic tapes. In many ways there was an archeological aspect to this task. Documentation for many of these files was neglected or lost, and key people in the development of data systems were retired or transferred. Considerable tenacity and cooperation were required to recover a data base going back 20 years. In all cases, agency staff were extremely cooperative in supplying information, despite their considerable burden of day-to-day operations.

Our initial objective in the data collection process was to assemble *event history records*[2] for educators located in each state. By *educator* we mean classroom teacher, instructional support staff (e.g., librarian), and school administrator. Close to 1 million individual records were so constructed. States vary in whom they track but, in general, the work force cohort consists of full-time elementary and secondary public school personnel. We compiled an event history of the work force from annual staff censuses and retirement system ledgers. And we extracted a complementary history of the reserve pool (i.e., those available to work) from certification data bases.

Figure 1 provides an example of an event history file, showing how the certification and staff files for the state of Connecticut were integrated to create a master record for each educator. Appendix A is an inventory of data collected over the region, and Appendix B indicates the range of years available in state archives. As can be seen, some states have detailed personnel records going back to 1968; others have records of considerably shorter duration. We admitted all available years rather than start at (or censor before) a common year.

DATA COLLECTION AND DATA PROCESSING

State administrative records are primarily used for specific accounting purposes. In many states, the educator data are rarely, if ever, examined in a longitudinal fashion. To estimate variables in our models, we had to transform the data into event history form (see Figure 1). To do this, we merged information over years and over data bases. This cross-year and cross-data-base merging created redundancy in the data, which provided opportunities to observe its reliability. Numerous correctable errors were discovered in this process, such as inconsistent data on gender, race, date of birth, and social security number.

We observed that data quality is often diminished by data collection and maintenance procedures. For example, some states record only the initial date of certification, and dates of subsequent certification or renewal are never entered. Therefore, information career development over time is lost. Other states record only the latest effective date of certificate renewal, which obliterates the original issue date, eliminating the possibility of modeling the time-dependent process from initial certification to entry into the teaching work force. The process of periodically purging data from files also degrades quality. Certification files seem particularly vulnerable to purging as individuals with expired credentials, those retired, and the deceased are often removed without archiving. This is simply lost history—of little administrative use but important for research, which may affect policy. An important matter for states to consider is the manifold uses for and potential

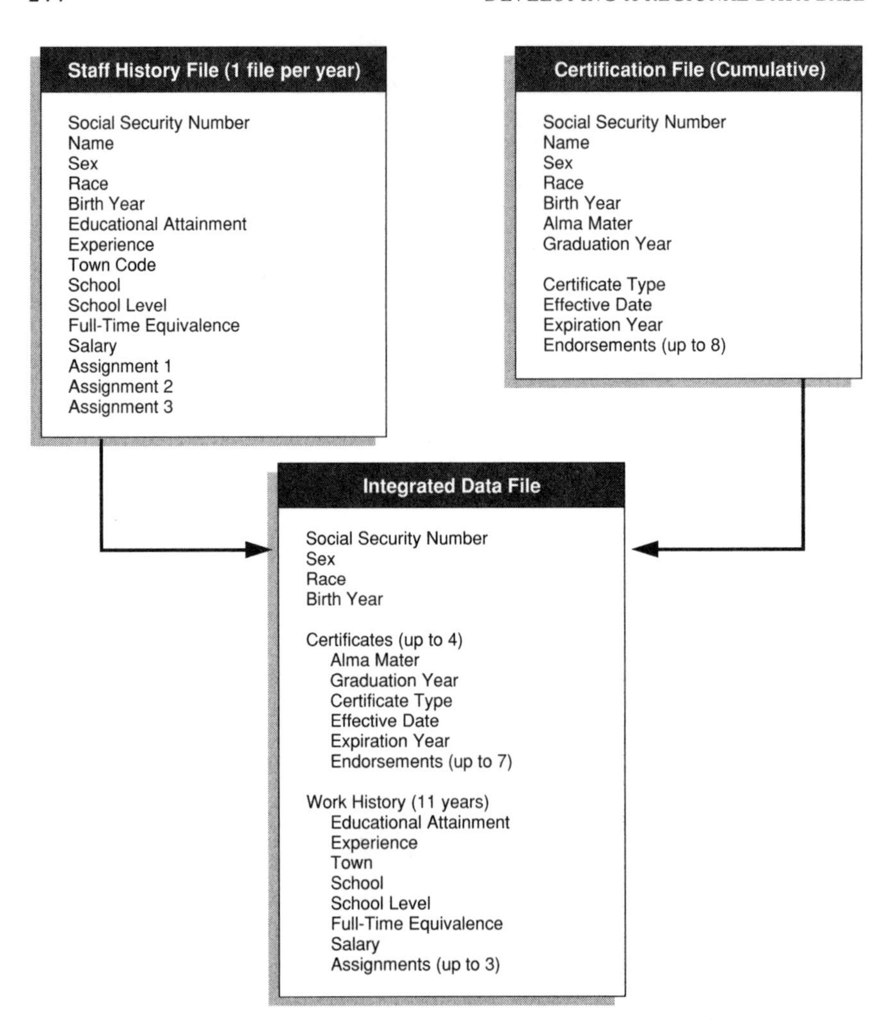

FIGURE 1 Connecticut Data Files.

of administrative records. Therefore, a broader perspective should guide data collection and maintenance procedures at the state level.

Assembling data from numerous states and agencies requires considerable documentation. Too often documentation was inadequate, particularly for items such as teaching assignment and certification endorsement codes, which change over time. When old code books were lost, codes were redefined on a "best guess" basis. In some cases, this was impossible because all personnel familiar with the changes had left state employment. A similar difficulty occurred when data bases migrated from one computer system to another, which inevitably altered the data structure. Old data was archived as is, and it fell on us to link and align old to new data. Such changes were often the occasion for states to abandon some data items and add others, creating discontinuities in the data. There were also exceptional problems. For example, one state in the region simply lost a year of data in the time series it provided.

Diversity of data collection among the states creates many deficiencies to reconcile and align. Some states had 22 years of data; others had but 10 years. Six states could identify what their teachers were teaching; one could not. Although one state could identify the quality of students in each class and whether the classroom had a video cassette recorder or computer, the other states had no record of what courses students were taking. The diversity of data collected throughout the region is reported in Appendices A and B.

There were also considerable differences among the states as to the number and type of certification and teaching assignment categories. To solve this problem, a regional certification working group established a classification framework, which was used to aggregate these categories. The final categories agreed on can be seen in Appendix C.

Descriptive statistics revealed additional problems with the data. For example, one state had significant underreporting on its staff census in a particular year. This surfaced as a low retention rate that year and a high reentry rate the next. As is customary, we resorted to imputation and collected additional data to validate results.

Data problems also emerged when we attempted enrollment projections. The cohort-survival ratios were quite small for certain grades. We therefore examined all the district grade data for potential problems. We discovered one district that put the total of its fourth, fifth, and sixth graders into fourth grade. After fixing this, the cohort-survival ratios fell into line and the accuracy of the enrollment projections improved.

Another concern in using administrative records for policy research on this scale is the timeliness of reports. Given available resources, we were constrained to assemble event history files one state at a time. When all were complete, some files were two years old. An important next step in improving timeliness is to standardize both the updating of the data files, as well as the production of statistics, model estimation, and software calibration. We believe it will take at least two production cycles before the turnaround time between data acquisition and data products becomes reasonably short.

A final issue is that the statistics generated from administrative records reveal the influence of policy changes. Thus, it is critical to recover the policy history of a state in order to understand patterns in the data. Changes in certification requirements, certificate types, job classification, fiscal environment, and salary enhancements must be well understood if statistics are to be correctly interpreted. For example, in one state we observed the retention rate of educators ages 20 to 24 drop from 84 percent in one year to 58 percent the next. An initial reaction to this might be that there was a problem with the data. However, this startling change in retention was the result of capping community property taxes leading to massive reductions in force throughout the state's public education system.

UTILITY OF ADMINISTRATIVE DATA FOR EDUCATOR SUPPLY, DEMAND, AND QUALITY MODELS

A regional data base offers numerous opportunities to answer questions about educator work force dynamics. In certain respects, a regional data base is superior to national data bases in that it can provide detail at the district and, in many cases, at the school level. Furthermore, the long time series on individual educators allows actual measurement of trends over time, such as rates of certification-to-entrance, retention, attrition, reentry, reassignment, and interdistrict and interstate transfer. It also provides an opportunity to study such trends by specialization, a type of analysis particularly useful in areas such as special education, which has great diversity among its several specializations.

Existing data are limited in that they provide little indication of educator quality. Data are generally available about experience and educational attainment. Yet these are dubious indices of quality that require ad hoc scaling to fit a model. Another indication of quality is whether or not a person is working within her or his field of certification and, if so, what type of certificate they hold. Teacher test scores (such as Scholastic Aptitude Test and core battery scores) would be very useful, as would college grade point average (GPA).[3]

Lack of data also restricts the modeling of demand. There are virtually no data on curriculum, class size, and student body composition.[4] To project enrollment by course, past participation rates by grade are required. Since the states estimate these rates, their reliability is obviously limited by the quality of the estimates.

Another weakness in this regional data base is that, currently, no data are collected on the number of graduates from programs leading to certification. A national data base collected by NCES, the Integrated Postsecondary Education Data System (IPEDS), does tally the number of graduates by postsecondary institution. In an earlier study on the Commonwealth of Massachusetts (Coelen and Wilson, 1987), a census of all programs leading to certification was undertaken. This microdata allowed the tracking of individuals into the education work force throughout the state. Five years of data provided enough information to identify trends over time in this yield. To undertake such a project in the Northeast region would have required a census of the approximately 110 postsecondary programs leading to certification. Although this data component is important for numerous policy reasons, it was not incorporated into the MISER regional data base due to cost considerations.

Although many elements of educator supply and demand can be modeled with existing administrative records, some basic questions cannot be answered. From administrative records there are ample data to estimate retention and attrition rates. We do know who was hired and when. We do have the two primary components of the reserve pool: individuals certified but never employed in education and experienced educators who left the system and may return. We know the entry rates from these groups, but we *cannot easily tell if the number hired are under conditions of supply constraints or demand constraints*. This is because we do not know the number of applicants denied due to demand constraints (not enough jobs) nor the number of positions unfilled due to supply constraints (no suitable applicants). Again, all we can observe from administrative records is hiring. Strong assumptions have to be made in modeling to identify available teacher supply.

Given these limitations, it is important to consider how a major national data base, the School and Staffing Survey (SASS) collected by NCES, can address some of these problems. SASS does provide data (a) on whether positions have or have not been filled, (b) on positions filled by individuals with emergency certificates, and (c) on positions withdrawn. Unfortunately, such constraints vary over districts and may occur for numerous reasons. We need to explore the representativeness of SASS data for estimating general supply and demand conditions when aggregated at the state level.

It may be problematic that factors influencing supply and demand are closely tied to geography and attributes of districts (urban, rural, socioeconomic status). For example, SASS provides information that may indicate, generally, what kind of districts suffered shortages in particular years of the survey, but it will not illuminate the range of supply and demand conditions within a state.

Furthermore, we do not know the reason for shortage if it occurs; that is, why the reserve pool is unresponsive to increased demand. To understand this necessitates an understanding of how the reserve pool is distributed geographically, and the competing job opportunities or life opportunities in local markets. SASS can begin to tell us about the propensity of individuals to reenter teaching with its Teacher Follow-Up Survey, but not the propensity for initial entry. The best work to date on this aspect of the reserve pool is Manski's analysis using the National Longitudinal Survey 1972 (Manski, 1987). This work sheds light on the causes of initial entry, but a complementary data base describing the size and composition of the reserve pool is needed before projections can be made. Here again, the linking of administrative records and national survey data may be fruitful.

In examining administrative records, one can observe the dynamics of education at the district, state, and regional levels. However, we need district-level data that go beyond salary differentials and urban/rural classification. Other data that could be linked are the decennial census data that identify, in a general way, the socioeconomic status of a district. Although not encountered in the Northeast, problems may arise in other states, where school districts are not coterminous with municipality boundaries. This creates difficult problems in allocating census[5] and other data such as births (used in enrollment projections) to school districts.

Interstate migration statistics are an important result of the Northeast regional study. While the magnitude of migration between states is known, the causes are as yet undetermined. For example, educator migration may be primarily driven by market forces acting on the educator's spouse. Furthermore, we should consider the change in real rather than nominal wages and factor in changes in retirement benefits and other incentives. The former are not available at the substate level and the latter are often difficult to quantify.

PROSPECTS FOR THE NORTHEAST REGIONAL DATA BASE

The northeastern states are tentatively committed to nurturing their nascent regional data base. With seed money spent and groundwork done, the cost of updates will be relatively low. With standardization, systematization, and software enhancement, the cost to benefit ratio will drop steadily.

A side issue is the improvement of the data collection by participating states. This ranges from adding some items, to improved archiving, to undertaking a census for the first time. This process of *continuous improvement* is a particularly difficult to sustain given the vicissitudes of the fiscal status of states.

In the course of the study, it was interesting to observe that education managers were quite uncertain about what data mattered and what did not. This arises, perhaps, from the culture of education, which has been largely bereft of accountability in a traditional management sense, and from the formidable problems in measuring the quality of education. If we are moving to a new period of accountability, then we are also entering a period of discovery regarding what information matters in educational management information systems (MIS). The regional common market forum exposed relative strengths and weaknesses in each state's MIS operation. The next steps are to identify useful data products, improve data quality, standardize data and reporting, and seek synergies in how administrative data are collected and organized.

REFERENCES

Coelen, Stephen, and James Wilson

1987 *Report on the Status of Teacher Supply and Demand in Massachusetts.* Amherst: Massachusetts Institute for Social and Economic Research, University of Massachusetts.

Manski, Charles F.

1987 Academic ability, earnings, and the decision to become a teacher: Evidence from the National Longitudinal Study of the High School Class of 1972. In David A. Wise, ed., *Public Sector Payrolls.* Chicago: University of Chicago Press.

NOTES

1. The project was funded by a number of organizations: the National Science Foundation, the National Center for Educational Statistics, the Council of Chief State School Officers, and the Regional Laboratory for Educational Improvement of the Northeast and Islands. The regional laboratory also provided support for the numerous committees that managed the Northeast Common Market Study. The Bank of New England generously provided access to their computing facilities.

2. Event history files, or panel data, are data that comprise time-independent and time-varying data on individuals.

3. New York records college GPA in its certification master file. Some states require certification applicants to pass prescribed tests. For example, Maine requires qualifying scores on the Core Battery of the National Teacher Examination.

4. Except in New York's personnel master file.

5. This difficulty is being addressed by NCES in creating a special extract from the decennial census that will provide summary data for tracts coterminous with school districts.

APPENDIX A Northeast Common Market Data Inventory

	CT	MA	ME	NH	NY	RI	VT
Personal							
Social security number	y	y	y	y	y	y	y
Sex	y	y	y	y	y	y	y
Race	y	n	y	n	n	y	n
Birth year	y	y	y	y	y	y	y
Name	y	y	y	y	y	y	y
Marital status	n	y	n	n	y	n	y
Certification							
Effective date	y	y	y	y	y	y	y
Date of first certification	n	y	y	y	n	y	n
Expiration year	y	n	y	y	y	y	y
Sponsor institution	y	n	n	n	y	n	n
Certificate type	y	n	y	y	y	y	y
Endorsed subject area	y	y	y	y	y	y	y
Grade level	y	y	y	y	y	y	y
Education							
Educational attainment	y	n	y	y	y	y	y
Alma mater	y	n	y	n	y	y	n
State of alma mater	y	y	y	n	n	n	n
Graduation year	y	n	y	n	y	y	n
Work History							
Town, district, or region	y	y	y	y	y	y	y
County	n	n	n	y	y	n	y
School	y	n	y	y	y	y	n
Type of school	n	n	y	y	n	n	y
Number of students taught	n	n	n	n	y	n	n
Position title	n	n	y	y	y	y	y
Grade level(s) taught	y	n	y	y	y	y	y
Occupation last year	n	n	y	n	y	n	n
Location last year	n	n	y	n	y	n	n
Years of experience	y	n	y	n	y	y	y
Work load (FTE)	y	y	y	y	y	n	y
Salary	y	y	y	y	y	y	y
Assignments	y	n	y	y	y	y	y
Enrollments							
School	n	y	n	y	y	y	y
Year	y	y	y	y	y	y	y
County	y	y	n	y	y	y	y
Town	y	y	y	y	y	y	y
Grades	y	y	y	y	y	y	y
Percent minority	n	y	n	n	y	n	n
Dropout rate	n	y	n	n	y	n	n

APPENDIX B Years of Data by State and Data Base

State	Databases	Years
CT	Births	74-87
	Enrollments	77-87
	Certifications	72-88
	Active teachers	77-87
MA	Births	68-88
	Enrollments	68-88
	Certifications	72-88
	Retirement board data	73-87
ME	Births	74-87
	Enrollments	79-87
	Certifications	73-89
	Active teachers	74-88
NH	Births	79-88
	Enrollments	84-88
	Certifications	72-89
	Retirement board data	68-88
	Active teachers	88-89
NY	Births	60-88
	Enrollments	67-88
	Certifications	82-88
	Active teachers	68-89
RI	Births	70-87
	Enrollments	75-88
	Certifications	84-90
	Retirement board data	79-88
	Active teachers	89-90
VT	Births	74-87
	Enrollments	77-87
	Certifications	74-88
	Active teachers	79-87

APPENDIX C Categories Suggested by Certification Working Group

General Categories

1	Agriculture
2	Art
3	Business
4	Early childhood
5	Elementary
6	English
7	English: second language
8	Health
9	Home economics
10	Librarian & media specialist
11	Mathematics
12	Marketing
13	Music
14	Physical education
15	Reading
16	Technology education
17	Other
75	Humanities
76	Bilingual Spanish
77	Bilingual other

Science

18	Biology
19	Chemistry
20	Earth/space science
21	General science
22	Physics
23	Other

Social Science

24	Anthropology
25	Economics
26	Geography
27	History
28	Political science
29	Psychology
30	Social studies
31	Sociology
32	Other

Languages

33	Asian
34	Classical
35	French
36	German
37	Italian
38	Russian
39	Spanish
40	Other

Vocational Education

41	Agricultural occupations
42	Health occupations
43	Office occupations
44	Technology subjects
45	Trade subjects
46	Other

Special Education

47	Blind
48	Deaf
49	Early childhood
50	Elementary
51	Generic
52	Intensive
53	Secondary
54	Speech & hearing
55	Other

Administrators

56	Principal
57	Assistant principal
58	Elementary principal
59	Secondary principal
60	Teaching principal
61	School business administrator
62	Special education director
63	Superintendent
64	Assistant superintendent
65	Associate superintendent
66	Supervisor/director
67	Vocational education director
68	Other

Support Staff

69	Guidance
70	Nurse/teacher
71	School nurse
72	School psychologist
73	Social worker
74	Other

Overview and Discussion of National Data Bases Relevant to Teacher Supply, Demand, and Quality

THOMAS L. HILTON

The amount of data available for educational research has grown exponentially during the last 40 years and much of it is relevant to research on teacher supply, demand, and quality. A number of such data files are reviewed in a recently published book by members of the research staff at the Educational Testing Service (Hilton et al., 1992); these files are listed here in Table 1. This paper will review and comment on several of these national data bases that have tended to be neglected in research on teacher supply, demand, and quality.

The first is the Longitudinal Study of American Youth (LSAY). This is an NSF-sponsored study being conducted by the Public Opinion Laboratory at Northern Illinois University, under the direction of Jon Miller. The study started with two national cohorts four years ago, a cohort of approximately 3,000 seventh graders and a cohort of 3,000 tenth graders. Thus, when the two cohorts are linked, complete data from the seventh grade to the twelfth grade are available, and the study is continuing.

The primary focus of LSAY is on the development of competence in mathematics and science, although the data base is comprehensive enough to permit a broader range of investigations of educational development. The study is unique in that annual student and teacher data are being obtained in both the fall and the spring. It thus avoids the problem of High School and Beyond (HS&B) in having measurements only every two years (Sebring et al., 1987). Also, fall and spring data make it possible to measure change and attributes that change to a specific teacher and that may obviate the problem of disentangling cumulative change from kindergarten to twelfth grade that has plagued so many studies of teacher effects. What a student knows as a high school senior represents the impact of 12 years of school (and nonschool) influences. Even HS&B does not solve the problem, for a student can be exposed to several teachers in a two-year period.

In LSAY, student data can be linked to particular teachers, textbooks, and syllabi, a capability that is unusual. The measurement of student behavior and characteristics relevant to science and mathematics is exceptionally broad. However, the measurement of teacher characteristics and behavior is less so, no doubt because the focus of the study is not primarily on teachers. But many questions concerning teacher effects can be addressed by means of this data base.

I emphasize the opportunity to study the dynamics of teacher quality

TABLE 1 Selected National Data Bases (in order of modal or initial age of subjects)

Data Base	Modal Age
Research Triangle Institute National Science Survey	6-12
National Assessment of Education Progress (NAEP)	9-17
Longitudinal Study of American Youth (LSAY)	13-19
National Longitudinal Surveys of Labor Market Experience	14-?
International Math Survey (U.S. Component)	14-18
National Education Longitudinal Study (NELS)	14-?
Project TALENT	15-30
Metropolitan Achievement Tests	16
Iowa Tests of Education	16
1980 High School and Beyond (HS&B)	16-?
Armed Services Vocational Aptitude Battery (ASVAB)	17
American College Testing Service	18
National Longitudinal Study of the High School Class of 1972	18-?
College Entrance Examination Board Admissions Testing Program (Scholastic Aptitude Test, Achievement tests, Advanced Placement Examinations)	18
High School Equivalency Test	19
Cooperative Institutional Research Program (CIRP)	19
Integrated Postsecondary Education Data System (IPEDS)	19-15
Current Population Surveys	All
Graduate Record Examinations	22
National Teacher Examinations	22
Recent College Graduate Survey	22
Graduate Enrollment Survey	26
Survey of Graduate Science Students and Postdoctorates	26
Survey of Earned Doctorates	26

SOURCE: Hilton et al. (1992).

with LSAY because this is so rare. Also, if one is interested in the antecedents of career choice, including the career of teaching, the LSAY data file is invaluable. By contrast, budget and wage variables have a common metric and can be found in several data bases. The data are all in the public domain and may be obtained from Jon Miller at no cost.

The second study I would mention briefly is Project TALENT, which only a few of us old-timers can remember (Flanagan et al., 1960). This was the first major longitudinal study in this country. The data collection was begun in 1960 and involved some 400,000 high school students. The data collection required 15 hours of school time, and the students were followed up for 15 years. It is hard to believe what they required of the students. Students apparently were a lot more compliant in 1960 than they are now. That may not have been a good state of affairs educationally but it was good from the point of view of educational researchers.

Since the original Project TALENT subjects are now 45 to 50 years old, I can easily imagine research questions for which the data would be indispensable, since the file has not only exhaustive individual student data, but also teacher and school data. The TALENT data are also in the public domain, obtainable from the American Institutes for Research in Palo Alto.

The third data source is the Graduate Record Examination (GRE). This data file includes not only test scores—important in terms of today's discussion—but also background information on the GRE takers. The most valuable of this information for teacher supply and demand are the items on the major field of the students' undergraduate study and the major field of their intended graduate study. Although these data are not routinely made available, arrangements can be made with the GRE program directors to obtain permission of the GRE board to use the data for only the cost of retrieving it.

Furthermore, it is not difficult to retrieve the scores on the Scholastic Aptitude Test (SAT) of GRE takers, including responses to the Student Descriptive Questionnaire. This introduces the possibility of relating the intended undergraduate majors of SAT takers to their intended graduate school majors. The possibility of using such data to develop a system of predicting graduate school enrollments by major from SAT data has intrigued me for a number of years. As far as I know, no one has done it.

While on the subject of GRE scores, I should also mention a little-known fact—namely that GRE scores were retrieved for 340 members of the 1980 HS&B senior cohort. This introduces the possibility of yet another linkage between a major data base and the GRE scores. These data were retrieved as part of a study of the postsecondary educational pathways followed by GRE takers, which was carried out for the GRE board (Hilton and Schrader, 1987). Although the sample is small, other researchers might find these data useful. GRE scores are an excellent indicator of the cognitive ability of students electing graduate school work in education relative to that of students in other fields. The worrisome fact is that the study just mentioned indicated that graduate students in education had no competition for bottom place.

With respect to national data bases, I will conclude with comments on the National Teacher Examinations (NTE). One might think that these files, which include several hundred thousand cases a year, would supply useful national data concerning the supply of teachers in this country. However, there are at least three problems in dealing with these data.

First, the teachers who take the exams are far from being representative of all teachers in the United States, even though the tests are taken throughout the country. Some states require the test for all entering teachers, while in other states the tests are voluntary, and state and district requirements keep changing. Also, the age level of individuals taking the test varies widely from one state to another. Thus, trend analyses are for most purposes out of the question.

The second problem encountered in using NTE data is that the format and content of the tests have changed over the years. Currently, the test is undergoing a thorough reexamination with the definite possibility that the NTE of the future will be a drastically different instrument.

Third, because of the history of lawsuits resulting from the way NTE scores have been used by some states, the NTE program direction has been somewhat gun shy—for good reason—about making NTE data available for research purposes. I think these reasons are sufficient for us to cross the NTE off our list of data files available for research on teachers. It's a pity, because it's a huge file of data.

I turn next to a consideration of selected annual and longitudinal data bases as diagramed in Figure 1. Notice the intersections of some of the commonly used tests. The top row, for the National Longitudinal Study (NLS) of the National Center for Education Statistics (NCES), indicates that SAT and ACT scores are available as part of the base year survey. Then moving down to 1979, the Department of Labor National Longitudinal Survey—different of course from NLS—is a very comprehensive file that is readily available. One of its unique features is the presence of scores on the Armed Services Vocational Aptitude Battery (ASVAB) (U.S. Department of Defense, 1976). This well-known test is taken by some 1,000,000 high school students, mostly juniors and seniors, every year.

Returning to the figure and going down to HS&B, you can see that SAT, ACT, and GRE scores are all available for HS&B subjects, as mentioned earlier.

Most of the large national cross-sectional or longitudinal data files with which I've been involved were designed with only a general notion of the uses that would be made of the data. This being the case, we tended to err

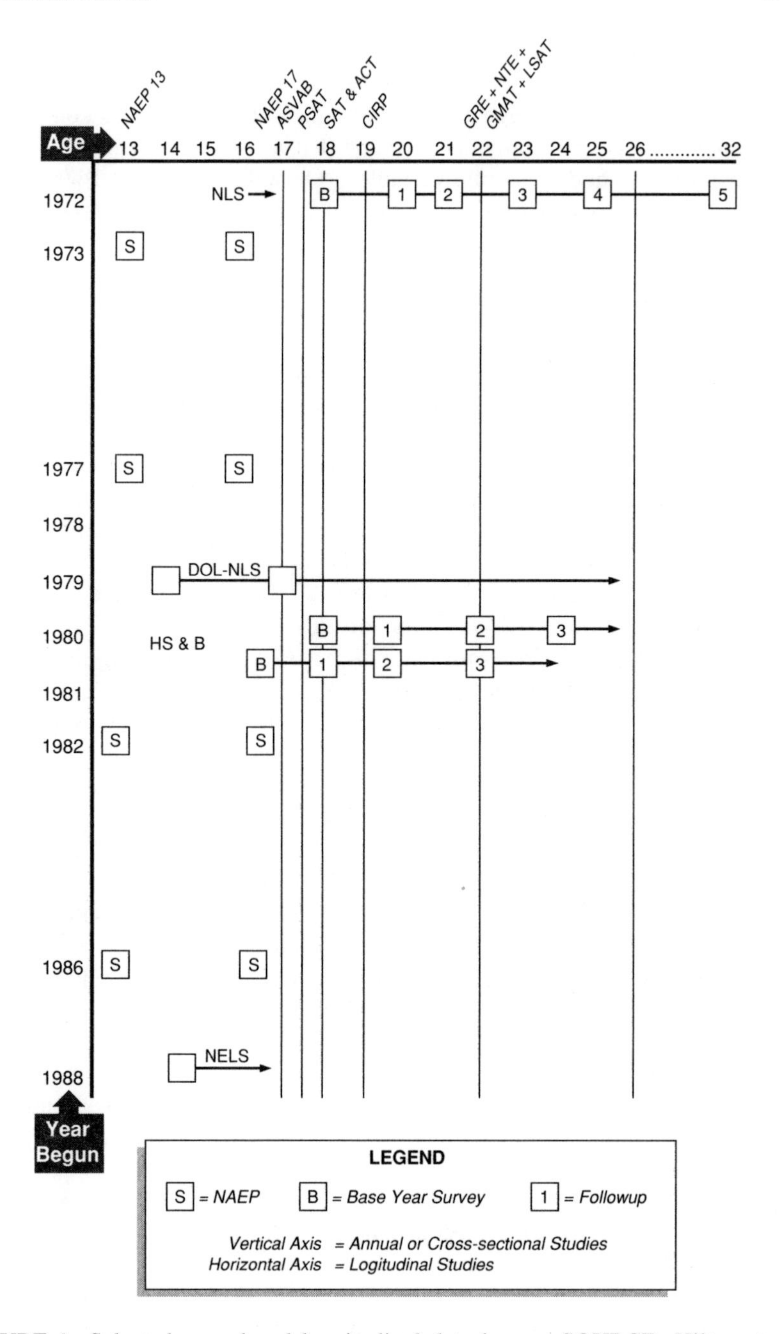

FIGURE 1 Selected annual and longitudinal data bases. SOURCE: Hilton et al. (1992).

on the side of overinclusion. We tended to include every questionnaire or interview item that might conceivably be of interest.

This circumstance suggests the importance of developing a comprehensive model of teacher supply and demand that includes relevant psychological, sociological, and economic variables. Only if such a model were available could the relevance of a particular source of data be judged. Whenever we ask about the validity of a data source, we have to ask "validity for what?" This question is unanswerable without at least a preliminary conceptualization of the phenomenon in which we are interested. Not only would such a model help us to decide whether a particular set of data is relevant, but it would also suggest data that may be missing from a particular data file—data that might be critical to investigations to be conducted by means of the data.

With the assistance of an adequate model of teacher supply and demand, future researchers would be able to be much more discriminating in choosing data files than they could without such a model. Furthermore it would enable them to select only the relevant parts of the large data files. The HS&B data file, for example, has grown to a mammoth size. Copies of the instruments and code books alone occupy two linear feet of shelf space in my office. Selecting relevant parts of the HS&B data file would be much easier with a model to guide the process.

Implementing a comprehensive teacher supply and demand model will probably require data from many different sources. This introduces the problem of merging data from multiple sources into one file if for no other reason than to reduce the cost of data processing. As a battle-scarred veteran of numerous efforts to do this, let me make a few comments.

Sometimes merging is straightforward, as for example when we merged the GRE and SAT data files. With a little caution we were reasonably sure we were dealing with the same students, that is, students with the same social security number, the same birth date, the same gender and the same spelling of their last names. It is disconcerting, however, to discover how many students do not know their social security number or do not write it down accurately. Or, when asked to give their birth date, they give the correct month and day but record the current year. Last names tend to be reliable—unless the sample includes women of marriage age—but matching on first names is useless, given the frequent use of nicknames.

Also one must be cautious about accepting apparent matches. It is a fact that in 1985 there were 18 John Smiths with exactly the same birth date in the SAT files for that year.

Usually, however, we want to compare categories of individuals in one data base with categories of similar individuals in another data base. For example, we may wish to compare high school seniors in the NLS sample who say they intend to go to college and major in secondary school teaching with similar students in the HS&B sample. This particular comparison is possible, but don't try it for prelaw students. The relevant questionnaire item was changed in 1980 in such a way that the comparison is now impossible. This is but one of a host of examples I could cite of minor changes by well-meaning questionnaire designers that have made certain desirable comparisons impossible.

Here and now I would like to make a fervent plea for noncreative questionnaire design. I have a vision of a group of gremlins sitting around a table gleefully asking themselves how they can make slight changes in a questionnaire item so that future comparisons will be impossible. Even the Senior and Sophomore Questionnaires of HS&B are not uniform. You cannot, for example, compute the transition probability from high school to first college for the senior cohort in such a way that it can be unambiguously compared to the probability for the sophomore cohort. There was some very creative item writing there. The moral is that one should make sure a proposed comparison is possible before committing oneself to making it. The research community needs to be vocal about the comparability in national surveys.

Finally, I would like to comment on the question of investigating teacher quality. As is widely recognized, this is a very complex topic. I know of no national data bases fully adequate for investigations of the characteristics of teachers related to effective teaching. I must explain, however, what I mean by this, for there are a number of well-done research studies that purport to accomplish this, including a study currently under way by Ronald Ferguson of the Kennedy School of Harvard University.

In that study, district-level data on teacher characteristics for the whole state of Texas are being related to gains in achievement by students in each district. Community data, such as mean parental income, are being taken into consideration, so Ferguson is able to covary community socioeconomic status out of any correlations. But even this promising work has shortcomings. I would agree that the ultimate measure of teacher effectiveness is the effect teachers have on their students. Before and after measurement is the best way of estimating this effect. But the measurement cannot be limited to change in scores on pencil and paper measures of achievement.

At the risk of being labeled hopelessly idealistic, let me propose that of equal, possibly more importance is the effect the teacher has on such elusive concepts as the student's ability to engage in higher-order thinking and creative problem solving. These qualities are hard enough to measure, but there are some even harder qualities that are important. Here I have in mind such attributes as appreciation of history, respect for scholarship, intellectual curiosity, tolerance, citizenship, and desire for lifelong learning.

Obviously, when I talk about quality, I have in mind something quite different from the economic models we have seen today. To me, a quality teacher is one who has a beneficial effect on the kind of outcomes that I've just listed. In contrast with this view, teacher quality is often regarded as qualifications or credentials. These may measure how much bargaining power a teacher has, and may be a perfectly good use of the word quality. I would only ask that we use "quality sub one" and "quality sub two", and that we be very clear about which kind of quality we're talking about.

I would also mention an incipient revolution in education in this country and that is the introduction in our schools of computer technology. Both performance testing and much of classroom instruction will be computerized in the future. Many unsolved problems stand in the way of widespread implementation in the schools, but it's inevitably coming.

This development may be a boon to empirical researchers: the record left in computer memory is likely to be an important source of research data. Any comprehensive file of school data in the future will want to take this powerful trend into consideration.

I would like to end on a real blue-sky note, just in case anybody is complacent. While we're on the subject of computerized data collection in the future, I see no reason why data relevant to teacher quality and some other teacher supply and demand variables cannot be obtained on line from classrooms throughout the country. The technology of electronic networking is highly developed. Theoretically NCES could have a standing national sample of elementary and secondary schools that routinely transmit data through an electronic network to a central repository where it is aggregated and displayed in such a way that teacher behavior and student learning can be observed as it happens. Why do I have to call this a blue-sky concept when highly developed electronic networking technology exists? Because this concept assumes successful resolution of the inevitable political, fiscal, union, and data processing problems entailed in attempting to implement such an electronic data collection system.

REFERENCES

Flanagan, J.C., J.T. Dailey, M.F. Shaycoft, W.A. Gorham, D.B. Orr, and I. Goldberg
1960 Designing the Study. Technical Report to the U.S. Office of Education, Cooperative Research Project No. 566. Pittsburgh, Pennsylvania: University of Pittsburgh, Project TALENT Office.

Hilton, T.L., A.E. Beaton, V.E. Lee, J. Pollack, D.A. Rock, W.B. Schrader, S.S. Swinton, W.W. Turnbull, and S. Urahn
1992 Using National Data Bases in Educational Research. Hillsdale, New Jersey: Lawrence Erlbaum Associates.

Hilton, T.L., and W.B. Schrader
1987 Pathways to Graduate School: An Empirical Study Based on National Longitudinal Data. Final Report, GRE No. 82-21-R. Princeton, New Jersey: Educational Testing Service.

Sebring, P., B. Campbell, M. Glusberg, B. Spencer, M. Singleton, and M. Turner
1987 High School and Beyond 1980 Senior Cohort Third Follow-up (1986): Data File User's Manual. Washington, D.C.: National Center for Education Statistics.

U.S.Department of Defense
1976 *ASVAB Specimen Test.* Washington, D.C.: U.S. Government Printing Office.

Who Will Teach?

RICHARD J. MURNANE

The purpose of this paper is to demonstrate how the administrative records of state departments of education can be used to inform a number of questions related to teacher supply. I do this by providing a number of examples of analyses that my colleagues (Judith Singer, John Willett, James Kemple, and Randall Olsen) and I have conducted using data provided by the North Carolina and Michigan state departments of education. All of these examples are taken from our book *Who Will Teach? Policies That Matter*, published by the Harvard University Press in 1991.

WHO PREPARES TO TEACH

Virtually every state in the country maintains information on the number of new teaching licenses granted each year.[1] Records on the number of licenses granted, the backgrounds of the licensees, and the distribution of teaching fields in which the licenses are awarded provide useful information in assessing how the supply of potential new teachers is changing. We illustrate this with several examples from North Carolina.

Trends in the Number of New Teaching Licenses

Figure 1 describes the number of teaching licenses granted by the state of North Carolina in each year from 1975-1982.[2] The total declined from more than 6,5000 in 1975 to less than 3,200 in 1982. This dramatic decline provides a strong signal that the supply of new potential entrants to the teaching profession in the state grew much more slowly in the early 1980s

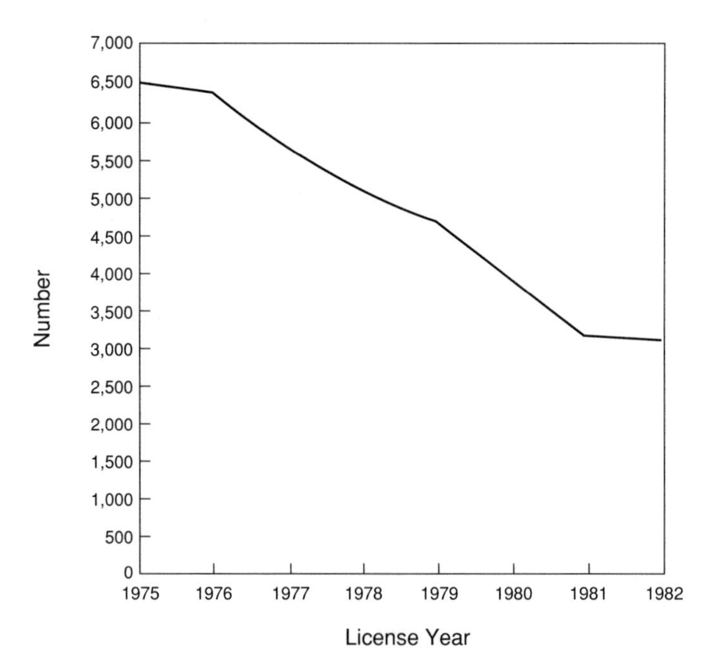

FIGURE 1 Number of new teaching licenses granted by North Carolina in each year from 1975 to 1982.

than in the mid-1970s. Is this a problem? There are many reasons why the number might have fallen. Was it because the number of college graduates in the state declined? Was it because changes in regulations made it more difficult to obtain a teaching license? Was it because changes in the attractiveness of teaching relative to alternative occupations reduced the number of graduates interested in teaching? Learning the answers to these questions is necessary to assess the policy significance of the decline in the number of licensees. Information on the trend in the number of new licensees does not answer the questions.[3] But timely provision of the trend data does highlight a potentially disturbing pattern and focuses attention on the need to explore the reasons for the decline in the number of new licensees.

The Trend in the Racial Composition of the Pool of Licensees

In many states there is growing concern that the representation of minority group members in the nation's teaching force is declining at the same time that the proportion of students who are minority group members is growing. One part of a strategy to identify the causes of this trend is to track the proportion of new licensees who are minority group members.

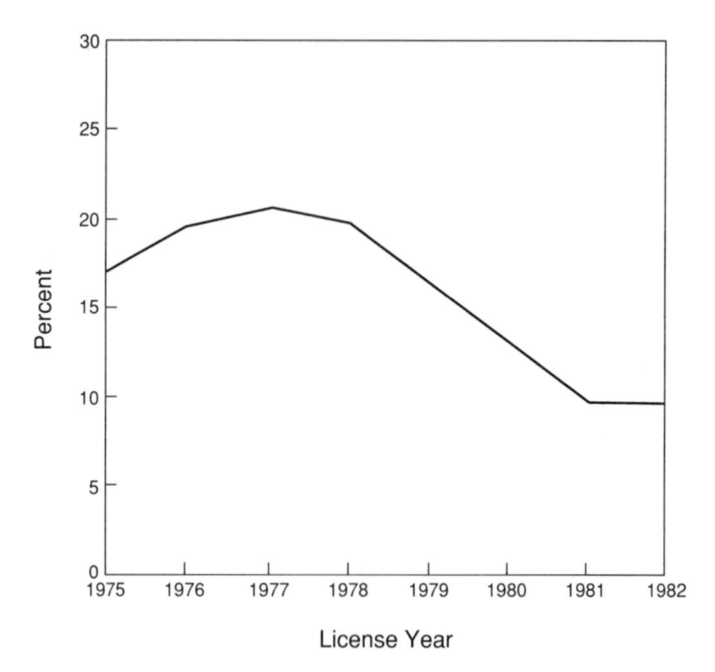

FIGURE 2 Percentage of new teaching licenses granted by North Carolina to black college graduates in each year from 1975 to 1982.

Figure 2 provides this information for North Carolina. In 1978, one out of five new licensees was black; by 1981, only one out of 10 was black. This dramatic decline raises the question of what happened in the late 1970s to cause the abrupt decline in the representation of black college graduates in the pool of new licensees. As my colleagues and I explain in our book, the answer concerns changes in the requirements for obtaining a teaching license in the state. The point I emphasize here is that the information on the racial distribution of new licensees is helpful in identifying a troubling trend.

The Trend in the Distribution of Teaching Fields

An obvious further use of state data on teacher licenses is to track the distribution of teaching fields chosen by new licensees. This may be of particular value as states attempt to stiffen licensing requirements *and* to eliminate the practice of out-of-field teaching, whereby teachers are asked to provide instruction in fields in which they are not licensed. If the number of new licensees in each field does not keep up with projected demand, it is unlikely that prohibitions against out-of-field teaching can be maintained. Identifying fields in which demand is growing faster than the number of new licensees may signal the need for policies to increase supply, such as scholarship aid or salary bonuses.

WHO ENTERS TEACHING

By coupling records on teacher licensing with records on who teaches in a state's schools, it is possible to learn a great deal about the influence that licensing requirements have on who teaches in our schools. For example, we found that college graduates who obtained provisional teaching licenses in North Carolina (which were only valid for two years) were much less likely to become teachers in the state than were graduates who obtained continuing licenses (which provided lifelong licensure). This raises the question of whether the provisional licensing program is worth the resources devoted to administering it. It also indicates that counts of the number of licensed teachers that do not distinguish between types of licensure are likely to be poor indicators of potential teacher supply.

A number of states, including California, Connecticut, and New Jersey, have introduced alternative routes to obtaining a teaching license. Typically these alternative route programs substitute a brief period of intensive training (often during the summer months) for the undergraduate teacher education required for conventional licensure. Debate surrounding the value of these programs is intense. Advocates argue that they attract to teaching academically talented college graduates who would not otherwise teach. Critics argue that the alternative route programs do not provide enough preparation to enable participants to learn to teach effectively. One part of a strategy for assessing the consequences of alternative route programs is to compare the proportion of graduates of these programs who enter teaching with the proportion of graduates of conventional programs. Other parts of an evaluation strategy include comparison of the types of school districts that graduates of different types of programs work in, and comparison of the lengths of time graduates of different programs stay in teaching. All of these analyses can be done with the data typically collected by state departments of education.

HOW LONG TEACHERS STAY IN TEACHING

The most critical determinant of the demand for new teachers is the length of time that teachers stay in the classroom. Consequently, learning about patterns of attrition is an important part of evaluating whether the supply of teachers is likely to prove adequate in the years to come. Information on teachers collected by many state departments of education can be linked to create longitudinal career profiles for teachers. This creates the potential to use these records to investigate how long teachers stay in teaching, and the factors that predict the likelihood that teachers leave the profession.

Career Lengths Vary by Subject Specialty

Table 1 provides predicted median lengths of stay in teaching for teachers with particular subject specialties who began their careers in Michigan or North Carolina.[4] The entries in the table illustrate that attrition rates differ quite markedly between the two states. They also show, however, considerable regularity in the role subject specialty plays in predicting length of stay in teaching. In both states elementary school teachers stay in teaching longer on average than do secondary school teachers. Among secondary

TABLE 1 Median Teaching Career Duration (in years) by Subject Specialty, Controlling for Age, Gender, and Race

Subject Specialty	Michigan	North Carolina
Elementary	5.9	11.0+
Secondary	3.9	7.8
Biology	4.5	5.9
Social Studies	4.0	8.8
English	3.7	6.4
Mathematics	3.6	11.0+
Chemistry/physics	2.2	5.6

school teachers, those teaching chemistry and physics tend to have particularly short teaching careers. As explained in *Who Will Teach?*, these patterns are consistent with the view that teachers with the best career options outside teaching are the most likely to leave it. The pattern displayed in the table illustrates the importance of paying attention to subject specialty in analyzing patterns of teacher attrition.

Salaries Affect the Likelihood of Attrition for Novice Teachers

One question often asked by taxpayers and school boards is whether salaries affect teachers' careers. It is possible to use state department of education records on teachers' annual salaries and careers to estimate statistical models (called hazard models) that address this question. Figure 3 illustrates the results of such model estimation. The curve labeled M shows the predicted hazard profile for a hypothetical Michigan teacher who started her career in 1972. There was a 3-in-10 chance that this teacher would

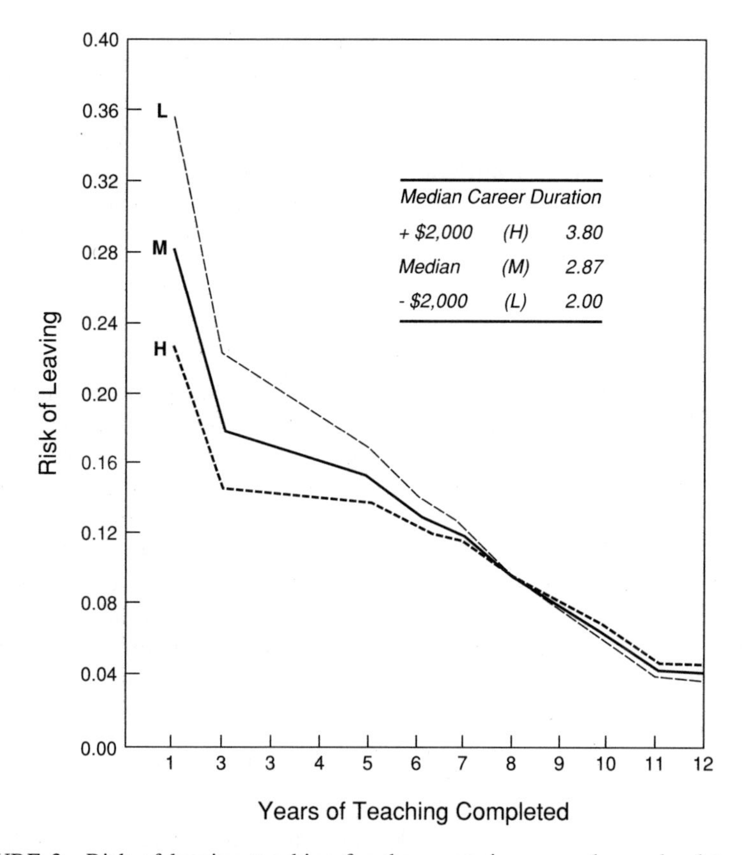

FIGURE 3 Risk of leaving teaching for three entering secondary school teachers in Michigan: in average, low, and high salary streams.

leave teaching at the end of her first year. If she did stay for a second year, there was approximately a 1-in-6 chance that she would leave at the end of the second year. The downward slope of the hazard curve means that the risk of leaving declines with each successive year of additional teaching experience.

The curve labeled H depicts the predicted hazard profile for a teacher paid $2000 above the median salary scale in the state in each year. The curve labeled L depicts the hazard profile for a teacher paid $2,000 below the median salary in each year. Comparison of the three hazard profiles reveals several patterns. First, salary makes an important difference in the risk that a beginning teacher leaves the profession. The risk that a first-year teacher paid $2,000 below the median salary leaves teaching is greater than 1 in 3. In contrast, the risk that a beginning teacher paid $2,000 above the median salary would leave teaching is less than 1 in 4. Second, the role of salary in predicting the risk of leaving teaching declines as teachers gain experience. Among teachers with more than seven years of experience, salary played no role in predicting length of stay in teaching. Third, the differences in the risk profiles associated with different salary profiles cumulate so that teachers paid $2,000 above the median salary scale in the state had a median length of stay in teaching (3.8 years) that was almost two years longer than the median length of stay for teachers paid $2,000 below the median salary scale.

WHO RETURNS TO TEACHING

Many analysts predict that the number of college graduates obtaining teaching licenses over the next 15 years will be far smaller than the demand for teachers needed to replace the large number of teachers expected to retire over this period. Whether the high predicted retirement rate and the low rate of new licensure results in significant shortages is likely to depend critically on the number of teachers who return to the classroom after career interruptions. Analysis of longitudinal records of teachers' career profiles created from state department of education records can provide information about the likelihood that teachers who leave the profession subsequently return after a career interruption.

Many Teachers Return

Figure 4 depicts the results of analyses of the likelihood that teachers in North Carolina and Michigan who left the classroom returned after a career interruption. The figure illustrates that, in both states, 1 in 6 teachers returns after an interruption of one year. Among teachers who stay out of teaching for a second year, approximately 1 in 20 returns. The downward slope of the curves illustrates that the longer a teacher is out of the classroom, the less likely he or she is to return. Although the likelihood of a return declines the longer a teacher is out of the classroom, the probabilities cumulate so that, in both states, 1 out of every 4 teachers who leave teaching returns within 5 years. Thus, returning teachers have been an important source of teacher supply.

The Probability of a Return to Teaching Varies by Subject Specialty

Table 2 displays the results of analysis exploring the extent to which the likelihood that a teacher returns to the classroom depends on subject specialty. In both states, elementary school teachers are more likely to return than secondary school teachers. Among secondary school teachers,

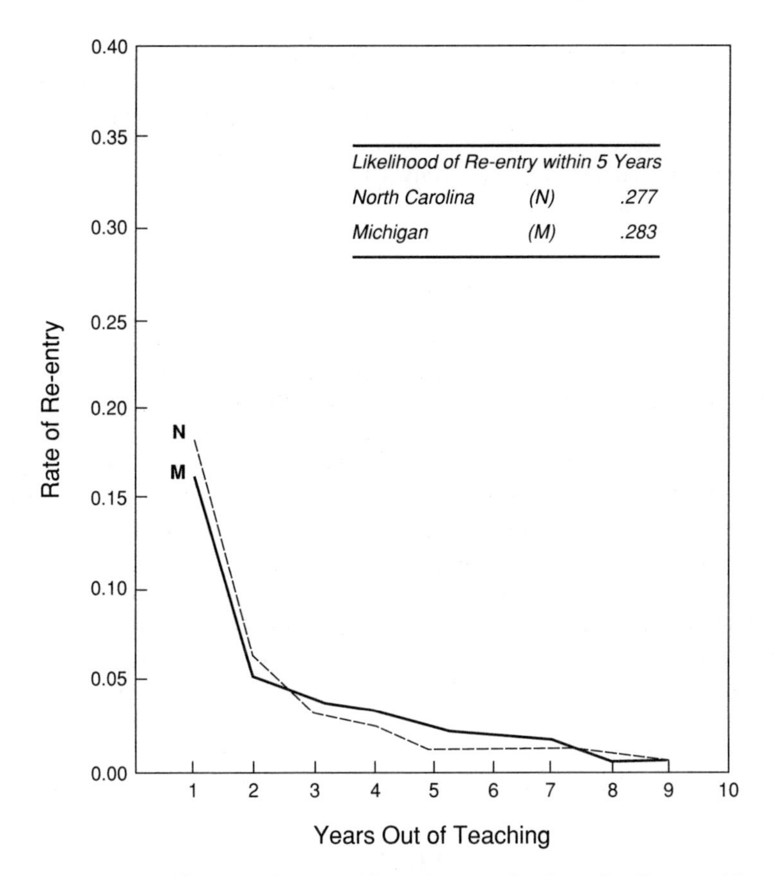

FIGURE 4 Rate of reentry into teaching after termination of a first teaching spell plotted against the length of time teachers have been out of the classroom in Michigan and North Carolina.

TABLE 2 Predicted Probabilities of a Return to Teaching in North Carolina and Michigan Within 5 Years of Terminating a First Teaching Spell, by Subject Specialty

Subject Specialty	Michigan	North Carolina
Elementary	.29	.31
Secondary	.24	.24
Social Studies	.28	.29
Biology	.26	.22
English	.23	.25
Mathematics	.21	.21
Chemistry/physics	.16	.17

those who taught chemistry and physics are less likely to return to teaching after a career interruption than are teachers of other subjects. The differences in probabilities of return are quite large. Approximately 1 out of every 3 elementary school teachers who leave teaching returns to the classroom within 5 years. In contrast, only 1 in 6 chemistry and physics teachers returns within 5 years.

SUMMARY

The examples provided in this brief paper illustrate only some of the ways data collected routinely by state departments of education can be used to inform questions related to teacher supply. Precisely what can be done with the data from any given state depends on the structure of the administrative records, on their accuracy, and on the extent to which they are kept up to date. It is also important to point out that the task of creating from administrative records data bases suitable for research is typically extremely time-consuming and resource-intensive. More than 5 years of work preceded the publication of *Who Will Teach?*. Much of this data preparation task stemmed from the fact that the state administrative record systems in Michigan and North Carolina were not designed to support research of the type we have described. Redesign of state record keeping systems could dramatically reduce the resources needed to use these records to address questions about teacher supply; it could also dramatically reduce the time needed to respond to queries posed by policy makers.

NOTES

1. We use the term *teaching license* instead of the more common term, *teaching certificate*, to differentiate the credential a candidate for a teaching position must possess (a license) from the credential that the National Board for Professional Teaching Standards hopes will designate superior teachers in the future (board certification).
2. Excluded from the count of number of licenses are licenses granted in vocational education and counseling, fields that have quite different licensing requirements from the following included fields: elementary education, special education, mathematics, English, biology, social studies, foreign languages, art, music, physical education, business education, and chemistry/physics (which is treated as one field because of the small number of licenses granted in these areas).
3. See Murnane et al. (1991: chs. 2 and 3) for answers to these questions.
4. These predictions are based on multivariate hazard models that hold constant characteristics of teachers and school districts. For further information, see Murnane et al. (1991: ch. 5).

Discussion: Teacher Supply and Demand Research With State Data Bases

DAVID W. GRISSMER

Data bases derived from state administrative records have proven to be very useful for research in the general area of teacher supply and demand. There are several issues in this general area that merit further research attention. In addition, there are some interesting future supply and demand scenarios that merit analysis.

ISSUES FOR FURTHER RESEARCH

Several topics that merit further research are:

- Specific supply and demand analysis for math and science teachers,
- Supply and demand analysis for minority teachers,
- Effects of early retirement offers on teacher demand,
- Effects of the declining number of returning and migrating teachers on the demand for teachers, and
- Supply and attrition of high-quality teachers.

Each of these topics is discussed in the following sections.

Supply and Demand for Math and Science Teachers

Several studies of attrition rates of mathematics and science teachers apparently reach different conclusions. Some report much higher attrition

Grissmer made a significant contribution to the conference with his remarks during the open discussion of the session. Those remarks have been formalized in this paper.

rates for physics/chemistry and biology teachers compared with other teachers; others conclude just the opposite. There are several hypothesis concerning differences in methodology, time periods of measurement, and definition of attrition that might explain the differences in conclusions, although these questions certainly need further empirical exploration.

Research based on state data sources from Michigan (Murnane and Olsen, 1989b), North Carolina (Murnane and Schwinden, 1990) and Indiana (Grissmer and Kirby, 1991, 1992) shows that physics/chemistry teachers have significantly higher attrition rates than the average of all teachers, and that biology teachers have the next highest rates. However, all three studies find that attrition rates for mathematics teachers are much lower than those for science teachers, although still above the average for all teachers. These studies all use entering cohort survival as the basis for their conclusions. The entering cohorts studied in the analysis are different by state. The Michigan analysis used entering cohorts from 1972 to 1980 followed through 1984, North Carolina the 1976 and 1978 cohort followed through 1986, and Indiana the 1966 through 1985 cohorts followed through 1988. The findings apply whether the definition of attrition includes or does not include teachers who subsequently return to teaching. However, the results are much stronger when teachers who return are not counted as attrition, since mathematics and science teachers return at much reduced rates than other types of teachers (Murnane et al., 1989; Grissmer and Kirby, 1992).

A recent analysis of attrition (Bobbitt et al., 1991), using the national sample of teachers from the Schools and Staffing Surveys (SASS) and the Teacher Followup Survey (TFS), concluded that chemistry/physics, biology, and mathematics had attrition rates below the average for all teachers. This data was based on attrition in a single year (1987-88 to 1988-89) from the base of all mathematics and science teachers.

Three differences that might explain these conflicting results are the use of different samples, different time periods, and different definitions of attrition. A cohort sample measures early attrition for younger teachers, whereas a cross-sectional sample of all teachers measures attrition for all age groups. Therefore, the state measurements and national measurements are not comparable. However, further work on each data base can develop more comparable measurements. The state data can provide cross-sectional estimates that would be more comparable with the national measurements. The national data can also be used to generate cohort attrition for one and eventually more years, which could then be compared with cohort rates from the state samples. In these comparisons, it is critical to control for, as a minimum, age and gender since small differences in sample composition can cause large differences in attrition rates. Thus a multivariate analysis is needed to perform these comparisons.

The second explanation is that the attrition measurements were for different time periods. The state cohort data measures average attrition for cohorts during the late 1960s, the 1970s, and early 1980s. The national sample measures attrition from 1987-88 to 1988-89. Evidence from New York and Illinois (Grissmer and Kirby, 1992) seems to indicate that teacher attrition rates have fallen over time, with the exception of a period in the late 1970s in which reductions in the teaching force occurred. Data from Michigan (Murnane and Olsen, 1989b) seem counter to this trend of lower attrition rates over time, with their initial cohorts from the early 1970s having lower attrition than the cohorts from the late 1970s. However, this may be due to the choice of the late 1970s as the second time period when reductions in force were present. Other data that continue into the 1980s indicate much lower attrition in the 1980s than the early 1970s. If this is true, then comparing rates for different time periods probably cannot be done.

The definition of attrition can also present comparison problems. The national sample measures annual attrition without taking account of returning teachers, while state analyses measure cohort attrition in two ways—with and without taking account of returning teachers. Since about one-third of teachers return (Murnane et al., 1989; Grissmer and Kirby, 1991), comparing attrition without comparable treatment of returning teachers can make estimates very different. This is especially true when comparing attrition rates of science/math teachers with other teachers. Science and math teachers return much less frequently than other types of teachers (Murnane et al., 1989; Grissmer and Kirby, 1991). This means that annual attrition rates for science and mathematics teachers could be similar or even lower, but the lower return rates would make permanent attrition rates higher for science teachers. While this may explain part of the discrepancy, it is also true that the state measurements shows higher annual cohort attrition for science teachers.

Other explanations are possible, but I think less likely. The particular states used in the analysis may have quite different attrition patterns and may not be nationally representative. However, many of the other results from the states and national data are not in conflict. It is possible that the age and gender distribution of science teachers in the states studied is different than in the national distribution. This could be easily checked on the different data bases.

It is also possible that the classifications used for science and math teachers are very different. The state cohort data classified teachers on the basis of what they taught in the first year of teaching. The SASS and TFS classified teachers on the basis of their main assignment in the initial year of the survey—1987-88. These might be very different groups. The cohort classification probably corresponds to certification area since they are newly hired teachers. Once teachers have some experience, there may be many science and math teachers not teaching in their main area, or conversely, teachers not having their main certification in science or math may be teaching these subjects. To the extent that (a) entering cohorts of science and math teachers teach other subjects or (b) individuals who were not initially certified in science and math are teaching these subjects, then the attrition rates for the state and national data could be different.

These discrepancies emphasize the need to perform attrition analysis within a common analytic context in which similar methodologies, similar controls, similar time periods, and similar definitions of attrition can be utilized. This common analysis needs to include data from several states and national data from the SASS and TFS. Otherwise these kinds of conflicting findings will arise over and over again, when common analysis could eliminate almost all of these conflicts.

There is a need to develop a complete supply and demand analysis for math and science teachers that includes identifying the sources of supply (returning, migrating, and inexperienced teachers), the paths into and out of teaching math and science, national return rates, and the effects of upcoming retirement eligibility and early retirement offers. We have not yet included these individual groups in supply and demand models to assess the potential for additional shortages.

This analysis is best done by combining data from several states, along with the simultaneous use of SASS and TFS data. SASS and TFS provide nationally representative data on math and science teachers, but sample sizes for newly entering teachers are rather small. In addition, supply and demand analysis is best done using long time series data whereby trends in key variables can be analyzed. Since at the present time SASS data will cover only a short time period, state data are best used to analyze these trends. The state data are based on very large sample sizes and on moderately long histories that allow better entering cohort analysis. Supply and demand analysis also needs to model the early stage of teaching careers most accurately since this is where attrition rates are high and more unpredictable.

Finally, more research is needed to discover the causes of the significant attrition differences among types of science and math teachers. One hypothesis is that it simply reflects differences in outside job opportunities (Murnane et al., 1989). The hypothesis is that mathematics teacher training may provide less job transferability than that of science training. This is especially true of those teaching lower levels of mathematics.

Another hypothesis is that laboratory teaching as opposed to classroom teaching is inherently harder, and there is greater sensitivity to the quality of equipment and facilities. Survey responses (Weiss and Boyd, 1990) from science and math teachers show differences in their sensitivities to working conditions. Science teachers—but not mathematics teachers—rate facilities and equipment and "time for hands-on instruction" as key aspects of their dissatisfaction with teaching. Finally, differences in attrition rate by subject may reflect variation in gender proportions in each area and their sensitivities. Men are more sensitive to lack of administrative support and low salaries than women (Weiss and Boyd, 1990). This sensitivity would be heightened by higher outside opportunities. Any teaching specialty with more men—other things being equal—would probably have higher attrition in situations in which where higher outside wage opportunities exist.

Minority Teachers

Declining proportions of minority representation in the overall teacher force could occur at a time when minority student enrollments are rising. The cause of lower minority teacher proportions may be more attributable to lower minority college enrollments and choice of education as a career rather than lower proportions of minority certified applicants obtaining jobs (Murnane and Schwinden, 1989). The studies of state data have not generally focused on the question of differences in attrition rates among racial/ethnic groups. Analyses of SASS and TFS generally show white and black rates to be similar, but lower attrition for Hispanic teachers (Bobbitt et al., 1991). More specific analysis of minority supply and demand is required.

Hispanic teachers especially merit analysis given the recent immigration trends. However, the sample sizes generally are small except in certain states. Two states stand out as having large enough populations of both black and Hispanic teachers to justify an analysis: New York and Texas. Fortunately, both of these states have fairly good data, and it has been edited and prepared for analysis (Texas by RAND and New York by the University of Massachusetts). Some joint analysis of these two larger states with the SASS and TFS data would provide a much clearer picture of minority teacher supply and demand behavior.

Teacher Early Retirement and Teacher Demand

The teaching force is unbalanced with respect to age and experience. Younger teachers—those under 35—are a smaller portion of the teaching force than at any time in the last 25 years, and half of all teachers are over 42, making them retirement eligible at age 55 within 13 years at the latest. An important supply and demand question is how soon these retirements will occur, and thus when replacement will be needed. Current retirement patterns show a strong tendency for teachers to stay until 62 or 65. If this is the case, then demand for new teachers will increase more slowly. Budget problems in states could make early retirement offers very attractive—in fact epidemic. Replacing older teachers with younger teachers significantly reduces education costs, even with somewhat increased retirement costs. Retirement costs are not generally paid out of operating budgets, which makes early retirement even more attractive to educational administrators.

Research is needed on the precise patterns of teacher retirement and the effects of early retirement offers on the decision to leave teaching. Massive early retirement could increase demand for younger teachers significantly. The federal government could also provide states with research on the effects of different types of early retirement offers. Research is also needed on quality issues inherit in early retirement offers. Is the tradeoff of younger for older teachers likely to increase or decrease teacher quality?

This research would again best be done in the context of combining data from several states with SASS and TFS data to find whether retirement patterns are similar across states. However, the state data may be especially valuable here because early retirement plans will be state specific. The effect of early retirement plans on retirement age could be obtained using time-series state data and/or comparing retirement behavior across states. Alternately, future SASS and TFS questions or a separate survey of teachers with regard to early retirement plans and the factors behind retirement decisions might be important.

The Declining Reserve Pool

Perhaps the most ominous trends for future shortages is the fact that the supply of returning and migrating teachers will be declining in future years. We currently depend on these teachers to fill about 50 percent or more of vacancies in any year. If there are fewer returning and migrating teachers, then we will need more younger teachers. Returning and migrating teachers will decline because of simple demographics. Teachers who return to teaching leave teaching most often between 25-35 years of age. Teachers over age 40 leave teaching less frequently. So as the average age of the teaching population increases, there will be a smaller reserve pool of teachers. Teacher migration also peaks during the 25-35 age span. Since there are going to be fewer teachers in this age span as the teaching force ages, there will be fewer returning and migrating teachers to fill vacancies.

We need more research on the patterns of returning and migrating teachers to determine the precise decline in these pools over the next 5-15 years. Data available from several states could be readily utilized to explore these patterns and the subsequent decline in the reserve pool. SASS and TFS data will have only limited utility here because they will not capture the longer time period in which many teachers return. Estimating the changing return rates of teachers would enable better estimates to be made of the reserve pool, and the timing of much stronger demand for new teachers. If this occurs about the time of massive early retirements, a problem in supply could result. So this research needs to be combined with the early retirement research to determine the relative timing of the two phenomena.

Supply and Attrition of High-Quality Teachers

Research has generally established the lower entrance rate and higher attrition rate of teacher graduates who score well on aptitude tests (Vance and Schlechty, 1982; Murnane et al., 1989; Manski, 1987; Murnane and Schwinden, 1989). The latter study however distinguishes between white and black applicants and shows that black applicants show the opposite effect, namely that higher NTE scores lead to increased chances of entry into teaching. There have been many programs within colleges to attract better students, and better induction programs into teaching may lower attrition rates (Hudson et al., 1991). But research is needed to discover differences in quality in teachers who stay and leave and the role of salary and working conditions in these decisions. There are several approaches that could be tried—case studies, surveys, and analysis of state data that include teacher test scores or teacher evaluations.

FUTURE RESEARCH DIRECTIONS

Much of the work of the last few years has focused on the collection, editing, and initial analysis of very large data bases. The SASS and TFS surveys have been designed and fielded. These surveys are an invaluable addition to the study of teacher supply and demand. The analysis of this data base is only beginning, and other waves of data will eventually be added to the 1987-88 and 1988-89 data.

SASS and TFS provide the only nationally representative data on teachers available for this purpose. The sample size of the survey is large and adequate for many purposes, although analysis of entering cohorts (or any age group such as retirees) within specialty categories can be a problem. The main drawback for analyzing teacher supply and demand issues is that it contains no time-series data, and therefore trends in key variables cannot be tracked.

There are three research centers that have invested in analysis of state data: Harvard University, the University of Massachusetts, and RAND. Harvard University has analyzed data from Michigan and North Carolina. The University of Massachusetts has data from eight New England states, and RAND has data from Indiana and Texas. A sizable investment has been made simply to assemble these data and prepare them for analysis. While some analysis has been done and published, this analysis has not yet tapped the potential of the data bases, partly because the initial costs of preparing the data was underestimated by all, and fewer resources were then available for actual research.

State data has the advantage of large samples (Texas has 180,000 teachers and New York has 240,000). The combined state data bases that have been prepared for analysis contain the records of approximately 1 million teachers—about 40 percent of U.S. teachers. These large sample sizes are critical when studying the behavior of age subgroups of teachers such as minority and science and math teachers. Data drawn from surveys is simply too expensive to allow for the sample sizes necessary to study many subgroups. In addition, state data are the only available data from which time-series and long-term longitudinal data can be constructed. Such data, as opposed to data collected at a single point in time, are critical to assessments of teacher supply and demand.

State and SASS/TFS data are basically complementary, and joint analysis can enhance considerably the analysis of several educational policy issues. I will provide two examples in which joint analysis can considerably improve our understanding of issues. The first is the question of attrition of science and math teachers described above. As reported, several conflicting results arose from analysis of the several data bases. It will be difficult to determine if these differences are an artifact of the analysis method or the time period or represent real differences among states and national samples in teacher behavior. However, joint analysis of data will be able to address many of these issues and avoid many unnecessary conflicts.

A second example is the analysis of early retirement behavior among teachers. The SASS data will be able to determine age-specific retirement rates that are nationally representative. However, since variation in pensions and early retirement offers exist at the state level, the sample sizes of retirement-eligible teachers within states that make such offers will be too small to determine how offers affect behavior. However, state data with its large sample sizes can track retirement rates over long time periods and reveal differences in retirement rates when offers are made. These data can also be used for interstate analysis of retirement rates and the relationship of these rates to differences in pension rules and amounts.

Research with data from several states is showing both similarities and differences in teacher supply and demand factors. There is similarity in age distributions and in some general attrition patterns among age groups and subject areas. There appear to be differences in (a) dependence on returning and migrating teachers to fill vacancies, (b) attrition levels, (c) capacity to generate new teachers, (d) proportions of minority teachers, and (e) early retirement programs and retirement patterns. These differences can arise from local or district policies, from state policies, and from differences in behavioral characteristics among teachers in different states.

Understanding these differences is important because teacher supply and demand factors, and the potential for shortages, will vary by state. It is also important because some states and districts have better policies and practices that can be identified and exported. Certain questions can also be better addressed by certain state data than others partly because data are available from some states for longer periods. Also, some states have implemented programs such as early retirement offers, while others do not.

The critical point here is that the analysis of state and national data needs to be done within an integrated framework that involves the following:

- Framing the same hypothesis as the basis for the research,
- Estimating attrition and other factors with the same model specifications,
- Using common definitions of variables across states,
- Estimating for similar time periods whenever possible, and
- Recognizing key differences across states that can explain differences in results.

If analyses of state and national data are done within this framework, then key national trends can be distinguished from within state trends. Trends that are supported by analyses of data from several states are more persuasive than from one state only. Moreover it is usually impossible to compare results derived from independent teacher supply and demand models because of different model specifications and variable definitions. This type of analysis would also allow us to identify key differences caused by particular state policies.

A research consortium also has significant cost advantages. Such analyses accomplished jointly would be less costly than if done independently and would result in a more interpretable set of findings. Exchange of models, ideas, hypotheses, and data handling techniques would benefit all research groups and would yield information of greater utility for education policy makers.

REFERENCES

Bobbitt, S.A., E. Faupel, and S. Burns

1991 *Characteristics of Stayers, Movers, and Leavers: Results from the Teacher Followup Survey, 1988-89*. NCES 91-128. Washington, D.C.: U.S. Department of Education, National Center for Education Statistics.

Grissmer, D. W., and S. N. Kirby

1991 *Patterns of Attrition Among Indiana Teachers: An Executive Summary*. R-4167-LE. Santa Monica, California: RAND.

1992 *Patterns of Attrition Among Indiana Teachers*. R-4076-LE. Santa Monica, California: RAND.

Hudson, L., D.W. Grissmer, and S.N. Kirby

1991 *Entering and Reentering Teachers in Indiana: The Role of the Beginning Teacher Internship Program*. R-4048-LE. October. Santa Monica, California: RAND.

Manski, C.F.

1987 Academic ability, earnings, and the decision to become a teacher: Evidence from the National Longitudinal Study of the High School Class of 1972. In D. A. Wise, ed., *Public Sector Payrolls*. Chicago, Illinois: University of Chicago Press.

Murnane, R.J., and R.J. Olsen

1989a Will there be enough teachers? *American Economic Review Papers and Proceedings* 79:242-246.

1989b The effects of salaries and opportunity costs on duration in teaching: Evidence from Michigan. *Review of Economics and Statistics* 11:347-352.

Murnane, R.J., and M. Schwinden

1989 Race, gender, and opportunity: Supply and demand for new teachers in North Carolina, 1975-1985. *Educational Evaluation and Policy Analysts* 11:93-108.

1990 The effects of salaries and opportunity costs on length of stay in teaching evidence from North Carolina. *Journal of Human Resources* 25:106-124.

Murnane, R.J., J.D. Singer, and J.B. Willet

1989 The influences of salaries and "opportunity costs" on teachers' career choices: Evidence from North Carolina. *Harvard Educational Review* 59:325-346.

Vance, V.S., and P.C. Schlechty

1982 The distribution of academic ability in the teaching force: Policy implications. *Phi Delta Kappan* 64:22-27.

Weiss, I.R., and S.E. Boyd

1990 *Where Are They Now?* Chapel Hill, North Carolina: Horizon Research, Inc.

General Discussion

The general discussion focused primarily on data bases relevant to teacher supply, demand, and quality (TSDQ) organized at three different levels: state, regional, and national. The characteristics of such data bases established at each level were considered, including information sources, methods used, and their strengths and limitations. The following paragraphs summarize the discussion pertaining to the five state data bases, national data bases, the relationship between data bases and modeling, and funding for data base development and maintenance.

Existing state data bases relevant to TSDQ typically have been derived from state administrative records containing information about teachers, students, and schools. States rarely use sample surveys of teachers to obtain TSDQ data. Several factors cause development of a teacher data base within a particular state to be difficult, time-consuming, and expensive. These factors include the sheer volume of detailed information available from multiple in-state administrative records, accessibility of data from these sources, and differences in definitions and time periods covered.

Once assembled, data bases support the investigation of a wide range of important TSDQ issues because of three characteristic strengths. First, state records contain a wealth of detailed data, often much greater detail than can be gathered reasonably by sample surveys. Second, these records are maintained year-by-year, thereby permitting examination of trends over time and permitting cohort studies of teachers as their careers develop. Third, state records incorporate entire populations of teachers, students, and schools. In contrast, surveys are usually based on samples of these populations, and limited sample sizes often do not permit the disaggregation needed for detailed analyses. Thus, at their best, state data bases provide opportunities for detailed, longitudinal analyses of TSDQ phenomena in teacher populations.

Unfortunately, state data bases are beset by a number of limitations. One is that teachers of a single state, or a combination of a few states, cannot provide national estimates. Furthermore, variations among states in definitions of variables as well as policies pertaining to teachers limit the generalizability of state-level findings. For example, definitions of second-year algebra and state policies pertaining to such factors as teacher certification, benefits packages, and collective bargaining vary a great deal among states. The conference participants discussed approaches to address the problem of differences in definitions. One is that cross-walks are sometimes successfully devised to bridge such differences. Another is that NCES is revising and developing, at the urging of many states, its handbook of definitions of teacher variables. Beginning with state and SASS definitions, the objective is to develop consensus definitions among the states and NCES and to use these in data base development. Of course, the definitions of many variables already are consistent, and much TSDQ research with data bases from different states has yielded consistent findings.

Another major problem is the quality of many state data bases relevant to TSDQ. In this context, quality includes the dimensions of data accuracy; breadth of variables covered; completeness of data for variables covered; timeliness of data; and difficulty in linking, and consistency *within* a state of, definitions across different sets of administrative records that contain the basic information used to create teacher data bases. It was generally agreed that most states will have to expand a great deal of effort to establish high-quality teacher data bases. However, this is a costly enterprise, which many states cannot afford.

A final limitation of state data bases is their inability to provide information on teachers migrating out of state. When a teacher discontinues teaching in the public school sector of a particular state, state records typically do not indicate whether the teacher left the profession, migrated to a school in another state, or transferred to a private school. Without this information, attrition studies lack precision and may yield misleading interpretations.

Turning next to the regional level, it was recognized that the only regional TSDQ data base currently operational has been developed for New York and the New England states by the Massachusetts Institute for Social and Economic Research (MISER).[1] In cooperation with these states, MISER has taken the lead in assembling seven useful state data bases by extracting information available from multiple sources within each of the seven states constituting its region. However, MISER has not generated "original" teacher data through sample surveys or other means.

With funding from federal, state, and private sources, MISER worked closely with the seven states of the northeastern region to improve and expand considerably the teacher data bases for each state, and has begun to create linkages among them for analytic purposes. These data bases probably go well beyond what the cooperating states would have developed on their own initiative. This regional interest and activity has had several beneficial results. First, it has stimulated these states to improve their collection and management of teacher data. As one commentator noted, this unlikely result suggests a new data base principle, namely, that "bad data begets good data," at least when comparisons and competition among states can occur. Second, the regionalization of the data has permitted the study of cross-state migration of teachers. Third, the generation of comparative state-by-state teacher data has stimulated intense interest among the chief state school officers and has led to policy changes such as regionalizing teacher credentialing.

With respect to the national level, a number of data bases useful for analyses of TSDQ issues now exist. Only one or two of these data sets are derived from data collected and reported by state or local education agencies. Most national data relevant to TSDQ have been generated by sample surveys with questionnaires—the prime example being the Schools and Staffing Survey (SASS), and its longitudinal component the Teacher Followup Survey (TFS), of the National Center for Education Statistics (NCES).

Since national and state data bases (including the one regional data base) differ greatly in their data sources and methods, their strengths and limitations also remarkably differ. For the most part, the strengths of national data bases relevant to TSDQ are the limitations of state data bases, and vice versa. At their best, national data bases, such as SASS, include a great deal of information about probability samples of teachers for each state and for the nation as a whole. In addition, the surveys define variables uniformly across all units sampled and use standardized procedures. Therefore, these surveys provide a national perspective of the teaching force, opportunity for state-by-state comparisons, and a basis for analysis of teacher migration among states.

National data bases, however, are as yet very limited in the extent to which they can support time-series analyses for teachers. In addition, practical limitations on the length of survey questionnaires do not permit the level of detailed information gathering that is typical of administrative records from which state data bases are derived. Finally, resources available for national surveys limit sample sizes, thereby either excluding many important cross-tabulations of data or producing estimates with large standard errors.

Since the best currently available state and national data bases are complementary in their respective patterns of strengths and limitations, there is great advantage not only in having both types, but also in being able to link data bases at these two levels. From the perspective of NCES, there is considerable potential for linking SASS with state data bases, and it is important to work toward achieving this dual strategy.

The reciprocal relationship between state data bases and MISER's regional TSDQ model was also discussed. It is readily apparent that data limitations (both quality and availability) constrain the variety of analyses demonstrated to be important by the model. However, this very fact was helpful in identifying data gap problems with the quality of state data. When these limitations became apparent, some states were stimulated to improve their state data collection and management.

Conferees recognized the limitations of funding data base development. States need to make major improvements in their teacher data collection and management. This is expensive. Several participants argued that all state money available for teacher data base development should be devoted to improving within-state data, and that none of it should be allocated to development of regional data bases. Even if this principle were adopted, most states probably would not have sufficient resources to produce high-quality data bases. It was therefore suggested that NCES, or some other federal agency, provide states with capacity-building grants. While this might seem to exclude the funding of regional data bases, it was pointed out that resources available to MISER to develop data in the Northeast were devoted primarily to working with individual states to improve and expand their data, and that this was carried much further than would have occurred had there not been a regional presence.

NOTE

1. In addition, the Southern Region Education Board (SREB) has explored the feasibility of developing such a data base for the Southern region of the nation. In a report delivered at the conference, Lynn Cornett and Robert Stoltz, both of SREB, stated that 11 SREB states were interested in cooperating in an effort to create a regional TSDQ data base derived from the records of each state. A preliminary survey of these 11 interested states found that 7 had excellent data for this purpose, one had satisfactory data, and three did not seem to have the minimum essential data available in readily usable form. SREB staff prepared a cost analysis for the project, but it is unlikely that it will start in the near future. There are several reasons for the delay: lack of state funds due to budget shortfalls, lack of high-level strong advocates within state education departments, lack of an immediate crisis involving TSDQ issues, and lack of external pressure on state education departments to produce TSDQ data and analyses. In view of these constraints, SREB is exploring the feasibility of an incremental low-cost approach to initiating the development of a TSDQ data base and model for the southern region of the nation.

VI

CONCLUSION

Directions for the Future

LEE S. SHULMAN

It is now time for all of us to think about suggestions for next steps the National Center for Education Statistics (NCES) might appropriately take with respect to teacher supply, demand, and quality data and, to the extent that it also is germane, to comment on some of the individual projects that have been described. I will leave this meeting remembering forever what I am now calling Stoltz's corollary to Gresham's Law, namely, that bad data actually encourage good data. This may be the longest enduring generalization from the meeting.

One of the questions that I did not hear discussed much is the purposes to which teacher supply, demand, and quality data are put, can be put, and ought to be put. If these data are the answers, as it were, what are the questions? It is clear that when you get chief state school officers together, they are enormously curious about data on teachers. I have been at some meetings with the chiefs, and they find those transparencies on supply and demand absolutely riveting. The chief from North Carolina immediately wants to compare his or her data to South Carolina and California and wherever.

But I am more concerned about how policy makers at different levels of the system actually use these kinds of data. Who are the relevant policy makers, first of all, and to what extent do they use different parts of the data? I think, for example, of the differences among chiefs, district superintendents, and state boards of education trying to decide whether or not to close a university school of education. The state of Oregon in 1991 substantially reduced the sizes of schools of education at Oregon State University and the University of Oregon, terminating all teacher training at the latter institution. That was ostensibly predicated on knowing something about supply and demand trends in the state of Oregon. I would hope quality of teaching also was a factor, but I frankly doubt that they really had access to data regarding quality.

So who makes the decisions? I think we would have to identify stake holders and policy makers, examine the kinds of choices and decisions they are making or intending to make, and then begin to map backward and ask, "What kinds of data would make it possible to render informed decisions instead of simply sticking a damp finger in the air?"

Dick Murnane commented on the misconceptions or misinterpretations that can readily be made by policy makers from looking at individual figures. He showed us an example of the hazard analysis that related number of years in teaching to the incentive value of salary, or at least, that is the way it would be interpreted. He smiled and said that you should not interpret this graph as a demonstration that after seven years one need not worry about teacher salaries.

Yet, that is exactly the misinterpretation that most policy makers will probably make. Therefore, an essential part of the question must be, "What are the most likely misinterpretations of these kinds of data? How can they be so collected and presented as to make it unlikely that they would have unintended and quite harmful consequences for those who are depending on them?" I am not sure how to conduct such research. I can imagine simulation studies in which we bring together policy makers at different levels, give them data, give them some problems to work on, and have them work together so we can study how they make use of the information. You can probably come up with other examples. But it is one thing to call certain data *indicators*; it is another to ask what they indicate to whom. How do they function for those who are using them as guideposts? We know very little about that.

A second general question is cross-occupational. Every time we saw an interesting data set about teaching, I found myself asking, "I wonder how that compares to nursing, social work, or other occupations?" I was not even sure what the comparable group ought to be. Is it public service occupations? Is it predominantly women's occupations? Are we observing in our data some universal characteristics of certain sorts of occupations? Is teaching a typical instance of a larger set of occupations, or is there something unique about teaching?

I shall now address the question of quality, which is the area of my own research. One question participants asked was how we could build indices of quality into surveys like the Schools and Staffing Survey (SASS). My first impulse was to say that we could not. Then I asked, "If we attempted something like this in medicine, could a small number of survey items tell us a lot about quality?" My answer, for medicine, was "yes."

If I were to ask about the quality of practice in internal medicine in a variety of settings, I could ask if respondents were board certified in internal medicine. To be board certified in internal medicine means an individual is already board certified nationally in general, has completed at least a three-year supervised residency in an approved training program in internal medicine, and has passed a set of examinations in that field.

There is no comparable question I can ask about teachers. There are no proxies for a comparable set of supervised and evaluated residency experiences in teaching. This observation leads to the desirability of NCES connecting their data-gathering initiatives with a number of emerging new programs that are going to provide those kinds of data over the next generation on teachers and their effects on kids.

I shall offer a few examples. On an experimental basis, the National Assessment of Educational Progress (NAEP) is now moving to a state-by-state examining system in reading and mathematics. This will probably not be a one-shot experiment. It will likely continue, and, in fact, all indications are that it will probably move to district-by-district, and maybe even school-by-school comparisons, although the matrix sampling scheme will have to change. If that happens, means should be sought to tie NAEP data to other kinds of data on teachers or on schools. This could become terribly complex, but it must be considered.

The National Board for Professional Teaching Standards will start slowly. It will be a voluntary teacher certification effort. The board will gather rich data on teachers' practices, including data on samples of their students' work. The virtue of starting slowly is that there will be time to determine how to link those data to SASS and other sources of school and teacher data that also will be collected.

The National Teachers Examination (NTE), published by the Educational Testing Service (ETS), will be much more widely used. The successor NTE, tentatively dubbed "Praxis," is advertised as a significant improvement over the current NTE, which is almost entirely composed of multiple choice items. ETS plans three components, much like the national board in medicine, to be given at three different times in a teacher's career. The current plan is for phase three, which unfortunately will be optional, to be based on observations or other documentation of teachers' classroom practices.

The NTE will report teachers' performance as scores. Hundreds of thousands of people will take that new NTE (though far fewer are likely to be observed in phase three). Discussions ought to begin to see how those data might be integrated into the larger data base. Unless a credible phase three attracts widespread use, however, NTE scores should be classified as predictors of quality rather than proxies *for* quality.

The current initiative in Vermont must be examined very carefully as a source of teacher quality data. They will use student portfolios in writing and math as an outcome measure at the fourth and eighth grades. How are those going to be scored and interpreted? How can those ratings be related back to teachers? Two things are important here. By their very nature, portfolios are jointly produced by pupils and their teachers. Hence, teachers are linked to student portfolios in very direct ways. This differs greatly from correlating a teacher's practice with a child's test scores nine months to three years later.

Second, Vermont's education superintendent, Rick Mills, intends that the next step is to initiate teacher assessment in Vermont using teaching portfolios that connect to those student portfolios. Here you directly tie together teacher assessment and student assessment. If I read the tea leaves correctly, California is going down this route as well, and California accounts for 10 percent of the nation's students and teachers. Connecticut is another state that has been moving in a similar direction.

It would seem useful for NCES to target a few states in which such experiments are under way to create new kinds of teacher quality data and to plan some collaborative efforts with them to discover how to include those data in a broader set of data bases.

Finally, we should consider the current discussions of a national examination system. I know it is just talk now, but, if that moves ahead, it will change the ball game entirely. If it goes in the direction that Lauren Resnick, Mark Tucker, and their New Standards Project are advocating, the major features of the new examination system will not be multiple choice tests, but rather forms of portfolios and projects. They will have to be scorable and they will be linked to individual teachers, much like Advanced Placement tests. They will be external examinations that students are taught and coached to pass by teachers. The teacher indicators and the student indicators can always be in the same data file. It will be a much tighter coupling than anything we have now.

I urge the NCES staff to plan ahead for these new forms of data that will become available over the next 10 years and to determine ways of accommodating to them.

APPENDIXES

A

Conference Agenda and Attendees

TEACHER SUPPLY, DEMAND, AND QUALITY
CONFERENCE ON POLICY ISSUES, MODELS, AND DATA BASES

March 21–23, 1991
National Academy of Sciences/National Research Council
2001 Wisconsin Avenue, N.W. — Green Building
Washington, D.C.

AGENDA

Thursday, March 21, 1991
Green Building, Room 130

6:00	Reception	
7:00	Dinner	
8:00	Opening Session	Lee Shulman, Chair
	Welcome	Emerson Elliott
	After dinner speaker	Albert Shanker

Friday, March 22, 1991
Green Building, Room 130

8:30 a.m.	Continental breakfast	
9:00	Opening remarks	Lee Shulman, Chair
9:05	The OERI Perspective on Teacher Supply, Demand, and Quality	Christopher Cross

9:20	What NCES Hopes to Learn from the Conference	Paul Planchon
9:30	Paper: On the Problem of Improving Teacher Quality While Balancing Supply and Demand	Mary Kennedy
	Invited discussants	James Stedman Arthur Wise
	Open discussion	
12:00	Luncheon	
1:00 p.m.	Paper: The State of the Art in Projecting Teacher Supply, Demand, and Quality	Stephen Barro
	Invited discussants	Gus Haggstrom Ronald Kutscher
	Open discussion	
3:15	Paper: National Data Bases Relevant to Teacher Supply, Demand, and Quality Models and Projection Methods	Ross Brewer Stephen Coelen James Wilson
	Invited discussants	Alan Fechter Thomas Hilton
	Open discussion	
5:30	Adjourn	

Saturday, March 23, 1991
Green Building, Room 130

8:30 a.m.	Continental breakfast	
9:00	Opening remarks	Lee Shulman, Chair
9:05	Panel on State Data	

	Who Will Teach?	Richard Murnane
	Developing a Regional Database for the Northeast: Problems, Products, and Prospects	James Wilson
	A Cooperative Project to Develop Teacher Supply/Demand Information in the Southern States	Robert Stoltz
	State Data on Teacher Quality, Supply, and Demand	Rolf Blank
	Open discussion	
11:30	Summary of Conference Findings	Lee Shulman
12:00 noon	Roundtable Discussion of Important Next Steps	
12:55 p.m.	Last Word	Dorothy Gilford
1:00	Adjourn Buffet Luncheon	

ATTENDEES

Chair

Lee S. Shulman, Charles E. Ducommun Professor of Education, School of Education, Stanford University

Speakers and Discussants

Stephen M. Barro, President, SMB Economic Research, Inc.

Rolf K. Blank, Project Director, Science/Mathematics Indicators Project, Council of Chief State School Officers

W. Ross Brewer, Director of Planning and Policy Development, Vermont Department of Education

Stephen P. Coelen, Director, Massachusetts Institute for Social and Economic Research (MISER) and Data and Decision Analysis, Inc.

Christopher T. Cross, Assistant Secretary, Office of Educational Research and Improvement

Emerson J. Elliott, Acting Commissioner, National Center for Education Statistics

Alan Fechter, Executive Director, Office of Scientific and Engineering Personnel, National Academy of Sciences/National Research Council
Gus W. Haggstrom, Senior Statistician, Economics Department, The RAND Corporation
Thomas L. Hilton, Senior Research Scientist, Educational Testing Service
Mary M. Kennedy, Professor of Education and Director, National Center for Research on Teacher Education, Michigan State University
Ronald E. Kutscher, Associate Commissioner, Office of Employment Projections, Bureau of Labor Statistics
Richard J. Murnane, Professor, Graduate School of Education, Harvard University
Paul Planchon, Associate Commissioner, Elementary/Secondary Education Statistics Division, National Center for Education Statistics
James B. Stedman, Specialist in Social Legislation, Education and Public Welfare Division, Congressional Research Service, Library of Congress
Robert P. Stoltz, Vice President and Director for Education Policy, Southern Regional Education Board
James M. Wilson, Senior Project Analyst, Massachusetts Institute for Social and Economic Research (MISER) and Data and Decision Analysis, Inc.
Arthur E. Wise, President, National Council for Accreditation of Teacher Education

Invited Participants
Susan Ahmed, Mathematical Statistician, Statistical Standards and Methodology Division, National Center for Education Statistics
Nabeel Alsalam, Chief, Indicators and Reports Branch, Data Development Division, National Center for Education Statistics
Elizabeth Ashburn, Schools and School Professionals Division, Office of Research, Office of Educational Research and Improvement
Sharon Bobbitt, Statistician, Elementary/Secondary Education Statistics Division, National Center for Education Statistics
Teresa Bunsen, Project Officer, Division of Personnel Preparation, Office of Special Education Programs
John G. Chapman, Program Analyst, Office of Planning, Budget, and Evaluation, U.S. Department of Education
Joseph Conaty, Education Research Specialist, Office of Research, Office of Educational Research and Improvement
Lynne Cook, Director, National Clearinghouse for Professions in Special Education
C. Emily Feistritzer, President, Feistritzer Publications and Director, National Center for Education Information

David Florio, Director of Policy Studies, Office of the Assistant Secretary, Office of Educational Research and Improvement
Debra Gerald, Mathematical Statistician, Statistical Standards and Methodology Division, National Center for Education Statistics
Milton Goldberg, Director, Office of Research, Office of Educational Research and Improvement
Jewell Gould, Director of Research, American Federation of Teachers
Jeanne E. Griffith, Associate Commissioner, Data Development Division, National Center for Education Statistics
David W. Grissmer, Deputy Director, Defense Manpower Research Center, The RAND Corporation
Ron Hall, Acting Associate Commissioner, Postsecondary Education Statistics Division, National Center for Education Statistics
Suzann R. Harrison, Executive Secretary, Georgia Professional Standards Commission
David Haselkorn, President, Recruiting New Teachers, Inc.
Terrence L. Hibpshman, Manager, Research Branch, Division of Research, Kentucky Department of Education
Edward Hurley, Research Specialist, National Education Association
Joseph S. Johnston, Jr., Vice President for Programs, Association of American Colleges
Daniel Levine, Study Director, Committee on Postsecondary Education and Training for the Workplace, National Academy of Sciences / National Research Council
Paul Lauritzen, Professor of Special Education, University of Wisconsin
David Mandel, Vice President for Policy Development, National Board of Professional Teachers
Marilyn M. McMillen, Statistician, Elementary/Secondary Education Statistics Division, National Center for Education Statistics
Jeffrey Owings, Chief, Longitudinal and Household Studies Branch, Elementary/Secondary Education Statistics Division, National Center for Education Statistics
John Ralph, Chief, Policy and Review Branch, Data Development Division, National Center for Education Statistics
Mary Rollefson, Acting Chief, Special Surveys and Analysis Branch, National Center for Education Statistics
Paul M. Siegel, Senior Education Analyst, Population Division, Bureau of the Census
John J. Stiglmeier, Director, Information Center on Education, New York State Education Department
Peter Stowe, Statistician, Postsecondary Education Statistics Division, National Center for Education Statistics

Miron L. Straf, Director, Committee on National Statistics, National Academy of Sciences/National Research Council

Larry E. Suter, Program Director, Assessments and Indicators, Office of Studies and Program Assessment, Directorate for Education and Human Resources, National Science Foundation

Bayla White, Senior Budget Examiner, Office of Management and Budget

Staff

Dorothy M. Gilford, Project Director, Conference on Teacher Supply, Demand, and Quality

Laura Lathrop, Research Assistant

Jane Phillips, Administrative Assistant

Consultant:

Erling E. Boe, Professor, Graduate School of Education, University of Pennsylvania

B

National Data Bases Related to Teacher Supply, Demand, and Quality

The American Freshman
Association of American Colleges Curriculum Database
Common Core of Data
Current Population Survey
Graduate Record Examination (GRE)
High School and Beyond (HS&B)
Integrated Postsecondary Education Data System (IPEDS)
Longitudinal Study of American Youth (LSAY)
National Assessment of Educational Progress (NAEP)
National Education Longitudinal Study of 1988 (NELS-88)
The National Longitudinal Study (NLS-72)
National Surveys of Science and Mathematics Education
The Private School Survey
Schools and Staffing Survey (SASS) and Teacher Follow-up Survey (TFS)
Status of the American Public School Teacher
Surveys of Recent College Graduates

THE AMERICAN FRESHMAN

The American Freshman survey is conducted annually by the Cooperative Institutional Research Program (CIRP), of the University of California at Los Angeles (UCLA). CIRP and UCLA's Higher Education Research Institute survey all incoming freshmen in full-time study in a sample of

These summaries rely heavily on descriptions in *Precollege Science and Mathematics Teachers* (Dorothy M. Gilford and Ellen Tenenbaum, Editors, National Academy Press, Washington, D.C., 1990) and on material provided by various sponsors of data bases.

colleges and universities. The data are stratified by type of college, public or private control, and selectivity. Longitudinal follow-up studies are conducted each summer to track students two and four years after college entry. Freshman surveys typically involve 300,000 students at 600 institutions; follow-ups are done with probability samples of 25,000 students from each cohort.

The 40-question survey instrument solicits data on high school background, including SAT or ACT scores and grade point average, intended major and educational goals, career plans, financial arrangements, and attitudes. Personal data include race/ethnicity, sex, and parents' income and occupations. Data from The American Freshman can illuminate the beginning stage of the supply pipeline—choosing a major and a career plan. The survey includes education as one of the "Probable Major Fields of Study." This broad category has a number of subcategories, including levels of education, subject matter, and special education. The longitudinal survey can provide some information about the stability of the early preference for teaching as an occupation. Questionnaire data, such as SAT scores and number of honors courses taken in high school, can be used to provide some measure of the qualifications aspects of quality.

Contact: Alexander W. Astin
Higher Education Research Institute
Graduate school of Education
University of California
405 Hilgard Avenue
Los Angeles, California 90024-1521
310/825-1925

ASSOCIATION OF AMERICAN COLLEGES CURRICULUM DATABASE

The Association of American Colleges (AAC) expanded what began as a small study in 1985-86 and 1987-88 to a large study that collected transcript data on all spring 1991 graduates from 200 institutions. These data provide the foundation for a curriculum database (CDB). To identify changes and trends, the AAC plans to collect and process such data every two years.

Of the 200 participating institutions, 100 were "friends" of the AAC and 100 were a stratified probability sample of 1,360 B.A.-granting institutions, which can provide national estimates. Twenty-four strata were used based on classifying the sampling frame by: control (public/private); type (liberal arts/comprehensive/doctoral/research); and geographic location (east/middle/west). The CDB does not use a questionnaire but takes electronic transcript and student record data.

Student data collected include: major/school, gender, ethnicity, date of birth, GPA, scores on the SAT and ACT, advanced placement credits, transfer credits, and transfer level (when applicable). In addition, data were collected on all course enrollments, including the year, term, campus, grade, and credits of each course. Each institution was asked to map its curriculum to clarify the field or discipline to which courses and majors belonged.

The CDB will provide information on course background as well as student variables that will be useful in longitudinal analysis of teacher preparation.

Contact: Joseph S. Johnston, Jr.
Association of American Colleges
1818 R Street, N.W.
Washington, D.C. 20009
202/387-3760

COMMON CORE OF DATA

The Common Core of Data (CCD) is a comprehensive, annual, national statistical data base for all public elementary and secondary schools and school districts. CCD is conducted by the National Center for Education Statistics, and the data base contains data that are comparable across states.

The CCD is comprised of five surveys that are sent to state departments of education. These five data sets can be used separately or in conjunction with one another in addressing issues of teacher supply and demand.

The data collected by the CCD surveys include three categories of information: general descriptive information on schools and school districts and state-level information on students and staff, and finances.

The information on students and staff includes enrollment by grade and race, full-time equivalent staff by major employment, and high school graduates and completers in the previous year.

Contact: John Sietsema
Elementary and Secondary Education Statistics Division
National Center for Education Statistics
555 New Jersey Avenue, N.W.
Washington, D.C. 20208-5651
202/219-1335

CURRENT POPULATION SURVEY

The Current Population Survey (CPS) is a continuing cross-sectional survey of a sample of U.S. households. The Bureau of Labor Statistics provides the major funding for the survey. It is conducted monthly by the Census Bureau and collects data on labor force status. The CPS surveys people age 15 or older on their employment status in the week prior to the survey. In most months the survey includes supplemental questions on such topics as income and work experience. Four of the monthly supplements collect data relevant to teacher supply, demand, and quality. The January supplement asks questions about skills improvement and training since obtaining their current (last) job, and the March supplement focuses on labor market information, migration patterns that can be used for planning schools, and income. The May supplement obtains information on multiple job holders, including information on hours worked at the main and second job and the reason for working a second job. The October supplement focuses on enrollment in formal schools, full- and part-time status in school, level of schooling, and tuition. It also includes questions about enrollment in business, vocational, technical, and correspondence courses. The October supplement is particularly useful in tracking trends in school enrollment, dropout rates, and relationships between educational attainment and labor force activity.

The sample design involves two stages. In the first stage the nation is divided into primary sampling units (PSUs). PSUs are comprised of larger counties and independent cities and groups of smaller counties. The larger PSUs are selected with certainty for the samples, while the smaller PSUs are grouped into strata and subsampled. In the second stage of sampling, clusters of two to four households are selected for interviewing from address lists developed by the Census Bureau. The CPS sample is designed to be state-representative for annual average data for most states.

Currently, the CPS sample includes about 60,000 eligible housing units, with 2,500 eligible housing units containing at least one adult Hispanic included in the March supplement. Information is collected for all the residents at each unit. The census rotates housing units into and out of the survey, replacing one-eighth of the sample each month. Each household is in the sample for 4 months, out for 8 months, and then in for 4 months, so that longitudinal data can be obtained for consecutive March or October supplements.

The Census Bureau plans to redesign the CPS samples based on the 1990 census. The newly designed samples will be implemented around 1994-1995. In addition, the Census Bureau expects to introduce an improved labor force questionnaire in the mid-1990s and to complete a new processing system that will take advantage of the quasi-longitudinal nature of the survey.

Contact: Ronald R. Tucker
Current Population Survey Branch
Demographic Surveys Division
Bureau of the Census
Washington, D.C. 20233
301/763-2773

GRADUATE RECORD EXAMINATION

The Graduate Record Examinations (GRE) include a General Test and Subject Tests in 16 subject areas. The GRE General Test measures verbal, quantitative, and analytical abilities. The Subject Tests measure knowledge and understanding of subject matter in specific fields. The GRE scores provide those graduate schools and fellowship sponsors who require the GRE with a common measure for comparing the qualifications of applicants from a variety of backgrounds.

In addition to test scores, GRE takers are requested to provide background information, including information on the major field of undergraduate study and of intended graduate study. It is possible to relate intended graduate majors to intended undergraduate majors (from the SAT of the same student) to develop a system of predicting graduate school enrollment by major. GRE scores are also useful as an indicator of the cognitive ability of students choosing graduate work in education relative to those in other fields.

Contact: Charlotte V. Kuh
Graduate Record Examinations
Educational Testing Service
P.O. Box 6000
Princeton, New Jersey 08541-6000
609/951-6506

HIGH SCHOOL AND BEYOND

High School and Beyond (HS&B) is a national longitudinal survey of high school seniors and sophomores conducted by the National Center for Education Statistics. A probability sample of 1,015 public and private high schools was selected with 36 seniors and 36 sophomores in each of the schools. A total of about 30,000 sophomores and 28,000 seniors participated in the base-year survey. The base-year data were collected in 1980, with follow-ups in 1982, 1984, and 1986, and another is planned for 1992. In addition, data from their parents and teachers and high school and postsecondary education transcripts were included. Currently the sample contains 14,825 participants from the 1980 sophomore cohort and 11,995 participants from the 1980 senior cohort.

The purpose of the survey is to observe the educational, occupational, and family development of young people as they pass through high school and college and take on adult roles. Data obtained can also help researchers understand the new graduate component of the supply pool and the incentives to which they respond.

The 1980 and 1982 surveys consisted of questionnaire data (on background characteristics, attitudes, postsecondary educational and career plans, and activities related to education, career, and family development). Cognitive tests developed for the sophomore cohort by the Educational Testing Service were administered in 1980 and 1982. The tests were designed to measure cognitive growth in three domains: verbal, mathematics, and science.

The 1984 and 1986 follow-up surveys contain similarly detailed questions concerning college courses and experiences, jobs (including salaries), attitudes, and marriage and family formation. An analysis file is being prepared containing transcripts and student responses for students indicating that they plan to become teachers.

The Administrator and Teacher Survey (ATS), which was given to a sample of High School and Beyond school staff in 1984, can be used for research on teacher supply, demand, and quality. It was designed to explore findings from "effective schools" research with a broadly representative sample. The effective schools literature identifies characteristics of schools in which students perform at higher levels than would be expected from their background and other factors. Prior to the ATS, measures of those characteristics were not available on any large national data set. The ATS provides measures of staff goals, school environment, school leadership, and other processes believed important.

A total of 457 public and private high schools (approximately half of the 1,015 High School and Beyond schools) were sampled for the ATS; separate questionnaires were prepared for principals, teachers, vocational education coordinators, heads of guidance, and community service coordinators. Up to 30 teachers in each of the 457 schools responded to the teacher questionnaire; only one respondent per school completed the other surveys. Respondents include 402 principals and 10,370 teachers.

The ATS was designed to measure school goals and processes that the effective schools literature indicates are important in achieving effective education. Questionnaire items describe staff goals, pedagogic practices, interpersonal staff relations, teacher workload, staff attitudes, availability and use of services, planning processes, hiring practices, optional programs designed to produce educational excellence, and linkage to local employers, parents, and the community.

The ATS asked teachers a number of quality-related questions concerning school environment, in-service experience, interruptions, autonomy, absenteeism, parent contact, hours spent teaching and nonteaching, and time use and practices in a typical class. The respondent's educational background and subject preparation, certification and salary data were also asked. NCES has not issued publications based on the ATS, but the data are available on tape and a code book is available.

Contact: Aurora D'Amico
Postsecondary Education Statistics Division
National Center for Education Statistics
555 New Jersey Avenue, N.W.
Washington, D.C. 20208
202/219-1365

INTEGRATED POSTSECONDARY EDUCATION DATA SYSTEM

The Integrated Postsecondary Education Data System (IPEDS), sponsored by the National Center for Education Statistics, is a single, comprehensive system that includes all identified institutions whose primary purpose is to provide postsecondary education. It includes programs whose purpose is academic, vocational, and continuing professional education. It excludes avocational and adult basic education programs. It includes the following types of institutions: baccalaureate or higher degree-granting institutions, 2-year award institutions, and less-than-2-year institutions. These three categories are further disaggregated by control (public, private nonprofit, and private for-profit), resulting in nine institutional categories.

Data are collected from approximately 10,500 postsecondary institutions. IPEDS has been designed to produce national, state, and institutional-level data for most postsecondary students. IPEDS collects data on fall enrollment (including enrollment in teacher training programs) including full and part-time enrollment by sex, racial, and ethnic data; age distributions (odd-numbered years); and residence status of first-time degree-seeking students (even-numbered years). In odd-numbered years, IPEDS also collects data on fall enrollment in occupationally specific programs by sex and race/ethnicity. It also collects degree-completion data by field or discipline, race/ethnicity, and sex. Specialized but compatible reporting formats have been developed for the different sectors of postsecondary education providers.

Contact: William H. Freund
Postsecondary Education Statistics Division
National Center for Education Statistics
555 New Jersey Avenue, N.W.
Washington, D.C. 20208-5652
202/219-1373

LONGITUDINAL STUDY OF AMERICAN YOUTH

The Longitudinal Study of American Youth (LSAY) is a longitudinal study conducted by the Public Opinion Laboratory at Northern Illinois University, sponsored by the National Science Foundation. The study began in fall 1987 with two national cohorts, one of approximately 3,000 seventh graders and the other of approximately 3,000 tenth graders. Thus, when the two cohorts are linked, complete data from the seventh grade to the twelfth grade are available.

Although the LSAY focuses on the development of competence in mathematics and science, the data base is comprehensive and permits a broad range of investigation of educational development. Background data are collected from parents, science and mathematics teachers, and principals as well as students. Student and teacher data are collected annually, in both the fall and spring, allowing student data to be linked to particular teachers, textbooks, and syllabi.

The data are good for studying the dynamics of teacher quality as well as the antecedents of career choice. Public release files as well as a User's Manual and data tape for the science and mathematics achievement test item data are available from the project by request.

Contact: Jon D. Miller
Longitudinal Study of American Youth
Northern Illinois University
DeKalb, Illinois 60115-2854
815/753-0952

NATIONAL ASSESSMENT OF EDUCATIONAL PROGRESS

The National Assessment of Educational Progress (NAEP) is a congressionally mandated study to continuously monitor the knowledge, skills, and performance of the nation's children and youth, directed and funded by the National Center for Education Statistics. The assessment is currently administered for NCES by the Educational Testing Service. It is referred to as The Nation's Report Card, the National Assessment of Educational Progress. Approximately 120,000 precollege students are randomly selected for the national assessment every two years. NAEP is required to provide objective data about student performance at national and regional levels.

Prior to 1990, NAEP was required to assess reading, mathematics, and science at least once every 5 years. Under current legislation, assessments in reading and mathematics are required at least every 2 years, in science and writing at least every 4 years, and in history or geography and other subjects selected by the National Assessment Governing Board at least every 6 years.

To comply with the legislation, NAEP has surveyed the educational accomplishments of 9-, 13-, and 17-year-old students in 11 subject areas, starting in 1969-70. NAEP first identifies counties as primary sampling units through a stratified sampling plan. Then for each age level, public and private schools are selected by a stratified sampling plan. Finally, within each school groups of students are selected to participate in NAEP. Student samples include both age- and grade-representative populations. A variation of matrix sampling (Balanced Incomplete Block Spiraling) is used in packaging and administering assessment booklets. In the 1990 assessment, data were collected from a national probability sample of over 45,000 students per age/grade or a total of about 146,000 students in nearly 2,100 schools, as well as their principals and a sample of their teachers. In 1990 representative state-level data were produced for the first time for participating states from the trial state assessment in mathematics at the eighth grade level.

Assessments are given in fall, winter, and spring, measuring achievement and gathering information on attitudes and classroom practices as students perceive them. The nonachievement measures (attitudes toward science or math, homework and grades, and home environment) are obtained through a companion background questionnaire.

Over the past three assessment cycles NAEP has developed scales for the subjects assessed. These scales allow NAEP to compare results across ages and across assessments. In addition, the scaling scores allow NAEP to report the proportion of students at different proficiency levels in various subject areas.

NAEP Teacher Questionnaire

In 1984, NAEP began collecting data on teacher attributes, as reported by teachers of the students participating in the NAEP assessments. At grades 7 and 11, teachers are identifiable by subject (e.g., mathematics, science). The 1986 assessment, for example, gathered information from 325 seventh grade science teachers and 289 eleventh grade science teachers who responded.

The teacher questionnaire asked for data on general demographic characteristics, certification, educational preparation, and teaching experience at various grade levels. These help to illuminate aspects of teacher qualifications. School environment indicators asked on the questionnaire include classroom activities and practices, homework, laboratory and other instructional resources, and autonomy. The questionnaire asks whether the respondent would become a teacher if he or she could start over again. Continuing education is touched on in one item, although not in detail. There are no questions tracing the teacher's career path, salary, or other nonteaching work. Thus, the NAEP teacher survey may provide some quality-related information, but little on demand or supply.

Contact: Kent Ashworth
Educational Testing Service
Princeton, New Jersey 08541
1/800/223-0267
Gary W. Phillips
Education Assessment Division
National Center for Education Statistics
555 New Jersey Avenue, N.W.
Washington, D.C. 20208-5653
202/219-1761

NATIONAL EDUCATION LONGITUDINAL STUDY OF 1988

The National Education Longitudinal Study of 1988 (NELS:88) is an education longitudinal study sponsored by the National Center for Education Statistics and designed to provide trend data about critical transitions experienced by young people as they develop, attend school, and embark on their careers. By initially focusing in 1988 on eighth graders and their schools, teachers, and parents, then by following up that cohort at two-year intervals, the NELS:88 data will be used to address such issues as persistence and dropping out of high school, transition from eighth grade to high school, tracking, and features of effective schools.

For the base-year survey conducted in spring 1988, a nationally representative sample of 1,000 schools (800 public and 200 private) was drawn. Within this school sample, 26,000 eighth grade students, 6,000 eighth grade teachers, and 24,000 parents were surveyed. Thus, the four major component surveys for the base year were directed at students, parents, school administrators, and teachers.

Students were asked about school work, aspirations, and social relations. They also took cognitive tests in four achievement areas: reading and vocabulary, mathematics, science, and social studies. The parent survey gauged parental aspirations for their children, commitment of resources to their children's education, and other family characteristics relevant to educational achievement. Analysis of these data may suggest young people's levels of interest and their parents' commitment to pursuing science/mathematics fields in the future.

School principals provided information about the teaching staff, student body, school policies and offerings, and courses required for eighth graders. For example, for science and for mathematics, the principal was to note whether a full year, a half year, less than a half year, or no specified amount is required. Whether a gifted-talented program is offered is also noted, by subject. School environment items, and particularly discipline indicators, are included. Staffing questions are general and not broken down by subject. From this survey, data on 8th grade mathematics or science required might inform demand in a general way. Course-taking data might inform preparation for high school mathematics and science. Indicators of quality of education offered at the eighth-grade level are somewhat more evident.

Teacher data include academic background and certification information, class size, time use, instructional materials used, laboratory use, and school environment information. The teacher questionnaire thus can shed light on a number of indicators of quality of education offered at the eighth-grade level by subject.

The science and mathematics teachers who participated in NELS:88 also participated in a National Science Foundation study, the NSF Teacher Transcript Study, under contract with Westat, Inc., in 1988. This study collected postsecondary education transcripts on a national basis for use in assessing the relationship between teacher qualifications and student achievement.

The NELS:88 First Follow-up, sponsored by the National Science Foundation as well as the National Center for Education Statistics, was conducted between February and May 1990. The follow-up survey included student, school administrator, teacher, and dropout questionnaires. Students took cognitive tests in reading, science, social science, and math. Selected teachers of each sampled student provided information about class size, the student's study habits and performance, instructional practices in the student's classes, teacher qualifications including how prepared the teacher feels to teach the subject matter in the course, and how satisfied they are with their teaching job, and whether or not they would become a teacher again. In 1992 the NCES plans a Second Follow-up Survey to survey this eighth-grade cohort, now in twelfth grade, again. In the 1992 survey, parent questionnaires will be used in addition to the student, school administrator, teacher, and dropout questionnaires.

Contact: Jeffrey A. Owings
Elementary and Secondary Education Statistics Division
National Center for Education Statistics
555 New Jersey Avenue, N.W.
Washington, D.C. 20208-5651
202/219-1777

THE NATIONAL LONGITUDINAL STUDY

The National Longitudinal Study (NLS-72), conducted by NCES and administered by the National Opinion Research Center, studies the high school class of 1972 in the form of a sample of 23,000 high school seniors (1972) enrolled in 1,318 high schools. Follow-ups were conducted in 1973-74, 1974-75, 1976-77, and 1979-80. A fifth follow-up was conducted on a subsample in 1986, with approximately 13,000 responding at this point they were about 32 years old. In each follow-up, data were collected on high school experiences, background, opinions, and attitudes, and future plans. Participants took achievement tests in the first survey. Follow-ups traced their college, postgraduate, and work experiences, including salaries. Reasons for leaving schools or jobs were also asked. In addition, respondents included data on marriage and family formation and military service.

A Teaching Supplement Questionnaire was sent to all respondents to the fifth follow-up survey (1986) who indicated they had teaching experience or had been trained for precollege teaching. In addition, persons with mathematics, science or engineering backgrounds (with 2-year, 4-year, or graduate degrees in those fields) were drawn into the sample. A total of 1,147 eligible individuals responded. Of these, 109 indicated they actually had no teaching experience, degree in education, or certification to teach. This left 1,038 completed teaching supplements to analyze, drawing on the wealth of previous NLS data on these individuals.

This sample of current and former teachers (and some who never became teachers) were asked about career paths, salaries in teaching and nonteaching positions, certification, continuing education, family formation, reasons for entry into teaching and attrition, and nonteaching jobs. This detailed information can be analyzed by subject area.

The data have been analyzed at NCES and by Heyns (1988) and contribute to knowledge of the characteristics of the supply pool, patterns of entry, exit, and reentry, and the role of salary and other incentives.

Contact: Aurora D'Amico
Postsecondary Education Statistics Division
National Center for Education Statistics
555 New Jersey Avenue, N.W.
Washington, D.C. 20208-5652
202/219-1365

NATIONAL SURVEYS OF SCIENCE AND MATHEMATICS EDUCATION

The 1977 and 1985 surveys were sponsored by the National Science Foundation and conducted by Iris Weiss of Research Triangle Institute. They involved a national probability sample of schools, principals, and teachers in grades K-12. The 1985 survey covered 425 public and private schools. From these schools a sample of 6,000 teachers was selected. The sample was stratified by grades K-6, 7-9, and 10-12. For grades 10-12 the sample was also stratified by subject to avoid the oversampling of biology. Of the teachers sampled, 2,300 were teaching at the grade 10-12 level. The survey used five different forms, one each for principals, elementary math teachers, elementary science teachers, secondary school math teachers, and secondary school science teachers. Response rates were generally high; for example, the response rate from principals was 86 percent.

Principals in schools selected for the grade 10-12 sample were asked to check the types and number of science and mathematics courses taught by each teacher: biology/life sciences, chemistry, physics, earth/space science, "other mathematics/computer science." They were also asked to evaluate teachers' competence. Principals also reported whether they had difficulty hiring fully qualified teachers for vacancies, by subject.

The survey requested science and mathematics course offerings and enrollment (by race, ethnicity, and sex), and information about science labs and equipment, instructional techniques, and teacher training. Information on achievement was not requested.

Teachers supplied in-depth information on curriculum and instruction in a single, randomly selected class. Time spent in instruction, lab, and amount of homework given are among the types of practices for which data were collected.

In addition, information on the demographics, salary, attitudes, assignment of teachers, and data on the detailed educational background of each teacher were requested. Information about advanced degrees earned, certification, and subject-matter courses taken, to compare with standards of the NSTA and NCTM, and teaching experience were also included. Teachers were also asked if they feel inadequately qualified to teach in one or more courses.

The next surveys will be conducted by Horizon Research, Inc., with data collection in the 1992-93 academic year and questionnaires in the spring of 1993. The report publication will be in 1993-94.

Most of the teacher data from the National Survey of Science and Mathematics Education are related to aspects of quality. The course offerings and enrollment data in the school-level data supplied by principals provides some indicators of demand.

Contact: Iris Weiss
Horizon Research, Inc.
111 Cloister Court, Suite 220
Chapel Hill, NC 27514
919/489-1725
Jennifer McNeill
Research Triangle Institute
P.O. Box 12194
Research Triangle Park, North Carolina 27709
1/800/334-8571

THE PRIVATE SCHOOL SURVEY

The Private School Survey, first conducted by the National Center for Education Statistics in 1989-90, collects data on private elementary and secondary schools. The survey reflects an increasing concern with alternatives in education. It will build a data base for private schools, generate biennial data on the total number of private schools, teachers, and students, and produce early estimates of private school characteristics.

The target population for the universe survey consisted of all private schools in the United States that meet NCES criteria of a school. The survey universe is comprised of private schools from a variety of sources. Periodically this list of schools is updated by matching it with other lists provided by private school associations, state departments of education, and other lists.

The early estimates portion of the survey is conducted with a sample of 1,200 schools selected from the list and area frame operations. The selected schools are stratified by affiliation (Catholic, other religious, and nonsectarian) and by grade level (elementary, secondary, combined). Schools will also be sorted by region and enrollment. Survey questions include information on religious orientation, level and size of school, length of school day and school year, total enrollment, number of high school graduates, number of teachers, location and year of beginning operation, and program emphasis. The early estimates section includes number of schools, teachers, students, and high school graduates.

Contact: Elizabeth Gerald
Elementary and Secondary Education Statistics Division
National Center for Education Statistics
555 New Jersey Avenue, N.W.
Washington, D.C. 20208-5651
202/219-1334

SCHOOLS AND STAFFING SURVEY AND TEACHER FOLLOW-UP SURVEY

Prime sources of data about teacher supply, demand, and quality are the Schools and Staffing Survey (SASS) and its longitudinal component the Teacher Follow-up Survey (TFS), both conducted by the National Center for Education Statistics. SASS was first administered during the 1987-88 school year, again in 1990-91, and is scheduled to be conducted every three years thereafter. In addition, one year after each SASS is administered, a subsample of SASS teachers is selected for the TFS. Data generated by SASS and TFS serve the following five purposes: (a) to profile the nation's teaching force; (b) to improve estimates and projections of teacher supply and demand by teaching field, sector, level, and geographic location; (c) to allow analyses of teacher mobility and turnover; (d) to enhance assessment of teacher quality and qualifications; and (e) to provide more complete information on school policies and programs, administrator characteristics, and working conditions. Accordingly, SASS includes a great deal of information about representative samples of teachers, school administrators, and schools from each state and from the nation as a whole.

Schools and Staffing Survey

The 1987-88 SASS was composed of four basic questionnaires, with minor variations for units in the public and private sectors, with content as summarized below:

SASS 1A—Teacher Demand and Shortage Questionnaire for Public School Districts (SASS 1B is the parallel private school form). District enrollment, hiring and retirement policies, and staff data. Number of teaching positions, by level and field, that are filled or remain unfilled. New hires, layoffs, salaries, benefits. High school graduation requirements by field.

SASS 2—School Administrator Questionnaire (public and private). Training, experience, and professional background of principals. School problems, including teacher absenteeism. Influence of teachers/principal/district on curriculum and on hiring. Methods of dealing with unfilled vacancies.

SASS 3A—Public School Questionnaire (SASS 3B is the parallel private school form). Teacher-student ratio, student characteristics, staffing patterns, and teacher turnover (entry, attrition). Supply sources of new entrants and destinations of leavers. Some data can be analyzed by academic subject area.

SASS 4A—Public School Teachers Questionnaire (SASS 4B is the parallel private school form). Education and training, current assignment, continuing education, job mobility, working conditions, career choices. Division of time, courses taught. Achievement level of students. Salary, other income. Opinions on pay policies, salary, working conditions, professional recognition, etc. What teachers did before they began teaching at this school. Data can be analyzed by teaching field.

The SASS design used schools as the primary sampling unit. Once a school was selected for the sample, the School Administrator Questionnaire was sent to the principal of the school, the Teachers Questionnaire was sent to a sample of four to eight teachers from that school, and in the public sector the Teacher Demand and Shortage Questionnaire was sent to the district in which the school was located. This design permits linking data from one questionnaire to another.

The 1987-88 SASS, as well as the 1990-91 SASS, includes approximately 12,800 schools (9,300 public and 3,500 private), 65,000 teachers (52,000 public and 13,500 private) and 5,600 public school districts. SASS was administered in the form of mail questionnaires, with extensive telephone follow-up. Consequently, questionnaire response rates were high—on the order of 90 percent in the public sector and 80 percent in the private sector.

Teacher Follow-up Survey

SASS also has a small but important longitudinal component termed the Teacher Follow-up Survey. During spring 1989, one year after the base survey, the Questionnaire for Former Teachers was sent to the approximately 2,500 teachers who left the teaching profession at the end of the 1987-88 school year. In addition the Questionnaire for Current Teachers was sent to a probability sample of approximately 5,000 teachers who remained active in the profession. This latter sample was divided equally into (a) teachers who remained in the same school and (b) teachers who transferred to a different school. The response rate for this survey was 93 percent for teachers who left and 97 percent for teachers who remained in the profession. Following the 1990-91 SASS, a second Teacher Follow-up Survey, similar to the first, was conducted in spring 1992. The content of the two follow-up questionnaires is summarized below:

TFS 2—Teacher Follow-up Survey (Questionnaire for former teachers sampled in SASS). Teacher attrition, salary, other factors or reasons for leaving teaching. What former teachers did after leaving. Comparison of teaching with current occupation with regard to salary, working conditions, and job satisfaction. Data can be analyzed by subject.

TFS 3—Teacher Follow-up Survey (Questionnaire for sampled teachers who remained in teaching). Factors in retention; reasons for possible change in school assignment. Salary, other income. Data can be analyzed by subject.

The Teacher Follow-up Survey provides the first data at the national level that permit the study of attrition from the profession and comparisons of "leavers," "stayers," and "movers" (i.e., those teachers who remain in the profession but move to a different school). Sampled teachers can be linked to SASS data to determine relationships among district and school policies/practices, teacher characteristics, and teacher attrition and retention. Furthermore, additional follow-up surveys of the teachers from the 1990-91 SASS are planned subsequent to the 1992 follow-up survey. Consequently, it will also be possible to study, from a national perspective, reentry to the profession of experienced teachers from the reserve pool.

Contact: Mary Rollefson
National Center for Education Statistics
555 New Jersey Avenue, N.W.
Washington, D.C. 20208
202/219-1336

STATUS OF THE AMERICAN PUBLIC SCHOOL TEACHER

In 1956 the National Education Association (NEA) developed the first of a series of surveys covering numerous aspects of U.S. public school teachers' professional, family, and civic lives. This survey project, titled The Status of the American Public School Teacher, has been conducted every five years since 1956. Although the questionnaire has been revised to update items of concern, the wording still provides comparable data on most items from survey to survey (except for 1961, which contained some differences in the wording of questions). The most recent survey was conducted in 1990-91 and will be published by the NEA in spring 1992.

The sample of respondents for 1990-91 contained 1,351 usable responses (73.5 percent of the questionnaires originally mailed). Participants were selected through a two-stage sample design: first, a stratified sample of public school districts was drawn with the districts classified by pupil enrollment into nine strata. All school districts in the sample were asked to submit a list of all their teachers. Using that list, systematic sampling with a random start was used. A 58-item questionnaire was then mailed, in spring 1991, to all teachers in the sample. Questionnaire items span teaching experience, educational background, subject(s) taught, income, workload, school environment, demographic and family information, and civic interests. Subject area taught is self-reported, with the teacher filling in a blank with the main subject taught (i.e., "science"). The sample size is large enough to provide regional data and data by school district size as well as national data.

Items related to supply include demographic data, number of breaks in service and (one) primary reason, salaries from teaching and from additional employment, what the person did the previous year, what he or she plans to do next year, and how long the person plans to remain in teaching.

Items related to quality include highest college degree and recentness of that degree; teaching and nonteaching loads; type of teaching certificate held, including emergency and provisional certificates; college credits earned in the past three years and how much of the teacher's own money was spent for credits and other school expenses; detailed information about professional growth activities (workshops, university extension, college courses in education/other than education, etc.); whether the person would become a teacher if he or she started over again; reasons for teaching; what helps/

hinders the teacher most in his or her position; and presence of teaching assistants.

Only the published statistics are available from these surveys.

Contact: Valencia Campbell
Research Division
National Education Association
1201 Sixteenth St., N.W.
Washington, D.C. 20036
202/822-7400

SURVEYS OF RECENT COLLEGE GRADUATES

The National Center for Education Statistics has conducted periodic surveys (1976, 1978, 1981, 1985, 1987, and 1991) on outcomes of college graduation. These surveys have primarily addressed the issues of employment related to individuals' field of study and their access to graduate or professional programs. The Recent College Graduates (RCG) surveys have concentrated especially on those graduates qualified to teach at the elementary and secondary levels, estimating the potential supply of newly qualified teachers and the number who were employed as teachers in the year following graduation. Education majors are thus oversampled for the RCG. The RCG surveys were not longitudinal, but in 1993 NCES will replace the RCG with the Baccalaureate and Beyond Longitudinal Study, a longitudinal survey of graduating college seniors. Recent studies were also designed to examine the relationship between courses taken, student achievement, and occupational outcomes.

The survey involves a two-stage sampling procedure, representative at the national level. First, a sample of institutions awarding bachelor's or master's degrees is selected and stratified by percent of education graduates, control, and type. Special emphasis is placed on institutions granting degrees in education and on traditionally black institutions. For each of the selected schools, a sample of degree recipients is chosen. Included are both B.A. and M.A. degree recipients.

The survey of 1974-75 college graduates was the first and smallest of the series. The sample consisted of 200 responding schools. Of the 5,506 graduates in that sample, 4,350 responded (79 percent). The 1981 survey was somewhat larger, covering 301 institutions and 15,852 students. The student response rate was 62 percent. The 1985 survey (which collected race/ethnicity data for the first time) requested data from 18,738 students from 404 colleges. The student response rate was an effective 70 percent, with just under 11,000 participating. Response rates in these cycles (except for the 1976 survey) tend not to be higher because of invalid mailing addresses, reflecting the difficulty in tracing students after graduation. The 1987 study (which included transcripts for the first time) was more effective in locating graduates as the file contains 16,878 respondents from 400 higher education institutions, representing an 80 percent response rate. The 1991 survey involved 400 institutions and 18,000 graduates. The RCG may thus be biased against more mobile graduates. Students are surveyed once, without additional follow-ups.

Questionnaire items request data including degrees and teaching certificates; continuing education; additional formal training; what job was held as of April 27, 1987, and its relation to educational training; subjects eligible/certified to teach, whether/when entered teaching; subjects taught; marital status and number of children; and further degree plans. The questionnaire asks whether the person taught in grades K-12 before completing the degree requirement. Subjects taught are phrased generally: mathematics, computer science, biological science, and physical sciences. Information on the graduates' incentives for choosing particular careers or jobs is limited.

Thus, the RCG offers a general, nonlongitudinal picture of the new graduates component of the supply pool. Its inclusion of items that may suggest incentives and disincentives to enter teaching make it a possible source of reserve pool information. In addition to supply related to potential teachers and potential minority teachers, a few aspects of the qualification component of quality may be touched on rather indirectly, such as grades (self-reported).

Contact: Peter Stowe
Postsecondary Education Statistics Division
National Center for Education Statistics
555 New Jersey Avenue, N.W.
Washington, D.C. 20208-5652
202/219-1363

C

Teacher Supply, Demand, and Quality Variables: National Data Base Sources

ERLING E. BOE AND DOROTHY M. GILFORD

Sources of TSDQ variables within national data bases are identified and organized in the tables of this appendix. Tables 1 and 2 contain dependent variables and independent variables respectively, related to teacher supply and quality. Tables 3 and 4 contain teacher demand variables, and Table 5 contains variables relevant to the student interest in and preparation for teaching careers. The definitions and procedures used in the construction of these tables, and certain qualifications of importance to potential users, are described in the following paragraphs.

National data bases are defined here as organized collections of data drawn from the nation as a whole. A total of 15 such data bases were identified and selected for inclusion because they contain national data on variables relevant to analyses of TSDQ issues and because they are generally accessible for data analysts. Representative examples of data bases included are the Schools and Staffing Survey (SASS) and the Common Core of Data (CCD) of the National Center for Education Statistics (NCES) and the Graduate Record Examination (GRE) data base. The 15 data bases were developed by various means, the principal methods being questionnaire surveys of national probability samples of teachers and schools (e.g., SASS), reports submitted by the population of public school districts in the nation (e.g., CCD), and self-selected samples of individuals (e.g., GRE).

A data base, as defined here, is composed of information drawn from a number of *particular sources*, some of which are very similar in content while others are very different. The SASS data base, for example, contains information from questionnaires completed by teachers about themselves, from questionnaires completed by school administrative personnel about school attributes, and from questionnaires completed by school district personnel about district variables. These different sources provide quite different sets of data. The SASS data base also contains information from questionnaires completed by one sample of teachers in 1988 and another sample in 1991. The contents of these two particular questionnaire sources are quite similar. Likewise, the National Assessment of Education Progress (NAEP) includes information from somewhat different versions of questionnaires for science and for mathematics teachers at the eighth grade level in 1990, each of which can be considered a particular source. Other data bases, such as CCD, amass similar data annually, each installment of which constitutes a particular source.

The five tables of this appendix were developed to provide helpful guidance for researchers, modelers, data base managers, and others interested in identifying sources of national data about variables relevant to analyses of teacher supply and demand issues. However, data bases are too complex internally to serve as the optimal unit of analysis for the purpose of providing helpful guidance. On the other hand, particular sources within data bases are too numerous to serve as a manageable unit of analysis, and, in any event, many particular sources contain a great deal of overlapping content.

In view of these considerations, an intermediate unit of analysis was devised—a unit more particular than a data base but broader than a particular source. This intermediate unit of analysis is a *cluster of particular sources* within a data base. To define such clusters, particular sources of data within data bases were analyzed to identify those sources that contained substantially overlapping information. For example, the teacher questionnaires of SASS for 1988 and 1991 were clustered together because there was a high degree of overlap of information collected. Similarly, the school questionnaires of SASS for 1988 and 1991 formed another cluster because of overlapping content. However, the differences between the teacher and school questionnaires were sufficiently great that they were treated as different clusters of particular sources. As a result of this type of analysis, the 15 national data bases were broken down into a total of 29 clusters of particular data sources. The particular sources contained within these 29 clusters are listed in the section preceding Table1.

Though useful, the strategy of consolidating particular data sources into 29 clusters was adopted at the cost of obscuring certain differences among sources included in a cluster. These differences are not revealed in the five tables of this appendix. For example, variations in similar questionnaires collected on two different occasions are not reported here, such as the differences between the teacher questionnaires of SASS for 1988 and 1991. Likewise, variations between similar questionnaires collected from different groups of teachers at a particular time (such as from eighth grade mathematics teachers and science teachers in 1990 for the NAEP) are not reported here. Interested users must review questionnaire forms to determine the specific information contained in each data base.

Although the rows of Tables 1 through 5 are termed *variables* and are intentionally very specific, different definitions of each variable may be used in different data bases, and sometimes for particular data sources within a data base. For example, the numbers of employed teachers are based on different operational definitions of a *teacher* and may be reported as either the number of full-time equivalent teachers, the number of full-time teachers only, or the number of full-time plus part-time teachers. Therefore, users of TSDQ data must review the original questionnaires and related documentation to determine specific definitions of TSDQ variables used.

In addition, some variables included in the tables are not recorded as such in their designated data base sources. These are derived variables. For example, combinations of questionnaire items included in the teacher questionnaires of SASS provide a basis for computing the percentage of teachers who transfer from primary teaching assignments in special education to general education from one year to the next even though there is no particular questionnaire item about such cross-field transfer. Of course, data users can generate many other useful derived variables.

Finally, some national data bases (such as SASS) have been structured to provide national estimates of TSDQ variables, while other data bases do not because they are not derived from national probability samples. For example, some teacher samples (e.g., from NELS:88, NAEP, and LSAY) have been formed by selecting teachers linked to national probability samples of students. Therefore, these teacher samples are not representative of the national teaching force. In another example, data on entering teachers from the Surveys of College Graduates are limited to graduates at the baccalaureate level. Since new teachers graduating at the masters level are not included, these surveys are not representative of all recently graduated new teachers. Therefore, users of data bases must determine the population represented in the TSDQ data.

For the several reasons described above, entries in Tables 1 through 5 should be viewed only as promising leads to data base sources of TSDQ variables. Users of this information should review the specific contents of data elements in each relevant data base before concluding whether needed information about particular variables is either available or is *not* available.

Data Sources Reported in Tables 1 through 5

1. Schools and Staffing Survey: Public School Teacher Questionnaire (1988 and 1991) (Sponsor: National Center for Education Statistics)

2. Schools and Staffing Survey: Public School Questionnaire (1988 and 1991) (Sponsor: National Center for Education Statistics)

3. Schools and Staffing Survey: Teacher Demand and Shortage Questionnaire for Public School Districts (1988 and 1991) (Sponsor: National Center for Education Statistics)

4. Schools and Staffing Survey: Public School Administrator Questionnaire (1988 and 1991) (Sponsor: National Center for Education Statistics)

5. Teacher Followup Survey: Questionnaire for Current Teachers (1989) (Sponsor: National Center for Education Statistics)

6. Teacher Followup Survey: Questionnaire for Former Teachers (1989) (Sponsor: National Center for Education Statistics)

7. Common Core of Data (1989-90) (Sponsor: National Center for Education Statistics)

8. National Education Longitudinal Study of 1988: Teacher Questionnaire (Base Questionnaire of 1988 and Following), Questionnaire for History, English, Mathematics, and Science Versions of 1990) (Sponsor: National Center for Education Statistics)

9. National Education Longitudinal Study of 1988: School Questionnaire (Base 1988 and 1990 Followup) (Sponsor: National Center for Education Statistics)

10. National Assessment of Educational Progress: Teacher Questionnaire for Grade 3, Grade 7, and Grade 11 (1986) (Sponsor: National Center for Education Statistics)

11. National Assessment of Educational Progress: Teacher Questionnaire for Grade 4 and Grade 8 (1988) (Sponsor: National Center for Education Statistics)

12. National Assessment of Educational Progress: Teacher Questionnaires for Math Teachers and For Science Teachers, both for Grade 8 (1990) (Sponsor: National Center for Education Statistics)

13. National Assessment of Educational Progress: Teacher Questionnaires for Grade 4, Mathematics Teachers and Writing Teachers, both for Grade 8 (1991-92) (Sponsor: National Center for Education Statistics)

14. National Longitudinal Study (NLS-72) (1972, 1973-74, 1974-75, 1976-77, 1978-80, and 1986) (Sponsor: National Center for Education Statistics)

15. High School and Beyond: Administrator and Teacher Surveys (1984) (Sponsor: National Center for Education Statistics)

16. Current Population Survey (March, May, and October 1991 and January 1992) (Sponsor: Bureau of the Census)

17. National Survey of Science and Mathematics Education: Teacher Questionnaire in (a) Elementary, (b) Elementary Mathematics, (c) Secondary, and (d) Secondary Mathematics (1985) (Sponsor: National Science Foundation)

18. National Surveys of Science and Mathematics Education: Principal Questionnaire (1985) (Sponsor: National Science Foundation)

19. Status of the American Public School Teacher (1991) (Sponsor: National Education Association)

20. American Freshman Survey (1990) (Sponsor: Cooperative Institutional Research Program, University of California, Los Angeles)

21. American Freshman Followup Survey (1991) (Sponsor: Cooperative Institutional Research Program, University of California, Los Angeles)

22. Association of American Colleges: Curriculum Data Base (1991) (Sponsor: Association of American Colleges)

23. Integrated Postsecondary Education Data Base (1991) (Sponsor: National Center for Education Statistics)

24. Survey of 1989-90 College Graduates (1991) (Sponsor: National Center for Education Statistics)

25. Survey of 1985-86 College Graduates (1987) (Sponsor: National Center for Education Statistics)

26. Graduate Record Examination (1991) (Sponsor: Educational Testing Service)

27. Longitudinal Survey of American Youth: Teacher Questionnaires (1987, 89, and 90) (Sponsor: National Science Foundation)

28. Longitudinal Survey of American Youth: Student Questionnaire (1987, 88, 89, and 90) (Sponsor: National Science Foundation)

29. Longitudinal Survey of American Youth: Principal Questionnaire (1988-89) (Sponsor: National Science Foundation)

TABLE 1 Supply of Teachers for Public Education: Dependent Variables and Data Sources

Teacher Flow Variables	Key to Data Sources[a]
I. Entering teachers hired into positions (inflow): Numbers of entering teachers disaggregated by	
A. Recent college graduates hired, disaggregated by	
1. Grade level	1 24 25
2. Major teaching field	1 24 25
3. Subject matter specialty	1 24 25
4. Total recent college graduates hired	1 24 25
B. Entering teachers hired from the reserve pool, disaggregated by	
1. Grade level	1
2. Major teaching field	1
3. Subject matter specialty	1
4. Total teachers hired from the reserve pool	1
C. Total entering teachers hired into positions disaggregated by	
1. Grade level	1 10 11
2. Major teaching field	1
3. Subject matter specialty	1 10 11
4. Total entering teachers hired	1 2 8 10 11 12 17
II. Retained teachers in public education classified by type of position shift from one year to the next (withinflow): Numbers of retained teachers disaggretated by	
A. Stable retention/no transfer (same school and teaching assignment): Numbers of teachers disaggregated by	
1. Grade level	1 5 8 10 11
2. Major teaching field	1 5
3. Subject matter specialty	1 5 10
4. Total teachers retained in same school and teaching assignment	1 5 8 10 11
B. Transfer retention within public education, disaggregated by type of transfer supply to different positions in public education: Numbers of teachers transferring to different positions disaggregated by	
1. Different school (school migration), same primary assignment dissaggregated by	
a. Grade level	1 5
b. Major teaching field	1 5
c. Subject matter specialty	1 5
d. Total migrating teachers	1 5
2. Same school, different primary assignment (reassignment) disaggretated by	
a. Grade level	1 5
b. Major teaching field	1 5
c. Subject matter specialty	1 5
d. Total teachers reassigned	1 5

continued on next page

TABLE 1 *Continued*

Teacher Flow Variables	Key to Data Sources[a]
3. Different school, different primary assignment disaggregated by	
a. Grade level	1 5
b. Major teaching field	1 5
c. Subject matter specialty	1 5
d. Total teachers migrating and reassigned	1 5
C. School transfer supply within public education: Numbers of teachers transferring to a different school (school migration) whether or not changing primary teaching assignment (sum of categories II.B.1. and 3. above), disaggregated by	
1. Grade level	1 5 8 10 11
2. Major teaching field	1 5
3. Subject matter specialty	1 5 10
4. Total migrating teachers	1 2 5 8 10 11
D. Total teachers retained in public education from one year to the next: Numbers of teachers retained disaggregated by	
1. Grade level	1 5 8 10 11
2. Major teaching field	1 5
3. Subject matter specialty	1 5 10 12 13
4. Total teachers retained in public education	1 5 8 10 11 12 13 17
III. Total teachers employed in public education in any one year (sum of I.C. and II.D.): Numbers of teachers employed disaggregated by	
A. Grade level	1 3
B. Major teaching field	1
C. Total teachers employed in public education	1 9 13
D. Total teachers employed in public education	1 2 3 8 9 13 17 27 29
IV. Attrition of teachers from public education from one year to the next (i.e., outflow): Numbers of exiting teachers disaggregated by	
A. Grade level	6
B. Major teaching field	6
C. Subject matter specialty	6
D. Total exiting teachers	6
V. Reserve pool component: Former teachers unemployed since leaving teaching	
A. Number of years out of work	16
B. Intention to look for work in next 12 months	16

[a] Numbers refer to preceding list of data source clusters.

TABLE 2 Supply of Teachers for Public Education: Independent Variables and Data Sources

Predictor Variables	Key to Data Sources[a]
I. Year of	
A. Most recent entry into teaching	1 14
B. Exit attrition (last year in teaching)	6 14
II. Employment Status	
A. Type of position	
1. Regular: Full time	1 8 10 11 15
2. Regular: Part time	1 8
3. Substitute	1 8 10 11 25
4. Itinerant	1
B. Percent of full time	1 2 5 14 24 25
III. Teacher characteristics: Demographic	
A. Age	1 8 10 11 14 15 16 17 19 24 25
B. Gender	1 8 9 10 11 12 13 14 15 16 17 19 24 25
C. Race/ethnicity	1 2 8 10 11 12 13 14 15 16 17 19 24 25
D. Marital/family status	1 5 6 14 15 16 19 24 25
E. Number of dependent children	1 5 6 24 25
VI. Teacher characteristics: Qualifications	
A. Degree(s) earned by	
1. Subject matter	
(1) Major	1 5 6 8 10 11 12 13 14 15 17 24 25 27
(2) Minor	1 5 6 8 11 12 14 15 25 27
2. Level	1 2 5 6 8 9 10 11 12 13 16 17 19 27
3. Year	1 5 6 14 15 19 24 25 27
B. Type of teaching certification held	1 3 5 6 8 10 11 12 13 15 17 19 24 25
C. Nonteaching experience	1 6 14
D. Prior teaching experience	
1. Any prior teaching experience	1 24 25
2. Number of years taught	
a. In public sector	1 15
b. In private sector	1 15
c. Both sectors combined	1 10 11 12 13 14 15 17 19 27
3. Last year taught	14 15
4. Grade level(s) taught	1 10 15
5. Major teaching field(s)	1 15
6. Subject matter specialty(s)	1
E. Teacher competence ratings	18
F. Inservice training	1 8 12 13 17 19 27
G. College GPA	24 25
H. Tested ability score(s)	—
V. Teaching practice variables	1 8 10 11 12 13 17 27

continued on next page

TABLE 2 *Continued*

Predictor Variables	Key to Data Sources[a]
VI. Financial Variables	
A. Teacher compensation (current year)	
1. Annual base teaching salary	1 3 5 19 24 25 29
2. Benefits provided	3 17
3. Salary/bonus inducements	1 5 9 19
4. Supplemental earnings opportunities	1 5 19
5. Extended contract	18
6. Subsidized retraining	17 18
B. Total family income	1 5 6
C. Relative wages by occupation	
1. Local	—
2. State	—
3. National	16
D. Former earned income	6 14 15
E. Income earned in year after leaving teaching	6
F. Local employment rates	—
G. District (LEA) financial variables	—
H. Retirement financial incentives	—
VII. School Variables	
A. Urbanicity	2 5 9 18 19 24
B. Total enrollment	2 9 18
C. Enrollment trends	2
D. Distance from high school home to school of employment	25
VIII. School transfer variable (from prior year)	
A. Different school, same district	1 5
B. Different school, different district within same state	1 5
C. Different school in contiguous state	1 5
D. Different school in noncontiguous state	1 5
XI. Distance from residence to school of employment	19
X. Working conditions	
A. Teaching load	
1. Number of teaching contact hours per week	1 10 13 19 27
2. Average number of students per contact hour	1 10 13 19 27
B. Availability of teaching assistant(s)	2 13 19
C. Adequacy of	
1. Instructional materials	1 11 12 13 27
2. Instructional equipment	1 5 12 19 27
3. Administrative support	1 5 8 27
4. Teacher authority over	
a. Instruction and marking	1 5 8 10 11 12 13 27
b. Student conduct	1 5 8 10 11 13 27
D. School safety	1 5 8 9
E. Student variables	
1. Academic performance	1 11 12 13 17 27
2. SES	2 9 18 29
3. Race/ethnicity	2 9 17 18 29

[a] Numbers refer to preceding list of data source clusters.

TABLE 3 Demand for Teachers in Public Education: Dependent Variables and Data Sources

Teacher Demand Variables	Key to Data Sources[a]
I. Funded positions for teachers disaggregated by status from prior year: Numbers of funded full-time (FTE) positions by	
A. Continued funded FTE positions from prior year: Numbers of continued FTE positions	—
B. Newly created and funded FTE positions for current year (i.e., new positions): Numbers of new FTE positions	—
C. Total funded FTE positions for current year: Numbers of total FTE positions disaggregated by	
1. Grade level	—
2. Subject matter specialty	—
3. Total funded FTE positions	3
II. Funded positions for teachers disaggregated by filled vs shortage positions: Numbers of funded full-time equivalent (FTE) positions by	
A. Positions filled by employed FTE teachers in current year, disaggregated by	
1. Grade level	—
2. Subject matter specialty	—
3. Total employed FTE teachers	3 7
B. Teacher shortage for current year as measured by	
1. Retained, but open, FTE positions for current year, disaggregated by	
a. Grade level	—
b. Subject matter specialty	—
c. Total open FTE positions	3
2. Unfunded (i.e., discontinued) FTE positions for current year due to inadequate supply of applicants, disaggregated by	
a. Grade level	—
b. Subject matter specialty	—
c. Total discontinued FTE positions	3
3. Total teacher shortage for current year, as measured by initially funded, but unfilled, FTE positions, disaggregated by	
a. Grade level	—
b. Subject matter specialty	—
c. Total unfilled FTE positions	3
III. Unfunded (i.e., discontinued) positions for teachers from prior year: Numbers of discontinued FTE positions	—
IV. Teacher shortage for current year as measured by: Degree of difficulty in filling funded, but open, positions, disaggregated by	
A. Grade level	—
B. Subject matter specialty	18
C. Overall difficulty in filling positions	4 18

[a] Numbers refer to preceding list of data source clusters.

TABLE 4 Demand for Teachers in Public Education: Independent Variables and Data Sources

Predictor Variables	Key to Data Sources[a]
I. Teachers required (i.e., needed) variables	
A. Student enrollment variables	
1. Student/population ratio	—
2. Student K-12 school enrollment	2 3
3. Public/private split of student enrollment	1 7
4. Public school student enrollment: Numbers of students disaggregated by	
a. Instructional variables	
(1) Level	2 3 7
(2) Subject matter	—
(3) Course	—
b. Student variables	
(1) Age	3
(2) Race/ethnicity	2 7
(3) Special needs	
(a) Handicap	2 7
(b) Limited English proficiency	2
(4) Free lunch eligible	2 3 7
B. Curriculum requirements	
1. Elementary school	—
2. High school graduation	3
C. Work load variables	
1. Planned teacher-pupil ratio	—
2. Teaching load: Number of teaching contact hours per week	—
D. Total teachers required (i.e., needed)	—
II. Financial variables	
A. Exogenous financial variables	—
B. District (LEA) endogenous financial variables	—
III. Employment obligations to teachers retained from prior year	—
IV. School variables	
A. Urbanicity	2 7
B. Student enrollment	2 7
C. Number of teachers	2 7
V. LEA Variables	
A. Urbanicity	7
B. Student enrollment	3 7
C. Number of teachers	3 7
D. Number of schools	7

[a] Numbers refer to preceding list of data source clusters.

TABLE 5 Student Interest In and Preparation for Teaching Careers

Student Variables	Key to Data Sources[a]
I. Student interest in teaching careers	
A. Educational level of interested persons	
1. Students in seventh grade	28
2. High school seniors	28
3. College freshmen	20
4. College upperclassmen	21
5. College graduates	26
B. Demographic characteristics of interested persons	
1. Age	20 21 22 26 28
2. Gender	20 21 22 26 28
3. Race/ethnicity	21 22 26
C. Tested ability scores of students interested in enrolling in teacher preparation programs	21 22 26
D. Grade point averages	
1. High school	28
2. College	26
II. Teacher education enrollments disaggregated by	
A. Subject matter specialty	22
B. Degree level	—
C. Total teacher education enrollments	22
III. Teacher education enrollments as a proportion of total higher education enrollments at the baccalaureate level	22
IV. Number of teacher education graduates disaggregated by	
A. Grade level	23
B. Major teaching field	23
C. Subject matter specialty	23
D. Degree level	23
E. Total teacher education graduates	23 24 25
V. Year of graduation from teacher education program	8 14 15 24 25
VI. Sources of college funding	24 25

[a] Numbers refer to preceding list of data source clusters.